Supply Chain Disruptions and Impact on Global Inflation

Syed Danish Bukhari
Sir Syed CASE Institute of Technology, Pakistan

Irfan Zafar
Sir Syed CASE Institute of Technology, Pakistan

IGI Global
Scientific Publishing
Publishing Tomorrow's Research Today

Vice President of Editorial	Melissa Wagner
Director of Acquisitions	Mikaela Felty
Director of Book Development	Jocelynn Hessler
Production Manager	Mike Brehm
Cover Design	Jose Rosado

Published in the United States of America by
IGI Global Scientific Publishing
701 East Chocolate Avenue
Hershey, PA, 17033, USA
Tel: 717-533-8845
Fax: 717-533-7115
Website: https://www.igi-global.com E-mail: cust@igi-global.com

Library of Congress Cataloging-in-Publication Data

Names: Bukhari, Syed Danish, 1986- editor http://id.loc.gov/vocabulary/relators/edt http://id.loc.gov/authorities/names/n2025019794 http://id.loc.gov/rwo/agents/n2025019794 | Zafar, Irfan, 1967- editor http://id.loc.gov/vocabulary/relators/edt http://id.loc.gov/authorities/names/n2025019797 http://id.loc.gov/rwo/agents/n2025019797
Title: Supply chain disruptions and impact on global inflation / [edited by] Syed Danish Bukhari, Irfan Zafar.
Description: Hershey, PA : IGI Global Scientific Publishing, [2025] | Includes bibliographical references and index.
Identifiers: LCCN 2025018900 (print) | LCCN 2025018901 (ebook) | ISBN 9798337319841 ebook | ISBN 9798337319827 hardcover | ISBN 9798337319834 paperback
Subjects: LCSH: Business logistics http://id.loc.gov/authorities/subjects/sh85018306 | Supply chain management http://id.loc.gov/authorities/subjects/sh2024000226 | Inflation (Finance) http://id.loc.gov/authorities/subjects/sh85066112 | Business cycles http://id.loc.gov/authorities/subjects/sh85018278
Classification: LCC HD38.5 (ebook) | LCC HD38.5 .S843 2025 (print) | DDC 658.7 23/eng/20250--dc26
LC record available at https://lccn.loc.gov/2025018900

British Cataloguing in Publication Data
A Cataloguing in Publication record for this book is available from the British Library.

Table of Contents

Detailed Table of Contents

The global supply network breakdown due to COVID-19 caused severe disruption which resulted in economic turmoil in addition to inflation. The implementation of lockdown restrictions generated transportation and human staffing problems that led to product deficiencies in healthcare sector and electronic products and food supply areas. Due to manufacturing systems operating via just-in-time methods prices increased and inflation occurred. Supply chain operations and workforce management and economic adaptation abilities suffered from exposure during the COVID-19 pandemic. Businesses need to reconstruct their supply networks alongside establishing secondary resources and enhancing their ability to manage uncertainties for operational interruptions.

World tensions born from trade wars and economic sanctions function now as major disruptors which disturb global trade operations and affect price stability. The analysis investigates inflationary effects caused by trade barriers and economic disputes because they break global supply networks while driving up business expenses and reducing operational market effectiveness. Imports become more expensive through tax impositions known as tariffs which drive companies between cost absorption and price increase to consumers thus magnifying inflation rates. The implementation of economic sanctions produces three detrimental effects on trade by blocking customer access to vital resources while simultaneously generating artificial shortages leading to price increases. Trade wars between nations triggered through retaliatory policies both worsen these impacts by breaking down world markets and creating constraints on economical product acquisition.

Preface

INTRODUCTION

The global economy has been undergoing a series of profound and complex transformations, many of which have been catalyzed or accelerated by disruptions in supply chains. From the COVID-19 pandemic to geopolitical tensions, energy price volatility, and rising pressures for sustainability, these disruptions have not only impacted the movement of goods and services but have also exerted significant inflationary pressure worldwide. This edited volume, *Supply Chain Disruptions and Impact on Global Inflation*, seeks to unpack the interplay between disrupted supply networks and inflation, providing a comprehensive, interdisciplinary exploration of causes, consequences, and innovative responses.

This book brings together scholars and experts from across the globe, each contributing context-specific insights and cross-cutting analytical frameworks. What emerges is a multi-dimensional picture of the inflationary mechanisms rooted in modern supply chain vulnerabilities, and how technology, policy, and strategic foresight can mitigate future disruptions. It serves academics, policymakers, business leaders, and students who seek to understand the evolving economic landscape shaped by global shocks and systemic changes.

CHAPTER OVERVIEW

Chapter 1: The Pandemic COVID-19 Case

Uzma Sarfraz examines the foundational disruption triggered by COVID-19. Lockdowns paralyzed logistics, human resources, and manufacturing systems, leading to sharp inflation due to supply shortages and increased costs. The chapter argues for re-engineering supply networks with redundancy, flexibility, and improved risk management.

Chapter 2: Geopolitical Tensions, Trade Wars, and Sanctions

Also authored by Sarfraz, this chapter investigates how geopolitical actions like tariffs and sanctions disintegrate supply chains and amplify inflation. It reveals how these measures artificially constrain supply, force firms to shift costs to consumers, and destabilize global markets.

Chapter 3: Energy Market Shocks: Effect of Oil Price Volatility on Supply Chain

Sudeept Maharana explores how oil price fluctuations directly affect manufacturing and logistics costs, increasing inflation. The chapter highlights AI as a vital tool for predictive analytics and energy market risk management, enabling supply chain agility in volatile conditions.

Chapter 4: Consumer Behavior and Demand Shocks

Maharana's second contribution delves into the behavioral economics of crises—panic buying, hoarding, and sudden shifts in demand. AI-powered forecasting and sentiment analysis are presented as essential tools for anticipating and adapting to such volatile consumer patterns.

Chapter 5: Logistics Bottlenecks in Nigeria

Frank Ojadi and Sheneni Maiyaki present a case study from Nigeria, where port congestion and infrastructural inefficiencies significantly increase costs and delays. Drawing on structuralist inflation theory, the chapter connects poor logistics infrastructure to persistent inflation and recommends strategic infrastructural investment.

Chapter 6: Role of Technological Innovation in Supply Chain

Lalitha Srinivasarao focuses on how emerging technologies such as Artificial Intelligence and Digital Twins are revolutionizing supply chain management. By enabling scenario planning, demand forecasting, and resource optimization, these tools offer inflation-mitigating potential in dynamic economic environments.

Chapter 7: Green and Costly – Decarbonizing Supply Chains

Muralidhar B. and colleagues analyze the economic paradox of greening supply chains amid inflation. The chapter outlines how policy frameworks and technologies can harmonize environmental goals with cost containment, emphasizing the importance of long-term resilience through sustainable innovation.

Chapter 8: The Rise of Circular Supply Chains

Md Mehedi Hasan Emon and Tahsina Khan illustrate how circular economy practices such as recycling and remanufacturing reduce dependence on volatile raw material markets. These approaches help stabilize costs and reinforce supply chain durability, offering inflation-resistant pathways to sustainability.

Chapter 9: Economic Nationalism and De-Globalization

Zerihun Alemu and Shashi Kant explore the resurgence of protectionism and reshoring as responses to supply chain fragility. While potentially boosting local employment, these shifts often raise production costs and consumer prices. The authors advocate for balanced, innovation-driven strategies that mitigate inflationary fallout.

Chapter 10: Preparing for the Next Disruption

Concluding the volume, Khan and Emon return to offer a synthesis of lessons from past crises. They propose a structured playbook for future disruptions, grounded in digitalization, AI, and sustainable business models, aiming to future-proof supply chains and soften inflationary shocks.

This volume illustrates that inflation, far from being a mere monetary phenomenon, is deeply intertwined with structural weaknesses and inefficiencies in global supply networks. As we move forward in an era of heightened uncertainty and complexity, understanding and managing supply chain resilience will be key to stabilizing prices and ensuring economic sustainability.

Syed Danish Bukhari
Sir Syed CASE Institute of Technology, Pakistan

Irfan Zafar
Sir Syed CASE Institute of Technology, Pakistan

Chapter 1
The Pandemic COVID-19 Case

Uzma Sarfraz Sarfraz
https://orcid.org/0009-0007-2342-1106
Minhaj University, Lahore, Pakistan

ABSTRACT

The global supply network breakdown due to COVID-19 caused severe disruption which resulted in economic turmoil in addition to inflation. The implementation of lockdown restrictions generated transportation and human staffing problems that led to product deficiencies in healthcare sector and electronic products and food supply areas. Due to manufacturing systems operating via just-in-time methods prices increased and inflation occurred. Supply chain operations and workforce management and economic adaptation abilities suffered from exposure during the COVID-19 pandemic. Businesses need to reconstruct their supply networks alongside establishing secondary resources and enhancing their ability to manage uncertainties for operational interruptions.

INTRODUCTION

The rise of global inflation during COVID-19 because of economic supply disruptions combined with decreased consumer spending across the world. The pandemic produced extensive consequences which disrupted worldwide supply networks and altered customer buying patterns as well as introduced complex monetary policy problems for governmental entities and central banks. The economic problems stemming from COVID-19 including lockdowns together with supply chain obstacles and employee shortages led to increased prices within multiple market sectors. Global supply chains suffered severe disruptions which functioned as the main force behind

DOI: 10.4018/979-8-3373-1982-7.ch001

inflation throughout the COVID-19 pandemic period. The pandemic resulted in factories becoming inactive because of decreased activity that reduced trade capability and produced transportation delivery problems. The disruptions immobilized available goods so that industries which produced electronics, automobiles and construction materials suffered from reduced product availability. The shutdowns of semiconductor factories due to COVID-19 led to an escalation of electronic and automotive product prices. The limited availability of products led to increased prices in the market which resulted in enhanced global inflation (Baldwin & di Mauro, 2020). The labor shortage caused by the pandemic served as an additional force that pushed up inflation levels. The pandemic prevented numerous workers from hospitality, retail and manufacturing sectors from resuming their jobs because they feared the virus or health dangers and had caregiving duties. The workforce deficits across multiple nations created by the pandemic made employers in the U.S. along with those in other countries raise their wage levels to seek qualified employees. Higher wages given to employees by businesses led to price increases on customer purchases throughout the pandemic (Coibion et al., 2020). The combination of increased wages in food production along with construction and transportation industries produced extra pressure on existing inflationary trends. The worldwide pandemic caused major behavioral alterations among consumers. The implementation of lockdowns along with social distancing requirements prompted home confinement for numerous people which shifted average household spending behavior. The rise of demand for fitness equipment alongside electronics and home renovating products occurred because people needed to adjust their lifestyles while staying inside. The demand for travel along with dining out services and entertainment fell to significantly low levels. The merging of rising consumer demand with temporary supply chain problems resulted in higher prices across the market because businesses faced difficulties adapting to these market fluctuations (Baldwin & di Mauro 2020). The worldwide economic crisis generated by COVID-19 led governments to launch comprehensive stimulus packages for their citizens and businesses. Stimulus plans consisting of cash payments and unemployment benefits with business subsidies delivered significant economic funding to the economy. The crisis measures directed at economic support throughout the pandemic generated higher demand yet struggling supply movements that increased inflationary pressures because of their implementation. Economic recovery required central banks to decrease interest rates while performing quantitative easing procedures. The broad monetary programs unintentionally triggered rising inflation because they expanded demand past the available supply of goods and services (Bordo & Levin, 2020).Energy prices fluctuated due to the COVID-19 pandemic thus escalating global inflation rates further. The worldwide reduction of global travel and industrial operations because of lockdowns caused an immediate decrease in oil together with other energy product demand during the early part of the pandemic. Energy prices increased when worldwide economic activity resumed because supply limited by geopolitical elements and constrained distribution capabilities pushed oil costs upward. Many nations saw their inflation levels increase due to the high energy price elevations during 2021 (IMF, 2021).The year 2021 and 2022 marked an intense spike in inflation levels throughout different nations across the globe. The United States experienced its highest inflation levels in 40 years because of supply chain disruptions together with rising utility costs and workforce problems. The Eurozone together with Canada and emerging markets experienced climbing inflation rates because the pandemic persisted and markets restarted their operations. The U.S. Federal Reserve and the European Central Bank needed to oversee inflation control measures during the recovery phase of economic performance. Such unprecedented circumstances have triggered public discussions regarding central banks' efforts to strike stability between their price management goals and economic recovery purposes (Coibion et al., 2020).

BACKGROUND OF PANDMEIC

Pandemic

Infected diseases which spread between multiple global regions characterize pandemics as they infect wide populations. Novel pathogens such as microorganisms and viruses and bacteria cause this epidemic spread because they transmit quickly between people with consequential severe disease outbreaks and excessive mortality levels. Pandemics extend beyond epidemics in their scale since they cross wider geographic regions which leads to extensive stress for global health structures and economic systems and social stability. Historical pandemics such as the Spanish Flu from 1918 as well as HIV/AIDS and SARS give modern society important insights to handle and minimize the effects of present-day pandemics. Early prevention alongside social distancing and vaccine development were critical factors which the Spanish Flu pandemic demonstrated could control disease transmission (Taubenberger & Morens, 2006). The worldwide approach to HIV/AIDS proved the significance of teaching public health to the public while building worldwide alliances for effective treatments development. Quarantine procedures along with travel restrictions proved effective during the SARS epidemic at stopping new outbreaks by containing the spread despite generating lower case mortalities than COVID-19 (Paltiel et al., 2009). Healthcare infrastructure investments remain paramount to cope with future health emergencies according to regional pandemic experiences. Health institutions must ensure disease monitoring tools operate efficiently alongside effective communication throughout the public sector to build quick response capabilities including vaccine development and distribution abilities. The understanding continues to grow that population resilience against pandemics depends on resolving health-related social factors including poverty and healthcare access and educational disadvantages. The full magnitude of pandemics emerges from their interconnected impact on economics together with their social disruption and their active role in political changes. Such expansive global events demand that responses need international cooperative efforts between governmental departments and academic fields. The global COVID-19 crisis has proven that public health systems must become stronger while international cooperation needs to improve together with the development of effective policy responses. Future pandemics can gain more manageable effects as well as enhance global health security by drawing wisdom from past pandemic experiences during current worldwide pandemic challenges.

COVID-19 Pandemic

The origins of SARS-CoV-2 are unclear although scientific evidence indicates that the virus initiated from a zoonotic transmission through bats while possibly passing through intermediate species before crossing to human populations (Zhou et al., 2020). Medical experts believe Wuhan developed from extensive markets selling live animals where COVID-19 transmission started initially. The first reported cases linked to Wuhan markets turned out to be a later development as scientific evidence showed the virus was circulating outside Wuhan before detection.The coronavirus spread rapidly across global borders because of international travel resulting in its fast spread from Asia to major areas of Europe and North America and many other regions worldwide. Often referred to as significant hotspots the earliest in the pandemic were nations that maintained a high level of international connectivity including the United States, Italy, and Spain. Fast worldwide virus transmission worsened because sickness carriers who displayed no symptoms made detection and control measures challenging (Rothe et al., 2020).The novel coronavirus SARS-CoV-2 responsible for COVID-19 started its global pandemic evolution from Wuhan China late in 2019. The respiratory system of human beings stands as the principal target for this virus which creates mild through severe symptoms from common cold symptoms to pneumonia and demise. WHO issued a public health emergency declaration about the outbreak in January 2020 before the pandemic status was confirmed worldwide in March of the same year. The virus quickly spread between people because it can transmit through respiratory droplets from infected patients as well as by touching contaminated surfaces (Rothe et al., 2020). The entire pandemic control effort was complicated by asymptomatic virus transmission because patients without symptoms carried and transmitted virus unknowingly to other people. COVID-19 generated dramatic effects which affected both medical systems worldwide and cities throughout the world economy. Several million deaths and above 200 million confirmed virus infections occurred worldwide up to 2021 (World Health Organization, 2021). Accidental spread from individuals with no active symptoms caused hospital systems to reach their capacity limits particularly in nations including Italy and also the United States and Brazil where critical COVID-19 cases depleted medical infrastructure and personnel (Ranney et al., 2020). Economic activities suffered severe contractions across the world as countless countries mandated travel restrictions and lockdowns that severely affected their economic growth. Tourism and hospitality together with retail experienced tremendous financial losses which coincided with high unemployment numbers because of extensive business shutdowns (Baldwin & di Mauro, 2020). The scientific community showed unprecedented speed in vaccine development which resulted in the late 2020 authorization of Pfizer-BioNTech and Moderna vaccines (Polack et al., 2020). Tests demonstrated that these vaccine candidates proved highly protective against serious illness and deaths which enabled an important weapon against the worldwide pandemic. The problems encountered during vaccine distribution in poor nations revealed the unequal global health care systems (Marmot, 2020). The pandemic highlighted multiple weaknesses in world health organizations in both health service delivery and governance while transparency capacity issues became most visible in underdeveloped Southern nations. International cooperation rose from the COVID-19 challenges through the establishment of COVAX which works to provide equitable access to vaccines throughout the world (Gostin et al., 2016). The COVID-19 pandemic forced societies to adapt totally new operating models while revealing weaknesses in healthcare delivery systems and requiring enhanced worldwide coordination and detailed pandemic readiness schedules for future protection of global health.

The COVID-19 pandemic stands as the most recent and prominent example of how pandemics affect the world as the SARS-CoV-2 virus displayed global impacts on public health together with challenges for both political structures and economic systems. Pandemics begin when pathogens develop new mutations to move from animal to human populations together with environmental changes that move humans closer to wildlife species and global connections that enable quick disease spreads. The history of disease outbreaks demonstrates that pandemics occur from different infectious agents under different suitable situations like HIV/AIDS around 1981 and then the 2009 H1N1 pandemic and finally the 2014 Ebola outbreak. The transmission of diseases between animals and humans known as zoonotic transmission creates numerous pandemic outbreaks. Deforestation combined with urbanization and increased animal farming practices has made such zoonotic incidents more frequent (Guan et al., 2020). The SARS-CoV-2 virus introduced the COVID-19 pandemic which appeared for the first time in Wuhan China during late 2019 before quickly becoming an international emergency early in 2020. Medical professionals first diagnosed the illness as pneumonia before establishing it as a widespread respiratory disease that spreads easily between people. The World Health Organization (WHO) issued the first global alert regarding COVID-19 by recognizing it as a Public Health Emergency of International Concern on January 30, 2020 before upgrading it to pandemic status on March 11, 2020. Respiratory droplet transmission of this virus generated worldwide epidemics which resulted in millions of illnesses and fatalities while damaging healthcare facilities and prompting massive public health together with economic measures (WHO, 2020). COVID-19 caused immediate health effects which proved especially dangerous to adults beyond sixty as well as those with pre-existing heart conditions, diabetes and respiratory problems. Large numbers of hospital admissions during the pandemic caused healthcare centers to reach their maximum capacity most severely in areas requiring extensive medical improvements. The virus quickly spread so much that keeping it contained proved challenging because people could be infected regardless of showing clear symptoms. Governments worldwide adopted lockdowns and travel bans alongside quarantine rules as pandemic control measures that produced major social and economic effects (Baldwin & di Mauro, 2020). Economically, COVID-19 caused widespread disruptions. The lockdowns produced quick economic contraction on a worldwide scale as the International Monetary Fund (IMF) predicted that the global GDP would decrease by 3.5 percent in 2020. Lockdowns combined with reduced consumer spending ruined the performance of tourism and hospitality along with retail operations. Business closures along with supply chain breakdowns triggered essential items shortages alongside increasing joblessness across workplaces. Governments launched economic stabilization programs which included combination fiscal stimulus and monetary relief packages and direct financial aid to stabilize their economies according to IMF (2021). COVID-19 revealed and made worse numerous societal inequalities throughout the period. Persons belonging to vulnerable groups who resided in poor communities or lived in close quarters or were part of ethnic minority groups experienced more intense economic hardship together with poorer healthcare outcomes. Education moved entirely online when schools and universities closed which created an expanded educational gap since numerous students did not possess adequate necessary technology (UNESCO, 2020). According to WHO (2021) the pandemic produced severe mental health problems because individuals experienced higher rates of stress and anxiety and depressive symptoms because of isolation and fear about getting sick as well as financial insecurity. The pandemic's response saw a major shift with the rapid vaccine development of COVID-19 vaccines during late 2020 and early 2021. Despite initial obstacles and vaccine resistance concerns vaccination programs emerged as essential components to fight against the transmission of the virus. The distribution of vaccines between wealthy and poor nations presented significant challenges because global cooperation remained necessary to provide equal access to vital healthcare treatments according to Gates (2020). The global pandemic resulted in significant permanent changes to worldwide systems and operations. Millions of people perished because of the virus whereas countless others endured health consequences from its attacks. The worldwide economic collapse triggered by COVID-19 generated permanent changes to businesses and jobs alongside lasting damage to public budgets. The virus intensified social gaps between different populations while revealing fundamental weaknesses in health services as well as educational facilities and mental healthcare systems. Future health crises will need to adapt their global response and recovery guidelines because of the permanent effects left by vaccines and the COVID-19 pandemic.

MAIN FOCUS OF CHAPTER: COVID-19, SUPPLY CHIAN AND INFLATION

Global Supply Chain and COVID-19

The modern interconnected manufacturing and distribution systems endured historic disruption because of the COVID-19 pandemic which struck the global supply chain deeply. Various industries including manufacturing, logistics, agriculture and retail experienced pandemic-induced effects which caused product shortages and delayed distribution and raised operational expenses. Global supply chains demonstrated their weaknesses and interconnectedness during COVID-19 because the world required enhanced systems that could handle international emergencies. As the first major effect of COVID-19 on worldwide supply systems production activity came to a sudden halt. The global manufacturing base faced production disruptions when social distancing requirements and lockdowns affected Chinese facilities specially since China remained the manufacturing center of the world. The world faced widespread distribution interruptions because China functions as a major source of both raw materials and component parts as well as finished products. The manufacturing industry faced extensive delays in production because industries that procure from China encountered shortages of critical components particularly in the semiconductor sector thereby affecting electronics and automotive and textile manufacturing (Baldwin & di Mauro, 2020). The pandemic damaged worldwide transportation and logistical networks to a severe extent. The decreased availability of air and sea cargo capacity together with travel restrictions and port restrictions and quarantine regulations caused shipping bills to soar while delays became routine. The lack of shipping containers for transporting goods while retail industries demanded more items caused widespread port congestion in major shipping locations such as

Los Angeles, Rotterdam, and Shanghai. Such logistical limitations created global delays in transporting goods which worsened product shortages while making prices rise for consumer items and unprocessed materials respectively (World Economic Forum, 2021). Through disruptions in international shipping the world saw the comprehensive dependency of global trade upon uninterrupted shipping of goods between borders. Modern supply chains across the globe encountered difficulties because of employee shortages throughout the COVID-19 pandemic. Manufacturing plants along with warehouses and transportation industries faced several obstacles because employee work was restricted by health concerns and quarantine measures along with employee illness which forced many workers to stop operating or maintain reduced working hours during lockdowns. The pandemic intensified labor shortage problems in agriculture and food processing operations which hampered the speed of harvesting and food delivery. The movement of goods suffered delays because shipping and logistics sectors received less labor input due to both employee disease cases and travel limitations (Mollenkopf et al., 2020). The lack of available workers caused operational delays along with reduced outputs and higher expenses among companies that depend on people to run their supply chain networks. Changes in consumer buying patterns because of COVID-19 affected the functionality of multiple supply chains. Lockdowns together with restricted movements along with decreased spending caused sudden market demand decline for luxury items and travel items and params from non-essential service sectors. The market witnessed a drastic increase in consumer demand for items which support home living as well as remote work and personal health needs. The pandemic triggered massive demand growth in electronic products and home exercise equipment and medical products which included face masks and sanitizers as significant examples. The combination of manufacturing interruptions and delivery métiers problems caused shortages of essential goods which worsened supply network conditions while making prices rise (Harrison & Watson, 2020). Most organizations use just-in-time (JIT) inventory management to decrease their inventory levels and minimize costs by making component orders when their usage demands it. The pandemic revealed weak points in this operational system which functions well under most situations. During peak demand times when supply disruptions occurred JIT inventory management systems faced significant challenges to meet operational needs. Organizations with this management system struggled with inventory supply shortages while facing delays in their reordering cycle. Many businesses involved in supply chain management changed their JIT approach after the pandemic because they sought inventory strategies that would protect them from future market disruptions (Christopher and Peck 2020). Global supply chain processes became more complex due to the pandemic as geopolitical tensions emerged strongly. Australia joined other major COVID-19 affected nations including the United States, India and European Union to experience escalated competition across essential medical supplies and vaccines along with vital products between nations. Nationalist policies which banned medical supply exports and vaccine exports triggered a race for resources which damaged global effort to work together. Between the United States and China diplomatic tensions escalated during the pandemic leading to additional trade barriers when both parties placed tariffs on each other while playing the blame game regarding virus spread and engaging in a competitive battle for scarce vital products (Huang, 2020). The world recovering from pandemic-related initial disturbances has enabled observation of permanent supply chain alterations on a global scale. Organizations together with public institutions demonstrate enhanced interest in making supply chains more resistant while they work to address weaknesses uncovered through COVID-19. Organizations need to expand their vendor networks while implementing digital systems along with better stock control and changing worldwide transportation approaches. COVID-19 accelerated the movement of businesses toward automation and near-shoring because they wanted to protect themselves against supply chain dependence and risks (Baldwin & di Mauro, 2020). People have started to understand the importance of developing sustainable and fair supply chains to handle upcoming global disruptions regardless of causes like pandemics or climate change or geopolitical complexities. The global supply chain proved vulnerable during COVID-19 because the pandemic exposed how interconnected modern production and distribution systems are between different regions. Multiple manufacturing stops and employee shortage problems with distribution problems and changing market demands combined to generate major supply chain breakdowns throughout numerous industrial sectors. The supply chain problems caused by the pandemic have led businesses and national authorities to examine their supply systems with an emphasis on building more robust systems with sustainability and flexibility. The world will apply the COVID-19 experiences to develop a future of more resilient global trade systems and supply chain management protocols.

Interplay between COVID-19, Supply Chain and inflation

The global supply chain became visible to widespread disruptions during COVID-19 because of shutdowns and products and labor shortages which created market inflation across production logistics and consumer behavior. Multiple consequences emerged because of country-wide lockdown measures and border closures and mobility restrictions which caused general product shortages along with price increases. Industrial disruptions showed the vulnerability of worldwide supply networks while causing inflationary impacts to emerge in various sectors. The vulnerabilities linked to COVID-19 together with inflation emerged through the following mechanisms. Globally spreading COVID-19 resulted in countries such as those in Asia to enact production and manufacturing restrictions. China operated as the primary manufacturing area for business operations until COVID-19 forced plants to close while limiting workplace employees leading to delayed deliveries. The interruption of essential items distribution primarily affected essential electronics together with machinery and automotive components and medical supplies production which led to global supply chip shortages. Firms running just-in-time (JIT) inventory systems experienced the most damage because they needed minimal stockpiling. Business operations faced manufacturing problems that prevented inventory replenishment which triggered product shortages together with cost increases (Baldwin & di Mauro, 2020). The pandemic produced substantial barriers for worldwide delivery systems and transport operations. Navigation restrictions and sealed ports along with social isolation policies decreased the total capacity of ships available for transport. Major ports like Los Angeles and Shanghai along with Rotterdam faced congestion because of delay-related container shortages and worker shortages. Production delays because of limited shipping container availability combined with slower transportation times increased business expenses so they needed longer time periods to deliver their products which boosted market costs. The manufacturing and delivery problems raised production expenses while consumer prices increased this produced inflation according to World Economic Forum (2021). COVID-19 created widespread labor shortages in production sectors and distribution businesses as well as manufacturing companies and warehouses alongside increases in employee pay rates. Numerous personnel remained out of the workforce since they either faced health perils or refused to resume their previous employment after lockdowns took effect. The lack of staffing became a challenge for food processing and retail businesses and transportation organizations which forced them to spend more on workforce compensation. Essential sector businesses increased employee compensation to recruit workers which they subsequently transferred to consumer costs through higher prices. The conversion to remote work operations generated new difficulties in education together with tech markets which made it tougher to find workers and pushed pricing points upwards (Coibion et al., 2020). The COVID-19 pandemic generated major changes in customer demand alongside new patterns of consumer spending habits. People consolidated their spending after they were confined to their homes. Consumer interest in products for home entertainment, remote work, home improvement, and personal health dramatically increased because travel-related services, hospitality and non-essential service demands decreased substantially. The elevated demand for particular products joined with persistent supply limitations resulted in additional difficulties for worldwide supply networks. The increased use of home fitness equipment as well as electronic products caused manufacturing delays which translated into higher prices. Building inflationary pressures continued between sectors since both travel and hospitality sectors had difficulty creating recovery during this period (Harrison & Watson, 2020). Energy prices along with raw materials went through tremendous fluctuations throughout the pandemic period. When the pandemic began the world diminished its energy and fuel demand as transportation became minimal and multiple manufacturing operations ceased. The restoration of global economies together with rising demand led to increased oil and energy costs. The rise in energy costs led businesses to raise product prices which consumers had to bear. The lack of essential raw materials including lumber and semiconductors and metals triggered delays and higher manufacturing expenses in both the manufacturing and building sectors. The global inflation increased because essential goods and raw materials experienced price increases (IMF, 2021). The worldwide economic decline created by COVID-19 led governments to establish expansive fiscal together with monetary policies for individual and business market support. Both direct cash payments and unemployment benefits and business lending formed part of these measures. These measures served the essential purpose of protecting the economy from severe damage yet they added significant monetary supply into the market which exceeded the restricted supply. Central banks including the Federal Reserve System of the United States and the European Central Bank simultaneously put forth low interest rate policies and quantitative easing measures to help economic recovery. These extensive monetary and fiscal policies caused inflation by raising demand beyond the available supply of goods and services according to Bordo & Levin (2020). The pandemic intensified geopolitical rivalries between nations because states elected to support their domestic needs ahead of international trade. The pandemic triggered many countries to use export restrictions and bans to control shipments of medical supplies and vaccines as well as other vital goods. Nationalistic trade policies and trade barriers locked down international supply routes thus limiting free passage between nations. Countries faced rising inflation issues because they fought to obtain restricted medical supplies and vaccines during the pandemic period (Huang, 2020). The global supply chain became exposed to critical vulnerabilities throughout 2020 because COVID-19 caused production limitations, employee shortages and delivery obstruction alongside consumer market shifts and enhanced costs for basic materials and operational energy. The global pandemic showed that the interconnected world economy remains extremely vulnerable to small disruptions which then generate worldwide propagation of consequences. The pandemic recovery phase has led numerous businesses together with nations to transform their supply chain frameworks into stronger adaptable systems to stop similar supply problems occurring in the future.

How COVID-19 exposed?

Global systems revealed their many weaknesses to COVID-19 through their incompetent healthcare structures and their inadequate economic systems together with their vulnerable political framework and their visible social disparities. The pandemic clearly illustrated how inadequate healthcare operations exist throughout the world when it exposed vulnerabilities across all healthcare systems. The health systems in various nations faced hospital surges due to rising COVID-19 infections which resulted in reduced availability of medical tools along with essential medical beds. Numerous healthcare delivery systems revealed their unpreparedness during the pandemic because resources already hit their limit in affected areas. Survey results reported the United States along with Italy and Brazil experienced hospital system collapse because doctor and nurse staff operated in difficult PPE and ventilator shortfalls (Ranney et al., 2020). Hospital capacity deficiencies became apparent while making clear how specific countries dominated global medical supply production thus requiring healthcare systems to become resilient. The global economy demonstrated unprecedented weakness throughout the COVID-19 pandemic because countries' economies remained deeply connected with each other. The global virus spread forced countries to lock down their territories while prohibiting travel and enforcing physical distancing protocols which disrupted worldwide commerce and supply chain operations. The tourism business together with hospitality and retail experienced extreme decline during the pandemic forcing the worldwide dismissal of numerous workers. The pandemic revealed critical weaknesses of workers in fragile employment situations and those holding jobs in the gig and low-wage sectors because they operated without job stability and health insurance coverage. Wealthier societies and individuals showed better capacity in weathering pandemic economic consequences but poor countries and disadvantaged groups among populations continued to experience worsened misfortune (Baldwin & di Mauro, 2020). The pandemic demonstrated that governments worldwide insufficiently addressed international emergencies from a political perspective. Governments worldwide faced the necessity to implement fast responses however their quickness and their efficiency in carrying out their actions faced significant difficulties. Public confusion along with decreased trust and reduced willingness for health guideline compliance emerged from nations which delayed their responses and failed to manage public health communications effectively and maintain clear messaging. The political leaders in the United States together with Brazil minimized the virus severity causing public health coordination problems and making the crisis worse (Vaughan & Tisdall, 2020). The global response became obvious during the pandemic because countries engaged in supply competitions that produced vaccine nationalism along with unbalanced treatment distribution between nations (Marmot,

2020). The pandemic of COVID-19 revealed and magnified previous health disparities in healthcare access together with social security networks alongside living environment inequalities. Both healthcare effects and economic consequences of the pandemic struck vulnerable communities such as working-poor workers alongside minorities and refugees. The disadvantaged groups experienced greater risk exposure because they lived in close quarters and carried out essential dangerous work and received limited health care services thus they faced increased infection risks and death probabilities. Many countries discovered their social support systems were not sufficient due to lacking unemployment insurance and reduced healthcare benefits that affected numerous population segments (Marmot, 2020). Systemic health inequalities became apparent because the virus mainly affected older adults together with people who had existing medical conditions. Toward the end of the pandemic modern society recognized its need for global cooperation since the virus spread universally necessitated worldwide coordination. Public health systems in countries including New Zealand and Taiwan managed to control the virus better than other nations which lacked proper coordination and sufficient resources. During the pandemic wealthy countries acquired vaccine supplies before developing nations obtained their doses due to global economic inequities (Gostin et al., 2016).In short, COVID-19 exposed deep flaws in healthcare systems, global economic structures, political governance, and social equity. The pandemic exposed critical health system weaknesses which demand immediate changes to global healthcare structures and international support systems and economic and social policies to develop stronger healthcare systems for future challenges.

Impacts

Pandemics create extensive economic problems as well as social disruptions. The economic effects of these events create extensive problems in worldwide business operations and distribution systems along with workforce-related problems. The combination of lockdowns with travel restrictions and health measures can strongly affect industry sectors that need personal contact including tourism and hospitality and retail. Many nations experienced major economic downturns along with unemployment disasters and consumer markets' complete failure during the COVID-19 pandemic (Baldwin & di Mauro, 2020). The problem of scarcity during pandemics causes price increases through goods and service scarcities that increases poverty levels while worsening economic disparities. The lives of communities along with the daily activities of their citizens undergo significant disruption because of pandemic events which produce general fear and insecurity throughout widespread populations. The transmission of infectious diseases prompts people to develop prejudices and spread false information and forces them into social isolation because they fear getting sick. Pandemics create significant mental health problems including expanded anxiety symptoms along with depression and post-traumatic stress disorder (PTSD) because people experience serious illness together with earnings loss and experience major lifestyle changes (Shultz et al., 2016). Pandemics put severe pressure on healthcare facilities which results in missing medical resources and hospital backlog and hinders healthcare delivery for both pandemically related and non-pandemic diseases. The stress causes healthcare disparities to worsen specifically among nations with low to middle economic status. The intensity of a pandemic disease together with governmental operational capabilities determine the various political response types which nations deploy. Healthcare infrastructure together with governance systems and international cooperation functions become apparent during pandemics through their weaknesses. The COVID-19 response became less effective because public health coordination failed during the first pandemic stages combined with delayed information exchange and decreased transparency. The pandemic showcased the necessity of strong transparent leadership and proactive planning and open communication for controlling pandemic consequences (Jasanoff, 2020). Globally occurring pandemics drive worldwide organizations including the World Health Organization (WHO) and the United Nations (UN) along with non-governmental organizations (NGOs) to work together for coordinated efforts and resource distribution and national guidance. National and worldwide health security improve through the Global Health Security Agenda because this initiative develops pandemic detection and response capabilities and surveillance networks and builds local abilities to fight epidemics (Gostin et al., 2016). Global pandemic responses face implementation obstacles because of international geopolitical power challenges alongside variations in resource distribution and healthcare infrastructure development capabilities which were especially evident in vaccine distribution during the COVID-19 pandemic. The health consequences from COVID-19 proved fatal in every aspect. COVID-19 targets patients' respiration leading to various outcomes from moderate breathing difficulties to dangerous pneumonia that progresses into acute respiratory distress syndrome which results in fatalities. Elderly people together with patients experiencing health complications and people with weak immune systems became the groups at highest risk. Medical records indicate that 200 million people developed COVID-19 infections globally which led to millions of deaths since the pandemic started (World Health Organization, 2021). The medical facilities throughout the world experienced extreme pressure because of high COVID-19 case counts. The healthcare system struggled with a lack of essential critical care items namely ventilators alongside intensive care unit (ICU) beds and personal protective equipment (PPE) as well as medical personnel working in hospitals during the pandemic. The strongest strain appeared in healthcare systems of Italy as well as Spain alongside the United States and Brazil (Ranney et al., 2020). The delivery of essential medical care for cancer patients together with elective surgery procedures became interrupted during the pandemic thus worsening the pandemic's health burdens. The pandemic produced big economic challenges that influenced almost every part of the world. The implementation of lockdowns together with travel bans and social spacing protocols by countries had devastating effects on tourism and hospitality and retail and entertainment which became the most affected industries during the pandemic. Manufacturing operations across the world faced shutdowns that disrupted global trading systems and caused supply channels to interrupt and maritime shipping routes to suffer breakdowns. Virtually all countries faced economic contractions because COVID-19 caused a 3.5% global economic contraction which stands as the deepest since World War II (World Bank, 2021). The sharp rise of unemployment across nations stemmed from both business shutdowns and economic downturns. The United States experienced job market conditions equivalent to those of the Great Depression when millions of people lost employment positions throughout various industries. The financial situation of small services-based businesses became critical because of decreased consumer consumption and business shutdowns alongside public distancing protocols. The economic crisis triggered governments to support individuals and businesses together with the healthcare sector through substantial economic stimulus funds. Central banks utilized two monetary instruments: decreased interest rates together with quantitative easing procedures to provide economic liquidity. The worldwide economic downturn exposed multiple weaknesses in the global economic framework which highlighted issues about social assistance programs while exposing financial gaps between rich and poor groups as well as supply chain dependencies (Baldwin & di Mauro, 2020). The COVID-19 crisis caused extensive social effects as well as major political disturbances. Current health disparities along with income and resource access problems became dramatically intensified during the pandemic. The health emergency and economic effects of COVID-19 hit vulnerable groups like racial minorities and refugees and members of low-income communities with excessive force. Members of these groups worked in exposed essential professions and frequently lived in limited space and faced multiple barriers to receiving quality healthcare care (Marmot, 2020). Politically, the pandemic exposed weaknesses in governance and international cooperation. Various nations encountered difficulties managing their responses during the outbreak phase since they operated without proper readiness and their communication failed and their reaction times lagged. The United States and Brazil endured criticism because their political leaders displayed incompatible direction and inadequate public health measures and underestimated the impact of the virus. New Zealand along with Taiwan gained recognition for their fast well-coordinated action which enabled them to stop the virus from spreading across their territorial boundaries according to Vaughan and Tisdall (2020).

Drawbacks of COVID-19

Many adverse effects from COVID-19 pandemic impacted people along with both businesses and entire social structures throughout the world. The immediate and greatest impact was death statistics combined with crushing stress on hospitals around the world. Healthcare staff endured both tremendous physical overload and emotional exhaustion while hospitals received overwhelming numbers of patients throughout the pandemic apex. Healthcare accessibility gaps became more apparent during the health crisis because marginalized communities endured increased suffering from inadequate resources coupled with their pre-existing medical issues (Vlassoff, 2020). The economic consequences of the pandemic created large-scale financial problems across the board. The rapid spread of the virus compelled governments to restrict public activities by imposing lockdowns which resulted in permanent shutdowns throughout various sectors especially hospitality, retail and travel industries. Massive job losses and temporary positions and substantial unemployment growth became the result of these government measures. The pandemic hit small and medium-sized enterprises particularly challenging due to their limited financial strength. Businesses shuttered down permanently because of this event creating lasting economic effects (Baldwin & di Mauro, 2020). The worldwide economic system demonstrated a sharp reduction because global production decreased in 2020. The global trading market declined because governments enforced border limits and restrictions on travel combined with factory closures and labor shortages alongside supply chain interruptions. The global pandemic caused disruptions throughout production lines which resulted in reduced availability of critical items such as food products while medical materials and technological items experienced price surges (IMF, 2021). Many countries faced growing inflation after the pandemic hit especially those nations which already demonstrated economic instability. COVID-19 had a severe adverse impact on educational systems. Schools and colleges throughout the world moved their operations online which introduced difficulties for students and their teachers. Young people from disadvantaged family backgrounds experienced additional barriers to education because they did not have sufficient home technology or suitable study spaces thus deepening existing educational gaps. Many experts predict that the educational results of millions of children will suffer permanent consequences because of this educational interruption (UNESCO, 2020). The global mental health situation deteriorated worse as a result of the pandemic. Lockdowns combined with the fear of contracting the virus and job uncertainty along with pandemic-induced uncertainty resulted in mounting mental health problems such as anxiety, depression and stress experienced by the population. WHO (2021) documented an escalation of mental health disorders because many people struggled to deal with economic and social disruptions. People suffered detrimental impacts to their health because of the heavy caregiving responsibilities combined with the emotional effects of the pandemic that affected their families. Significant weaknesses in worldwide supply systems became apparent during the pandemic as this situation resulted in rising prices across various sectors. The pandemic disrupted production and shipment networks and disrupted raw material logistics which caused inventory shortages along with higher market expenses that increased worldwide inflation levels. Production delays and rising material expenses along with semiconductor shortages negatively impacted technology, automotive and construction industries to create additional stress for the world economy (Baldwin & di Mauro, 2020). The COVID-19 pandemic led to prompt medical discovery and digital advancements and worldwide collaboration but also produced extensive negative impacts on global operations. The worldwide crisis left significant marks on the globe through large-scale deaths along with economic breakdown while education systems endured many disruptions and supply chains collapsed which led to long-lasting recovery needs.

Effects of COVID-19

COVID-19 produced extensive multiderivative modifications to global conditions which extended through all social domains including medical services and the economy together with national institutions and international affairs. The swift virus transmission revealed worldwide connections because it demonstrated structural weaknesses in resilient systems which people had formerly viewed as sturdy. Public health systems across the world experienced their most rapid and destructive consequences directly from COVID-19. At the beginning of the pandemic healthcare systems across numerous countries faced operational limitations because of excessive healthcare demand. Speedily advancing COVID-19 cases exceeded Italian and US and Brazilian hospitals' operational ability which led to simultaneous care challenges for patients infected with the coronavirus and their counterparts needing treatment for other healthcare requirements. The worldwide shortage of medical supply equipment and personal protective equipment and ventilators and intensive care beds exposed fundamental issues within public health emergency readiness (Ranney et al., 2020). Disproportionate health outcomes alongside restricted medical care emerged throughout the pandemic except broadly along marginal populations consisting of racial minorities and low-income families and senior citizens (Marmot, 2020). COVID-19 triggered an economic downturn which was the most severe worldwide since the Great Depression. Worldwide business closures and travel restrictions along with far-reaching lockdowns stopped all global economic operations. Tourism, hospitality and retail sectors lead other industries in suffering massive job losses when the pandemic hit worldwide. The year 2020 witnessed a 3.5% economic contraction across the world according to the International Monetary

Fund (IMF, 2021). The employment figures surged in numerous countries where workers devoted to low-wage and temporary positions faced the most significant job losses. Fiscal stimulus packages introduced by governments contained unemployment benefits together with business support and monetary interventions while the uneven recovery continues to burden many countries with economic difficulties. The economic upheavals exposed several weaknesses in international supply chains because factories shuttered down and shipping routes became unreliable while supply delays brought about critical shortages of food and medical supplies (Baldwin & di Mauro, 2020). COVID-19 produced dramatic social repercussions because it intensified societal gaps and caused harm to the most disadvantaged population segments. Daily life suffered through lockdowns together with social distancing policies which enhanced social isolation while increasing mental health problems and domestic violence incidents across communities. The children faced significant hardships due to school closures because their education suffered interruptions together with food security and safety issues impacting children from poor families (UNICEF, 2020). Students from rural and disadvantaged regions faced problems with remote learning because many did not have the required technology and internet access needed for distance education. Low-income workers faced a higher risk of virus exposure because they mainly worked as essential and frontline personnel during the pandemic. This exposure led to greater inequality across the society. Researchers documented how racial and ethnic populations from the United States suffered maximum COVID-19 health consequences alongside worse economic outcomes (Marmot 2020). Systemic problems in healthcare and employment and social protections revealed themselves through these disparities making the world focus on implementing social equities and structural changes. Politically, COVID-19 exposed weaknesses in governance, particularly in crisis management. Multiple countries failed to manage the crisis efficiently because their lockdown procedures were delayed while public messages about health spread uncertainty and testing and tracing programs remained unclear. Some political leaders refused to acknowledge the full danger of the virus which counteracted public trust in health guidelines while extending the delay of coordinated national responses. The political management of the coronavirus crisis by the United States along with Brazil encountered extensive criticism from public audiences leading to increased fatalities of citizens and heightened discontent (Vaughan & Tisdall, 2020). The current pandemic proved that crises require speedy and effective command from leadership teams. The decisive political decisions of New Zealand and Taiwan involving border restrictions together with broad testing strategies as well as strong quarantine procedures allowed these countries to achieve lower infection rates (Vaughan & Tisdall, 2020). Governance practices together with the actions of leaders demonstrated that effective strategies reduce the pandemic's effects on communities. COVID-19 introduced major repercussions which restructured both international cooperative initiatives between nations and power relationships between nations. The pandemic made clear that medical challenges need worldwide cooperation during such global health emergencies. The COVAX initiative demonstrated the essential role of international partnership in delivering fair COVID-19 vaccine distribution to poor nations thus highlighting the need for worldwide health equality. Medical supplies and vaccine distribution ignited political tensions between nations as they started to compete with each other. Wealthier countries acquired most of the initial vaccine supply through "vaccine nationalism" approaches during vaccine development thus creating and increasing global inequalities (Gostin et al., 2016). The worldwide order proved vulnerable during COVID-19 because nations adopted patriotic measures to pursue domestic healing instead of united international solutions. Major international relationships including U.S. relations with China became tense because both nations continued to accuse each other regarding virus origins and pandemic responses as explained by Huang (2020).

SOLUTION AND RECOMMENDATIONS

Strategies to Control Pandemics

Pandemic control demands an extensive methodical design to simultaneously handle medical emergencies and create societal disaster readiness. Control measures for managing pandemics operate at various locations from global to local together with public health protocols and messaging and medical infrastructure and policy frameworks. Several effective control strategies operate to manage COVID-19 pandemics and other epidemic outbreaks. Timely identification of new infectious diseases becomes vital for stopping their spread on a large scale. Strategic disease detection networks operating on regional and international scales need to become stronger for effective surveillance purposes. The implementation of early warning systems enables detection of emerging health threats which enables immediate prompt actions to be triggered. National governments together with health systems need to establish funding for real-time data collection systems which should enable disease trend monitoring and international information sharing across national borders. Through effective surveillance authorities gain the ability to respond when outbreaks first emerge (Heymann et al., 2020). An effective management of pandemic requires a well-developed healthcare system infrastructure. The required components consist of appropriate hospital bed capacity along with medical supplies and healthcare equipment that need skilled medical personnel. Healthcare facilities suffered widespread overwhelmment because COVID-19 created an increased burden of patients. The management of infection waves becomes achievable through upgrading healthcare system capabilities such as building more intensive care units alongside ensuring proper availability of personal protective equipment (PPE) and optimizing healthcare facility effectiveness. Attracting funds to develop healthcare technology including telemedicine and digital health records enables better care access throughout pandemic situations (Baldwin & di Mauro, 2020). Vaccines represent an optimal approach to limit pandemics along with their spread. Mass vaccination efforts became essential for controlling COVID-19 spread when scientists rapidly developed vaccines throughout the global pandemic. Governing bodies need to dedicate resources towards developing vaccines alongside developing their distribution networks and fostering scientific innovation. The global pandemic control requires assuring that vaccines remain accessible for every country irrespective of their economic level (Gates, 2020). Social distancing combined with lockdowns and quarantine measures functions to control the spread of infectious diseases that break out. These severe social and economic impacts of these restrictions become necessary for slowing down virus spread while protecting healthcare capacity during the first pandemic waves. Governments should carry out these measures by designing effective strategies which prioritize public health alongside population welfare. The combination of proper isolation protocols for those who show symptoms and proper quarantine protocols for their contacts will reduce transmission rates according to Ferguson et al. (2020). Public health crises require open and straightforward sharing of information to achieve proper management. Health organizations together with governments have to deliver specific and timely information which shows the pandemic nature with detailed risk details and protective measures for people. Unclear or false information causes people to panic while they join the fight against health guidelines and develop opposition to vaccination programs. Public health campaigns must be culturally sensitive such that they allow their messages to reach each population segment (Gollust et al., 2020). The nature of pandemics as global crises demands full international collaboration to control their spread. Collaboration leads to equal distribution of required resources by guaranteeing equitable sharing of vaccines together with medical supplies and professional expertise. As a leading health organization the World Health Organization (WHO) supports worldwide disease management through its fundamental role in both response coordination and technical support as well as its guidance for international public health policies. Officials should exchange genomic sequencing data together with research results because these enable more rapid development of interventions (Heymann et al., 2020). The prevention of additional infections requires both widespread testing and contact tracing which help identify people infected with the virus to isolate them effectively. Monitoring COVID-19 provided authorities with rapid early identification of both hidden symptomatic cases combined with prevention of numerous outbreaks. Contact tracing enables healthcare workers to discover individuals who exposed themselves to sick persons so they can stop virus spread. When pandemic situations occur governments must establish easy-to-scale testing and contact tracing systems which will enable fast deployment (Kretzschmar et al., 2020). The COVID-19 pandemic reveals how essential preparedness measures are during emergencies. A system of pandemic preparedness planning must exist for governments to maintain current policies with precise declarations regarding duties and budget allocations and strategic action steps. The plans need to establish comprehensive frameworks for supply chain operation along with healthcare capability expansion and protection of critical personnel doing essential work. Key outbreak response times can be cut down significantly through both pre-placement of medical supplies and vaccines and medicines as well as training healthcare professionals to handle emergencies (Baldwin & di Mauro, 2020). Economic pandemics disrupt markets to such an extent that they create massive joblessness alongside business shutdowns and financial crises for populations and companies. Government authorities need to create financial assistance programs which strive to safeguard businesses and employees with unemployment payments in combination with business subsidies and loan programs. Economic recovery plans must concentrate on strengthening economies while providing support to intensive-hit industries and building resilient economic foundations that can fight future unexpected disturbances (OECD, 2020).

Pandemics and Controlling Inflation

The diverse economic disruptions from COVID-19 make inflation control during and after the pandemic extremely complex because supply chains break down while labor shortages emerge alongside changes in consumer spending patterns. Government entities together with central banks can use several operational approaches to combat inflationary effects in such crisis situations. The approaches aim to sustain economic growth along with stopping inflation from becoming uncontrolled. The management of inflation falls primarily on central banks which achieve this by adjusting the interest rates. Pandemic situations lead central banks to reduce interest rates as a way to motivate borrowing and spending for economic development. The strategy of interest rate adjustments by central banks requires a shift toward increased rates if inflation increases because this policy action helps to tame economic growth and fight rising price levels. Interest rates that rise slowly are effective for controlling inflation but do not interrupt economic growth (IMF, 2021). Proper attention to timing during interest rate increases becomes essential since large changes might disrupt economic growth or prolong recovery periods. Public authorities utilize funds from budget resources to support citizens through direct payments together with business relief programs along with unemployment benefit programs to fight economic decline. Short-term demand boosting through increased spending generates inflationary effects when goods and services availability fails to catch up with the rising consumer demand. Governments should concentrate their inflation management efforts on specific fiscal policies that send support to pandemic-impacted industries rather than implementation of general stimulus measures. Stimulus spending will effectively support economic recovery because it avoids creating unnecessary economic overheating according to Baldwin & di Mauro (2020). The breakdown of international supply systems function as a primary factor driving inflationary trends by producing shortages and boosting prices in consumer markets during pandemic period. Public authorities alongside businesses should work on creating stronger supply chains with varied operations to prevent future breakdowns. Nation-states should provide production incentives and build digital as well as logistical systems while establishing international partnerships for creating stronger supply chain networks. The effectiveness of addressing supply-side issues about worker shortages and production delays will increase as governments boost work labor markets and establish better mobility systems (OECD, 2020). Supply bottleneck-induced price increases will decrease when this method is applied. Energetic price volatility has become a major factor behind inflationary pressures due to the pandemic recovery period because it affects transportation-dependent sectors alongside their production activities. The management of stable energy supply combined with investments in renewable power generation along with energy pricing stability measures constitutes a government strategy to fight inflationary effects. Crisis situations require governments to launch energy price controls or establish subsidies that will protect consumers from expensive energy bills (Bordo & Levin, 2020). Energy reforms implemented for the long-term will serve as a fundamental factor to minimize exposure to volatile energy prices. The combination of workforce deficiencies has emerged as an essential driver of inflation throughout the pandemic due to business difficulites in finding enough workers to satisfy market requirements. Governments need to pursue strategies that promote workforce involvement through improved child care solutions and worker-focused training schemes and better payment benefits for essential roles to control inflation rates. Expansion of the active workforce will resolve supply shortages which leads to lower wages thus enabling inflation control (IMF, 2021). The manner in which consumers behave becomes difficult to predict in uncertain moments. Consumer-sividual spending drives inflation but simultaneous demand reduction because of anxiety creates obstacles for recovery. Governments together with central banks need to preserve consumer trust through routine discussions and economic relief initiatives as well as programs that decrease economic ambiguity. Consumer spending at appropriate levels alongside national confidence growth will prevent inflationary pressures because it matches supply to demand (Gollust et al., 2020).

Inflation control during a pandemic requires close coordination between fiscal and monetary policies. Central banks need government collaboration to develop stimulus approaches which target specific sectors while adjusting interest rates promptly. The implementation of immediate taxpayer and business aid programs must coincide with economic expansion strategies to prevent inflation growth. The economic recovery's strength depends on policy coordination because it helps control inflation respectively (Baldwin & di Mauro, 2020). Extreme conditions allow governments to use limited price control methods on critical goods to stop inflation from growing out of control. Price controls serve to stop excessive price increases in food markets as well as medical supply and transportation industries. The implementation of price controls should be handled with caution since they might disturb supplier operations by making it difficult for them to recover expenses. Governments should identify the core drivers behind inflationary concerns like supplier delays and workforce shortages because these problems should be handled directly (Bordo & Levin, 2020). Price controls remain suitable only as emergency tools. The worldwide factors of commodity price increases along with supply chain breakdowns and trade blockades tend to intensify inflation during pandemic times. Rational border collaboration serves as an instrument to reduce negative consequences from these impacts. Nations should collaborate to steal away market restrictions and guarantee the unimpeded circulation of products alongside services while fixing worldwide vaccine distribution irregularities that limit developing countries' economic growth potential. The joint management of recovery between countries supports controlled inflation prevention in each nation while maintaining sustained economic health between regions (Gates, 2020). Controlling inflation during a pandemic requires a delicate balance of fiscal and monetary policies, supply-side interventions, and international cooperation. Central governments should combat inflationary developments at their sources while preserving economic recovery by confronting supply restraint and labor shortages and energy price problems. Sustained financial investment in supply chain resilience and energy stability together with workforce development fundamentals will ensure economic recoveries from pandemics do not produce severe inflationary impacts (Gates, 2020).

CONCLUSION

The COVID-19 pandemic made current economic systems show their weaknesses which resulted in supply chain breakdowns alongside rising prices across markets. Operational slowdowns occurred together with limited access to essential products because of the supply chain disruptions caused by lockdowns and movement restrictions and social distancing protocols. The sudden disruptions caused severe operational problems to Just-in-time inventory sectors including automotive and electronic industries. The manufacturers responded to this situation by launching price hikes which caused global inflation to rise extensively. When economies reactivated businesses people made a sudden and massive surge in their buying habits for remote working tools along with home entertainment goods and healthcare essentials. The lack of available raw materials combined with increased transportation costs made inflation worse. Together with central banks governments employed monetary policy tools along with stimulus measures to minimize the economic damage which in turn increased inflation rates. Future business operations together with governments need to prioritize supply chain diversification as well as domestic manufacturing and digital infrastructure development for future prevention of price escalations.

REFERENCE:

Baldwin, R., & di Mauro, B. W. (2020). *Economics in the Time of COVID-19.* CEPR Press.

Bordo, M. D., & Levin, A. T. (2020). [*Pandemic and the Economic Response: A Global Perspective.* NBER.]. *COVID*, 19.

Christopher, M., & Peck, H. (2020). Building the Resilient Supply Chain. *International Journal of Logistics Management, 31*(3), 389–409.

Coibion, O., Gorodnichenko, Y., & Weber, M. (2020). *The Impact of COVID-19 on Consumer Behavior: Evidence from the US.* NBER.

Ferguson, N. M., et al. (2020). *Impact of Non-Pharmaceutical Interventions (NPIs) to Reduce COVID-19 Mortality and Healthcare Demand.* Nature.

Gates, B. (2020). *The Case for COVID-19 Vaccines and Global Health Equity.* Gates Foundation.

Gollust, S. E., Nagler, R. H., & Fowler, E. F. (2020). *The Influence of COVID-19 News Coverage on U.S. Public Opinion.* Journal of Health Politics, Policy, and Law.

Gostin, L. O. (2016). Global Health Security and the WHO: Assessing the International Health Regulations 2005. *Journal of the American Medical Association, 315*(10), 1039–1040. PMID: 27623457

Guan, Y., (2020). Zoonotic origins of human coronavirus infections. *Journal of Clinical Virology, 127*, 104406.

Harrison, A., & Watson, P. (2020). *COVID-19 and Supply Chain Disruption: Lessons Learned and Strategies for Future Resilience.* McKinsey & Company.

Heymann, D. L. (2020). Pandemic Preparedness and Response: The Role of International Cooperation. *Lancet.*

Huang, Y. (2020). Geopolitics of COVID-19: An Overview of China's Political and Economic Response. *Asian Perspective, 44*(4), 561–577.

IMF. (2021). *World Economic Outlook: Managing Divergent Recoveries.* IMF.

International Monetary Fund (IMF). (2021). *World Economic Outlook: Managing Divergent Recoveries.* IMF.

Jasanoff, S. (2020). The COVID-19 Pandemic: A Global Crisis of Trust. *Science, 368*(6497), 1431–1432.

Jones, K. E.. (2020). Global Trends in Emerging Infectious Diseases. *Nature*. PMID: 18288193

Kretzschmar, M. E., et al. (2020). *Impact of COVID-19 Control Measures on the Spread of the Virus*. Science.

Marmot, M. (2020). The COVID-19 pandemic and the social determinants of health. *Lancet, 395*(10238), 1181–1183.

Mollenkopf, D., Stolze, H., & Tate, W. (2020). Managing Supply Chain Risks During the COVID-19 Pandemic. *Journal of Business Logistics, 41*(2), 103–121.

OECD. (2020). *The Economic Impact of COVID-19 on Global Economies and Strategies for Recovery*. OECD.

Paltiel, A. D., Zheng, A., & Walensky, R. P. (2009). Assessing Cost-Effectiveness in HIV Prevention. *Journal of the American Medical Association, 302*(10), 1095–1101.

Polack, F. P., Thomas, S. J., Kitchin, N., Absalon, J., Gurtman, A., Lockhart, S., Perez, J. L., Pérez Marc, G., Moreira, E. D., Zerbini, C., Bailey, R., Swanson, K. A., Roychoudhury, S., Koury, K., Li, P., Kalina, W. V., Cooper, D., Frenck, R. W.Jr, Hammitt, L. L., & Gruber, W. C. (2020). Safety and Efficacy of the BNT162b2 mRNA Covid-19 Vaccine. *The New England Journal of Medicine, 383*(27), 2603–2615. DOI: 10.1056/NEJMoa2034577 PMID: 33301246

Ranney, M. L., Griffeth, V., & Jha, A. K. (2020). Critical Supply Shortages—The Need for Ventilators and Personal Protective Equipment during the Covid-19 Pandemic. *The New England Journal of Medicine, 382*(18), e41. DOI: 10.1056/NEJMp2006141 PMID: 32212516

Rothe, C., Schunk, M., Sothmann, P., Bretzel, G., Froeschl, G., Wallrauch, C., Zimmer, T., Thiel, V., Janke, C., Guggemos, W., Seilmaier, M., Drosten, C., Vollmar, P., Zwirglmaier, K., Zange, S., Wölfel, R., & Hoelscher, M. (2020). Transmission of 2019-nCoV Infection from an Asymptomatic Contact in Germany. *The New England Journal of Medicine, 382*(10), 970–971. DOI: 10.1056/NEJMc2001468 PMID: 32003551

Shultz, J. M.. (2016). The Impact of Pandemics on Mental Health: A Global Perspective. *Current Psychiatry Reports, 18*(12), 121.

Taubenberger, J. K., & Morens, D. M. (2006). 1918 Influenza: The Mother of All Pandemics. *Emerging Infectious Diseases, 12*(1), 15–22. DOI: 10.3201/eid1209.05-0979 PMID: 16494711

UNESCO. (2020). *Educational Disruption and Response*. UNESCO. *COVID*, 19.

UNICEF. (2020). *COVID-19 and Children: Impact and Recommendations for Action*. UNICEF.

Vaughan, R., & Tisdall, M. (2020). *Taiwan's COVID-19 Response: A Model for the World*. Financial Times.

Vlassoff, C. (2020). *Pandemic and Health Inequalities*. International Journal for Equity in Health. *COVID*, 19.

WHO. (2020). *Timeline of WHO's Response*. World Health Organization. *COVID*, 19.

WHO. (2021). *Mental Health and COVID-19: Impacts, Concerns, and Solutions*. World Health Organization.

World Bank. (2021). *Global Economic Prospects: January 2021*. World Bank Group.

World Economic Forum. (2021). *The Impact of COVID-19 on Global Supply Chains*. World Economic Forum.

World Health Organization. (2021). *Coronavirus Disease (COVID-19) Dashboard*. World Health Organization.

Zhou, P., Yang, X. L., Wang, X. G., Hu, B., Zhang, L., Zhang, W., Si, H.-R., Zhu, Y., Li, B., Huang, C.-L., Chen, H.-D., Chen, J., Luo, Y., Guo, H., Jiang, R.-D., Liu, M.-Q., Chen, Y., Shen, X.-R., Wang, X., & Shi, Z.-L. (2020). A pneumonia outbreak associated with a new coronavirus of probable bat origin. *Nature*, *579*(7798), 270–273. DOI: 10.1038/s41586-020-2012-7 PMID: 32015507

Chapter 2
Geopolitical Tensions, Trade War, and Sanctions

Uzma Sarfraz Sarfraz
https://orcid.org/0009-0007-2342-1106
Minhaj University, Lahore, Pakistan

ABSTRACT

World tensions born from trade wars and economic sanctions function now as major disruptors which disturb global trade operations and affect price stability. The analysis investigates inflationary effects caused by trade barriers and economic disputes because they break global supply networks while driving up business expenses and reducing operational market effectiveness. Imports become more expensive through tax impositions known as tariffs which drive companies between cost absorption and price increase to consumers thus magnifying inflation rates. The implementation of economic sanctions produces three detrimental effects on trade by blocking customer access to vital resources while simultaneously generating artificial shortages leading to price increases. Trade wars between nations triggered through retaliatory policies both worsen these impacts by breaking down world markets and creating constraints on economical product acquisition.

INTRODUCTION

Political economic and military together with ideological elements produce national. Conflicts and struggles known as geopolitical tensions. Nations develop tensions because of historical conflicts and contested territories as well as power struggles between nations and resource competition. The major geopolitical tensions of the present day involve both U.S.-China relations and the Russia-Ukraine conflict plus the tensions which emerge in the South China Sea. Major disputes

DOI: 10.4018/979-8-3373-1982-7.ch002

result in economic restrictions together with expanded military forces and cyberattacks and trade confrontations which weaken economic progress and harm global peace (Mearsheimer, 2019). Nationalism together with protectionist strategies has produced geopolitical cleavages which damage worldwide joint work especially for security measures and climate change solutions (Allison, 2017). Nations now prioritize competitive technological developments regarding artificial intelligence as well as cyber capabilities because they seek national dominance in these fields (Goldstein, 2020). Geopolitical tensions need diplomatic approaches together with conflict resolution systems alongside international cooperation for preventing conflicts from growing into full-scale wars. Global affairs have been defined by geopolitical tensions throughout centuries while these tensions establish guidelines for economic policies and military plans as well as diplomatic ties. Different factors produce tensions between regions such as history-based tensions and disputes about boundaries and extraction of natural resources as well as variations in philosophies. The major geopolitical disputes of modern times are formed by U.S.-China diplomatic friction and Russia's ongoing war against Ukraine as well as the disputes centered in the waters of the South China Sea. The existing conflicts generate severe implications for worldwide balance along with worldwide trade relationships and worldwide safety (Mearsheimer, 2019). The analysis of geopolitical tensions' origins and consequences helps international stability navigators within policy positions and global organizations alongside multinational enterprises.

Causes of Geopolitical Tensions

The formation of geopolitical tensions results from multiple historical economic military and ideological elements which influence global international relations. The ongoing conflicts across different areas stem from historical grievances which include unsolved territorial claims coming from colonial eras. India and China persist in Himalayan border conflicts because of historical land claims and developing patriotic feelings (Kaplan, 2014). Countries pursue essential resources together with commercial supremacy and advanced technology leadership through their economic contests. Rising competition between China and the United States in semiconductor and artificial intelligence production sectors has led to intensified economic breaking points alongside trade warfare (Allison, 2017). The demand for energy security stands as a critical factor because fuel-importing states attempt to expand their energy mix and resource-abundant countries leverage their energy resources as national power tools. Economic and geopolitical strategies combine when Russia manipulates its natural gas supplies to control Europe (Mearsheimer, 2014). The rising military capabilities as well as power projection intensifies regional tensions in regions where opposing blocs encounter each other. The eastward expansion of NATO has generated Russian concerns which prompted aggressive foreign policy behavior along with military intervention in Ukraine (Mearsheimer, 2014). The growing military activity of China in the South China Sea has generated concern among bordering nations which triggered stronger U.S. military involvement in the Indo-Pacific (Kaplan, 2014). Nuclear weapons systems make geopolitics tougher to manage because states that possess these weapons practice strategic deterrence to prevent large-scale dangerous conflicts. Alliances formation and conflicts development demonstrate a strong link to the ideological differences between authoritarians and democracies. Democratic nations with liberal principles and human rights values face external independence from authoritarian states which focus on internal power accumulation. The ideological gap between nations is currently manifesting in Japan-China and United States-Russian relations due to election tampering and cyber attacks as well as political control activities that weaken bilateral relations (Keohane, 1984). Geopolitical tensions within today's highly interconnected global environment grow as nations use technology advances for cyber warfare purposes. The pursuit of leadership positions by nations includes emerging technologies such as AI and quantum computing and space research because these areas hold both economic and military value (Allison, 2017). Cyber attacks against critical infrastructure together with financial institutions and government systems now serve as typical weapons in geopolitically driven conflicts affecting the United States as well as Russia China and Iran. Modern globalization together with the emerging multi-polar world order system transformed conventional global power arrangements into new power blocs and competitive relations. Global affairs remain defined by national interests and historical legacies and strategic competitions that challenge diplomatic attempts and multilateral institutions to reduce conflicts (Keohane, 1984).

Territorial and Border Disputes

The source of numerous geopolitical tensions derives from border disputes between nations. Governments assert control over regions through three main factors which include historical background as well as economic advantages or strategic value. The South China Sea territorial dispute between China and its regional neighbors and the United States has led to confrontations because China claims this area while the U.S. supports open maritime navigation (Goldstein, 2020). A significant factor behind the Russia-Ukraine war is their territorial dispute regarding Crimea and the eastern Donbas region which became a full-scale conflict in 2022 according to Sakwa (2022).

Economic Competition and Trade Wars

National economic battles function as a leading factor that creates geopolitical strains between countries. Trade wars between the United States and China have emerged through their economic conflict which has disturbed international supply chains and economic development (Allison, 2017). Wars in both the Middle East and Africa began because of competition between nations to gain control of oil resources as well as gas resources and rare earth metals. The political leadership of countries like Russia and Saudi Arabia utilizes their energy supplies as strategic diplomatic instruments to control foreign policymaking decisions (Friedman, 2021).

Technological and Cyber Warfare

Technology has transformed into a strategic power tool for countries who seek to maintain their supremacy in present-day international relations. Different countries pursue global leadership positions in artificial intelligence and 5G networks as well as semiconductor fabrication. Because of espionage concerns and cybersecurity issues U.S. along with its partners restrict Chinese technology enterprises such as Huawei (Segal, 2021). Cyber warfare stands as a vital geopolitical component of present-day conflicts because authoritarian governments orchestrated digital assaults against essential national infrastructure combined with financial sectors and global democratic organizations (Rid, 2020).

Impacts of Geopolitical Tensions

Global stability, economic development, security measures as well as international relations suffer extensive adverse effects due to geopolitical tensions. Major geopolitical conflicts produces two instant consequences in the form of economic disruptions and trade limitations through sanctions and supplies networks interruptions. The U.S.-China trade war established billion-dollar tariffs which simultaneously affected technology and agricultural businesses (Allison, 2017). Market stability throughout Europe and worldwide experiences considerable destabilization when Europe implements economic sanctions against Russia for its Ukrainian invasion (Mearsheimer, 2014). Nations which depend on foreign oil and gas supplies must confront unstable oil prices together with the fear of interrupted delivery. Due to critical dependence on political adversaries the international community now strives toward renewable energy adoption and alternative supplier acquisition to escape geopolitical dominance (Keohane, 1984). Security risks grow more pronounced because military clashes and rising potential for conflict expansion continue to threaten regions. The South China Sea has become more dangerous for naval activities because global superpowers engage in military disputes in this disputed region (Kaplan, 2014). The conflict in Ukraine compels NATO together with European nations to bolster their military strength while altering security frameworks because of Russian attacks (Mearsheimer, 2014). National tensions have reached new heights through cyber warfare and technology competition because states now use cyberattacks to target their infrastructure and institutions and financial systems. The digital threats create substantial risks against global financial infrastructure and critical economic systems in addition to diminishing national security (Allison, 2017). Geopolitical stability creates global humanitarian disasters and war demands that displaced persons leave their homes while food scarcity and human rights offenses occur. Large-scale refugee movements happen due to wars and political instability in the Middle East and Africa which puts major strain on both international organizations and neighboring countries. Economic sanctions designed to penalize threatening countries create increased hardship for civilians since they restrict their access to basic items (Keohane, 1984). The existing geopolitical tensions between nations create barriers to achievement of international collaboration on vital global matters including climate change response and pandemic control and economic development measures. The realignment of national defense and economic interests between states makes it harder for cooperative solutions to address united problems. Countries push past other nations in their pursuit of artificial intelligence and space control through technological supremacy which newest research shows leads to decreased collaborative innovation (Allison, 2017). Despite the obstacles that exist geopolitical conflicts still enable diplomatic progress through negotiations and strategic partnership formation. When nations want to offset more powerful countries they develop strategic relationships through which global power alliances shift. Bringing effective diplomatic engagement to the table keeps negative geopolitical tensions from creating extensive economic downturns and military conflicts and humanitarian crises (Keohane, 1984).

Regionally escalating political conflicts produce economic instability which harms international commerce together with investment activities. The global energy markets underwent price increases after economies implemented sanctions against Russia during its assault of Ukraine as per Sakwa (2022). Supply chain disruptions mainly affect industries that depend on Chinese manufacturing because of these rising tensions (Goldstein, 2020).

Geopolitical tensions between countries usually evolve to military warfare as observed with Russia's invasion of Ukraine. The growing investments in military strength together with arms competitions between major nations including the USA, China and Russia creates prospect of future wars according to Friedman (2021). Hypersonic weapon programs nuclear weapons capabilities alongside artificial intelligence warfare development systems create advanced security complexities for global dynamics (Segal, 2021).

Challenges in Addressing Geopolitical Tensions

Many obstacles block the resolution of geopolitical tensions because of how intertwined global conflicts have become. Definite national interests functions as one main barrier because states continue to place their strategic goals and their economic demands and their security aims ahead of global peace and security. National sovereignty stands in the way of reaching political agreements about important matters including military reductions and settlements regarding territorial disputes (Keohane, 1984). Historical resentments combined with severe mutual distrust between states increase the difficulties of diplomatic solutions through negotiations. The sustained tensions between India and Pakistan due to Kashmir disputes as well as the South China Sea confrontations between China and its neighbors persist in fouling international mediation efforts (Kaplan, 2014).

The utilization of economic policy tools such as trade restrictions and currency manipulations and sanctions turns into a major geopolitical difficulty because it intensifies tensions instead of achieving resolution. The purpose of sanctions is to make aggressive countries comply yet they primarily destroy national economies while driving targeted states to join new alliances thus diminishing the impact of these measures (Mearsheimer, 2014). The increasing global trend of economic nationalism alongside protectionist strategies damages worldwide trade operations causing additional international friction between nations. The economic rift between the U.S. and China together with Russian economic sanctions resulted in worldwide market fragmentation which made nations reevaluate their foreign market dependencies (Allison, 2017).

Defensive alliances as well as defense plans create obstacles when trying to reduce geopolitical tensions. States sometimes consider NATO's expanding eastern borders as direct threats that drive them to take defense measures which result in increased global instability (Mearsheimer, 2014). Weapons proliferation along with modern military technology requires precise deterrance policy management due to its potential to lead to deadly misinterpretations. Governing bodies now face advanced geopolitical challenges because states abuse cybersecurity threats to launch information warfare through attacks and espionage and broadcast misleading content for strategic reasons. The strategies develop new unregulated combat methods which simultaneously destroy mutual national trust (Allison, 2017).

Diplomatic and Political Barriers

The process of addressing geopolitical tensions meets strong opposition during diplomatic discussions. Intensive power conflicts among major nations block their ability to achieve peace through negotiations. The United States and China maintain a competitive relationship which makes global cooperation difficult to achieve (Allison, 2017).

Technological and Cybersecurity Threats

The advancement of cyber warfare along with escalating technological races creates a critical global issue regarding cybersecurity. Cyber attacks against governments and businesses and infrastructure operations threaten many key assets thus warranting enhanced multinational laws and inter-governmental partnerships (Rid 2020).

Rise of Nationalism and Protectionism

Protectionist and nationalist movements throughout the world have reduced global engagement which limits major cooperation on climate change among other subjects. Social policies focused on local development goals disrupt global cooperation since they reduce worldwide consensus on essential problems (Friedman, 2021).

Geopolitical tensions create complex results that influence worldwide peace along with national economic development and national security levels. Different sources of tension emerge from territorial conflicts as well as economic competition and technological competitions and ideological divergences. The consequences resulting from these situations span from armed conflicts to both economic chaos and damaged worldwide associations and human rights situations. The resolution of these difficulties demands direct diplomatic work together with various conflict resolution systems while promoting enhanced worldwide teamwork. The upcoming global power dynamics will need proactive management of diplomatic tensions to create both stability and prosperity in the future.

TRADE WARS

Trade wars joined with economic sanctions serve as essential tools for geopolitical conflicts which control the course of international relations while affecting market stability and worldwide economic systems. Governments implement economic tools as methods to influence opponents politically or to carry out national objectives and respond to national security concerns. Economic wars through trade restrict imports and exports and impose tariffs whereas sanction programs specifically focus on nations or businesses and economic entities to stop economic activities. Global trade and diplomatic relations experience significant impacts because of U.S.-China trade hostilities and Russian sanctions and Iranian and North Korean economic restrictions (Allison, 2017). The crucial evaluation of global geopolitics requires a complete comprehension of trade war origins and mechanisms together with their resulting impacts.

Nations employ trade wars together with economic sanctions to secure geopolitical power as they fight for protection of domestic economies and political dominance. A trade war through economic rules includes countries who implement border tariffs together with import restrictions in addition to offering subsidies to counter perceived unfair trade conditions. Nations and organizations and individuals face economic sanction when punitive measures such as asset freezes and travel bans and trade restrictions are used to obtain political and security-related aims (Allison, 2017).

The world has witnessed substantial geopolitical changes because of trade wars and sanctions throughout the last few years. The intensifying U.S.-China trade war started when America placed tariffs on Chinese imports due to its accusations about Chinese unfair trade practices and intellectual property theft during 2018. The Chinese response with tariffs created worsening relations between these two worldwide economic powers while affecting worldwide manufacturing networks (Goldstein, 2020).

Russian has faced sanctioning since its Crimean annexation in 2014 together with its 2022 Ukrainian invasion. Russian banks together with its energy exports and core industrial activities faced broad international sanctions through a joint U.S.-European Union-allied diplomatic program. The economic measures caused major damage to Russia's economy but brought China and Russia closer together in economic cooperation (Sakwa 2022).

Trade Wars: Causes and Implications

International trade conflicts develop from the fusion of economic forces together with political elements and strategic purposes which stem from national interests and trade restrictions and geopolitical power conflicts. Economic protectionism stands as one main reason why countries create barriers to block out international market competitors. Every government imposes trade barriers with subsidies and tariffs to protect their manufacturing and technological sectors from international market fluctuations. Intelligent Property theft as well as trade imbalances and unfair Chinese government subsidies towards local enterprises ignited the United States and China trade dispute in 2018 (Allison, 2017). Nations embark on initiatives to decrease their dependence on foreign items and services especially in vital sectors such as energy and semiconductors and pharmaceuticals (Keohane, 1984) because it represents another major factor that leads to trade wars. Global companies exhibit a pattern of supply chain relocation and diversified operations because they aim to safeguard their businesses through minimizing reliance on sole trade partners.

The execution of economic policies through strategic competition leads to trade wars especially due to geopolitical tensions and national security considerations. Rival nations face economic constraints by imposition of trade limitations and economic sanctions which impede their economic and military progress. The European Union with the United States implemented economic restrictions against Russia after the Ukraine invasion that specifically focused on isolating the energy sector and defense fields and financial services (Mearsheimer, 2014). Trade disagreements between countries intensify because nations battle to dominate rising industries including artificial intelligence as well as 5G networks and semiconductor manufacturing. Huawei together with other Chinese telecom assets continue to face operating constraints from governments as trade policies have merged with national security considerations (Kaplan, 2014).

Trade wars produce substantial consequences that influence worldwide economic advancement and market sustainability together with international political relations. The immediate result of trade restrictions and tariffs leads business entities to change their supply networks which drives up manufacturing expenses and purchasing prices. The US-China trade war caused prices to increase across electronics and automobiles and agricultural products thus affecting global businesses together with their customers (Allison, 2017). Increased conflict results from trade wars because nations tend to counter initial trade restrictions with additional retaliatory measures. It generates mutual damage between involved parties. The Chinese government retaliated against U.S. tariffs through export restrictions that particularly harmed their agricultural sector impacting all businesses conducting international trade activities.

Economic effects lead only to a fraction of trade wars' consequences since these conflicts damage international diplomatic associations and restructure worldwide political blocs. Trade disputes between countries result in partner shifts which cause trade network systems as well as economic unions to adapt new frameworks. The heightened tensions between the United States and China have led China to enhance relationships throughout Asia and Africa and Latin America while undertaking Belt and Road Initiative projects (Kaplan 2014). Trade wars that extend in duration create financial market instability because investors become less certain about tariffs and economic policies while making business and financial decisions. The intense U.S.-China trade war caused major stock market price swings due to ongoing trade agreement uncertainty according to Keohane (1984).

Economic instability along with deteriorated international collaboration emerges as unexpected results from actions that nations initiate to defend their national interests during trade wars. The resolution of trade disputes accompanied by prevention of extended economic conflicts depends on continuing multilateral agreements and diplomatic negotiations. Trade wars persist as a major international relations challenge as global power structures change because they continuously influence national economic policies and strategic frameworks for the coming years (Keohane, 1984).

Trade wars originate from three main factors which include economic competition together with national security concerns along with political disagreements. The U.S.-China trade war began in 2018 through American trade restrictions placed on Chinese products due to claims about unfair competition along with intellectual property theft and substantial trade imbalance between nations (Goldstein, 2020). The dispute led China to levy tariffs on American exports thereby intensifying economic tensions between America and China as the two biggest global economies. The U.S. has been implementing tariffs against European Union steel and aluminum imports because of national industry protection and economic powers goals (Bown, 2019).

ECONOMIC SANCTIONS

The enforcement of economic sanctions functions as a vital geopolitical intervention method which allows nations together with international organizations to implement pressure against states and other subject matters that violate global security principles or international laws or human rights standards. The targeted governments encounter trade barriers together with financial prohibition systems along with asset seizure regulations as well as trade boycotts to modify their political behavior through non-military means. International bodies deploy economic restrictions to stop countries from beginning conflicts while they simultaneously penalize serious human rights abuses and seek to harm economic strength of their opponents through trade embargoes. The United States alongside the European Union launched heavy sanctions against Russia due to its Crimean annexation in 2014 that escalated through more harsh measures after Russia attacked Ukraine in 2022 through market restrictions and oligarch asset seizures and energy export barriers (Mearsheimer, 2014). International agreements remain an objective of sanctions against Iran through measurements that block Iranian market participation in banking systems and oil markets (Keohane, 1984).

The effectiveness of economic sanctions in pressuring governments comes with serious difficulties that have unfavorable side effects. Economic sanctions negatively affect common people worse than governments because such trade and financial restrictions primarily damage the general citizenry. Food scarcity and rising prices along with economic turmoil within civilian populations became worse because countries like North Korea Venezuela and Iran faced international trade restrictions (Kaplan, 2014). Targeted nations use sanctions as motivation to find alternative economic connections which makes the penalties less effective. Following international western sanctions Russia made strategic economic pacts with both China and India as well as non-western partners thus avoiding economic restrictions and maintaining essentially economic stability (Allison, 2017).

The deployment of sanctions leads to major effects on worldwide commercial activities and worldwide financial stability systems. The SWIFT ban on Russian banks demonstrates how financial system weaponization threatens both worldwide monetary network stability and the possible split of the international financial structure (Keohane, 1984). Stringent economic measures have caused multiple nations to create supplemental payment methods because they want to decrease their financial reliance on Western organizations. Prolonged economic sanctions cause geopolitical divisions when different economic groups form opposite the Western financial restrictions. The United States alongside its coalition partners increased their sanction use which led China along with Russia to establish independent financial organizations and trade pacts to avoid Western dominance (Mearsheimer, 2014). Economic sanctions retain their status as a top choice for geopolitical crisis management because they create substantial adverse effects for opponents even when avoiding actual military engagement. Their success rate depends on three vital elements that include global support and action together with the enforcement system strength and targeted regions' adaptive capacity to handle financial limitations. The use of sanctions will persist to influence global political and economic development patterns that affect international relationships and trade systems as well as worldwide power dynamics according to Keohane (1984).

Purpose and Types of Sanctions

Various geopolitical purposes motivate countries to use economic sanctions with the goals to prevent military aggression and punish human rights violators while denying access to vital resources. Sanctions can be classified into:

- Unilateral Sanctions: Imposed by a single country (e.g., U.S. sanctions on Iran).
- Multilateral Sanctions: Coordinated by multiple nations or international organizations (e.g., EU and UN sanctions on North Korea).
- Targeted Sanctions: Focused on individuals, companies, or specific industries (e.g., freezing assets of Russian oligarchs after the Ukraine invasion).

- Entire economies experience broad-based restrictions through comprehensive sanctions as the United States currently applies to Cuba through its embargo.

Case Study

The response from the U.S. and EU together with allies generated a broad range of sanctions against Russia after its Crimea annexation in 2014 and 2022 Ukraine invasion (Sakwa, 2022). The sanctioning measures imposed substantial economic downturns upon Russia which created currency instability and forced foreign institutions to pull investments and blocked technological import operations. Russia has adopted two approaches to counter the economic challenges by establishing new trading relationships with China and India and implementing parallel financial mechanisms (Mearsheimer, 2019).

Because of its nuclear program development and backing of terrorist organizations Iran maintains continuous exposure to sanctions from global powers. The economic sanctions imposed on Iran have blocked its oil exports while limiting bank operations and damaging international trade relations which produced harsh economic consequences (Friedman, 2021). The international community imposed major sanctions on North Korea that target its nuclear weapons advancement capabilities. Strategic economic sanctions have led to weakened economic conditions in the target countries but not stopped their military activities because of the constraints of economic tools in modern geopolitical strategies (Allison, 2017).

Challenges and Effectiveness of Trade Wars and Sanctions

Trade wars along with economic sanctions function as common geopolitical instruments although experts continue to question their effectiveness because they create multiple obstacles and adverse results. Both trade wars and economic sanctions pose economic self-damage risks because they inflict considerable harm to both the target nation and their imposing counterparts. Tariffs imposed within the U.S.-China trade war elevated costs for Americans across both consumer and business sectors and harmed supply chains supporting advanced technology and farming operations (Allison, 2017). The European nations suffered because Russia imposed energy price increases after Ukraine sanctions (Mearsheimer, 2014). Global economic systems demonstrate an interdependent structure since trade limitations generate adverse impacts which affect both involved parties.

These safety measures demonstrate restricted durability when viewed from a long-term perspective. The purpose of trade limitations and economic sanctions is to drive political change in targeted governments but these measures commonly trigger an economic shift instead of forcing the release of control. Sanctioned states attempt to bypass economic restrictions by creating domestic production capacities and establishing new business relationships with non-embargoed countries and conducting illegal trading operations. Economic sanctions have failed to dissuade Iran from pursuing its nuclear program as the country continues development while Russia turns towards Asian markets in response to Western economic pressure (Keohane, 1984). Under authoritarian rule the implementation of sanctions serves to create internal nationalism through propaganda to gain power rather than surrendering to foreign conditions (Kaplan, 2014). Sanctions lose their ability to produce political alterations when faced with such situations.

Economic and Humanitarian Consequences

Political sanctions alongside trade wars usually produce unforeseen results which affect ordinary residents to a greater extent than officials. The Iranian and North Korean populations face escalating prices together with product shortages and deteriorating standards of living because their movements in trade and banking sectors remain restricted according to Goldstein (2020). Global food and energy pricing surged worldwide following Russia sanctions which threatened the well-being of grain-importing developing nations and all global markets (Sakwa, 2022).

Adaptation and Countermeasures

The targeted nations tend to build various countermeasures which let them bypass economic trade barriers. Russia increased its economic relations with China as well as other non-Western partners to reduce the harm caused by Western economic sanctions (Mearsheimer, 2019). Iran has found ways to avoid economic restrictions by creating shadow banking networks and illegal trade systems for commercial operations (Friedman, 2021). Political conflicts often extend in time because these strategic changes lower the success rate of economic urban development tools.

Risk of Escalation and Retaliation

The implementation of trade wars along with sanctions tends to intensify diplomatic tensions as the affected parties adopt retaliatory actions that carry on conflicts for extended periods. The U.S.-China trade war triggered multiple escalating tensions through technological transfer limitations and essential goods import taxes together with diplomatic tensions which badly damaged their bilateral relationship according to Segal (2021). The nuclear pursuit of North Korea proceeded uninterrupted throughout decades under economic restrictions according to Allison (2017).

Geopolitical conflicts employ trade wars together with economic sanctions as potent weapons to affect worldwide trade relations and economic stability and diplomatic ties. When applied by foreign powers to change governmental practices they produce negative financial ripple effects and worsen human suffering and create defensive actions that diminish their desired outcome. The ongoing U.S.-China trade war, sanctions on Russia, and restrictions on Iran and North Korea highlight both the strengths and limitations of these economic strategies. Global power shifts require political leaders to combine diplomatic solutions with economic practices which will minimize enduring conflicts while preserving international stability.

Role of Tariffs in Trade Wars and Economic Policy

Tariffs function as essential defensive and offensive instruments in economic policy by safeguarding home-based industries and reaching worldwide policy objectives. Governments deploy tariffs against imported goods to increase their cost level so consumers tend to select local alternatives over foreign ones. Governments implement this strategy to defend important industries at the same time they work to maintain employment numbers and shrink international trade imbalances. The United States began placing import tariffs on Chinese products in 2018 to fight against the U.S.-China trade war because they wanted to stop intellectual property theft and address unfair trade practices and growing trade imbalances (Allison, 2017). The implementation of protective measures brings temporary help to domestic companies but it causes unwelcome repercussions through price hikes and diminished market competition while third parties respond with countermeasures.

Government entities use tariffs extensively in trade policies to control imports while safeguarding industries at home while creating tax income for public funds. Any country can implement tariffs through which it adds costs to imported products thus steering domestic consumers towards choosing domestic alternatives (Irwin, 2020). Economic relations between countries and worldwide trading patterns experience lasting effects because of tariff usage in trade wars. Tariffs provide protective measures to national industries but they trigger retaliation and output price rises that develop into disputes between major global economies.

One fundamental economic policy reason for imposing tariffs consists of safeguarding newly emerging businesses using the infant industry protection approach. National protection of local companies through trade barriers creates an environment where domestic firms develop into international competitors. Extended use of trade barriers causes domestic firms to become inefficient and less innovative and promotes unwillingness among them to improve their operations. The historical implementation of high tariffs through the Smoot-Hawley Tariff Act of 1930 during the Great Depression triggered counterreactive policies which resulted in worldwide economic slowdowns (Keohane, 1984). The current trade disputes between U.S., China and the European Union have triggered reciprocal protective measures which disrupt worldwide production lines while causing business expenses and consumer costs to rise throughout the world (Kaplan, 2014).

Developing economies use tariffs as a financial resource because they find it difficult to collect income or corporate taxes. The use of tariffs as an economic revenue tool becomes less impactful than the negative economic effects which diminish both imports and exports while generating inflation and delaying growth in the economy. Through tariffs on steel and aluminum imports the Trump administration triggered rising manufacturing costs that impacted both construction sector as well as automobile production (Mearsheimer, 2014). The initiative aimed to rekindle home-based metal production yet many companies experienced higher expenses which they needed to transfer to their customers.

Nations use trade sanctions through tariffs because this method functions as a negotiating instrument to push other countries toward accepting trade agreements. Countries intend to use strategically imposed tariffs on political industries for diplomatic leverage during international disputes. China applied tariffs to U.S. agricultural exports specifically aiming at soybeans in order to challenge American farmers because they form a vital political group in the United States (Allison, 2017). Through such instances of strategic tariff implementation nation-states demonstrate how economic policy measures serve as geopolitical tools that change alliances and economic interdependency.

Types of Tariffs and Their Economic Impact

Protective Tariffs

Protective tariffs defend domestic industries through price-increased imports which limit foreign competition. In 2018 the United States introduced trade barriers against Chinese steel and aluminum shipments to support American manufacturing firms (Bown, 2019). The protective policy intensified the cost structures for American businesses because they needed imported raw materials during this period.

Revenue Tariffs

The main purpose of revenue tariffs is to actualize earnings for governmental bodies instead of blockade foreign imports. Before income taxation became the primary revenue source for governments tariffs functioned as a dominant method of financial income generation in the past. Friedman (2021) explains that modern developing countries maintain tariffs as their primary method to finance both public services and infrastructure development.

Retaliatory Tariffs

Such trade measures represent the enactment of punitive duties which another country establishes against imports. Trade wars typically involve these measures as one of their main characteristics. China implemented trade barriers against American farm products throughout the U.S.-China trade conflict especially against strategic industries in pivotal political states within the United States (Goldstein, 2020). When implemented these measures create an upward spiral in trade tensions simultaneously destroying global business connections.

Tariffs in Modern Trade Wars

In current international trade disputes countries employ tariffs which serve as economic instruments and geopolitical weapons to achieve advantage during geopolitical confrontations. Modern global trade disputes have witnessed rising government-imposed tariffs which serve to defend home industries and modify economic exchanges in response to international trade disputes mainly due to escalated diplomatic negotiations regarding business dealings. Modern geopolitical battles show the United States has weaponized its trade wars with China and Europe as well as additional trade partners during the past decade.

The ongoing U.S.-China trade war initiated in 2018 demonstrates how tariffs function as instruments for reducing trade discrepancies and fighting suspected unfair trade methods. The United States released hundreds of billions of dollars in Chinese product tariffs following accusations that China conducted intellectual property theft and forced technology sharing along with additional unreasonable trade practices (Allison, 2017). China applied retaliatory trade tariffs to several American products such as agricultural goods as well as electronics and automobiles. The trade tariffs damaged worldwide supply networks and triggered higher expenses for buyers while generating business uncertainties among operations which depend on international commerce. The trade conflict enhanced our understanding of the easability of global supply chains when tariffs create obstacles for businesses as they try to redirect their sourcing methods to dodge imposed duties. Producers such as Apple and Samsung which operate in technology and manufacturing experienced increased production expenses when trade tariffs were applied to Chinese products (Keohane, 1984).

The implementation of modern trade war tariffs enables nations to use economic penalties against trading partners for both statutory and diplomatic objectives. As part of the U.S.-China trade conflict tariffs served both economic purposes and functions as a strategic tool to pressure China into reforming its trade policies. The U.S. deployed trade policies to minimize commercial deficits with China while sustaining American intellectual creations from piracy and impeding Chinese authority across fields such as wireless network infrastructure and AI innovation (Kaplan, 2014). The U.S. government used its tariffs on Chinese products to negotiate with China about markets and intellectual property protections and additional issues. Although the economic impact was severe the escalating trade war failed to deliver swift relief to both countries making permanent industry supply chain disturbances along with increased costs and diminished market standing (Mearsheimer, 2014).

The use of tariffs extends beyond the U.S.-China trade conflict because these tools have shaped numerous trade disputes between the United States and both the European Union as well as Mexico and Canada and other international trading partners. American tariffs against European steel and aluminum have been justified by national security concerns while the government has implemented tariffs against Mexican and Canadian products during NAFTA renegotiation attempts. These tariffs have triggered major trade conflicts between nations which caused more countries to adopt retaliatory tariffs to worsen the existing tensions. European governments responded to United States steel and aluminum tariffs by targeting American bourbon whiskey and motorcycles and jeans thus disrupting worldwide trade and causing global industry disruption (Keohane, 1984).

Current trade wars through the implementation of tariffs create essential economic evaluations for worldwide markets. Taring protectionist policies give industries brief domestic assistance at the expense of higher customer and business rates and slower economic expansion and financial instability. Consumer prices increased due to the U.S.-China trade war since tariffs elevated production prices and blocked affordable imports of electronics clothing and food products (Allison, 2017). The implementation of tariffs results in market fragmentation because countries instead prefer regional agreements rather than global trade frameworks thus hindering international trade efficiency.

U.S.-China Trade War

Tariffs acted as the primary element of the trade conflict between the United States and China which started in 2018. The United States started placing trade taxes on an extensive value of Chinese merchandise accusing Beijing of stealing intellectual property and conducting unfair business methods. China issued trade tariffs which affected American soybean imports together with cars and technological items.

The trade dispute between the United States and China continued indefinitely and created higher costs for buyers as well as halted supply routes and global economic instability (Segal, 2021).

Tariffs on European Goods

The U.S. government applied levies on European metals and aluminum during 2018 because its security needs demanded them. The European Union chose to impose customs duty restrictions on American whiskey and motorcycles and farming products (Bown, 2019). The trade measures between America and Europe created tensions between the two blocs and negatively impacted their industrial sectors.

India's Tariffs on Agricultural Imports

The agricultural sector of India has used protective tariffs for historical protection through trade policy. India applied trade restrictions to American almonds alongside apples and walnuts after the U.S. ended its Generalized System of Preferences benefits. The use of tariffs demonstrates their dual purpose that serves defensive protection and retaliatory response (Irwin, 2020).

Economic and Political Consequences of Tariffs

Tariff measures spread extensive consequences throughout political and economic systems which affect countries both implementing and experiencing the trade restrictions. The application of tariffs through economic protectionist measures and geopolitical bargaining creates various market disturbances which lead to unforeseen diplomatic impacts.

Economic Consequences of Tariffs

From an economic point of view tariffs generate immediate impacts and established long-term results. The direct outcome of introducing tariffs results in elevated costs that consumers must pay. By implementing tariffs on imports a nation forces manufacturers to increase product prices because importers tend to transfer the added expense to their purchasing customers. During the U.S.-China trade war the American public along with businesses faced higher consumer prices on Chinese electronic products and textiles besides machinery because of the implemented trade tariffs according to Allison (2017). The restriction of imported goods through tariffs creates negative effects for consumers due to elevated prices which diminishes their purchasing ability and could reduce market consumption.

Tariffs substantially impact global supply chains by disrupting their operation. Manufacturers in numerous modern industries connect multiple stages of their production facilities across international borders. The trade barriers implemented through tariffs create disruptions that augment the expenses across supply chain operations from resource acquisition to finished goods. When tariffs occur certain organizations must choose between new suppliers or moving their manufacturing operation resulting in higher production expenses. Economic growth becomes slower and global trade declines while production efficiency decreases as a result. Technology firms in the United States experienced higher production expenses after U.S. government-enacted tariffs against Chinese electronics manufacturers thus causing rising customer prices for electronics and reducing U.S. technical sector competitiveness (Keohane, 1984).

When countries reciprocate with their own trade barriers the result becomes trade barriers that get steadily worse and damage both economic sides involved. The U.S.-China trade war retaliatory tariffs negatively affected America's agricultural sector by decreasing Chinese demand for U.S. exports in China (Kaplan, 2014). Chinese imports of U.S. soybeans, pork and agricultural products made the agricultural sector highly sensitive to tariff changes resulting in economic disruption throughout this industry. Tariffs become harmful for both nations because they cause industries in each country to suffer while trade disputes may stretch over multiple years.

Long-term usage of tariffs tends to divide the world economy into separate market blocs. Countries respond to bilateral trade barriers through dual action. They establish new localized trade pacts instead of using the global multilateral framework. The changes could diminish the effectiveness of the World Trade Organization (WTO) along with its mission to eliminate trade hurdles while fostering free trade. Modern economic growth could decline because greater emphasis on bilateral and regional trade agreements would fragment and decrease efficiency of the global business system (Mearsheimer, 2014).

Political Consequences of Tariffs

Countries tend to use tariffs strategically in their diplomatic relations for political gains. Taxes on imports serve governments to penalize foreign countries when they perform practices that conflict with national interests such as intellectual property violations or aggressive geopolitical practices or when engaging in unfair trade practices. The United States applied tariffs to China for two purposes: resolving trade deficits and enforcing Chinese reforms of intellectual property protection and market participation (Allison, 2017). When countries apply tariffs as an economic coercive tool they try to force opposing nations into discussions for policy changes. The effectiveness of political pressure through tariffs becomes limited because target nations usually choose resistance or retaliation that creates a continuous pattern of trade conflicts.

The implementation of trade barriers generates significant political impact throughout domestic territory. Throughout their campaigns politicians frequently implement these trade barriers to support groups of citizens whose jobs are endangered by foreign market competition in industrial production. Governments use tariffs to show their dedication to defending domestic businesses together with employment opportunities to gain increased backing from these voting groups. Despite the initial political backing of higher prices and industry problems caused by retaliatory tariffs. The support from affected constituencies becomes weaker. The U.S. steel and aluminum import taxes were intended to protect American metal producers but provoked increased expenses for automotive manufacturers and other industries dependent on these raw materials. According to Keohane (1984) political support for tariffs will diminish when economic conditions of the country deteriorate.

High tariffs frequently create serious diplomatic problems that damage bilateral relationships and eventually lead governments to end their mutual support programs. External trade battles go past economic priorities since they entwine with both security threats and political perspectives along with large-scale geostrategic competition. According to Mearsheimer (2014) the U.S.-China trade war extended beyond trade imbalances to include competition for global supremacy particularly regarding technological advances and military expansion. Broader political or security interests undergo the process of politicization when they influence economic decisions in trade relations thus making diplomatic resolutions more challenging to achieve.

Tariff implementation leads to deterioration of trade dispute arbitrating institutions established internationally. International trade disputes are now handled by the World Trade Organization (WTO) together with other global organizations that work to advance international collaborative practices. The implementation of unilateral tariffs together with protectionist policies threatens to diminish institutional power making the global trading system rules-based structure collapse according to Keohane (1984). International organizations find it challenging to resolve disputes because countries choose unilateral action which leads to political and economic conflicts becoming worse.

Role of Sanctions in Global Trade and Geopolitics

Countries together with international organizations utilize economic and political sanctions as their crucial method to put stress on foreign governments and entities or single persons. Sanctions differ from tariffs because their primary purpose goes beyond economic use for coercion because they function to implement international rules and penalize agreement violations alongside limiting enemy operational capabilities (Drezner, 2019). The various forms of sanctions include commercial trade barriers as well as freezing assets and prohibiting movement and enforcing monetary penalties. These economic barriers appear when international bodies respond to security threats and human rights breaches as well as geopolitical tensions and nuclear developments. Sanctions rarely fail to modify national behavior but they challenge civilians through economic constraints and inspire nations to create countermeasures and generate unexpected diplomatic impacts.

Types of Sanctions

Trade sanctions serve to block both international goods shipments into and out of countries. Countries employ these economic tools to diminish access to vital resources which harms their domestic economies. The U.S. and European Union (EU) and their partner states implemented large-scale trade limitations against Russia after it seized Crimea in 2014 as well as after the Ukraine invasion in 2022 which banned the export of cutting-edge technology products while blocking Russian market participation (Sakwa, 2022).

Nations receive financial exclusion from worldwide financial systems as the main purpose of financial sanctions. Such restrictions involve blocking access to bank accounts in addition to stopping transactions and prohibiting investment activities. The United States together with the European Union placed financial sanctions against Russian banks that block their ability to work with the SWIFT international financial system resulting in Russian economic instability (Gould-Davies, 2022).

Under targeted "smart" sanctions programs economic measures specifically target persons or organizations and particular business sectors rather than applying general limitations. Political leaders lose their financial assets while businesses related to corruption receive operating bans as government officials see limitations in their mobility. The U.S. as well as the EU have used their economic sanctions to target Iranian political figures and Chinese authority officials who violate human rights (Pape, 2021).

Sanctions in Global Conflicts

Western powers implemented extraordinary economic restrictions that targeted Russian banking operations and oil exports while striking major industrial facilities after Moscow started the war in Ukraine. Sanctions resulting from these measures have triggered a downward trend in the economy, financial currency weakness and fewer opportunities for foreign investment. Sanctions have not managed to cripple

Russia entirely since the country succeeded in building stronger diplomatic partnerships with China and India according to Sakwa (2022).

The United States has maintained sanctions against Iran throughout many decades with primary emphasis on its nuclear program development. When pulling out of the 2015 Iran Nuclear Deal America put in place heavy sanctions which targeted Iranian exports of oil and its banking institutions. Although the sanctions created severe economic problems in Iran they were not sufficient enough to completely halt its nuclear progress (Pape, 2021).

The Effectiveness and Consequences of Sanctions

Sanctions can greatly hurt an economy by preventing them from being able to trade and therefore getting financial aid. For instance, such as Iran's economy which went through supply cuts to oil sales and North Korea, illustrated in the food shortages as a result of embargo on trade (Gould-Davies, 2022).

Sanctions hit governments, not people, but they inevitably span the breaches and cause inflation, unemployment and shortages of essentials for ordinary citizens. Sometimes, humanitarian carve outs are included to let in food and medicine, but implementation is challenging (Pape, 2021).

Sanctions might pressure the target countries to align themselves with other countries. Russia for instance has also stepped up trade with China and India after Western sanctions. Meanwhile, Iran has improved its political and economic ties with China and Russia as a way of going around the U.S. restrictions (Sakwa, 2022).

While sanctions can influence governments into bargaining, they do not always swell into definitive policy adjustments. Countries from North Korea to Iran have these kinds of policies, disregarding sanctions for years. Excessive use of sanctions may diminish diplomatic initiative (Drezner, 2019).

Sanctions have become a major player in global geopolitics as so-called soft tool of warfare to shape international behavior. They can be used to a meaningful degree to break economies, constrain the ability of adversaries, or enforce norms of international behavior. Their impact, however, is not always straightforward because the targeted countries usually come up with countermeasures. In addition, hardship comes from sanctions and proliferation of global alliances. As geopolitical tensions keep changing, effectiveness of sanctions is still a subject of a discussion among politicians who are trying to find a balance between strategic benefits and unexpected consequences of these economic and other restrictions.

Trade Conflicts: SOURCE and EFFECTS and GLOBAL IMPLICATION

Trade disputes occur when countries disagree on tariffs, import and export blocks and trade policies capable of impairing their economic relations. These trade wars normally originate from protectionism, unfair trading practices, currency devaluation and competition in geopolitics. Trade is conceived as a means of promoting economic cooperation, but disputes disturb world markets, breed supply chain uncertainties and sometimes lead to larger economic or political disputes. Well-known trade conflicts have influenced International economic policies, for instance U.S.-China trade war, U.S.-EU tariffs frictions, as well as trade controversies between Japan and South Korea (Bown, 2019).

Causes of Trade Conflicts

Protectionism and Tariffs

Protectionist policies, like tariffs and importers of restriction, are published to safeguard the domestic industries from international trade. And yet when one nation adopts protectionist policies increase tariffs another nation may respond in the following way trade conflicts. By way of illustration, the U.S.-China trade war started in 2018 when the U.S. imposed tariffs on Chinese products as Beijing failed to follow fair practices and commit intellectual property theft. In retaliation, China applied tariffs on United States exports rebutting and amplifying tensions and destroying global supply chains (Irwin, 2020).

Unfair Trade Practices and Subsidies

Councils sometimes at the fore accuse one another or of engaging in competitive unfair trade practices -- subsidize the domestic government industry, currency manipulation, and dumping (selling goods below the cost of production to destroy rivalry). The U.S. and EU have long subjected competing over subsidies, especially in the aviation sector. Dispute between Boeing (U.S.) and Airbus (EU) continued to litigate for years to World Trade Organization (WTO) and then the counter tariffs on aircrafts and other goods (Krugman, 2021).

Intellectual Property Disputes

Intellectual Product (IP) theft and technological transfer appeals are tough sources of trade disputes. US accuses China of compelling US firms to hand over tech to enter China. The Trump administration claimed this as a main cause for imposing tariffs on Chinese goods. These disputes have raised worries about economic espionage as well as national security threats to the technology sector (Goldstein, 2020).

Trade Agreements and Policy Differences

Trade agreements too can spark dissensions and conflict. States frequently seal free trade agreements (FTAs) that curtailing tariffs and boosting market access. A however, disputes arise when one party asserts the other's breach of the agreement or tortfeasor, or potentially gaining an unfair competitive edge. Brexit is a poster child as the UK and EU fought subsidy will contend over commission regulation, customs rules, and founded chains (Baldwin, 2021).

Geopolitical Rivalries and Economic Sanctions

Trade war is frequently linked to geopolitics. Countries employ economic sanctions and trade embargoes as instruments of political leverage against their foes. To illustrate, U.S. has declined to trade with Iran and Russia, microbes their access to worldwide commercial networks and trades. Correspondingly, Japan and South Korea have a trade dispute over historical legacies and security issues, impacting on semiconductor supply chains (Sakwa, 2022).

Major Trade Conflicts in Recent History

U.S.-China Trade War

One of the biggest trade conflicts in recent times, the US-China trade war started in 2018 when the US imposed tariffs on some Chinese merchandise worth in billions, citing trade deficits and unfair trade practices. China retaliated with taxes on US goods including soybeans, cars, and electronics. This conflict have caused global supply chain disruption, cost increase of production, and spillover to economic uncertainty all around the world. Although some partial accords, underneath of tensions continues between both economic superpowers (Segal, 2021).

U.S.-EU Tariff Disputes

The US and the EU have been engaged in the trade war, especially on issues on steel and aluminum tariffs. US imposed tariffs on European metals in 2018 citing national security concerns. The EU retaliated with tariffs on US products including motorcycles, whiskey and agricultural products. Bown (2019) also went on to mention that because of the long-standing Boeing-Airbus dispute which ultimately resulted in retaliatory tariffs on goods across the pond affecting transatlantic trade (Transatlantic Trade by the Numbers, 2018).

Japan-South Korea Trade Dispute

In 2019, Japanese export restrictions on sensitive materials crucial in the manufacture of semiconductors, including memory chips and processors of notebooks and mobile phones, citing security risks over South Korea's treatment of sensitive technology. For South Korea this was seen as a politically motivated effort related to contested history. The conflict also weakened economic relations between the two biggest technology powers and brought anxieties about worldwide hair film dispatch lines (Mearsheimer, 2019).

India-China Border Dispute and Trade Restrictions

After their border clashes in 2020, India has barred Chinese investments and banned several Chinese mobile apps, citing national concern. China in return decreased imports of Indian goods. This conflict in trade serves to illustrate how political tensions between neighboring countries can interfere with economic relations(Goldstein, 2020).

How Trade Conflicts Contribute to Inflation

Tariffs Increase Costs for Businesses and Consumers

Tariffs are a common trade conflict tool – they are import taxes. When a country applies tariffs on foreign goods, the imported goods become more costly. This increased cost is often capitalized to companies which made rely on imported materials, and amounts to eventually to consumers in rising cost of their goods. For instance, in the U.S.-China trade war (2018-2020), the United States imposed tariffs on Chinese imports worth over $350 billion covering items such as electronics, apparel and house-hold items. Because of this, American businesses paid more for raw-materials and components, which, in turn, created higher retail prices (Irwin,

2020). And not misled by China counter-attacking tariffs on U.S. agricultural products and causing food price shake ups.

Supply Chain Disruptions Result in Shortage And Higher Price

Trade wars frequently lead to logistical disruptions, such as shortage of critical raw materials, goods parts, and completed items for businesses. When supply is in short supply and demand remains strong, prices will elevate. An influential example is the semiconductor shortages prompted U.S. limitations on Chinese technology businesses, such as Huawei - Global supply chain of microchips which is essential for automobile, smartphones and all other electronics were impacted as these import restrictions. As outcome, the car and electronics market prices rose since shortages happened Goldstein, (2020).

Currency Devaluation and Inflationary Effects

Trade tensions can spark currency fluctuations that adds up even more to inflation. When tariffs and sanctions lower exports, the countries affected by this may devalue their currency to increase their competitiveness. A decline in currency value, raises the cost of imports, as well as the price of goods which contain foreign alloys. In the course of the U.S.-China trade war, the Chinese yuan fell (depicted in dollar terms) against the U.S. dollar, raising the price of imports from China to U.S. consumers. Throughout, this devaluation added to inflationary pressures across sectors of business needing Chinese goods, for example consumer electronics and garments (Segal, 2021).

Energy Price Shocks Due to Trade Disputes

Trade disputes impacting oil- and gas-producing countries can cause oil and gas prices to surge. For example, sanctions enforced on Russia after its 2022 invasion of Ukraine compromised the global oil and gas supply. As western countries have scaled back on their usage of Russian oil, the world has seen fuel prices rise, aggravating inflation in energy-reliant economies (Gould-Davies, 2022). Equally, the US's unfaltering squeeze on Iran's oil exports in 2018 – cut oil into global supplies – go driving up fuel costs. Because energy expenses affect transportation and production expenses in virtually all industries, price increases of this character are responsible for adding to the level of inflation (Krugman, 2021).

Food Price Inflation Due to Trade Restrictions

Trade disputes in agriculture can be important contributors to the food price increases. When large scale food exporting countries implement restrictions, it shrinks the global food supply and sharpens prices. For instance, the complications with India and Malaysia over palm oil shipments resulted in uneven prices of edible oil streams around the world. Apart from that, Russian's decision to cap its grain exports after the Western sanctions led to a world-wide wheat price hike, affecting the affordability of food worldwide (Sakwa, 2022).

Business Cases Show How Trade Wars Cause Inflationary Pressures

U.S.-China Trade War and Consumer Goods Inflation

An intensive price rise happened to multiple consumer goods in the United States because of the ongoing U.S.-China trade war. According to Bown (2019) the Federal Reserve demonstrated that household prices increased by $1277 annually because of tariffs. The costs of washing machines combined with furniture pieces and clothing items rose substantially because of additional tariffs implemented.

Brexit and Rising Import Costs in the UK

After the UK departed from the EU new trade barriers and customs rules as well as import taxes raised business expenses for EU imports. British food consumers dealt with both higher prices and disrupted supply of perishable items such as fresh fruits and vegetables during the examined period (Baldwin, 2021).

Russia-Ukraine Conflict and Global Energy Inflation

Russia endured record-breaking high levels of oil and gas prices as an outcome of international sanctions after its Ukrainian invasion in 2022. European power markets suffered from increasing electric and heating expenses because they depended heavily on Russian energy supplies which drove manufacturing industry inflation rates higher. The global escalation of food prices happened because Ukraine lost its position as one of the biggest wheat exporters worldwide (Gould-Davies, 2022).The escalating trade disputes trigger inflation through manufacturing expense increase while damaging supply networks together with marketplace instability. The implementation of trade barriers together with regulatory limitations causes price rises across consumer products as well as energy sources and food items. Understanding how trade conflicts create inflation plays a crucial role in creating economic stability policies that maintain trade security between nations during economic and geopolitical challenges.

CONCLUSION

The rise of global inflation affects businesses and consumers together with national economies because of increasing trade conflicts and geopolitical tensions between nations. Market prices shift because of economic challenges which include tariffs as well as supply chain problems and currency exchange rate movements. Multiple disputes between the US-China and Brexit nations together with Russia-Ukraine have resulted in increased costs for imported products and energy and food supplies thus deepening worldwide economic uncertainty. The disputes between Russia and NATO and the tensions in the South China Sea region lead to disruptions of supply chains as well as disruptions of energy. Nation-states should create a balanced alignment of economic measures while working together with strategic economic policies to deal with inflationary problems. The reduction of worldwide armed clashes depends on diplomatic efforts and multilateral meetings and regional cooperative agreements which foster international cooperation. Protective tariffs provide immediate industrial development and negotiation power yet they lead to economic problems that result in market segmentation and delayed international growth.

REFERENCES

Allison, G. (2017). *Destined for war: Can America and China escape Thucydides's trap?* Houghton Mifflin Harcourt.

Baldwin, R. (2021). *The great convergence: Information technology and the new globalization*. Harvard University Press.

Bown, C. P. (2019). *The trade war and its effects on global supply chains*. Peterson Institute for International Economics.

Drezner, D. W. (2019). *The sanctions paradox: Economic statecraft and international relations*. Cambridge University Press.

Friedman, T. L. (2021). *The world is flat: A brief history of the twenty-first century*. Farrar, Straus and Giroux.

Goldstein, A. (2020). *China's rise to power: Conceptions of state governance and global influence*. Stanford University Press.

Gould-Davies, N. (2022). Economic sanctions and international power struggles. *International Affairs*, *98*(2), 305–321.

Irwin, D. A. (2020). *Clashing over commerce: A history of U.S. trade policy*. University of Chicago Press.

Kaplan, R. D. (2014). *Asia's Cauldron: The South China Sea and the End of a Stable Pacific*. Random House.

Keohane, R. O. (1984). *After Hegemony: Cooperation and Discord in the World Political Economy*. Princeton University Press.

Krugman, P. (2021). *Arguing with zombies: Economics, politics, and the fight for a better future*. W. W. Norton & Company.

Mearsheimer, J. J. (2019). *The great delusion: Liberal dreams and international realities*. Yale University Press.

Pape, R. A. (2021). Why economic sanctions do not work. *International Security*, *22*(2), 90–136. DOI: 10.1162/isec.22.2.90

Rid, T. (2020). *Active measures: The secret history of disinformation and political warfare*. Farrar, Straus and Giroux.

Sakwa, R. (2022). *Frontline Ukraine: Crisis in the borderlands*. I.B. Tauris.

Segal, A. (2021). *The hacking of the American mind: Cybersecurity and global conflicts*. PublicAffairs.

Chapter 3
Energy Market Shocks:
Effect of Oil Price Volatility on Supply Chain

Sudeept Maharana
https://orcid.org/0009-0004-3777-5042
School of Management and Entrepreneurship, Indian Institute of Technology, India

ABSTRACT

Oil price changes disrupt global supply chains, raise manufacturing costs, and fuel inflation. Energy-intensive industries face instability, impacting consumer spending. AI uses predictive analytics to manage energy market shocks, improve supply chains, and mitigate inflation risks. Volatile oil prices create confusion for businesses and policymakers. AI models enable accurate oil price forecasts, helping companies adapt logistics and operations to energy price shifts. Rising energy costs drive inflation by increasing production and distribution expenses. AI-powered financial planning adjusts to market conditions, aiding inflation control. AI ensures economic stability by predicting market trends and adapting to energy market uncertainty.

INTRODUCTION

The economic activities require substantial amounts of energy to function. The availability of energy resources is the main limitation that restrains economic growth. In the energy market, each transaction involving energy takes place. Every trader in the market has an essential interest in sustaining a stable energy market output. Business production and market trading can benefit from specific insights into how the energy market behaves under extreme circumstances—the market value fluctuations in energy influence business operations, which in turn helps lower economic

DOI: 10.4018/979-8-3373-1982-7.ch003

risk factors. Economic performance influences the energy market functionality, yet access to energy resources establishes the basis for economic achievement. The 2023 yearbook of World Energy & Climate Statistics reveals that the worldwide average growth of energy consumption reached a level of 1.4% throughout the period from 2010 to 2019. An economic recovery following the pandemic caused global energy consumption to increase by 4.9% in 2021 and another 2.1% in 2022. Economic activities drive most of the performance indicators in the energy market. In recent years, the world economy has experienced increasing threats to its stability. Worldwide economic activities experienced extreme shocks that created substantial uncertainty and produced extreme market volatility in the energy sector. The West Texas Intermediate (WTI) crude oil price declined approximately 300% when COVID-19 shattered global markets and registered a negative value on April 20, 2020. This brought financial losses to millions of market traders (Liu et al., 2023).

The AI industry's leading role during the industrial revolution has sparked research about technological innovations within the energy sector in the last few years. New technological developments create motivation for digital transformation, which has fundamentally transformed how people produce and use energy. One of the primary effects of the modern industrial revolution is the development of the AI industrial sector. AI serves various economic sectors through its deployment, which extends to energy-related operations. AI technology currently handles various data sets connected to the energy industry. When energy users and producers apply AI-based data management tools for decision-support systems, these systems achieve enhanced convenience and effectiveness while providing superior efficiency. Machine learning, deep learning, and natural language processing are the leading AI algorithms for processing energy-related data. The ongoing economic operations and the potential destruction of economic growth can be prevented by this practice (Liu et al., 2023).

BACKGROUND OF ENERGY MARKET WITH IMPACT AND SHOCKS

Energy Market

The majority of energy consumers understand retail markets because they get to select from multiple suppliers along with their rate options. Homogeneous commodity exchanges permit traders to exchange energy products through future oil and gas contracts. Investors acquire the choice to buy or sell specified quantities of oil products instead of conducting physical sales or purchasing physical barrels. The understanding of the wholesale energy market depends on the unfeasibility of electric power storage at scale. The constant task of grid operators involves adjusting power production output from generators against consumer electricity requirements. The electricity value exchange happens among generators who make power and suppliers delivering electricity to end users as trader conduct transactions between them. Such market arrangements sustain a properly functioning wholesale electricity system through the steady fulfilment of supply and demand dynamics. The energy exchange between generators and energy suppliers operates under pre-established contractual terms in bilateral market trades. The generators and suppliers maintain pre-established agreements which define how they should proceed with each electricity deal. Different electricity contracts embrace diversity regarding purchase agreements while setting prices according to established general principles. Generators use the grid operators to report their upcoming electricity trading volumes, enabling the Transmission System Operators (TSO) to maintain supply and demand balance. The TSO maintains observation of all activities occurring within the Day-Ahead Energy Market. Suppliers purchase electricity for tomorrow using price rates set by marginal principles and current supply-demand dynamics. The national grid engages in real-time purchasing through different balancing services as its last step before the transaction. Ancillary services such as demand response act as supplementary operational tools that maintain power supply and demand control above transmission and generation levels. These measures are the last defence to maintain stability and protect security in the power grid. The rise of renewables in the world's energy supply creates a need for ancillary services that counteract the inconsistent nature of solar and wind resources (Antonova, 2024).

Prices of Global Energy Market

- The price structure for natural gas in main global markets, including the United States, Europe, and Japan, remained attached to oil prices throughout the initial half of the 2000s. The forward and backward price movements of natural gas and oil occurred uniformly, and both commodities maintained equivalent energy-based cost structures. During that time, natural gas and crude oil markets operated as a single integrated system under regulatory and non-market-based pricing schemes. The independent price of coal maintained rates of approximately one-third lower than the oil values when measured in terms of energy content. The rising energy prices during the early 2000s transformed every aspect of these situations (World Bank, 2013).
- Energy linkages between U.S. natural gas prices and Asian natural gas prices and oil prices disappeared due to this change. The market transition established a difference between WTI (the mid-continent U.S. price) and Brent (the international marker). The oil price boom directly connected natural gas and coal prices in the United States. All conditions change direction in their

current patterns. The convergence between WTI-Brent prices is set to occur during 2014 or, at most, 2015. The U.S. coal mass transfer system shows indicators which suggest it will stay joined to natural gas prices in the future (World Bank, 2013).

- Implementing natural gas price convergence requires multiple policy and investment decisions, so achieving this goal will likely take a long time. The analysis of natural gas and oil price relationships becomes intricate because it depends on unknown factors regarding induced innovation development, which cannot be assessed or predicted. U.S. Natural gas extraction rates increased when the region started using horizontal drilling and fracking technologies, so supply rose, resulting in lower domestic natural gas prices. The low natural gas prices encouraged U.S. industries to opt for this energy source, particularly electricity generators, which are beginning to replace coal plants with natural gas facilities. From 2006-08 to 2009-11, the United States decreased its coal usage by 10.5%, though global coal consumption expanded by 9%. Natural gas price coupling across markets requires removing market constraints from demand and supply forces and policy barriers that, should occur in the future run (World Bank, 2013).
- The worldwide supply of unconventional natural gas resources outside the USA has expanded. Production of unconventional gas has only occurred in the United States by itself. Numerous areas worldwide possess sufficient unconventional natural gas resources, particularly Asia Pacific and South America and regions across North America. Research from the industry indicates unconventional gas reserves, counting half of available recoverable natural gas reserves at current market rates and existing technical capabilities. Slow technology adoption occurs because of weak property rights management and insufficient knowledge concerns (World Bank, 2013).
- A total of 31% of natural gas flows between international borders through pipeline trade 21% and liquefied natural gas (LNG) delivery 10%. This figure exceeds foreign crude oil trades that reach approximately two-thirds of international exports 46% of oil exports and 20% of product exports. New LNG facilities and gas pipeline development increase prices in natural gas-producing areas while lowering pricing levels in the consumption markets. The expenses of liquefying and transporting natural gas will always generate higher trade prices than traditional pipeline gas (World Bank, 2013).
- The relocation of manufacturing industries to the United States from other markets demonstrates how businesses exploit the natural gas opportunity instead of following work cost advantages that resulted in previous industry migration to Asia. Four energy-intensive industries use the United States for their production facilities because of its reduced energy prices and these sec-

tors include paper manufacturing alongside aluminum production and steel manufacturing as well as chemical manufacturing. These industries allocate between 5% to 9% of their material costs towards energy expenses (World Bank, 2013).

- The increased coal trading will improve the natural gas price convergence between regions while accelerating the existing merger of coal and natural gas price trends. The global coal export market increased substantially by 258 million tons in seven years (2005-2012) until reaching almost 758 million tons, pushing the percentage of coal in total production to nearly 15%. Various available data observations suggest natural gas prices have the potential to rise even more (World Bank, 2013).
- The policy areas influencing natural gas trade and price convergence include U.S. energy exports, nuclear energy, and property rights. Implementing three policy types will enhance natural gas trade growth, supporting market price convergence. The United States plans to eliminate energy export limitations from the post-1970s oil crisis because of energy safety worries. After the Tohoku disaster in Japan, numerous states reviewed their nuclear energy strategies because some countries wanted to let ageing nuclear units reach end-of-life without replacement. Yet, others want to remove power units ahead of schedule. The worldwide reduction of atomic power participation in energy resources since 2001, when nuclear power reached its maximum of 6.4%, has resulted in increasing coal and natural gas utilization and limited adoption of renewables. States with abundant unconventional resources will establish new measures to protect property rights since this absence often leads to non-development decisions. The United States executed fracking and horizontal drilling techniques in the oil industry, triggering equal supply effects (World Bank, 2013).

Oil Prices

The contemporary global economy depends heavily on oil as its primary energy source. Even though alternative energy sources such as wind, water nuclear and solar power have increased in popularity, they remain secondary to oil as the worldwide energy staple. Energy use through oil has been the most critical source from the middle of the twentieth century until today. The global economy depends heavily on oil; therefore, its market value serves as a standard measurement for every country. Low international oil prices offer multiple positive effects to nations that import oil since these lower prices decrease production costs and raise consumer activity, accelerating economic growth. The populations of oil-exporting nations experience benefits from elevated oil prices because these prices boost export income and produce more significant investments and improved welfare across their countries. The patterns of oil price evolution have undergone substantial changes throughout the historical period. A stock exchange market has controlled oil price settings since 1986, following many years of oligopolistic control in the market. The stock exchange market influences daily oil price changes by multiple geopolitical and natural events, weather patterns, and transportation variables. Minor price changes in the oil market do not extensively affect the economic stability of countries that export oil, yet sudden price shifts can create instability within national economies (Aladwani, 2024).

Energy Market Shock

The extensive military confrontation between Russia and Ukraine began on February 24, 2022, which triggered Western countries to launch sanctions through US leadership. The designed target of these sanctions worked to stop Russian energy exports and ultimately triggered an extensive energy emergency. Political events at this level generate extensive and enduring effects, especially in worldwide energy markets. The economic evaluation of these crises becomes vital for all governments and their policymakers to manage appropriately. The imposed sanctions unified to stop Russian energy exports, triggering a major power crisis. US President Biden declared through a March 8, 2022 announcement that Russia would no longer receive products incorporating oil, natural gas and coal as imports. The United Kingdom soon joined President Biden by announcing a Russian energy product import ban for the same year, and Japan declared a restriction on exporting energy technology to Russia. The European Union (EU) began its fifth wave of Russia sanctions in April 2022 by banning Russian ships from member port entry, restricting national investments into Russia's energy sector, and eliminating trade of listed refining items and technologies to Moscow. The EU announced extra restrictive measures through its sixth round of sanctions against Russia on June 3, 2022, including banning select petroleum products and placing sanctions on Russian oil shipping operations and their supporting finance institutions. The combined actions of the Western government pressured major Western energy corporations, including BP, Royal Dutch Shell, ExxonMobil, and Equinor, forcing them to end their business and technological partnerships with Russian energy companies. The UK, alongside EU nations, imposed restrictions that barred home-based insurance providers from assuring the transportation of Russian oil via ships, which prevented maritime access to international oil markets for Russia (Sun et al., 2024).

Economic restrictions primarily target Russian fossil fuel exports because they underpin the country's currency income generation and supply its energy needs to Western regions, specifically Europe and the United States. During 2021, Russia exported oil, which represented 11.4% of global total oil exports. Coal exports total 17.8%, and natural gas exports reached 19.1%. Russia exports substantial oil, gas and coal products to Western markets, including European Union member states, the United States and Japan. Western nations headed by the United States enacted sanctions against Russia that caused worldwide energy prices to surge rapidly through the international energy market. The energy crisis exposed fundamental weaknesses in global energy systems, which led to evaluations of future energy sustainability possibilities. The global economy experienced profound impacts through the wild swings between supply and demand for international energy resulting from Russia's sanctions and the dramatic price increase. Economic projections from Germany's Federal Ministry for Economic Affairs and Climate Protection show a 1.4% reduction from January expectations to reach a 2.2% growth rate in 2022. The Russia-Ukraine military conflict and current energy price spikes constitute the main reason behind this reduction. Energy prices have risen to a level that has substantially inflated household budget expenses. The statistical data released by Eurostat shows that the Eurozone's inflation rate reached 8.5% in March 2022. The rising living expenses have greatly exhausted residents, triggering widespread demonstrations among European nations. Developing economies and less prosperous nations continue to suffer from the same situation (Sun et al., 2024) .

The Sri Lankan government faced worsening economic conditions after losing its dependence on imported energy, which led to power rationing and soaring electricity and fuel prices. The economic crisis has caused the public to demonstrate intense displeasure through demonstrations, which resulted in domestic unrest. The economic situation in Sri Lanka represents a common problem, according to World Bank Chief Economist Carmen Reinhart, who observes that many other developing countries will soon encounter similar economic troubles. The Russia-Ukraine war outbreak has led to a lasting increase in major commodity prices, particularly in oil and natural gas. The ongoing price trend has generated major economic inflation across countries, strongly affecting global energy market transactions. Local geopolitical conflicts now project that global crude oil costs will rise along with worldwide energy prices, which will impose elevated energy expenses on countries, further increasing business costs and thus affecting domestic economies. The US dollar's current strength strengthens exports of crude oil and natural gas from the United States in such localized geopolitical standoffs. Global energy markets' rising instability and non-sustainable nature create significant barriers to attaining the United Nations Sustainable Development Goals (SDGs). The complexity requires the worldwide organization to take multiple actions to guarantee a stable and sustainable energy supply at reasonable prices and achieve sustainable development targets. Research on the Energy Crisis Triggered by the Ukraine Crisis must be an immediate priority (Sun et al., 2024).

Impacts of Energy Market Shock

The military invasion of Ukraine by Russia in February 2020 started a sequence of Western economic restrictions, which the United States led as the primary actor. The export of Russian energy products became the main focus of Western economic limits. Russian energy supplied about 40% of natural gas to the EU, a significant import market for Russian resources. European power infrastructure faced critical difficulties finding alternative energy sources because of restricted supplies from other areas, demonstrating that global markets reacted strongly to geopolitical disruptions. Similar importance has been identified regarding energy within geopolitical conflicts before. Energy supply security became a pressing issue throughout EU countries because various political and economic circumstances presented challenges. Worldwide energy market disruptions force governments to operate under considerable strain. The direct and substantial effects of the Russia-Ukraine conflict touch each nation that maintains significant economic and financial bonds while allowing free movement across both countries. The essential basis of energy is that it is a fundamental foundation supporting all economic activities and social functions. Global economic stability depends heavily on commodity price increases triggered by rising energy expenses, which leads to limited availability of crops and cereals in the food market. The worldwide rise in energy expenses would generate universal cost-of-living emergencies and numerous social conflicts, which could trigger social chaos. The crisis has consequences which surpass price increases. The Russia-Ukraine military conflict produced food supply shortage problems that increased hunger levels, particularly in developing nations (Sun et al., 2024).

International energy prices have soared since the start of the Russia-Ukraine conflict, triggering massive disruptions throughout global energy operations. This price surge triggered many long-term effects that spread worldwide and produced enhanced prices throughout the globe alongside geopolitical challenges while slowing economic growth and mounting inflation and debt, making existing problems harder to address. Positive macroeconomic developments have emerged in nations such as Canada, Russia, Mexico, Southeast Asia, Australia, and Middle East oil-producing countries, but a range of other nations, including China, Japan, South Korea, the United States, the United Kingdom, the European Union, South Asia, Middle East non-oil-producing countries, and Africa experience significant adverse effects on their macroeconomic interests. The EU faces a substantial situation with Russia and Ukraine trade because of its strong commercial relations and dependency on Russian and Ukrainian food and energy imports. The increase in international energy prices created massive economic impacts on Russia's economy. The United States and other Western countries have tried to reduce Russian economic power by limiting oil exports, yet there remains no explicit agreement on the actual effects.

The export revenue from Russian energy sectors increased by a staggering 93 billion euros, according to the Finnish Center for Energy and Clean Air Research reports on these 100 days of the Russia-Ukraine conflict. European Union's dependence on Russian energy allows Russia to avoid Western sanctions because it accepts payments through alternative currencies such as the ruble. The Russian economy receives meaningful foreign exchange revenue through this option, which moderates the damage of Western sanctions. Residents worldwide share similar income and consumption patterns with GDP since Middle Eastern nations subsidize their energy prices, thus protecting household spending (Sun et al., 2024).

Oil price boosts pending in the market will drive substantial price rises throughout South Asia and increase inflation while raising living expenses across Japan, China, and South Korea. Domestic investment patterns experience effects due to the energy price surge. Energy-exporting nations supporting China, Japan, and the United States, including the European Union, the United Kingdom and Middle East oil states, and South Asian territories, increased their domestic investments. The decreasing trend in investment exists for Russia, Africa, Latin America, Mexico, Middle East non-oil-producing countries, Canada, Southeast Asia, and Australia. Multiple elements influence these patterns because they relate to energy dependence, tile energy markets fiscal income, interest rates, capital flows, and geopolitical instability. Rising international energy prices prompted multiple nations along with territories to expand their exports because they could enhance their energy product output capabilities. Rising prices across different parts of the world due to this surge led to more significant quantities of exported products. The export growth in the energy sector stems primarily from Southeast Asia and Middle East oil-producing countries while South Asia and Latin America and Middle East non-oil-producing countries and the European Union have followed. The escalating energy import expenses have forced Russia, Southeast Asia, South Asia and Africa to curb their energy purchases with additional funds. Several nations and areas show higher import market activity because they benefit from raised budgetary funds and improved foreign exchange assets. The price increases have produced worldwide impacts that mainly affected South Asia while causing significant life changes for its inhabitants. Chinese and South Korean residents and Japanese citizens have experienced substantial price increases, which may destabilize their economic systems and elevate expenses for people and businesses (Sun et al., 2024).

Different parts of the world have experienced varying decreases and increases in social welfare based on how changes influenced economic income and consumer spending patterns. Russia's rising domestic price levels have caused a deterioration of social welfare for its residents. Australia and the Middle Eastern oil-producing countries used the energy pricing situation to secure significant portions of the energy market while improving public welfare. The global economic winners and losers become evident through this dual system due to rising and falling resource price values. The rising energy prices during the Russia-Ukraine conflict are expected to reduce the overall industrial output of China, Japan, South Korea, the United States, the European Union, the United Kingdom, Russia, the Middle East non-oil-producing countries, South Asia and Africa. Rising oil production enhancing output occurs in Canada, the Middle Eastern oil-producing countries Mexico, Australia and Southeast Asian nations, leading to distributional changes in regional sector production levels. The United States has the potential to gain advantages through energy sanctions against Russia even though it would experience limited economic consequences. During the Russia-Ukraine crisis, the United States possessed a unique opportunity to reach its strategic goal of controlling Russia while weakening European economic power. A plausible result emerges from America's efforts to produce stronger political and economic relationships with Europe and enhance its energy exports to the region. The Russia-Ukraine conflict presents a massive challenge to global energy trade because it will substantially transform worldwide energy provisioning systems. The current strife allows China to enhance its economic and energy cooperation with Russia because of the containment activities conducted by the United States and European Union. The existing geopolitical struggle demands organizations to review their entire trading structure along supply chains to establish new global agreements. The de-globalization trends, the world has become fragmented into semi-autonomous regional blocs; thus, value chains will likely undergo decentralization. The Russia-Ukraine military conflict, combined with increased global energy prices following Western economic restrictions against Russia, has brought substantial financial impact to both Western and developing countries. Global uncertainties will continue to unfold because of the prolonged Russia-Ukraine conflict while Western nations enforce additional export restrictions against Russia. Competitiveness in the euro area faces continued deterioration through the medium term because the European economy remains vulnerable to recession. (Sun et al., 2024).

MAIN FOCUS OF CHAPTER: INFLATION AND ENERGY MARKET SHOCKS

Inflation and Oil Prices

The fluctuations in global output and oil prices are linked with inflationary shifts. Several advanced economies, emerging markets and developing economies (EMDEs) experienced rising inflation from the early 1970s to the mid-1990s because of higher oil prices, strong output fluctuations, and financial crises, including debt and currency destabilization. The mid-1980s and early 1990s saw brief oil price collapses, which caused short-term inflation declines within both advanced economies and EMDEs. These relationships have regained attention as inflation rates have risen across various countries. Inflation rates dropped during the early COVID-19 pandemic before their upward climb within multiple nations starting from mid-2020. Inflation levels in different countries rose at similar rates because of a strong post-implementation market recovery, worldwide supply difficulties, and irregular food and petroleum price shifts. Global inflation has strengthened due to rising oil prices after Russia invaded Ukraine in February 2022 (Ha et al., 2023).

Global Shocks and Inflation

During the 1970–2022 period, the global shocks, including demand and supply conditions and oil prices, explained 26% of the inflation changes across the median countries. The combined influence of demand shocks 18% and oil price shocks 4% generated significant inflation variations stemming from global shocks. Three-quarters of the countries demonstrate significant oil price shock effects, which produce changes in inflation rates despite their seemingly minor inflation-contributing role in typical countries. The median country experiences a two-year inflation increase of 1.2% points due to a positive one-standard-deviation oil price shock similar to the early 2022 oil price change during the Russian invasion of Ukraine. In advanced economies, the sources of inflationary variance from global demand and oil price shocks exceed those in Emerging Markets and Developing Economies. Global shocks particularly global demand together with oil price shocks became major factors in explaining inflation changes when global economies experienced recessions or faced significant oil market disruptions. Oil price shocks during the period from the third quarter of 1973 to the first quarter of 1974 raised overall year-on-year inflation by 3.4% points out of the 7%-point increase. The rise in inflation from the second quarter of 2021 to the second quarter of 2022 was primarily driven by oil prices to a degree of about 10% (Ha et al, 2023).

The impact of international shocks expanded throughout the years such that global shocks became responsible for approximately 36% of inflation variations, whereas they contributed only 20% of inflation before 2000. Research shows that oil price shocks became doubly important between the pre-2000 period, with a 4% influence, and the post-2001 period, with a 9% influence. The analysis is influenced principally by economic global demand and oil price effects that developed during global recessions in 2009 and 2020 and through extreme periods of extreme oil market volatility. Various country features determined how important oil price shocks were when explaining inflation variations. In economies with well-established international trade and financial bonds, the inflationary impact of oil price movements became more statistically significant. Among countries primarily dependent on commodity imports, oil price shocks gave rise to a substantially more substantial impact on their inflation levels. Therefore, the inflation variance from oil price shocks proved statistically significant in monetary policies without inflation targeting, which operated under fixed exchange rates combined with high levels of government debt (Ha et al., 2023).

In the average nation from 1970–2022, global demand fluctuations and petroleum price changes emerged as the two essential elements that jointly explained 22% of all inflationary changes. Results from this research verify the earlier findings published by other authors. The substantial influence of global demand disturbances (oil price disturbances) stemmed partly from significant inflation fluctuations that followed global economic downturns and oil market disruptions in all decades over the past fifty years. During 1970–2022, global shocks produced 35% of inflation variance in advanced economies, while EMDEs experienced 19% of global shock-induced inflation changes. The worldwide economic demand disturbances contributed 25% of the inflation volatility across advanced economies but only reached 14% in EMDEs. Advanced economy oil price shocks established themselves as inflation influencers at an extent twice the measurement of 3% found in EMDEs. The results may stem from the higher similarity level between advanced economies, while multiple system characteristics of unified monetary policies and deep trade and financial connections explain these findings. Advanced economies display uniform monetary policies, resulting in much higher homogeneity of their inflation expectations when compared to EMDEs. EMDEs show greater diversity among their member states since inflation in these countries mainly reacts to local economic conditions (Ha et al., 2023).

Oil Sector and Price Volatility

The oil sector's vital global economic foundation experienced significant shifts, including unstable prices that affected several economic segments throughout history. A complete understanding of oil sector dynamics requires thorough studies of historical developments and the analysis of price variations alongside current business advantages and difficulties resulting from considerable data utilization. The oil sector's price volatility throughout history has deeply affected macro and microeconomic parameters. The oil sector underwent significant structural changes starting from the 1970s oil shocks, and different industries produced varying responses to oil price fluctuations. Japan, which ranks as the third-largest crude oil purchaser in the world, has demonstrated a high level of sensitivity to oil price changes among its commercial, industrial and transport sectors, but oil price changes barely affected residential usage. Oil price volatility impacts more than traditional sectors because it creates a noticeable effect on the renewable energy market. Stock market indices faced significant impacts from the COVID-19 pandemic as it darkened the clean energy sector. During the pandemic, investors and policymakers discovered that infectious disease volatility indexes require evaluation in renewable energy market planning. Libyan economic sectors experience positive or negative impacts due to oil price movements, affecting agriculture, construction, manufacturing and transport industries. The rising oil prices had minimal overall effects on the manufacturing sector. The world devotes much research to oil price volatility because it has global economic consequences. Economists have introduced multiple theories to explain market movements in oil price levels. The oil market is a multilayered system controlled by numerous economic features and influences from the business sector. Japanese economic sectors demonstrate different responses to changes in crude oil prices because Japan is the third-largest oil-consuming nation globally. The residential industry showed minimal reaction to shifting oil prices. However, commercial and transport, as well as industrial sectors showed significant sensitivity to oil price changes, particularly after the 2011 Fukushima event resulted in higher dependency on imported oil and less sensitivity to oil price volatility (Okogwu et al., 2023).

Oil Price Changes and Supply Chain Reactions

Within the worldwide energy framework, the oil industry is a foundational element because its price points keep changing, affecting Supply Chain (SC) modifications in subsequent years. Investigating oil market prices from the past gives insight into sector development alongside methods used to deal with market complexity. Since ancient times, the oil and gas sector, alongside other fossil fuels, has displayed various effects on economics, society, and the environment. Regular operating practices of fossil fuel SC generated the majority of world-warming effects through Co_2 emissions from fossil fuel combustions. A complete comprehension of oil market shifts and supply logistics happens through analyzing the modern and past fossil fuel distribution paths. A sustainable energy transition needs the development of policies which will improve its economic viability. A new corporate law proposal would impose legal responsibility on shareholders to face the environmental consequences of their investment companies. The proposed policy seeks to use capital resources more efficiently for clean technology development to drive sustainable energy innovations. The method explains that investment behaviour determines supply chains' responses during oil price variations. The coal sector includes significant energy domain components that demonstrate adjustments through the development of both human civilization and industrialization processes. The analysis examined the coal industry's future directions along with key elements that would substantially impact its development path. The new coal production technologies demonstrated significant potential to clean up the industry and make it more competitive, which affected the global market structure and supply chains. The evaluation of invisible economic impacts from natural disasters possesses exceptional value in studying supply chain responses. Economic activities that did not stem from damaged enterprises were evaluated to understand how disruptions affected local SC losses. The approach provides valuable insights into the diverse range of indirect losses the SC can face due to disruptions through a complete analysis of oil price alterations and chain reactions. The past analysis of crude oil pricing effects and SC reactions delivers significant insights into the intricate relationship between economic matters and social structures with environmental elements. Analyzing historical trends and present-day developments allows this section to provide in-depth insights into the methods used to handle the complicated oil price fluctuation environment (Okogwu et al., 2023).

Research on Supply Chain and Past Oil Price Crises

The essential oil position throughout the world's economy brings many crises through varying petroleum prices that demand well-built supply chain approaches to support sustainability while reducing adverse outcomes. Nigeria faces economic challenges from unstable oil prices since its business climate remains exposed to oil demand- SC risks and disruptions. The solution proposes strengthening economic diversity and trading alongside non-trading markets to protect Nigeria from SC failures. The strategy targets reducing the long-lasting consequences of oil price fluctuations affecting economic performance and business conditions. The Environment of businesses' impact assessments of oil production was crucial in developing sustainable SC models. The bio-gasification was the best method for extra virgin olive oil (EVOO) extraction since it generated superior environmental advantages compared to composting. The research examined how rising oil prices affect commodity prices by analyzing energy supply chain systems. Through decades-long secondary data evaluations, the researchers examined the origins of oil price rises before designing strategies to address energy-based SC perils. Moreover, a study delved into sustainable green service Supply Chain Management (SCM) in the oil and gas industries. The research developed an assessment framework for sustainable green service SCM through evaluation from an organizational and environmental perspective. The research showed that green logistics combined with enhanced environmental performance across service SC is an important sustainable competitive resource that enables better environmental, social, and economic risk management and creates sustainable services (Okogwu et al., 2023).

The current global economy heavily relies on the oil sector as its central element because oil price movements produce extensive economic consequences. Price fluctuation heavily impacts the SC sector, so adaptability is a leading method to reduce the negative results of oil price instability. The changes in the oil market price have solid economic growth effects, which can be observed in Ghana's economy. The analysis utilizes dynamic stochastic general equilibrium modelling to research what affects oil prices and monetary policy fluctuations that create Ghana's economic growth. The authors revealed a complicated relationship between interest rate disturbances and price movements, emphasizing why flexible SC approaches are necessary for dealing with oil price volatility in complex economic systems. SC designers must integrate sustainability principles because this approach helps build adaptability within SC systems. This approach demonstrated a sustainable method to create the best biodiesel/diesel SC by assessing economic sustainability alongside environmental and social factors. The researchers presented tactics to determine the best quantities, dimensions, and placement of bio-refineries and solid waste plants, creating an adaptable supply chain system (Okogwu et al., 2023).

SOLUTION AND RECOMMENDATIONS: ARTIFICIAL INTELLIGENCE AND ENGERY MARKET

Artificial Intelligence in Energy Market

The AI industry is a key force for the 4th industrial revolution because it helps transition digital economies while supporting economic operations. The study of AI deals with objects that sense environmental signals before executing operational commands. Technology handles many tasks that human beings should perform with their intelligence. AI industry functions through data technology systems that parallel data status to new oil resources. The AI algorithm allows the world to achieve greater processing efficiency for its data. AI researchers extensively investigate AI's economic effects, including interrelated domains like economic development, corporate production and innovation, public management, social and household welfare, and sustainable development. Recent research indicates that AI technologies transformed all parts of modern human existence (Liu et al., 2023).

The addition of AI with smart grids impacts energy sector alteration because it makes well-organized electric distribution networks which also boosts working dependability and conservational sustainability. Smart grids operated by machine learning and advanced analytics in conjunction with AI technologies process data from real-time monitoring points across the grid infrastructure network. The system integration enables operators to obtain improved demand predictions, automated demand responses, and equipment maintenance predictions that enhance operational stability with cost reductions. Smart grids grew in popularity from modern infrastructure development combined with renewable energy implementation since conventional power systems struggle to meet these new demands. Brilliant grid technologies experience increased funding support from governments and energy companies because regulation forces these organizations to develop carbon emission reduction programs and improve energy efficiency metrics. AI systems achieve better prediction and decision abilities through increasing Internet of Things (IoT) devices and their sensors, which gather high-precision data. The energy sector transforms because these trends develop power grids which unite management capabilities with strong operational features that align with future sustainable energy needs (P, 2023).

AI achieves its optimization potential using advanced computational methods and algorithms to achieve energy generation consumption and distribution optimization in the sector. The four core components of AI implementation within this context are machine learning with deep learning, natural language processing, and data analytical capabilities. Structured information from smart meters and sensors and stored energy consumption patterns become accessible to energy companies using these technologies for decision-making. AI technology enables the energy sector to perform three key functions: predictive maintenance, future equipment failure prediction, real-time energy management, and grid management for network stability improvements. The four groups of energy users benefit from AI through utility providers, grid management personnel, energy supply generators, and final electricity consumers. The implementation of AI by utility companies enables them to forecast demand patterns to run their supply structures effectively. Their clients enjoy automated smart homes with AI-controlled energy efficiency, which leads to lower expenses and fewer losses. AI has enhanced total energy system efficiency through energy-saving innovations that deliver improved reliability and sustainability benefits from end to end. Market advancement occurs because of the progressive development of highly sophisticated AI solutions that generate renewable energy(P, 2023).

The leading companies in the energy market sustain rapid strategic development and dynamic business expansion through their AI sectors. Energy companies put significant funding into research to improve their AI systems. At the same time, the main areas of focus include predictive analytics, machine learning algorithms, and IoT system connections. The organizations devise these tactics to enhance operational effectiveness and build market domination by creating innovative solutions. Regulatory requirements push businesses toward AI-driven solutions, which they implement due to their need for sustainable and efficient energy operations leading to market expansion. Business success relies heavily on strategic partnerships because they enable organizations to combine technology resources to expand market reach. Manufacturers focus on making their AI solutions expandable by developing cost-effective basic digital infrastructure that supports energy systems while their staff continues to refine these products. AI technology progress urges producers to create sophisticated products that deliver service to broader customer bases. Two key drivers of future AI for energy market expansion include new technological developments alongside technology collaborations and heightened demand for environmentally sustainable solutions (P, 2023).

Trends of Artificial Intelligence in Energy Market

AI in the Energy sector generated USD 13,164.4 million in revenue in 2023 before it is forecasted to earn USD 15,228.6 million in 2024 and advance to USD 46,188.9 million in revenues by 2031 with an anticipated annual growth rate of 17.18%. Platforms that use AI to power renewable energy solutions experience increasing development because the power grid requires improved renewable energy integration through more reliable and efficient methods. Solar panels and wind turbines receive AI-based optimization technology for the operational enhancement of renewable energy systems. AI solutions make predictions about weather patterns to optimize renewable energy source operation, enhancing energy output and reducing time-based interruptions. Renewable energy's growing acceptance stems from the worldwide initiative of decreasing carbon pollution and increasing renewable energies. Governments worldwide and organizations continue setting higher renewable energy targets while recognizing the importance of AI as their essential achievement instrument. Renewable energy technologies have become more affordable through reduced costs because of simultaneous advancements in AI technology. AI systems help utilities optimize power grid operations by forecasting and calibrating irregular production levels from renewable energy sources, which results in stable and dependable electricity distribution. The growing practice is essential for developing a sustainable power system of the future (P, 2023).

Segmentation Analysis

The global market implements segmentations through component, deployment, application, end user and geography. The market is divided according to components into solutions and services. AI solutions control seventy-seven point three-five percent of the AI in energy market share in 2023 due to their extensive advantages across the energy sector. The solutions area of application includes predictive maintenance, energy management systems, innovative grid technologies, and renewable energy optimization. Through their broad scope of operation, AI solutions help energy companies resolve multiple business issues at once to create more efficient, enable, and sustainable energy systems. The adoption of AI solutions is spread broadly throughout the energy sector because of escalating energy requirements combined with regulatory constraints and because business operations require better analytics capabilities and real-time decision support systems. Wider adoption of AI solutions results from the ability to merge them with existing infrastructure platform solutions and build intuitive user interfaces. The dominant market position of AI stems from significant investments in AI research and essential strategic partnerships that advance the deployment of innovative solutions (P, 2023).

By Application

The market separation based on application includes robotics, renewable management, demand forecasting, safety & security, infrastructure and other applications. The forecast period indicates a spectacular 18.49% CAGR for the safety & security segment because of rising requirements to protect critical energy infrastructure from new security threats. The growing digitalization of energy infrastructure creates new weaknesses against cyber incidents and security breaches. AI technologies have become a priority for security enhancement because they offer strong threat detection and real-time monitoring systems that provide rapid emergency responses. Energy companies perceive cybersecurity awareness growth and strong security frameworks as necessary drivers that require significant spending on AI-powered safety and security solutions. The need for enhanced security compliance at regulatory and industry standards levels drives the market demand for advanced AI-based safety and security systems. Through AI security operations, organizations stop unauthorized intruders and reduce possible threats to safeguard essential infrastructure and sensitive data. These upcoming factors will drive the projected growth of the safety & security segment (P, 2023).

By End User

AI in the energy market divides itself into four segments based on end-users: energy transmission, energy generation, energy distribution, and utilities. The AI energy transmission sector reached USD 3,185.7 million in 2023 revenue due to its essential function in SC energy delivery systems and the broad adoption of AI technology for transmission operation optimization. Growing electricity requirements make it necessary to maintain dependable power transfer methods which link electricity generation facilities to power consumers. AI technologies enhance the performance of transmission networks through developed grid management solutions that produce real-time monitoring alongside predictive maintenance capabilities. Energy companies can detect and solve upcoming issues through these technologies before they materialize, thereby minimizing operational disruptions and maintenance costs. Complex transmission management solutions for renewable energy integration are needed because these sources demonstrate variable characteristics. AI solutions help utility companies distribute their load more effectively, reduce energy transmission losses, and improve flow efficiency to maintain stable energy transmission (P, 2023).

Regional Analysis of Artificial Intelligence in Energy Market

The international AI in energy market segments itself by geography into North America, Europe, Asia-Pacific, MEA, and Latin America. Global research shows that the Asia-Pacific AI in the energy sector maintained a 40.20% share with a market value of USD 5,291.7 million in 2023. Market leadership emerges from rapid industrial development, growing urbanization, and the essential demands of sustainable energy solutions needed for national economic progress. Several countries, especially China, India, and Japan, use their financial resources to implement AI systems that improve energy management and smart grids and optimize renewable energy generation. Implementing AI systems happens through state-funded projects in modern energy infrastructure development and direct financial investments. Asia-Pacific must immediately deploy advanced AI solutions to enhance efficiency and reliability as the region increases its power consumption across many users. The proactive collaboration between public agencies and private entities in installing AI solutions for energy applications makes Asia-Pacific lead the AI in the energy market. The European market will experience remarkable growth at a 17.10% CAGR in the various years through its stringent sustainability framework and comprehensive renewable energy commitments. The European nations actively use sophisticated AI technology to boost operational energy efficiency and merge renewable power capabilities with their power systems. Clean energy promotion and carbon emission reduction policies from the European Union are fundamental drivers behind this market expansion. Significant financial support fuels investments for innovative grid technologies, energy storage solutions, and AI predictive maintenance systems to develop the power sector. The regional market expands through mutual partnerships between technology providers, academic institutions, government bodies, and private corporations. European nations achieve better domestic market results through digital transformation platforms with innovative energy solutions by enhancing their energy networks to reduce operational expenses and ensure reliable power supply (P, 2023).

Competitive Landscape

A market research report for the energy market AI segment provides crucial information related to sector division rules. Leading market companies use merger and acquisition partnerships, joint ventures, and product development methods to boost the range of their products while strengthening market dominance across different geographical areas. Manufacturers enhance market competition by implementing research and development investments and creating new facilities with improved supply chain operations (P, 2023).

Problem/Challenges in Artificial Intelligence for Energy Market

Innovative energy implementations of AI lead to communication problems, including difficulties in managing data quality and scarcity, parameter optimization of AI, structural complexity demands, workforce shortages, integration challenges, and legal accountability. Busy work remains to detect and evaluate system errors while building energy systems. Many research documents point to unstable data and insufficient information as the main obstacles that challenge energy systems. The system's trustworthiness and performance decrease due to poor detectors working with regulators and controlled bias, which leads to diminished data estimation and energy system operation. Recent requirements need solutions to address power grid data relationships and manage complex data from high-dimensional simulation grid information. Managers of energy networks encounter many challenges during the complex procedures required to implement wind and solar renewable power systems. Several IT organizations have established amount computing as one of the most efficient supercomputers in present-day use. Quantum technology offers improved machine learning capabilities at increased computational speed, resulting in higher algorithmic randomness along the way. The sustainable management of AI development results in significant carbon emissions due to its direct impact on production scale. A single AI learning algorithm produces emissions equivalent to running five buses during a single operation period. AI systems use diverse energy data types for processing that directly contribute to IT infrastructure carbon emission totals. Decision makers in the energy sector face two significant energy-related AI challenges: Non-theoretical history and lack of crucial AI competencies. Most institutions need technological specialists to develop strategies for using artificial intelligence operations. A severe shortage of experts exists despite business organizations struggling to find staff capable of handling their computer infrastructure independently (Rinku & Singh, 2023).

The market lacks experts capable of developing robust, stable AI systems that lead to concrete business outcomes. However, electric companies face difficulties handling data processing through contemporary operational programs to maintain their data systems. The main drawbacks are the combination of data loss, poor configuration and device malfunction, and unauthorized access to energy company systems. Organizations refrain from launching aggressive new business plans because they must carry higher costs which result from energy sector errors. The traditional power system infrastructure is the biggest hurdle hindering modern energy development. Sector. The data aggregation conducted by mileage companies presents difficulties because they do not grasp proper data management methods. The business sector maintains massive information collections throughout its numerous unorganized storage areas that house data locally. Implementation of the assiduity demonstrates notable advantages, whereas its old-fashioned organizational models create persistent challenges. Implementing advanced energy technology appears to be the most lucrative answer, but the cost of investing in this framework proves to be exorbitant. Additional time and substantial financial resources are required to acquire established software vendors, conduct development work for configuration, and maintain qualification documentation for management functions. Significant financial backing and personnel support are needed to execute energy technology, which involves continual software supervision with long-term funding requirements. The strategy encompasses decolonization and energy force expansion through decentralized distribution. The expansion of AI capabilities and more significant demand requirements produce intricate energy production problems: energy transmission, energy distribution, and cargo consumption in all countries. Many developing agricultural industries, poverty-stricken nations, herding territories, and unattended regions restrict AI significance because these communities depend on mobile phone technology. The popularity of cyber attacks has emerged as a significant concern affecting automatic control systems and innovative meter systems. The digital segment represents ten per cent of the global power grid construction while requiring \$30 billion in yearly funding for new infrastructure. The AI-based operation remains invisible to consumers since regular people know nothing about its internal workings or development processes, thus creating an inherent safety risk. The protective mechanisms will benefit the power systems because existing practices fail to satisfy necessary safety standards (Rinku & Singh, 2023).

Opportunities

Modern AI technology developments create substantial transformations within the energy industry, producing more intelligent energy system management approaches. Reliable energy management depends on the solutions of machine learning deep learning, and data analytics because these technologies help companies handle large volumes of data to reveal strategic findings. Modern technology enables precise forecasting of electricity needs to opt, optimized power station control, and extended maintenance prediction capabilities. Technological development in AI happens fast and expands the abilities of AI in energy applications altogether. Modern AI models benefit from greater computational power and extensive available technical data. The energy sector benefits from continuous research and development that generates special-purpose AI algorithms designed to address particular energy sector issues.

Energy efficiency and sustainability needs have made these technological advancements essential, so AI remains a critical management solution in future energy operations. The energy sector faces problems in adopting AI technologies because of the substantial implementation expenses during startup. The deployment of AI systems demands high initial costs to procure advanced equipment and program software systems alongside qualified staff expertise. The deployment costs become challenging to handle for organizations with small budgets, including utilities whose resources are limited. Implementing AI technology with current infrastructure systems demands complex customization work and upgraded systems that boost the initial cost level. The financial investment requirements dissuade firms from adopting AI technology, although such solutions provide long-term advantages. The high level of risk perception about these investments because of uncertain returns on investment and technical complications limits companies from adopting new technologies. The high initial expenditure deters businesses from obtaining stakeholder approval because they lack evident quick returns. The barrier is overcome by developing new financing schemes combined with official government support programs and experimental installations, which prove the potential worth of AI energy solutions. The demonstration of AI success and financial burden reduction enables leading players to conquer this significant obstacle that drives transformative AI technology adoption (P, 2023).

AI-based claims processing generates operational efficiency and sustainable management practices through data delivery into strength systems. Predictive maintenance applications achieve their solutions through AI technology implementations. The correct execution of transformer units and circuit breakers and similar electrical equipment needs regular maintenance to achieve operational safety. The evaluation of sensor data by AI algorithms allows operators to forecast maintenance duration for scheduling preventative instances that prevent equipment breakdowns. AI applications in power systems establish forecast energy as an essential opportunity because the sector receives meaningful gains from it. The process of energy forecasting demands simultaneous predictions of renewable power output from wind and solar resources and simultaneous customer energy consumption estimates. The combination between weather sensors and smart meter smart meters from various monitoring systems enables AI systems to deliver exact energy forecasts to optimize power management operations. The use of AI systems grants utility customers specific benefits which result in decreased energy consumption at times of peak demand. Trend identification technology used by AI systems analyzes matching data between sensors and smart meters besides optimizing demand response programs. AI controls voltage independently while it independently optimizes power flow operations and performs fault identification processes. AI algorithms using entire power grid sensor data enables them to detect upcoming network faults so they can trigger immediate protective action. The establishment of optimal energy trades in deregulated power market networks depends on AI technology for success. AI algorithms enable energy market participants to execute efficient deals through their ability to acquire critical market information and environmental data and market signals (Hamid & Ganne, 2023).

Future Direction

AI continues to progress rapidly while producing various possible implementations for both energy markets and power system applications. The following potential future uses of AI technologies for the domain represent several options among others:

- Progressive AI advancement allows developers to create better predictive analytics solutions that analyze transformers and generators and transmission lines with enhanced precision. The system fulfills better planning of asset operations to avoid system disturbances and extend operational life while improving reliability with cost savings (Hamid & Ganne, 2023).
- The management of Distributed Energy Resources (DERs) obtains substantial advantages through Artificial Intelligence because it enables complex integration between these decentralized resources and the power grid. The latest AI technology optimizes DERs processes through weather-dependent dispatch capabilities used for optimizing system stability as well as demand response control. Through its partnership with blockchain technology AI obtains advanced analytical capabilities for improving transaction processes simultaneously with contractual operations and verifying exchange authenticity. AI enables the delivery of secure energy markets with transparent operations (Hamid & Ganne, 2023).
- At the same time the power grid management system uses AI to execute monitoring operations and control activities efficiently. The application creates stable power grids and shorter operational disturbances that result in improved system reliability. AI creates improved human-operated decision making collaboration through its integration with operational power systems and energy markets (Hamid & Ganne, 2023).
- The connection between humans and artificial intelligence systems enhances operational efficiency while improving both situation understanding and precise decision-making capabilities to build sustainable effective energy management systems (Hamid & Ganne, 2023).
- AI has become increasingly powerful in energy markets and power systems so organizations need to adopt ethical approaches for responsible AI usage that supports sustainable operation. The deployment of AI in energy markets

and power systems needs evaluations about fairness and transparency of AI algorithms as well as data privacy and security measures along with responsible AI usage to match societally important values and address possible ethical issues (Hamid & Ganne, 2023).

- Research involving AI in energy markets and power systems demands interdisciplinary collaboration between experts who specialize in AI together with those who specialize in power systems as well as energy economics and policy. Future work needs to develop joint research initiatives between different disciplines to develop new AI solutions that tackle complicated issues within the energy sector (Hamid & Ganne, 2023).

CONCLUSION AND REFERENCE

Conclusion

Constant price flux in oil markets produces economic disarray and supply disruption which drives national inflation increases. The energy market shocks generate difficulties that expand throughout multiple sectors resulting in higher production expenses and transportation expenses and retail pricing. AI turned into a vital instrument to counter global financial shifts by developing better prediction models and supply chain optimization programs and risk management solutions for these turmoil response purposes. Implementing AI technology enables businesses to handle both energy market evaluation and supply chain management operations that help control oil price volatility together with its related effects. Through progressive analytics businesses and traders gain economic resilience and better supply chain operational efficiency together with inflation control capabilities as real-time data processing systems and automation mechanisms operate. The evolution of artificial intelligence technology will establish basic requirements to preserve stabilized energy markets by enhancing predictive modeling along with reducing inflation possibilities because these components promote lasting economic development and market stability.

REFERENCES

Aimer, N. M. M. (2017). The effects of oil price volatility on the economic sectors of Libya. *International Journal of Business and Social Research, 6*(12), 13. DOI: 10.18533/ijbsr.v6i12.1017

Aladwani, J. (2024). Oil volatility uncertainty: Impact on fundamental macroeconomics and the stock index. *Economies, 12*(6), 140. DOI: 10.3390/economies12060140

Antonova, N. (2024, Nov 12). *Sympower*. Retrieved January 22, 2025, from https://sympower.net/articles/what-are-energy-markets#understanding-Energy-markets

Foroutan, P., & Lahmiri, S. (2024). Deep learning systems for forecasting the prices of crude oil and precious metals. *Financial Innovation, 10*(1), 111. Advance online publication. DOI: 10.1186/s40854-024-00637-z

Ghosh, S. (2022). COVID-19, clean energy stock market, interest rate, oil prices, volatility index, geopolitical risk nexus: Evidence from quantile regression. *Journal of Economic Development, 24*(4), 329–344. DOI: 10.1108/JED-04-2022-0073

Ha, J., Kose, M. A., Ohnsorge, F., & Yilmazkuday, H. (2023). Understanding the global drivers of inflation: How important are oil prices? *Energy Economics, 127*, 107096. DOI: 10.1016/j.eneco.2023.107096

Hamid, M., & Ganne, A. (2023). Artificial Intelligence in energy markets and power system. *International Research Journal of Modernization in Engineering Technology and Science*. Advance online publication. DOI: 10.56726/IRJMETS35943

Hesary, F. T., Rasoulinezhad, E., & Kobayashi, Y. (2015). Oil price fluctuations and oil consuming Sectors: An Empirical analysis of Japan. SSRN *Electronic Journal*. DOI: 10.2139/ssrn.2670444

Jahanshahi, H., Uzun, S., Kaçar, S., Yao, Q., & Alassafi, M. O. (2022). Artificial Intelligence-Based Prediction of Crude Oil Prices Using Multiple Features under the Effect of Russia–Ukraine War and COVID-19 Pandemic. *Mathematics, 10*(22), 4361. DOI: 10.3390/math10224361

Liu, M., Liu, H., & Lee, C. (2023). An empirical study on the response of the energy market to the shock from the artificial intelligence industry. *Energy, 288*, 129655. DOI: 10.1016/j.energy.2023.129655

Okogwu, C., Agho, M. O., Adeyinka, M. A., Odulaja, B. A., Ufoaro, O. A., Ayodeji, S. A., & Daraojimba, C. (2023). Adapting to oil price volatility: A Strategic review of supply chain responses over two decades. *International Journal of Innovation and Scientific Research*, *X*(X), 68–87. DOI: 10.51244/IJRSI.2023.101007

P, A. (2023). *Artificial Intelligence in Energy Market Size, Share, Growth & Industry Analysis, By Component (Solutions and Services), By Deployment (On-Premises and Cloud-based), By Application (Robotics, Renewable Management, Demand Forecasting, Infrastructure, and Others), By End User, and Regional Analysis,* https://www.kingsresearch.com/artificial-intelligence-in-energy-market-849

Rinku, N., & Singh, N. G. (2023). Artificial intelligence in sustainable in energy industry: Status quo, challenges and opportunities. [IJMR]. *EPRA International Journal of Multidisciplinary Research*, *234–237*, 234–237. DOI: 10.36713/epra13323

Sun, M., Cao, X., Liu, X., Cao, T., & Zhu, Q. (2024). The Russia-Ukraine conflict, soaring international energy prices, and implications for global economic policies. *Heliyon*, *10*(16), e34712. DOI: 10.1016/j.heliyon.2024.e34712 PMID: 39247264

World Bank. (2013). GLOBAL ECONOMIC PROSPECTS | July 2013 Commodity markets Outlook. *GLOBAL ECONOMIC PROSPECTS*. https://thedocs.worldbank.org/en/doc/114641587674023619-0050022020/original/CMO2013Julyanalysis1.pdf

Chapter 4

Consumer Behavior and Demand Shocks:

Role of Panic Buying, Stockpiling, and Shifts in Consumer Preferences

Sudeept Maharana

https://orcid.org/0009-0004-3777-5042

Indian Institute of Technology, India

ABSTRACT

Consumer behavior is increasingly shaped by external shocks like economic crises, pandemics, and supply chain disruptions, leading to panic buying, stockpiling, and demand fluctuations. This chapter examines how Artificial Intelligence (AI) analyzes, predicts, and manages these shifts to enhance market stability and organizational resilience. AI-driven predictive analytics and sentiment analysis help businesses anticipate panic buying and stockpiling, enabling proactive inventory and supply chain management. AI-powered recommendation systems and real-time market analysis track shifting consumer preferences, optimizing pricing and engagement strategies. By integrating AI into demand forecasting, organizations improve supply chain resilience, reduce market volatility, and enhance customer retention. As AI evolves, its role in mitigating demand shocks and behavioral shifts becomes critical for economic and business sustainability, fostering adaptive, customer-centric markets.

DOI: 10.4018/979-8-3373-1982-7.ch004

INTRODUCTION

The global financial system regained strength after overcoming the effects of COVID-19 yet the delivery chain issues grew worse leading to higher prices. Organizations faced difficulties serving clients because of wide supply chain disruptions and delivery delays so widespread that they hindered their ability to meet customer needs. The shortage of raw materials created by the Covid-19 health emergency led to essential supply limitations which raised the expenses of these resources. The combination of traits and their inflationary impact became worse because of delayed manufacturing operations and decreased stock levels and workplace congestion and labor shortages which resulted from COVID-19 containment measures. Inflation has increased substantially due to Supply Chain (SC) bottlenecks which occurred after the COVID-19 pandemic and the Russian-Ukrainian crisis. The disturbances initiated in April 2020 reached a brief lull until they regained intensity during December 2021. The EU originally reduced Russian energy imports based on projected electricity price hikes which happened after EU authorities made a decision about their heavy dependence on Russian power supplies. During the first quarter of 2022 the prices of crude oil skyrocketed to double their value while coal expanded to three times its original cost alongside a natural gas price increase exceeding 500 percent from early 2021. The agricultural exports of Ukraine caused multiple commodities to rise in price. In October 2022 the annual inflation expenses rose in both the U.S. and the U.K. and Germany while Japan displayed a 2% annual inflation rate. Inflation grew during global delivery disruptions due to their negative impact on customers (Jama, 2024).

The impact of global SC shocks on the euro place commercial business corporation cycle and find out that a worldwide SC marvel causes a drop in real financial interest in the euro area and a boom in client costs. However, SC indicates that inflationary consequences may likely be international, searching ahead to similar effects for regions other than the euro region and the U.S., which includes Japan and the U.K. Moreover, a nicely functioning delivery chain is based now not satisfactory on transportation but on the availability of enter materials for the production gadget. In terms of a global SC, commodities are the primary input for big sort of industries all around the globe. A supply shock in a commodity marketplace, which includes a geopolitical occasion, represents a disruption to the distribution chain, in which the resulting rate increase will not handiest electricity inflation higher but depress financial interest. There is widespread literature documenting the vast effect of power costs on inflation expenses. In the unexpectedly evolving virtual era, agencies throughout sectors increasingly count on information to make strategic choices. Deep knowledge of purchaser conduct is pivotal for companies to design advertising strategies, improve product services, and improve popular purchaser delight. However, the complexity of patron statistics and the want to adapt to changing styles rapidly necessitate a more effective method. Artificial Intelligence (AI) systems are a fashion and an aggressive necessity in this digital generation for assessing client behavior. Moreover, AI can deal with and examine records suddenly and as it needs to be, surpassing human capabilities. This empowers agencies to stay ahead of the opposition and make better-informed predictions about future client choices (Jama, 2024).

BACKGROUND OF CONSUMER BEHAVIOR

Consumer conduct describes a customer's journey as they study, select, and purchase a service or product. Enterprises need to recognize why customers select to buy or reject their products. It is beneficial to format private products better, which can enhance profits and develop the enterprise. It is critical for gaining earnings, so purchaser behavior needs to be predicted. Culture, schooling, existence style, and many different things impact customer behavior. The prediction of client behavior by using the selection of key elements. For every employer, the elements most carefully associated with their customers were exceptional. Survival psychology acknowledges that individuals may also go through behavioral changes due to the superiority of specific activities, along with natural screw-ups, healthcare crises, and terrorist assaults. These behavioral adjustments may include poor herd mentality, panic shopping, adjustments to discretionary buying behavior, and investment preference making (Loxton et al., 2020).

Factors that exchange Consumer Behavior

Panic Buying

According to established practice panic buying occurs when customers purchase abnormally big amounts and diverse assortment of products before or during or after a natural disaster or perceived emergency or before anticipated price surges or supply shortages. When panic shopping occurs carriers receive enormous demand for requirements and scientific substances that results in limited or complete removal of these products from the marketplace thereby denying both vulnerable groups including the elderly and negative access to these goods. Panic shopping can occur both when customers expect products to disappear or when fear of personal freedom limitations arises from not owning the items. This practice also begins when buyers may feel regret for non-positive behaviors or non-purchase which leads them to pre-purchase the desired items. Customers transform their limited knowledge of crises into comforting and safety-boosting behaviors and stress reducers through panic shopping activities. Trust development is influenced by social elements and psychological aspects which drive panic buyers to act based on the way businesses and organizational authorities and governments present themselves to consumers. The adoption or public discussion of exceptional behaviors by consumers can lead to a social mistrust phase. Consumer behavior theories demonstrate to explain the coping mechanisms of people who use product purchase and panic shopping to gain control during uncertain times (Loxton et al., 2020).

Herd Mentality

The formation of community member behaviors without official management direction is often termed herd mentality. This process provides marketing opportunities through social interactions between participants. Onset of herd mentality results in a misdirected distribution of assets which causes economic price fluctuation because buyers purchase items at high speed although delivery times remain too long to improve sufficiently or when market volatility occurs. Information motives about herd mentality should assist authorities develop strategies to fight this harmful consumer behavior. Behavioral economics sets out how customers automatize their buying decisions based on social choices made by others. During scarcity events the normal objects undergo unjustified market price surges owing to heightened consumer demand which follows scarcity heuristics principles. Weak societal decision-making results in stockpiling of everyday goods such as red wine along with iodine tablets and salt while customers follow each other without caring about overall societal standards (Loxton et al., 2020).

Maslow's Hierarchy of Needs Model

Maslow's ladder functions according to economic conditions which determine its level structure and customers in growing economic markets adapt their lifestyles in parallel. Analysis of customer conduct in high-pressured situations becomes a result of implementing Maslow's theoretical structure. The sales pattern of non-durable products that people consume has shown that these items directly relate to GDP declines because they typically align with commercial sector downturns. When crises happen Maslow says people delay fulfilling their higher needs. The market introduction of expensive durable electronic systems and devices in 2008 presented greater risks than the launch of essential non-durable products. Studies indicate that during full recessions Australian GDP dropped 2.6% simultaneously while expensive durable items sales rose 5.7% and the purchase of essential durable materials remained unchanged. Consumer buying patterns align with Maslow's model which establishes essential requirements should be met before consumers consider discretionary purchases. The financial growth combined with commercial business interest of the post-GFC decade strengthened people's financial capabilities while the panic decreased across the period. Customers who achieved fulfillment at the lower levels of Maslow's hierarchy shifted their focus to seek satisfaction at his top tiers of needs satisfaction. Growth in worldwide consumer spending along with wealth-based income defined the performance of both the Global Car and Automobile Sales Corporation and other non-durable industries during the five years after the GFC (Loxton et al., 2020).

Media in Influencing Consumer Behaviour

In the age of facts, mass media plays a pivotal characteristic in forming, remodeling, and maintaining public opinion. This relationship will become even more apparent at some point in disaster situations, wherein the media can inform and dispel incorrect information or belief hysteria through headlines. Initial panic permeates organically from unfolding crises; the media contributes disproportionate anxiety by emphasizing aspects of news stories that garner extra attention, predominantly via provocation of worry. Social media has become an increasing number of influential sources of facts; national statistics coverage continue to be the primary framing mechanism of public and insurance debates regarding protection and fitness emergencies. Hence, developing information on the manner in the media would possibly affect or affect consumer choice making, whether this be on the dimensions of inflicting changed behaviors or, in truth, informing client sentiment, is critical for expertise motivations in the again of tremendous behaviors (Loxton et al., 2020).

Consumer Behavior during COVID-19

The emergency period creates specific psychological changes among residents that lead their purchasing behaviors to exhibit four basic buying traits: panic shopping behaviors, impulse purchasing behaviors, compulsive buying behaviors and online shopping behaviors. Immediately after the first COVID-19 outbreak phase, direct exposure to the event affected specific individuals yet society received its bad emotions through social media channels. Irrational emotions affect the public since they can include elements of tension together with melancholy. Rising public concern about widespread epidemics makes negative emotions spread throughout society in a relatively easy way. Customers sense increased uncertainty regarding shortages and severity together with specific intellectual factors which pushes them to implement panic purchasing behavior. Inventorying key requirements and buying less essential products forms the core performance aspect of managing panic buying behavior. Customers developed a stronger need to stock up products because of COVID-19 supply disruptions which led to out-of-stock situations. People who show a poor understanding of the COVID-19 outbreak experience stronger internal stress which drives them to make spontaneous fitness merchandise purchases. COVID-19 has increased client stress levels along with making specific purchasers develop compulsive purchase patterns. Elevated shopping patterns function as a method to decrease internal tension as well as the tension (Tao et al., 2022).

Besides, online purchasing behaviors have become increasingly popular with customers after the COVID-19 outbreak. In the face of the government's home isolation measures, it has become increasingly commonplace for customers to apply online shopping for meals and other items. People privy to the risks of going out are inclined to buy clean food online. Consumer buying behavior is not confined to the useful resource of time and vicinity, and clients use cell equipment, including cell telephones, to achieve purchasing freedom. Therefore, the COVID-19 pandemic is caused by outside stimuli, which will change human beings' intake psychology and, finally, their purchase behavior regarding buying items, purpose, place, time, body, and technique. In terms of buying objects, the epidemic has made customers recommend better necessities for services or products. Customers who face an emergency choose trouble-solving products or services over emotional recuperation services or products. Utilitarian products, rather than hedonic objects, are extra effective in addressing customers' instantaneous needs. Consumers stuck during the pandemic should increase their purchases of utilitarian merchandise, including disinfectants, masks, and fitness food (Tao et al., 2022).

On the other hand, even as human beings are under pressure or are nerve-racking about outdoor threats, in preference to immediately address the problems, they regularly spark off a mental safety mechanism—the cognitive and behavioral tendencies that human beings unconsciously adopt within the face of frustration or war so that can relieve anxiety and anxiety to shield themselves. The COVID-19 pandemic has introduced people's mental safety mechanisms, mainly to greater caution looking. Consumers are not the best charge-sensitive; however, they are similarly named for higher quality and additional dependable merchandise. In terms of purchasing devices, purchasers pay greater attention to the first-class of the devices they buy. The boom in online buying sports activities has made customers extra inclined to reveal their records (Tao et al., 2022).

Consumer Purchase Behavior Changes and Business Model Design

People's worry and tension regarding the pandemic are not all likely to bog down in the near destiny, and the resulting adjustments in consumer calls might subsequently damage the delivery chain's ordinary overall performance of purchaser services agencies. The corporations have already been experiencing extensive demanding situations with their current business enterprise models because of strict social isolation, not on-time return-to-paintings, and disrupted logistics. The pandemic is putting a few essential businesses to the test because customers may not repair their preceding looking for conduct every time fast. According to the Expectation Confirmation Theory, consumer offerings organizations must modify their commercial enterprise models to satisfy new customer expectancies if they want to attain consumer satisfaction. Changes in client purchase behavior during the COVID-19 pandemic have impacted the layout of novelty-targeted enterprise fashions (Tao et al., 2022).

Novelty-targeted commercial enterprise fashions emphasize exploiting new opportunities in new methods, and their essence is to meet new consumer charge propositions, want or revel in through innovations within the content material, shape, or governance of the interest system. Although the COVID-19 pandemic has brought about a decline in customers' purchase power, the requirements for product first-rate improvements will not be exchanged. Changes in buying objects drive patron service companies to lay out novelty-centered industrial agency fashions. With the development of clients' ordinary intake level, the enhancement of electricity consumption, and the enhancement of intake opportunities, their delight with standardized merchandise gradually decreases, and the trend of pursuing more diverse and personalized services or products will hold. As client alternatives boom in diversification, corporations must release new products and price them as they should be in a fiercely aggressive marketplace, specifically in environmental uncertainty exacerbated by the COVID-19 pandemic. Novelty-focused commercial enterprise fashions can supply clients with better merchandise and revel in modern techniques based on product-era innovation. When it entails buy motive, clients opt for merchandise from organizations with a good picture or a strong sense of social obligation. Branded merchandise boosts clients' perceived usefulness; that is precisely what novelty-centered business enterprise models should accomplish. Therefore, purchasers assume groups should lay out novelty-centered industrial employer models. In phrases of purchase method, purchasers determine upon novel purchase techniques and offerings at the side of mobile fee and contactless transport. It shows that customer calls for novel rate techniques have not been really glad (Tao et al., 2022).

People exposed to the same services or products repeatedly will become bored due to the diminishing marginal software of overexposure. Bored customers will ultimately enjoy much less glad. Thus, consumer offerings organizations have to undertake a novelty-centered agency model layout to re-establish consumer pride. Moreover, clients commonly tend to choose a shorter buy time-body and a more secure purchase area, indicating their expectation to reduce perceived dangers. To meet that expectation, corporations are better served with novelty-centered business enterprise model layouts. Changes in purchase behavior have impacted the layout of performance-targeted enterprise fashions during the COVID-19 pandemic. Consumer purchase behavior is a procedure from information acquisition to the formation of buy aimed at buying choice-making trouble. Consumer buying purpose is an important detail determining the last purchase selection. Facts are critical factors that influence purchasers' shopping aims and buying choices in the long run. Generally speaking, customers are risk-averse, so they will gather much applicable information before buying to turn the uncertainty of purchasing a positive product into fact. With the fast improvement of records technology, whether the contradiction of some of the explosive boom of data and the constrained interest of purchasers can be resolved has become an inevitable requirement for organizations to gain an aggressive advantage (Tao et al., 2022).

The fast improvement of the information era also brings the risk of private records being infringed on clients always in the transaction, especially within online consumption; the black corporation chain of stealing and unlawful use of clients' private information shows an explosive growth fashion. Whether agencies can preserve clients' private data accumulated in business sports strictly or personally has become a close challenge to customers. Efficiency-centered employer fashions emphasize that businesses can improve industrial organization efficiency by decreasing transaction costs, improving records transparency and sharing, and enhancing transaction security. With this, data may be efficaciously shared among clients and corporations, and the facts may be reduced so that consumers can believe corporations and generate buy intentions. Regarding purchasing objects, humans are more rational in selecting what to shop. It will increase calls for performance in the products or offerings purchased from customer offerings corporations. In this case, corporations need to pick a performance-targeted commercial enterprise model layout as it emphasizes improving the performance of business organization transactions. Customers are satisfied, and their expectancies are confirmed when they perceive that the performance of the goods or offerings exceeds the predicted performance. In addition, regarding purchase reasons, clients tend to favor brands that might be properly rated and contribute to society. Consumers understand branded products as permitting them to make the right desire more rapidly. Efficiency-targeted organization models are constant with this purchaser notion. In phrases of purchase place, people choose to store online or on social media systems, highlighting their expectations for a steady and available shopping environment. Efficiency-targeted business enterprise models are essential for companies to meet such purchasers (Tao et al., 2022).

MAIN FOCUS OF CHAPTER: CUSTOMER DEMAND SHOCKS AND INFLATION

Understanding drivers within the pre-pandemic generation modified into the knowledge of underlying demographic trends of the customers and brief-run rate and advertising and marketing choices of the company. Given that purchaser alternatives and trends alternate slowly over the years, charges and promotions have temporary results on call. These strong relationships have all been damaged during the pandemic. Though conventional elements determine demand to a quantity, new drivers grow to be more vital as people make sudden choices with the changing environment. It makes a name for making plans for manufacturing and distribution hard in consumer markets (Hoda et al., 2020).

Demand Shock within the route of COVID-19

The pre-COVID-19 literature on epidemics and the discussions of the present-day catastrophe make it clear that epidemics strongly influence consumer spending. In addition to growing their call for fitness services, clients may also be looking to lessen their hazard of publicity to the virus and reduce names for services and products that comprise close contact with others. In the early days of the outbreak, stockpiling behavior also drove an instantaneous boom in retail locations. However, there are three exceptional properties of consumption shocks (Del Rio-Chanona et al., 2020).

The COVID-19 pandemic has an extremely good impact on societies around the arena. The governments mandate social distancing practices and educate non-critical agencies to shut to the unfolding of the outbreak, there may be massive uncertainty about the impact such measures may have on lives and livelihoods. While healthcare has skyrocketed in modern-day weeks, precise sectors collectively with air transportation and tourism have seen the call for their services evaporate. At the same time, many sectors are experiencing problems with delivery, as governments curtail the sports of non-crucial industries and employees are related to their homes. Many economists and commentators accept as authentic that the economic effect may be dramatic. Around half of the US financial system may consider every critical or capable characteristic without growing risks of discussing the virus. Shutting down in Tokyo might also motivate a lack of output in exceptional components of the financial system supply chain linkages, and it is estimated that after a month, everyday output decreases (Del Rio-Chanona et al., 2020).

Inflation and the Behavior of Consumers

Consumer conduct is increasingly inspired by the beneficial resource of outdoor shocks, which encompass economic crises, pandemics, and supply chain disruptions. Balancing Act: Exploring the Relationship Between Inflation and Consumer Behavior delves into the dynamic interaction among the important factors that form the cutting-edge-day market. Customers navigate a complex monetary tapestry as charges range and look for strength wavers. Consumers exhibit predictable behaviors to address declining search-out strength and developing prices. Common strategies encompass substituting much less costly manufacturers, looking for in bulk, reducing discretionary spending, and purchasing for and selling all of the manners in a manner proper down to lower-priced stores. High inflation will bring about biased consumption as customer boost purchases to avoid future higher costs. However, a few show irrational behaviors like stockpiling or recognition-searching for purchases regardless of inflation constraints. Vroom's expectancy principle explains purchaser alternatives based on calculated assumptions about a product's ability to benefit from favored consequences. This cognitive view indicates that, at the same time as inflation rises, customers rationally have a check charge and affordability. However, inflation provokes emotional responses like worry and tension that generate reactive behaviors. Integrating economic and intellectual views offers a nuanced knowledge. Consumer reactions to inflation are based mostly on cultural, economic, and demographic elements. For example, people with regular incomes and restrained economic and financial savings will generally be predisposed to less spending extra appreciably (Gartner). Younger customers with monetary instability can also adjust more outcomes than older cohorts. More studies are needed on phase-particular outcomes (Lakshmanamoorthy & Athinarayanan, 2024).

Factors for Inflation and Consumer Behavior

Expectancy Principle of Motivation: Purchaser Conduct

Consumer behavior theories are set to offer some primary commands and conclusions about how consumers may behave, specifically when seeking to shop for products. Researchers claim that in terms of customer behavior, pupils and practitioners lack consensus on the large, influential determinants that might be great to guide human beings' buying behaviors or how the determinants are interrelated.

Consumers' motivation is the precept source governing their shopping for behavior alternatives amongst opportunity types of products, offerings, and awesome procurement accomplishments. Motivation is the cause for which human beings initiate, keep, revive, pause, or terminate conduct at a given time. According to the expectation idea of motivation (Negm, 2023):

- Purchaser conduct is a cognitive system: intellectual motion or device of acquiring expertise and information through concept, enjoyment, and the senses. Consumers make picks based mostly on assumptions that have been calculated and assessed concerning well the predicted consequences of a given product/logo are going to come up with or, in the long run, bring about the popular effects that they need to achieve behavior choice shows their movement (Negm, 2023).
- Selected aspiration: If the customer believes that there may be an excessive high-quality correlation, the product/ logo will bring about a suitable reward, which will fulfill a vital need, and/or the outcomes satisfy their need sufficiently to take some time profitably. Based on the expectation concept, students have clarified several expectancies that describe client purchases at some point during inflation. When charges of products leap, fear and tension may be an adaptive response, leading to mental or irrational shopping (Negm, 2023).
- During instances of marketplace uncertainty and monetary turmoil, clients normally are searching to buy huge portions of a specific product or commodity due to unanticipated worries of a functionality scarcity or price spike; proudly owning a top-notch sort of merchandise results in the expectation of contentment echoing delight/happiness/utility (Negm, 2023).

Compulsive looking for

Inflation permits any product to be valued by the patron until it is unavailable or unachievable; consequently, purchasers are attempting to find and shop for as good a buy as possible for the goods they choose as they nonetheless maintain freedom of preference among products. This compulsive conduct among customers is known as panic shopping. It has been generally practiced at some stage in several instances of emergency, collectively with epidemics, economic disasters, or natural disasters. During instances of panic, humans understand an item to be limited or that there may be a threat that the charge could likely increase further inside the destiny; because of this, they end up inspired to buy the item now (in choice to later) due to its availability and coherent charge; they may be trying to find for to shop for the manufacturers that they may be acquainted with or if there are different alternatives which can be attractive to the customers (Negm, 2023).

Sense of Tension

According to the Weber–Fechner law of psychophysics, clients do not respond to cost adjustments under a fine threshold degree. However, customers reply to a boom in rate, which can be immoderate and above the threshold diploma. Early and current research claim that when clients are aware that there is a threat that product charges will similarly grow within their destiny, they seeming experience terrible feelings, together with anxiety. Consumers face anxiety because of suspense, anxiety, and apprehension bobbing up from a diffused enjoyment of danger. Thus, physiological tension, deficiency, or imbalance will emerge, pressing customers to do so to shop for numerous merchandise and brands; they are trying to find to shop for the essential products and brands that they anticipate will reduce the negative feelings. When clients study trade-in product fees, they may experience demand, which, in flip, will inspire them to do something fantastic about it, both accepting buying and selling down manufacturers or purchasing smaller quantities (Negm, 2023).

Value Buying (rewards and discounts)

Comparing prices and planning a listing earlier than purchasing can offer the purchaser giant money and time financial savings, especially when consumers look for products that maintain fees. Consumers will hold to hold, but in hard monetary times, they will trade their purchasing for conduct in conjunction with excessive inflation. This trade-in habit can tackle many office works; for example, some clients may buy from other manufacturers near extra costly options. During times of excessive inflation, rewards and distinct incentives are a huge factor influencing customers' purchasing conduct; fee which is probably supplied to clients certainly influences client conduct on the pinnacle of the purchase funnel and the lowest; with rate services, the goods and types are located above the indifference curve, making clients glad and seeking out to buy and devour (Negm, 2023).

Attitude toward non-Public Label

The turbulent surroundings encourage the consumers to look for new techniques to fulfill their intake wishes. Inflation, financial crises, and espresso-dwelling top-notch purpose clients end up touchier to fees, and they started to expose interest in non-public manufacturers, supporting the economists' theories. Private labels are manufacturers of shops and groups furnished exceptional in their chains. Many clients are seeking to shop for private label products within the presence of large forms of products with respective elegance because of their better rates; private label manufacturers are commonly considered a reasonably priced and modest opportunity to top-rate branded merchandise. Personal labels are primarily modified to be produced for low-income and price-sensitive customers; currently, many customers are considering shopping for those merchandise as the manufacturers are owned via well-known stores with reputations and big marketplace percentages (Negm, 2023).

Materialistic Behavior

Income inequalities have improved globally in cutting-edge years. A horrible final result of earnings inequality is the growth in materialistic behavior among poorer people. Materialism reflects the importance someone places on possessions and their acquisition as an essential or relevant form of conduct to reach favored quit states, which encompass happiness. In literature, studies have hinted that people expand materialistic conduct as they prefer to make amends for financial deprivation. Although the shopping for power of all clients is limited to some extent and the electricity is reduced due to immoderate inflation, a few customers, who are probably monetarily wounded, are much more likely to enjoy horrific feelings, which translate into low arrogance; therefore, they searching for to have interaction in ostentatious intake or pursue products that act as symbols of wealth to sturdy their low vanity. Other research has provided empirical evidence that clients' materialistic behaviors increase once they revel in non-public relative deprivation. The idea that monetary deprivation results in materialistic tendencies is usually supported in literature on the path of countries, showing that humans count on acquiring several brands past their monetary acquisition. Materialistic clients are endorsed to buy producers, which might give them greater popularity and reward, helping the expectancy concept (Negm, 2023).

Monetary Policy for Inflation and Consumer Behavior

Consumer sentiment, which is brought about by the effect of exogenous variables on the propensity to devour, represents a vital trouble in economics, and it has an effect on macroeconomic variables, which has been extensively noted in the literature. Economic analysts interpret customer sentiment records as an early indicator of future patron behavior, cautiously watching it within the course of recessions as ability signs of the stop of financial despair. Among the characteristics blanketed with the resource of using consumer sentiment are clients' inflation expectancies, which play a key function inside the financial transmission mechanism, making it important to examine the perceptions and expectancies of said inflation, which can be vital for the economic gadget for the reason that they affect the effectiveness of financial and monetary policy. The relationship between monetary growth, inflation price, and economic base has been analyzed by various researchers, with the conclusion that the financial base may be beneficial in sentiment as the most carefully monitored indicator of monetary behavior, suggesting that each component can be significantly related. Though many specialists agree that a 10% increase inside the monetary base choice to 5% may motivate prolonged-term inflation, which does now not provide enough information on how large banks must act. During financial expansions, immoderate client self-perception encourages extra spending. Low customer self-warranty values spark off the decreased intake, likely leading to reduced earnings volumes and a financial recession. In this context, the validity of the customer sentiment index as an accurate predictor of economic hobby proof that an increase in inflation is possible because of a boom in the economic base in comparison to a productiveness increase, putting forward that growth in the cash supply reduces the want to shop, slowing down and growing cash balances. Along the equal traces, the software program of a latent detail model to patron records affected their expectations regarding monetary situations, unemployment, and family rate range. It pondered that once a shock in monetary recommendations produced an adjustment in consumer expectancies inside the route anticipated through favored fashions, there was an uneven reaction to insurance tightening or easing. It is viable that monetary rules can stimulate intake via inflation expectations, demonstrating how expansionary policy shocks will be predisposed to increase the willingness to spend on extra expected inflation outside the zero conditionally decreases certain. To examine the effect of monetary rules and inflation on the conduct of patron sentiment, really certainly one type of methodology has been used inside the literature, the side of Panel Vector Auto regression and Quantile Vector Auto regression, to focus on the importance of financial coverage in determining clients' monetary expectancies, evidencing an impact of economic regulations on patron sentiment inside the Eurozone (Monge et al., 2024).

Case Study

Egypt for Inflation and Consumer Behavior

The present-day global market features inflation at the forefront of economic and political and societal dialogues because media outlets and public audiences extensively cover it. Although inflation happens naturally on a global scale and in statistical records it presents indications about a nation's development yet serious inflation damages financial systems by raising living costs and diminishing economic power across the population. The post-COVID-19 era and Ukraine and Russian warfare conditions have activated profit and wealth transfers through inflationary pressure. In February 2023 the inflation rate in Egypt rose to 31.9% compared to 25.8% in January 2023. Statistically the inflation reading exceeded market projection levels which indicated 26.9% for that period. The year 2023 marks the most severe inflation level in the history of Egypt which began in August 2017. Egyptians demonstrate rapid reaction to continual foreign exchange devaluations in present-day months as unstable commodity costs rose by 40.26% between February 2023 and the previous month. The Consumer Price Index (CPI) monitors the price shifts of a preset set of goods and services as used by urban family members in Egypt; the measured figures represent price change throughout one year in 2023. Food and beverages together with meals and drinks rates contributed 40% to the general consumer price index with housing utilities of strength and water sustaining 18.4% and training, hospital remedies, public transportation, home items and clothing following with 4.6%, 6.3%, 5.7% and 3.8% respectively. Research demand continues to increase due to updated knowledge about how consumers evaluate logo buying odds and react to search under stress and anxiety or scarcity which leads to shopping during price increases and so on (Negm, 2023).

Uzbekistan for Inflation and Consumer Behavior

The financial variable of inflation deeply affects how customers behave in Uzbekistan and determines the course of financial policy design. Since Central Asia hosts this country observers have watched recent financial shifts with attention focused on inflation alignments which catch the interest of both policymakers and economists and analysts combined. Sustainable economic growth in Uzbekistan requires full comprehension of how inflation operates through customer conduct and monetary policy formulation. The figure sits at the lowest position of all time as it existed in August 2016. Food expenses underwent a 9.7% rise during 2023 based on information from the Statistics Agency. Consumer prices for beef and lamb rose by 9% but flour experienced a 1% drop while sunflower oil with a useful resource experienced an 18% decrease and surrender result and nuts went up by 37%. The cost of fuel increased by 19% while methane fees rose by 22% throughout the year. The Statistics Agency has reported on December 31 that Uzbekistan recorded an 8.77% rate of inflation for 2023. Since August 2016 the country has experienced its lowest actual inflation fee. The price of instruction in public kindergartens decreased through 2.8% during the last 365 days while non-public kindergartens showed a 3.3% reduction while non-us of a better instructional establishment observed a 1% fee increase along with tutoring costs growing 10.3%. The fees used by hair salons have reached a 17% increase since last year. Statistics Agency determines annual inflation by investigating expenses of 250 non-meal products and ninety paid services along with 250 food items. Each month between the tenth and twentieth day the price sheet becomes available for viewing. Each combination inflation rate element receives an influence and percentage determination by evaluating price adjustments for specific products and their spending value. The annual inflation rate experienced its largest influence from rice and red meat combined with grapes and pomegranates and methane as the other key factors. Onions and sunflower oil together with cottonseed oil and potatoes and carrots are inflation-reducing products. During March 2024 the inflation rate in Uzbekistan decreased to reach 7.98% while February recorded 8.35%. The inflation rate of Uzbekistan maintained an average of 10.10% throughout 2006 until 2024 whilst reaching its most elevated mark at 20.10% in January 2018 and descending to its minimum at 40% in March 2018. The State Statistics Committee reported extreme inflation rate changes throughout 2018 to 2020 in Uzbekistan. The inflation rate reported in 2018 reached 14.4% during that time period which became the start of a persistent inflationary phase. The inflating economic problems within the kingdom's economy continue to persist according to 15.2% inflation statistics from 2020. The accelerating inflation trends emphasize the critical need to investigate fundamental inflation elements which affect different economic interests. Consumer conduct within Uzbekistan has strongly reacted to the inflationary patterns that emerged during this period. The rising costs pushed customers to reorganize their spending therefore leading them to change their purchasing preferences toward essential items and services. Government-run purchaser expenditure surveys show conclusive proof regarding changes in buying practices. The surveys show an impressive increase in expenditures for essential commodities that include food and housing along with healthcare due to inflation-based monetary limitations affecting Uzbek consumers. The worrying financial stability issues prompted Uzbekistan policy makers to create powerful monetary strategies that both reduced the negative inflation consequences while developing sustainable financial growth. The Central Bank of Uzbekistan leads this role with its several financial insurance instruments which help reduce inflation symptoms. Financial insurance measures join forces with the existing strategies by prioritizing three essential areas that support economic stability and optimize public spending (Gafurdjan, 2024).

Demand shocks, Supply Chain Disruptions, and Inflation

As the worldwide financial device recovered from the COVID-19 pandemic, deliver chain disruptions intensified, exerting upward stress on charges. Many agencies struggled to keep up with surging clients, fueled by immoderate economic, monetary financial savings and pent-up name for – amid large-based delivery shortages and delays. Supply-call for imbalances arising from the COVID-19 health surprise brought about an essential scarcity of uncooked materials and area transportation, which in turn caused an increase in their expenses. These trends and their effect on inflation have been exacerbated by congested global ports and factories, hard artwork shortages, low stock levels, and production delays due to COVID-19 containment measures. While an uncommon event earlier than the COVID-19 pandemic, disruptions in international delivery chains have become increasingly unusual at some stage in many nations (Ascari et al., 2024).

Nowadays, geopolitical tensions and the COVID-19 pandemic have attracted policymakers' interest to the risks underlying this worldwide financial community and the extreme repercussions that supply chain shortages and disruptions may additionally have on monetary interest. However, regardless of the developing evidence of the importance of supply chain shocks, it recognizes little about how groups respond to deliver chain shortages and the consequences of man or woman company conduct for industry shape and macroeconomic outcomes. To the quantity that the most critical agencies in a business enterprise, which label superstars in keeping with in advance literature, have extra complicated and worldwide delivery chains, they will be more negatively affected and reduce quite to their smaller opposition whilst deliver chain shortages rise. On the other hand, large organizations should go through a good deal less from delivery chain shortages because they have greater resilient supply chains and additional bargaining strength to benefit from preferential treatment from their companies. If that is the case, supply chain shortages must cause a larger growth in manufacturing expenses for particular, smaller groups. It ultimately delivers chain shortages advantage to large corporations; they ought to test greater attention and markups, especially in industries with some superstar corporations competing with smaller organizations (Franzoni et al., 2023).

Geopolitical dangers may also have influences that are no longer best at the home inflation of nations affected by such dangers but also on specific economies (and because of this worldwide inflation), worldwide change, and finance linkages. In addition, geopolitical risks can foster an imbalance between consumer calls for and commercial enterprise supply that might spill over to worldwide places. Similarly, supply chain strain disruptions can also affect inflation through the transportation price channel, in which delays in shipping or better charges are handed at once to the client as better costs. Moreover, the disruption within the delivery chain may result in better inflation via aggregate calls for shocks. Consumers pay more because of an imbalance between delivery and demand, increasing international costs. Supply chain strain disruptions can also affect inflation through the transportation charge channel. The process of delays in shipping or higher rates is handed without delay to the customer as higher costs. In addition, the disruption in the supply chain results in better inflation via aggregate call-for shocks, and consumers pay more due to an imbalance between supply and call-for, resulting in higher expenses (Asadollah et al., 2024).

Oil is applied in production, business enterprise, and transportation. The price-push channel affords a mechanism in which oil charges strain up the producing charge and charge of assets. Oil costs can affect inflation through exchange charges as well. Therefore, imports can be extra luxurious for oil-importer countries like China and us. Research has established that most of the upward thrust inside the rate of oil is surpassed immediately by customers within the shape of higher costs for almost all goods and offerings. While some gadgets are directly affected by the rate of petroleum, like fuel and adventure, others are laid low with the downward shift in the supply curve because of higher production expenses. The inflationary impact of higher oil prices may be maximum time-honored in the short term; however, it also can have much less of an effect within the medium and prolonged terms. It is a common financial coverage to lessen inflation by raising the coverage interest fees, while discussing international inflation, this could become more complex, as more than one government, which incorporates the European Central Bank, makes insurance independently. However, worldwide capital flows inside the more and more covered economic markets have led the Federal Reserve Bank to have a developing impact, as it plays a function because the banker to the area and masses of policy-makers endure in mind its present-day actions (and expected destiny moves) at the same time as deciding on their home guidelines. In addition, the worldwide effect of domestic signs and symptoms is considered with the resources of policy-making bodies. Central banks keep in mind key financial signs in unique worldwide locations while figuring out their recommendations, including synchronizing worldwide pointers in stopping global inflation. (Asadollah et al., 2024).

SOLUTION AND RECOMMENDATIONS: ARTIFICIAL INTELLIGENCE AND CONSUMER BEHAVIOR

Artificial Intelligence (AI)

In Demis Hassabis's words, AI is the era of making machines smart. AI refers back to the ability of a PC or a laptop-enabled robotic gadget to process statistics and bring results in a way similar to the manner of people getting to know, making choices, and solving problems. AI can remedy complex troubles using logic and reasoning, just like humans. AI transfers human intelligence to machines so that it may deal with simple and complex obligations. AI includes three easy standards: device learning, deep reading, and impartial getting to know. Numerous authors describe AI using several techniques. However, all have highlighted the primary characteristics of non-human intelligence that are programmed to perform particular ventures. When AI was introduced, it was modified and considered as suddenly evolving, studying, speaking, getting to know, and feeling feelings. AI is the idea and development of a laptop device capable of acting on a mission that typically requires human intelligence. The fundamental point highlighted is that AI can perform the maximum of the obligations that humans do in the place of their jobs and within society. AI has entered all fields collectively with the ones that had been solely treated with the resource of human beings. AI presents the salesperson with accurate predictions and smart hints through reading beyond facts and priorities, which can be likely to convert. AI is associated with computer systems with talents that can assume and act more efficaciously than humans. It can understand photos or voices, make decisions, and translate the language.AI can discover, determine, and increase. Detection is the ability of AI to grow and be privy to the maximum predicted and main characteristics in a topic recall. The decision is the potential of AI to decide after evaluating a large style of traits, which decides the most vital one. Development refers to the electricity AI has to software with the aid of considering new information and the assessment of research collectively with how it evaluates every element and then alters its view. In the virtual era, clients show their wishes, wants, and attitudes in one-of-a-kind bureaucracy through searches, comments, blogs, motion pix, and conversations through numerous channels like the net, mobiles, or face-to-face. AI can convert such information into significant consumer notions. AI is predicated upon such insights to advocate shops regarding product presentations and cataloging. AI can help marketers apprehend and attain customers at many degrees of the consumer journey (Nasirian & Taheri, 2019).

Artificial Intelligence and Consumer Behavior

The AI technology delivers enhanced online platform evaluation experiences from customers. The technology provides customized recommendations for consumer surveys across e-commerce websites by processing customer data for business value assessment while performing future forecasting. Real-time monitoring of website visitor behavior allows the AI to learn device learning techniques which adjust results ranking to better display relevant products while maximizing profits. Technological advancements help online shops maintain daily competition by allowing them to offer premium selection in trade, industrial, business, enterprise strategy, revolutionary era and intuitive organization designs enhancing customer satisfaction. Artificial intelligence accelerated many business approaches which led to the development of exceptional industrial organization management practices at a large scale. The AI system handles customer queries and provides personalized notifications concerning their wish lists and product deals to users. Organizations leverage AI to develop fresh active customer-engagement platforms through which they can interact dynamically with their audience. AI helps e-trade shops match their products to the ideal consumers through its accurate database capabilities. Every industrial sector encounters AI-driven transformations across the entire duration of their business operations. Humans would classify artificial intelligence as the method of training computers to execute tasks such as problem solving and learning and reasoning and perception. Systemwide AI penetration has prompted different businesses to utilize AI for building strategic competencies. AI technology manifests through Google Assistants and Siri and Alexa along with Tesla smart cars and YouTube effect systems which operate based on user actions and behaviors. The information provided by artificial intelligence enables marketing departments to develop advertising strategies while consumption patterns show similar AI-driven responses from clients. The impact of synthetic intelligence on customer behavior becomes our topic of analysis (Ramya & Karthikeyan, 2024).

AI evolution has added new value to clients and preference makers. AI affects customers' conduct through automated approaches, making them patron-centric and less difficult to use. Despite the advantages, because statistics processing is closer to segmentation, AI concentrates on and makes suggestions that are considered a risk to customers' free will and autonomy. Consumers' autonomy in locating out for themselves and making their picks appears to affect their health. AI technology consists of 3 stakeholders: the clients, the choice makers, and the algorithms. Consumers can locate products or services to cover their wants at low fees by no means in advance. On the other hand, selection makers agree with that because consumer segmentation lowers the hunt volumes, and boom custom, custom-designed guidelines will truly boost transactions and make choice-making techniques less tough. AI algorithms gather, keep, phase, have a look at, and pattern huge every day generated client datasets, allowing selection makers to make greater balanced picks. Consumers consider the liberty of desire, which is vital to their lives. Free will reinforces people's belief that they can make alternatives, proving their lifestyles and independence. AI's contribution to client autonomy should aim to serve human beings. Autonomous alternatives are balanced, run beneath nice regulations and boundaries, and endure self-determined alternatives. Sure elements impact customers' autonomy to pick out the high-quality desire for them; however, unexplained preference for preference, although the choice approach calls for no attempt. Consumers not only feel an experience of hedonism at some level in the shopping system and the choice of desire, but they also considerably weigh the self-sustaining desire as crucial. Finally, it appears that AI-driven customized content material and audience segmentation are at the customer's side, supporting them to revel in qualitative services by way of responding to their wishes for comfort, lower fees, product availability, higher suggestions, and integrity (Gkikas & Theodoridis, 2021).

Purpose of Artificial Intelligence in Consumer Behavior

Increase clients spending

There is no doubt that customer spending will boom as one of the core elements of AI, i.e., Machine studying allows the teams to decode the huge records accumulation that narrows down the statistics in a manner that lets them pick out target audience, what are clients looking as much as, do fashion assessment after which creating funnels which may be greater character targeted ultimately lessening the time spent and in the long run will convert prospect into conversion. Customers' spending is much more likely to boom because as quickly as advertising groups have identified their audience, they can construct their marketing strategies around it. They comprehend when to do email marketing and at what time customers are more likely to open the email. With growing opposition, corporations are paying extra attention to what they offer and whom they provide. If any individual needs to start an organization, he/she may be able to understand the present-day traits of the customers. If any man or woman desires to propose to girls and teenage women and wants to recognize their hobbies, they can attain the information through AI. They can also begin up conventional style fashion emblems and promote make-up merchandise. This way, they can have accurate information and maximize their earnings by building strategies around it (Ramya & Karthikeyan, 2024).

Personalized Consumer Experience

Through AI, the information about customers is driven by the number of times a purchaser undergoes positive internet sites, what they look for, about their geo-area, and the devices they are signing in. Predictive personalization has helped the brand to offer a more custom-designed client experience. Now, customers do not need to take their day trip to visit a shop to buy a positive product. With the statistics available, brands will come up with a mind that complements what purchasers enjoy. There has been a fashion of virtual buying in which a precise product is shipped to the client's vicinity even before shopping to try it out and then motivate them to determine whether or not they want it. This way, clients feel that reveling in or trying is truly made for them. Personalization is crucial to transforming prospects into conversions (Ramya & Karthikeyan, 2024).

Boosting Customers loyalty

With the help of insights about customers' conduct patterns, producers who are arising with more customized clients reveal that it is more likely that customer loyalty will shift closer to that specific emblem. According to Microsoft, 97% of customers say customer support is crucial once they choose a brand. AI has helped enhance customer support similarly through chatbots. Clients get a quick reaction as they can deal with a couple of queries at a time and are to be had 24/7. Through clustering and facts gathered, approximately clients' possible results easily show their likes and dislikes and propose their specific desire for products or services. These little nuances can convert clients into regular clients (Ramya & Karthikeyan, 2024).

Great comfort to clients

AI has delivered awesome consolation to customers. In truth, they are now familiar with comfort. We have not even thought booking appointments, virtual buying, or monitoring property protection could be only a click away. Face and fingerprint popularity is one of the upgrades that result from AI. More importantly, it has saved instances as its abilities in a way that does not comprise human intelligence. Imagine how much time we can deliver to extraordinary subjects if we are not certain to do responsibilities that can be operated via artificial intelligence. Artificial Intelligence has created a horizon of the latest possibilities (Ramya & Karthikeyan, 2024).

Customers will shift to voice era

Several main retail and economic groups will shift closer to voice technology because clients feel comfortable with the use of this. Voice searchers are less difficult for customers to query and get higher effects than textual queries. In addition, using a virtual assistant in day-to-day existence makes people more open to using voice-over generation in their daily lives. The oldest barrier has long passed, and now humans have decided to use voice-over texting (Ramya & Karthikeyan, 2024).

Influence of Artificial Intelligence in Consumer Behavior

The development of synthetic intelligence is categorized into four crucial components. Viz is a real-time product focused on Visual Search, Chatbot, and commercials. In the modern age, client purchases and effects are decided and managed using synthetic intelligence. It offers advertising answers, and business software helps many international marketplace leaders (Ramya & Karthikeyan, 2024).

Real-time product targeted on

Product focus has been practiced in complete online retail globally. Here, customers were segmented and targeted with merchandise based mostly on their options and purchase facts. It shows product pointers and shopping for process purchaser movement on every buy. It communicates to the clients in actual time and focuses on shoppers with custom-designed product tips. Machine analyzing platforms are supported to recognize the buyer's intent-based totally on their actions, in real-time, and a list of endorsed products. Real-time product focus is also known as cognitive product-focused. Real-time products concentrated on issues are solved artificially shrewd. It starts with evolving with historical consumer information know-how and eating patron clicks in real-time (Ramya & Karthikeyan, 2024).

Visual search

It lets customers search online through photos instead of textual content or key phrases. It presents the answer for people when unknown matters are being discussed. Visual seek lets in to simplify the quest technique and permits aim-orientated customers to discover the proper products faster and simpler (Ramya & Karthikeyan, 2024).

Chatbot

Chatbots assist customers in discovering facts by asking questions and requests through text input, audio entry, or each—without human intervention. It commenced with the smart audio device at the domestic level and moved to messaging packages at the administrative center. The AI chatbots are known as virtual assistants or digital shops. Examples are Apple's Siri, Google Assistant, and Amazon Alexa. Users commend the assistants through questioning or controlling domestic automation gadgets or media playback voice and dealing with recurring responsibilities consisting of e-mail, to-do lists, and calendars with verbal commands. This technology enhances patron-centric commercials and helps to build deeper connections with audiences (Ramya & Karthikeyan, 2024).

RESEARCH, IMPACTS AND CONCLUSION

Research on Artificial Intelligence and Consumer conduct

The impact of AI on client behaviors inside the retailing quarter is a massive relationship between AI and client conduct. The version can highly expect and offer a reason for patron purchase behavior AI. The researcher recommends that online shops hire AI in each step within the consumer journey, from need reputation, statistics seeking for, evaluation, and purchase decision-making to place up-purchase behavior to expecting patron purchase behavior inside the online platform. Advances in technology and AI's ability to do virtual advertising and advertising are on the boom; therefore, the opportunities are endless. AI is increasingly used in operational markets to identify threats, undertake marketing studies, and figure out business corporation features to coordinate with intended clients. While the use of AI in digital advertising will impact marketing strategies, enterprise fashions, marketing and advertising and marketing strategies, and customer company options, it will also affect customers' behavior. The fundamental interest of AI in digital marketing is not based totally on replacing human dynamics in critical choices but on developing a better dynamic digital advertising environment. It will allow advertisers to quickly examine the needs of a likely purchaser and regulate the AI they hire in virtual marketing to grow earnings. The trade-in customer behavior with the assistance of AI to analyze and count on the client's goals. Further, this test enlarges the manufacturers to expand higher promoting techniques to the customers and purchase it. AI follows client behavior to determine if customers will buy products and services from the market in the coming days—the assignment of AI reasoning in internet enterprise and its utility in numerous zones of online commercial corporations. Computerized reasoning has the outstanding functionality of acquiring and observing massive records and providing alternatives to hobbies. Web-based enterprises receive this innovation from recognizing designs depending on perusing, buying statistics, credit score tests, and account statistics. The impact of AI on consumers and industry is turned on by the usage of AI in retail, healthcare, crime investigation, and employment (Ramya & Karthikeyan, 2024).

AI Benefits in Consumer Behavior

AI revolutionizes how clients act and the way companies perform. AI influences users' experience and conduct. Organizations use AI to enhance client experience and increase patron pride. The use of AI improves the company's overall performance, including high-quality advantages that affect the dimensions and electricity of marketing techniques that support industries in performing their company desires.

These advantages include sales boom, purchaser loyalty, client consolation, and patron consideration. AI can identify customers behavior, wishes, feelings, selections, and dreams. By segmenting these records, it can intentionally provide customized solutions mainly to a certain huge variety or institution of clients, increasing the opportunity for better conversion charges. Customer segmentation concentrated on suggestions for creating a win-win relationship between clients and brands. AI can increase patron loyalty to the degree that every buyer and supplier will experience a wealthy enterprise relationship. Effective patron centered on mixed with immoderate splendid services or products may also grow patron loyalty so that the clients will keep re-engaging with the emblem gambling its offerings. On the other hand, the brand will enlarge their satisfied customer's funnel. Since AI has been embedded in industries, the growing clients' convenience will advise e-commerce with the support of faster orders and purchases, appropriate guidelines, and robot delivery. Patron privacy and records protection coverage are essential elements of brand success. Both denote the trustworthiness of the logo. How a brand keeps, protects, processes facts, lives transparent, and defends customer statistics determines the quantity of achievement. When the services or product description responds as promised to the deliverable, the brand grows the possibility of constructing strong bonds with the customers. AI contributes to that path by offering offerings that clients discover as precious and realistic to their wishes based totally on state-of-the-art statistics manipulation and information dealing with algorithms (Gkikas & Theodoridis, 2021).

CONCLUSION

The intersection of client behavior, the name for shocks, and AI reshapes present-day markets in profound techniques. The function of panic attempting to find, stockpiling, and shifts in purchaser options has become increasingly obvious, especially in response to monetary uncertainties, pandemics, and worldwide crises. These phenomena spotlight customer names delicate yet adaptive nature as intellectual elements, supply chain disruptions, and technological enhancements strain buying styles. As the worldwide marketplace continues to adapt, the combination of AI in purchaser conduct assessment is essential for correctly predicting, responding to, and managing calls for shocks. Businesses that leverage AI-powered insights can navigate uncertainties, optimize inventory strategies, and foster customer remember, ultimately developing more resilient and adaptive supply chains. While panic searching for and stockpiling can also in no way be in truth removed, AI's predictive skills can mitigate their terrible consequences, making sure of an extra strong and consumer-centric marketplace. Understanding and searching beforehand for shifts in client behavior with AI will be a defining difficulty in retaining commercial enterprise boom, enhancing customer satisfaction, and keeping marketplace equilibrium in an era of fast monetary and technological transformation.

REFERENCE

Asadollah, O., Carmy, L. S., Hoque, M. R., & Yilmazkuday, H. (2024). Geopolitical risk, supply chains, and global inflation. *World Economy, 47*(8), 3450–3486. DOI: 10.1111/twec.13585

Ascari, G., Bonam, D., & Smadu, A. (2024a). Global supply chain pressures, inflation, and implications for monetary policy. *Journal of International Money and Finance, 142*, 103029. DOI: 10.1016/j.jimonfin.2024.103029

Ascari, G., Bonam, D., & Smadu, A. (2024b). Global supply chain pressures, inflation, and implications for monetary policy. *Journal of International Money and Finance, 142*, 103029. DOI: 10.1016/j.jimonfin.2024.103029

Del Rio-Chanona, R. M., Mealy, P., Pichler, A., Lafond, F., & Farmer, J. D. (2020). Supply and demand shocks in the COVID-19 pandemic: An industry and occupation perspective. *Oxford Review of Economic Policy, 36*(Supplement_1), S94–S137. DOI: 10.1093/oxrep/graa033

Detmers, G., Ho, S., & Karagedikli, Ö. (2022). Understanding Consumer Inflation Expectations during the COVID-19 Pandemic. *The Australian Economic Review, 55*(1), 141–154. DOI: 10.1111/1467-8462.12460 PMID: 35601136

Diaz, E. M., Cunado, J., & De Gracia, F. P. (2024). Global drivers of inflation: The role of supply chain disruptions and commodity price shocks. *Economic Modelling, 140*, 106860. DOI: 10.1016/j.econmod.2024.106860

Dulam, R., Furuta, K., & Kanno, T. (2021). Consumer panic buying: Realizing its consequences and repercussions on the supply chain. *Sustainability (Basel), 13*(8), 4370. DOI: 10.3390/su13084370

Franzoni, F. A., Giannetti, M., & Tubaldi, R. (2023). Supply chain shortages, large firms' market power, and inflation. SSRN *Electronic Journal*. DOI: 10.2139/ssrn.4586302

Gafurdjan, Z. (2024). Inflation and its Effects on Consumer Behavior and Economic Policies. *Deleted Journal, 10*(10), 3–6. DOI: 10.54613/ku.v10i10.895

Gkikas, D. C., & Theodoridis, P. K. (2021). AI in Consumer Behavior. In *Learning and analytics in intelligent systems* (pp. 147–176). DOI: 10.1007/978-3-030-80571-5_10

Hoda, S., Singh, A., Rao, A., Ural, R., & Hodson, N. (2020). Consumer demand modeling during COVID-19 pandemic. *2021 IEEE International Conference on Bioinformatics and Biomedicine (BIBM)*, 2282–2289. DOI: 10.1109/BIBM49941.2020.9313281

Hu, Z. (2022). Consumer behavior prediction based on machine learning scenarios. In *Proceedings of the 2022 International Conference on Bigdata Blockchain and Economy Management (ICBBEM 2022)* (pp. 410–419). DOI: 10.2991/978-94-6463-030-5_43

Jama, I. (2024). Understanding the consumer: AI-Driven predictive analytics and the transformation of purchasing behavior. *Proceeding of International Student Conference on Business, Education, Economics, Accounting, and Management.*, *2*(1), 2174–2190. DOI: 10.21009/ISC-BEAM.012.157

Lakshmanamoorthy, S., & Athinarayanan, S. (2024). Balancing Act: Exploring the Relationship between Inflation and Consumer Behaviour. *Shanlax International Journal of Economics*, *12*(2), 8–12. DOI: 10.34293/economics.v12i2.7194

Lorenzoni, G. (2009). A theory of demand shocks. *The American Economic Review*, *99*(5), 2050–2084. DOI: 10.1257/aer.99.5.2050

Loxton, M., Truskett, R., Scarf, B., Sindone, L., Baldry, G., & Zhao, Y. (2020). Consumer Behaviour during Crises: Preliminary Research on How Coronavirus Has Manifested Consumer Panic Buying, Herd Mentality, Changing Discretionary Spending and the Role of the Media in Influencing Behaviour. *Journal of Risk and Financial Management*, *13*(8), 166. DOI: 10.3390/jrfm13080166

Madanchian, M. (2024). Generative AI for Consumer Behavior Prediction: Techniques and applications. *Sustainability (Basel)*, *16*(22), 9963. DOI: 10.3390/su16229963

Monge, M., Lazcano, A., & Infante, J. (2024). Monetary policy and inflation rate in the behavior of consumer sentiment in the us. A fractional integration and cointegration analysis. *Research in Economics*, *78*(3), 100981. DOI: 10.1016/j.rie.2024.100981

Nasirian, K., & Taheri, H. (2019). *EPRA International Journal of Research & Development (IJRD). EPRA International Journal of Research & Development.* IJRD., DOI: 10.36713/epra2016

Negm, E. M. (2023). Consumers' purchase behavior reactions: A focus on the steady devaluation of currency, compounding increase in inflation rates in Egypt. *Journal of Humanities and Applied Social Sciences*, *5*(5), 383–401. DOI: 10.1108/JHASS-05-2023-0054

Ramya, K., & Karthikeyan, K. (2024). A study on the usage of Artificial Intelligence technology in influencing consumer Buying Behavior with special with special reference to online shopping. *Proceedings on Engineering Sciences*, *5*(4), 13–20. DOI: 10.24874/PES06.01.002

Singh, P., Arora, L., & Choudhry, A. (2022). Consumer Behavior in the Service Industry: An Integrative literature review and research agenda. *Sustainability (Basel)*, *15*(1), 250. DOI: 10.3390/su15010250

Tao, H., Sun, X., Liu, X., Tian, J., & Zhang, D. (2022). The impact of consumer purchase behavior changes on the business model design of consumer services companies over the course of COVID-19. *Frontiers in Psychology*, *13*, 818845. DOI: 10.3389/fpsyg.2022.818845 PMID: 35310236

Chapter 5
Logistics Bottlenecks:
Port congestion, Shipping Delays, and the Inflationary Effects of Transportation Challenges

Frank Ijem Ojadi
Lagos Business School, Pan-Atlantic University, Nigeria

Sheneni Felix Maiyaki
https://orcid.org/0009-0006-1955-0637
Lagos Business School, Pan-Atlantic University, Nigeria

ABSTRACT

Logistics bottlenecks increase the time it takes to get products to their final destination. In addition to the time, logistics bottlenecks have cost implications. Consequently, this chapter explores the connection between logistics bottleneck and inflation in Nigeria. Utilizing the structuralist inflation theory and the just-in-case inventory management strategy, this study shows that logistics bottlenecks transcend operational setbacks and are drivers of inflation. This study uses a qualitative methodology through secondary data from extant literature and government information sources. This chapter shows that structural inefficiencies, like cumbersome port clearing processes, inadequate port infrastructure, and inadequate intermodal transportation, contribute to inflation in Nigeria. The study indicates capacity building, policy consistency, and intermodal transportation infrastructure development, among others, as means of reducing logistics bottlenecks and consequently curbing cost-push inflation in Nigeria.

DOI: 10.4018/979-8-3373-1982-7.ch005

1. INTRODUCTION

Global supply chains are the backbone of international trade. It has enabled businesses to reach consumers hundreds of miles away and improved the living conditions of individuals globally. The globalisation of supply chains has experienced tremendous growth in the last decade of the twentieth century (Vidrova, 2020). The technological advancements of the twenty-first century have caused it to grow exponentially (Yang et al., 2021). Despite the continued growth of global supply chains, it has been plagued by inefficiencies in logistics that continue to undermine economic growth, particularly in developing countries. Port congestion, shipping delays, and transportation bottlenecks create ripple effects across industries, thus increasing operational costs, supply shortages, and inflationary pressures (Eddrgash, 2022). These challenges are more pronounced in regions with poor infrastructure, bureaucratic red tape, and inefficient customs processes across borders, consequently causing delays and escalating costs for businesses and consumers (Nwokedi & Nwachukwu, 2022). And as a result, the timely and efficient distribution of goods and services have proved elusive.

Developing countries, particularly Nigeria, face unique logistics constraints due to their underdeveloped transport networks, port infrastructure and policy inefficiencies (Agbigbe, 2016). This is evident in the land-side part of Apapa and Tin Can Island Ports, which are responsible for handling most of the country's imports. These ports are plagued by congestion, cargo handling issues, and high demurrage charges. These logistics challenges come with exorbitant cost implications that contribute to inflation, making goods more expensive and reducing economic competitiveness (Ye et al., 2023). Therefore, this chapter will explore the nature of logistics bottlenecks in Nigeria and their inflationary consequences. The chapter draws insights from the Structuralist Inflation Theory and the Just-in-Case Inventory Management Strategy. The theories will provide insights on how structural rigidities and challenges impact countries and the ramifications of the coping strategies businesses employ.

2. BACKGROUND

Supply chain integration has risen to promise as the world continuously transforms into a global village. Global supply chain networks have become critical to international trade, instrumental to increasing access to goods and services and healthy economic performance (Vidrova, 2020). This is due to its ability to enhance delivery speed, reduce trade barriers, and facilitate economic growth. However, while developed countries continue to advance their logistics processes and infrastructure to enjoy their benefits, developing countries grapple with several logistics challenges.

In Nigeria, the port system has undergone significant organisational transformations throughout its history. Initially, the functional organisation of the ports had a decentralised governance structure. Different ministerial departments of the Federal Government controlled various aspects at different times. The Nigerian Railways Corporation handled cargo at terminals, while the Marine Department managed vessel movements. This fragmented approach contributed to some coordination challenges, leading to the establishment of the Nigerian Ports Authority (NPA) through the Port Act of 1954. The NPA was vested with comprehensive responsibilities, including the design, construction, and development of ports, docks, and associated infrastructure. They also handled the management of port labour, the provision and maintenance of port facilities, and the regulation of port use. The establishment of the NPA effectively centralised the control and development of ports. For decades, the NPA operated primarily under a model where it controlled the port infrastructure, employed the workforce, and regulated all port activities, which came with its own challenges.

The organisation of the Nigerian ports system experienced a significant shift with the port reforms initiated in the early 2000s. These reforms were in response to persistent operational inefficiencies, congestion, and the need to attract private sector investment and expertise. Prior to these reforms, the NPA's powers were extensive. It was mandated to operate profitably while still controlling virtually all public and private tasks within the sector. However, despite these powers, issues like high tariffs, low productivity, and endemic corruption persisted. This resulted in a comprehensive technical and financial assessment spearheaded by the Bureau of Public Enterprises (BPE) with support from international consultants. The overarching goal of the reforms was to enhance efficiency, reduce costs for port users, and attract private investment. The resolution reached was the transition of the system to a Landlord Port model. This model meant that the public sector (NPA) retained ownership of the port land and basic infrastructure (acting as the landlord) while private companies were granted concessions to operate and invest in terminal superstructure, equipment, and service delivery.

Consequently, the current organisation of the Nigerian ports system is characterized by this Landlord Port model. The NPA's primary role has evolved to that of a technical regulator and provider of common user infrastructure and marine services, such as pilotage. The operational aspects of cargo handling and terminal management have largely been the responsibility of private terminal operators. This is based on concession agreements for specific terminals within the major ports, such as APM Terminals and Tin Can Island Container Terminal Ltd. in Lagos. This unbundling of port operations into numerous concessioned terminals was intended to foster competition, drive economic efficiency and investments. The Bureau of Public Enterprises (BPE) played a crucial role in implementing these concession transactions. Part of their responsibilities included setting criteria for evaluation and defining the fee structures for concessionaires. The Federal Ministry of Transport retains overall supervisory responsibility for maritime transport and its associated agencies, including the NPA and the Nigerian Shippers' Council, which is increasingly positioned to take on the role of an economic regulator for the ports sector. With the port reform, a more efficient and commercially oriented port system capable of supporting Nigeria's trade ambitions was birthed (**Figure 1**).

Figure 1. Nigeria's Port Framework Analysis

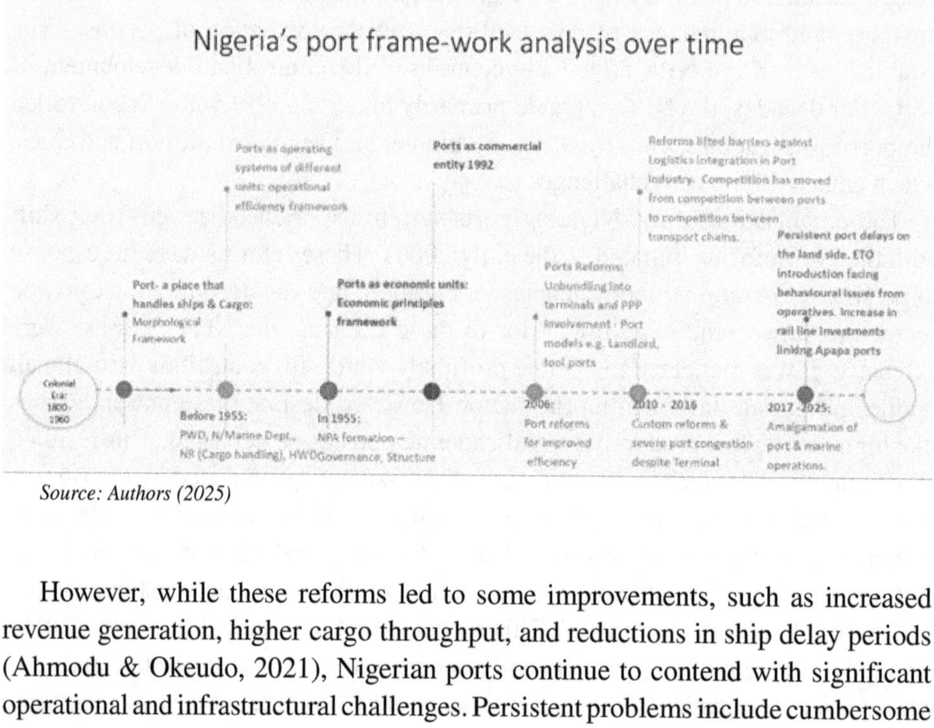

Source: Authors (2025)

However, while these reforms led to some improvements, such as increased revenue generation, higher cargo throughput, and reductions in ship delay periods (Ahmodu & Okeudo, 2021), Nigerian ports continue to contend with significant operational and infrastructural challenges. Persistent problems include cumbersome documentation processes, the multiplicity of agencies operating at the ports, severe port congestion, prolonged cargo dwell times, and pervasive behavioural issues, such as corruption, still exist (Oyewole, 2019). The key ports of Apapa and Tin Can Island in Lagos are described as overstretched. A symptom of this is attendant delays in cargo handling and processing. This is further exacerbated by the failure to adequately develop other national ports like Calabar, Onne, Port Harcourt, and Warri to deep-sea standards capable of accommodating larger vessels and decongesting the Lagos axis (Ndalu & Umennaihe, 2024). This has led to a scenario where neighbouring countries with better-developed deep-sea ports are increasingly serving as hubs for West African cargo (Emenyonu et al., 2016). Although the lekki seaport became operational in early 2020s.

The efficacy of Nigerian ports is also undermined by the deficient state of inland transportation infrastructure, which creates severe bottlenecks in cargo evacuation and distribution. Road transport remains the major means for moving goods to and from the ports and across the country. However, a significant proportion of Nigeria's road network, particularly rural and port access roads, is in a deplorable condition (Aboyeji & Aguda, 2024). The access roads to major ports like Apapa are notoriously inadequate and often gridlocked. This results in substantial delays in cargo movement and increased operational costs for businesses (Oritse & Bivbere, 2018). The reliance on a poorly maintained road system leads to prolonged transit times and high transport costs (Aboyeji & Aguda, 2024). The rail system has historically played a role in freight movement, but its capacity to handle substantial container traffic from the ports has diminished. Currently, efforts towards revitalization of the rail system are ongoing. Nigeria also possesses an extensive network of inland waterways with significant potential for freight transport, yet this mode remains largely underdeveloped and underutilised. This is due to challenges such as insufficient dredging and inadequate facilities. These collective deficiencies in inland transport infrastructure severely constrain the logistics chain, place immense pressure on the road network, and ultimately hamper the efficiency of national and international trade (Ihugba et al., 2014). Of recent is the proliferation of airports across the states. These airports are designed and constructed by the state governments some, partly with the aim of handling cargo while others target both cargo and passengers. An interesting development is the Lagos international airport, which is just about an hour away by road from the airport in Ogun state. Both of the airports are underutilised. The said airports are ultimately handed over to the Federal government. A closer look at the airports suggests a lack of integration with the other transportation modes.

3. METHODOLOGY

This chapter employs a qualitative research methodology to explore the interplay between logistics bottlenecks and inflationary pressures within the Nigerian economy. Adopting a qualitative approach is rooted in the need for an in-depth exploration and understanding of the structural and institutional factors and their inflationary effect. The study draws from secondary data, drawing insights from a diverse range of credible sources. These sources include a thorough review of extant academic literature, comprising scholarly articles, books, and policy papers that address logistics, supply chain management, port operations, structural economics, and inflation theory, with a particular emphasis on the context of developing countries and Nigeria. Complementing this academic foundation are publications and reports from relevant Nigerian government agencies, such as the Central Bank of Nigeria (CBN), World Bank, and the National Bureau of Statistics (NBS), which provide essential official data, policy perspectives, and historical context on economic indicators and sectoral performance. The chapter utilises only qualitative methodology as it is suitable for addressing our objective which at this stage remains exploratory. Subsequent studies could measure empirically the extent of the inflationary pressures of logistics bottlenecks.

The analysis within this chapter proceeds by first establishing a detailed understanding of the nature and manifestations of key logistics bottlenecks in Nigeria, based on evidence from the secondary data sources and observations. This foundational step identifies the specific challenges within the logistics system, such as port congestion, shipping delays, and inadequate infrastructure. Subsequently, the chapter utilises two distinct theoretical lenses, namely the Structuralist Inflation Theory and the Just-in-Case (JIC) Inventory Management Strategy. These theories aided in interpreting and explaining how these identified bottlenecks contribute to inflationary pressures in Nigeria. The Structuralist Inflation Theory provides a framework for understanding how underlying structural rigidities and supply-side constraints translate into non-monetary driven inflation. Simultaneously, the Just-in-Case inventory strategy offers insights into the coping mechanisms adopted by firms in response to an unreliable logistics environment. It further demonstrates how the resulting practice of holding excess inventory adds to costs within the supply chain.

4. LOGISTICS BOTTLENECKS

4.1 Port Congestion

Port congestion in Nigeria is a persistent and complex issue that affects the efficiency of maritime trade. Unfortunately, this state of inefficiency has far-reaching implications for economic stability, business operations, and inflation. Congestion at Nigeria's ports, especially Apapa and Tin Can Island Ports in Lagos, is an issue for serious concern. Congestion in these ports is driven by capacity issues, poor planning, and regulatory inefficiencies (Chinedum, 2018). These ports, which collectively handle more than 80% of Nigeria's imports, have long struggled to keep up with the increasing volume of cargo amid limited expansion in physical and operational capacity.

The journey of goods through Nigeria's trade corridors is plagued by a myriad of logistics bottlenecks, each turn presents new delays, unforeseen costs, and frustrating inefficiencies. These bottlenecks are woven into the very fabric of the import and export processes. They stem from a confluence of overly complex procedures, chronic infrastructural challenges, unpredictable policy environments, and deeply ingrained behavioural patterns among key stakeholders. The cumulative effect is a trade environment that is significantly more challenging and costly than it needs to be, acting as a drag on economic activity and international competitiveness.

Chief among these bottlenecks are the procedural and documentation hurdles that define Nigerian trade. Importers and exporters consistently lament of the multiplicity and repetitiveness of documentation required by various authorities. Prior to the port and customs reforms a single import transaction can involve completing forms with over fifty distinct line items of information. Whilst the practice has reduced, this meticulous, yet often duplicative, demand for paperwork is a significant time sink. The frustration is amplified by the common practice where hard copies of documents are still insisted upon by numerous agencies. This becomes more frustrating because electronic submissions have been made to the same organizations. It further negates many of the potential efficiencies of digitalisation. These inefficiencies are further deepened by corruption and unethical behaviour. The Maritime Anti-Corruption Network (MACN) ranks Nigerian ports among the highest in informal payments and facilitation requests globally. Importers and clearing agents are often forced to make undocumented payments to expedite inspections, secure approvals, or bypass certain administrative hurdles. This informal system creates unpredictability in port operations, further slowing legitimate cargo movement and fostering distrust.

The Nigeria Customs Service (NCS), which is responsible for the cargo clearance process, is frequently identified as a locus of major bottlenecks. Stakeholders describe NCS clearing activities as semi-manual, painstakingly slow, and plagued by inconsistency. A key issue is the perceived misuse of discretionary powers by customs officials in interpreting HS codes for tariff classification and valuing goods for duty assessment. These interpretations can vary significantly, which leads to frequent and often arbitrary upward revisions of payable duties, and importers are then compelled to contest or pay to avoid further delays. The official channels for seeking redress for such disputes are protracted and burdensome. The process is perceived as being designed to encourage informal settlements rather than transparent resolution. This perception fosters an environment where "facilitation payments" can become an expected part of the clearance process. The operational hours and work practices within customs, such as late resumption of duties by officers and early closure, as well as a reluctance to delegate key responsibilities for cargo release, further contribute to daily backlogs and slow processing times. The often overriding of PAAR also introduces duplication of effort and extends the clearance timeline.

The policy and regulatory environment itself is a source of significant logistics bottlenecks. Importers and other stakeholders lament because of sudden and uncoordinated changes in import and export policies. These policy shifts range from alterations in inspection regimes to new documentation formats or revised tariff structures. These are sometimes implemented with little to no prior consultation with the trading community or even among different government agencies operating at the ports. Consequently, importers may only become aware of critical changes when their consignments are already en route or undergoing clearance. The consequence of this is disruptions, urgent re-documentation (sometimes involving overseas suppliers), and unforeseen delays. There have been instances of abrupt changes in the destination inspection scheme and the introduction of new electronic clearance platforms with insufficient lead time for stakeholder adaptation. This unpredictability undermines planning, increases business risk, and adds layers of complexity to the international trade process.

Beyond procedural and policy issues, infrastructural deficiencies create bottlenecks that affect the supply chain. The deplorable state of inland road transport infrastructure, poor utilisation of barges and inadequate rail infrastructure are key drivers of this. Dilapidated roads, severe traffic congestion within port cities and along inland routes slow down the movement of imports and the delivery of exports to the ports. This issue is a consequence of road quality, traffic management and the lack of viable alternatives like a well-functioning rail freight system or efficient inland waterway transport. For exporters, the challenge is compounded by the limited availability of modern, functional warehouses in proximity to production areas. The non-standardised procurement processes for export commodities add further layers of complexity and potential delay before goods even reach the port. The operations and behaviours of other critical players, like terminal operators, shipping lines, and various inspection agencies, also contribute to the bottlenecks. Terminal operators, despite improvements post-concession, are blamed for deficiencies in cargo handling equipment. These deficiencies lead to slow loading/unloading of trucks and inadequate space or coordination for container examinations. The process for booking physical examinations or scanning can be protracted. Given the limited daily capacities at terminals, queues and extended cargo dwell times are inevitable. Exporters also face challenges in obtaining empty containers from shipping lines in a timely manner for stuffing their goods. Furthermore, the interactions between stakeholders sometimes have an adversarial nature rather than a partnership geared towards collective efficiency. Importers and exporters frequently recount experiences of dealing with officials who seem more focused on personal gain than on trade facilitation. Another pervasive factor is corruption and indiscipline that undermine adherence to procedures and timelines. The lack of robust and fully integrated IT systems across all port community stakeholders also means that many processes remain manual and prone to error and delay. All these frustrate the realisation of a truly streamlined and efficient logistics environment. These interconnected bottlenecks create delays and costs, ultimately hindering Nigeria's ability to fully leverage international trade for economic advancement.

Nigeria ranks poorly in the Logistics Performance Index, due to inadequate infrastructure and customs performance, which are directly tied to port efficiency (World Bank, 2022). However, government and private sector actors have made efforts to address port congestion. The Nigerian Port Process Manual (NPPM) was a significant step toward standardising port operations and eliminating corrupt practices. The Presidential Enabling Business Environment Council (PEBEC) has also introduced several port reforms to improve transparency and efficiency. However, implementation has been inconsistent, and systemic change has been slow. A public-private partnership has also developed infrastructure initiatives such as the Lekki Deep Sea Port. The port began operations in 2023 and promises to decongest existing ports by offering modern cargo handling facilities and deeper berths for larger vessels. Nevertheless, unless complementary investments are made in rail, road, and digital systems, the benefits of the new port may be limited. Especially as the implications of port congestion affect other sectors. Manufacturing firms, for instance, experience production delays due to the late arrival of raw materials and retailers face stockouts.

4.2 Shipping Delays

Shipping delays are a pervasive and costly reality in Nigerian maritime trade. The late arrival of goods can deeply impact the entire logistics chain. This fosters the predictability of supply for importers and the ability of exporters to meet deadlines. These delays are not attributable to a single cause but arise from several factors involving pre-arrival and clearance procedures, the efficiency of port services, the operational practices of shipping lines and terminal operators, and the preparedness of shippers themselves. The consequences are significant, contributing to increased operational costs for shipping lines (which are often passed on to shippers), extended cargo dwell times, heightened uncertainty in supply chain planning, and a reduction in the overall competitiveness of Nigerian ports as transhipment hubs or even efficient gateways

One of the initial points where shipping delays can originate is in the pre-arrival and clearance processes for vessels. Shipping lines have highlighted the burdensome requirement of distributing numerous hard copies of voluminous cargo manifests to multiple government agencies, including the NPA (20 copies), NCS (7 copies), and NIMASA, among others (Ojadi & Walters, 2015). This manual distribution must occur despite the simultaneous provision of electronic copies to the NCS command at the port of entry. Such a repetitive process is arduous and expensive, as well as time-consuming. The process can potentially delay the issuance of the crucial rotation number by the NCS, which is necessary for accessing the Data Trade Input (DTI) system to commence pre-clearing activities by the clearing agents. While vessels on direct call from origin ports might submit manifests up to seven days prior to arrival, those on looped services calling at multiple West or North African ports before Lagos often only submit their updated manifests about two days prior to arrival. This compressed timeframe is often insufficient to complete the pre-clearing process (including data capture and duty payment). This also stalls timely inspection arrangements upon cargo discharge. This positions Lagos more as a feeder port susceptible to transhipment delays, rather than a proactive hub.

The efficiency of port services provided by the Nigerian Ports Authority (NPA) is another significant factor influencing shipping schedules. Pilotage services, essential for navigating vessels into and out of the Lagos ports, are a frequent source of complaint from shipping lines. The method of booking pilotage is described as cumbersome, requiring physical presence at the NPA harbour office and manual contact with pilots for each movement. Shipping lines report that failure to maintain these direct contacts, even if a schedule is released, can lead to delays in obtaining these crucial services. Shipping lines indicated that it can take an average of up to four hours to secure pilotage. This claim, however, varies with NPA's own assessments, but it directly impacts vessel turnaround time. Furthermore, perceived inadequacies in the number of available tugboats, mooring launches, and pilot cutters are impediments to the speedy pilotage and berthing of vessels, especially considering the growing number of vessel calls. Even the daily berthing meetings convened by the NPA to coordinate vessel arrivals and resource allocation can be constrained by tidal and seasonality issues, as well as the available capacity of pilots and watercraft. Delays in berthing a vessel directly translate to additional, unproductive time spent by the ship at port, incurring costs and disrupting schedules.

Once a vessel is berthed, the "break bulk" process, which involves joint inspection by port health, immigration, NCS enforcement, NDLEA, and other statutory agencies, before discharge operations can commence. This is another point where significant delays occur. Shipping lines report that coordinating these various agencies to conduct a joint inspection and issue the break bulk certificate can be very time-consuming. Requests for these activities made late in the day are reportedly often deferred to the following day. Consequently, adding a 24-hour delay to the commencement of cargo discharge.

The operational efficiency of terminal operators also directly influences how long a ship stays at berth. While private terminal operators have invested in equipment and systems, the actual vessel discharge and loading rates are critical. The coordination between quay crane operations, yard handling, and the readiness to receive or load containers determines the speed of turnaround. For instance, APMT reported an average crane productivity of 15 Moves Per Hour (MPH) and an average berth productivity of 30 MPH, with a vessel turnaround time of two to three days, depending on the cargo (Ojadi & Walters, 2015). While these figures represent an improvement over past performances, any inefficiency in these operations, such as equipment breakdown, labour issues, or yard congestion, will directly translate into longer port stays for vessels. This is because any issue impacts the ability to quickly move containers to and from the quay.

Shipping lines themselves, and the preparedness of shippers (importers/exporters), can also contribute to delays. For instance, incomplete declarations on shipment instructions provided by buyers can lead to export processing delays. Exporters also face pressure to meet tight shipping line cut-off dates for cargo availability, and any upstream delays in getting goods to the port can result in missing a vessel's deadline. Conversely, bringing cargo too early to avoid missing deadlines can lead to additional storage costs if the vessel itself is delayed. Some shipping lines are also reported to invoice exporters for additional storage days if export cargo remains at the terminal due to the late arrival of the nominated vessel, a frequent point of contention. The issue of overtime cargo also has an indirect impact on shipping because it ties up terminal space and can affect the overall fluidity of port operations. This eventually affects the berth availability and the speed at which new vessels can be processed. The non-manifestation of Form M numbers on bills of lading by some lines, a requirement confirmed by the Central Bank of Nigeria, can also create downstream clearance problems. These myriad sources of shipping delays collectively reflect a maritime environment where time is a costly and unpredictable variable, which is critical to the smooth flow of international trade. Shipping companies, anticipating these delays, often add additional lead times to their delivery schedules or impose congestion surcharges. In the end, these strategies inflate the cost and duration of shipping goods to Nigeria. Importers bear these additional costs and ultimately pass them on to end consumers, contributing to the inflationary spiral (Ye et al., 2023).

The inland transport system is another major contributor to shipping delays. The movement of cargo from the port to its final destination is hampered by poor road conditions, traffic congestion, and the absence of efficient alternative transport modes. The collapse of Nigeria's rail system has placed an unsustainable burden on road transport. This leads to long queues of trucks around the ports and increased transit times. The overdependence on trucks for cargo movement in a country with poor road infrastructure has also led to logistics inefficiency and high costs (Agbigbe, 2016). In Nigeria, inland container depots have remained underdeveloped. These inland ports can decongest seaports and speed up the movement of goods, but have not been fully established. These facilities act as extensions of seaports by facilitating customs clearance and container handling closer to the final point of delivery. However, delays in their operationalisation and lack of supporting infrastructure have limited their effectiveness in mitigating shipping delays.

The consequence of these delays is higher costs and reduced reliability in the eyes of international trading partners. The inability to ensure the timely delivery to Nigeria is a significant risk factor for international trading partners. Some firms have bypassed Nigeria entirely, rerouting shipments through neighbouring countries such as Ghana, where port operations are more efficient and predictable. This diversion results in lost economic opportunities and reinforces Nigeria's negative reputation as a challenging logistics environment. Shipping delays also affect domestic supply chains. Local manufacturers who rely on imported raw materials face production downtime when inputs are delayed. Retailers and distributors also face stockouts, which lead to lost sales and frustrated customers. The case of perishables is even more precarious. They are rendered unusable due to prolonged exposure during transit or delays in customs clearance. These inefficiencies constrain the supply chains, push up prices, undermine business confidence, and discourage investment.

5. ECONOMIC IMPACT OF LOGISTICS BOTTLENECKS - CHANNELS THROUGH WHICH THEY IMPACT.

5.1 Inflation

Logistics bottlenecks are a major contributor to inflation in Nigeria. Inflation, which refers to the general increase of the prices of goods and services over a period of time, is often attributed to monetary policy, demand-supply imbalances, or global commodity price fluctuations. In the case of Nigeria, however, logistics inefficiencies profoundly influence the price of goods and services. It is a typical case of cost-push inflation where prices increase due to higher production and distribution costs. Transportation and logistics form the backbone of product distribution and market integration. When this backbone is compromised by structural inefficiencies such as poor road networks, congested ports, and delayed shipments, it directly affects the final price of goods and services. In Nigeria, transport costs are among the highest in sub-Saharan Africa. These costs account for as much as 30 to 40% of the final consumer price of goods. This is further exacerbated by Nigeria's dependence on imported goods for industrial inputs, food products, electronics, and pharmaceuticals (Unegbu & Ugwunna, 2024).

Furthermore, one way through which logistics disruptions drive inflation is the upward pressure they place on the cost of doing business. Importers, wholesalers, and retailers incur additional costs due to prolonged port dwell times, demurrage charges, warehousing fees, and informal payments to expedite cargo movement. These added costs are transferred down the supply chain to the end users. For instance, when a container sits at the port for days beyond the grace period, demurrage fees accrue, sometimes exceeding the value of the goods for low-margin products. Such scenarios create a distorted pricing structure that artificially inflates market prices across sectors. Moreover, transportation bottlenecks significantly affect food inflation, a significant component of Nigeria's Consumer Price Index (CPI). Food inflation has consistently outpaced core inflation in recent years, with logistics constraints being a central driver (Thomas et al., 2023). Bad roads, extortion by security operatives, and a lack of cold chain facilities hinder the movement of agricultural produce from rural production centres to urban markets. Perishables such as tomatoes, fruits, fish, and dairy products arrive in the market in spoiled condition, leading to shortages and sharp price spikes.

In addition, manufacturing firms that rely on imported raw materials face higher costs and longer lead times due to shipping delays. These inputs are crucial for producing goods ranging from construction materials to packaged foods and pharmaceuticals. Manufacturers delay production or source more expensive substitutes when delivery timelines are extended. In both cases, the cost per production unit increases, pushing up final product prices. The inflationary effects of logistics bottlenecks are not uniform across all segments of society. Low-income households are disproportionately affected because they spend much of their income on food and necessities, making them more sensitive to transportation costs. This results in declining purchasing power, reduced food security, and worsening inequality. Businesses are also impacted unevenly. Large corporations may have the resources to expedite bureaucratic processes or absorb additional costs. Small and Medium Enterprises (SMEs), on the other hand, often struggle to stay afloat. They resolve to reduce their output, raise prices unsustainably, or exit the market altogether. This ultimately shrinks the supply base and fosters inflation.

The ripple effects also extend to service industries, particularly logistics and retail. Logistics companies adjust service fares and rates in response to rising fuel prices and maintenance costs caused by deteriorating roads. These changes indirectly influence the cost of labour and services, feeding into the overall inflationary trend. Transport sector workers, including truck drivers and freight handlers, often demand higher wages to compensate for delays and the physical toll of navigating poor infrastructure. Similarly, Inflation triggered by logistics inefficiencies can also lead to macroeconomic instability. When price levels rise uncontrollably, central banks typically respond by tightening monetary policy, raising interest rates or reducing the money supply to reduce inflation. However, such interventions can stifle economic growth. This is even more important when inflation is not primarily monetary but structural. Nigeria's Central Bank has implemented these interventions multiple times, only to find that prices continue to climb due to non-monetary pressures such as transport costs, fuel shortages, and currency devaluation (CBN, 2021). A more sustainable approach would be to address the root causes of inflation, among which transport and logistics infrastructure play a critical role. Globally, efficient logistics systems lead to lower inflation volatility and higher economic resilience. For example, countries with well-integrated transport networks, reliable intermodal systems, and digitised port operations tend to have more stable pricing environments, even during global supply chain disruptions (World Bank, 2022). Nigeria's inability to replicate these efficiencies has made it especially vulnerable to internal and external shocks.

5.2 Effects on the Supply Chain

The ripple effects of logistics bottlenecks extend beyond immediate cost implications and manifest across the entire supply chain. In Nigeria, the disruptions caused by logistics bottlenecks trigger a ripple effect on procurement, production, distribution, inventory management, customer satisfaction, and even long-term strategic planning for businesses. The result is a series of inefficiencies and vulnerabilities that impact firms and the broader economy. One of the most immediate ripple effects is inventory planning and management distortion. In unpredictable shipping schedules and unreliable delivery timelines, businesses procure excess inventory as a buffer against disruptions. This practice, known as the Just-in-Case (JIC) inventory strategy, which contrasts with the more cost-efficient Just-in-Time (JIT) model employed in developed logistics systems. While JIC provides short-term resilience by ensuring the availability of goods, it significantly increases holding costs, including warehousing, insurance, and risk of product obsolescence (Coslett, 2022). For businesses in Nigeria, especially SMEs, JIC creates a financial strain. Capital that could be invested in innovation, expansion, or human resources becomes tied up in inventory.

Production processes are also adversely affected especially, manufacturing firms that rely on imported raw materials or components that must arrive on time to maintain production schedules. Delays in receiving inputs lead to production downtimes, underutilisation of labour and machinery, and protracted turnaround times. In sectors such as pharmaceuticals, food processing, and construction, disruptions can result in loss of market share, reputational damage, and in some cases, contract termination. The compounding effect is a decline in industrial output, which undermines sectoral performance, amplifies unemployment, and reduces GDP contributions from the manufacturing sector. Furthermore, frequent logistics delays also undermine supplier relationships and trust dynamics. Inconsistent supply timelines damage the reliability of Nigerian firms in the eyes of international partners. This makes it difficult to secure long-term contracts or favourable payment terms. Suppliers may impose higher premiums, shift to more reliable markets, or demand upfront payments to mitigate their risks. These conditions further strain the working capital of Nigerian firms.

On the distribution end, stockouts and supply gaps become common in retail environments. Goods that are delayed in transit or stuck in clearance processes fail to reach retailers on time. This is particularly true in the fast-moving consumer goods (FMCG) sector, where turnover speed is essential to profitability. Retailers often increase prices due to scarcity or face empty shelves, which hurts consumer retention. This unpredictability disrupts consumer behaviour, creates frustration, and reduces brand loyalty. In parallel, these supply chain disruptions create significant pricing volatility. Frequent adjustments to pricing, driven by changes in transport costs or availability of goods, undermine pricing strategy and forecasting. Businesses cannot plan effectively or maintain consistent margins. This volatility disproportionately affects lower-income households and vulnerable populations in inflation-sensitive food, transportation, and healthcare sectors.

Another critical aspect is the increase in operational complexity. Many firms diversify their supplier base or establish multiple shipping channels to mitigate the risks of delays. This approach can reduce reliance on any single node in the supply chain. It, however, also introduces additional coordination challenges, compliance requirements, and quality control risks. This increased complexity can lead to internal inefficiencies and strategic drift for smaller firms with limited managerial capacity. There are also environmental and societal implications. Frequent road congestion caused by port-bound trucks contributes to urban pollution, fuel wastage, and deterioration of public infrastructure. The delay in clearing goods often necessitates round-the-clock truck movement, increasing road accidents and driver fatigue. Moreover, informal practices such as roadside bribery, offloading in unauthorised locations, and warehousing in unregulated facilities become normalised. These reinforce a shadow logistics economy that operates outside legal and ethical standards.

From a policy perspective, accumulating these ripple effects undermines national development objectives. Economic plans that rely on efficient logistics are rendered less effective. For instance, the African Continental Free Trade Area (AfCFTA) presents significant opportunities for intra-African trade. However, without efficient logistics systems, Nigeria risks becoming a peripheral rather than a central player in the emerging continental market. The financial sector also feels the reverberations. Banks and credit institutions become cautious in extending trade finance or invoice factoring services to firms that demonstrate poor delivery timelines or inventory instability. When they do, long durations lead to increased interest payments. Insurance firms face rising claims related to cargo damage, loss, and delays, leading to higher premiums for logistics-related coverage. These added financial burdens further erode profitability and deter investment.

6. THEORIES

6.1 Structuralist Inflation Theory

The Structuralist Inflation Theory provides a critical lens for understanding the root causes of persistent inflation in developing economies. Originating from the Latin American structuralist school of thought in the mid-20th century, this theory challenges the conventional monetarist view that inflation is solely a result of excessive money supply. Instead, it posits that inflation in developing contexts is driven mainly by structural bottlenecks and supply-side constraints that prevent economies from efficiently responding to rising demand (Baer & Kerstenetzky, 1964)[1].

In Nigeria, the relevance of this theory is evident in how logistical inefficiencies generate inflationary pressures. The Structuralist view contends that the ability of the economy to expand production and distribution is limited when critical infrastructure is under-developed and institutional inefficiencies abound. As a result, even modest increases in aggregate demand can trigger disproportionate price increases due to rigid supply mechanisms. For instance, Nigeria's port infrastructure is grossly inadequate for efficiently handling the volume of imports and exports. The poor state of intermodal transport systems and prolonged customs procedures mean that the supply of goods to markets is frequently delayed or disrupted. These limitations, embedded within the economy's structure, align with the theory's foundational assumption that inflation is often systemic rather than short-term.

Another important component of Structuralist Inflation Theory is the role of sectoral imbalances. In Nigeria, there is a heavy dependence on imports for consumer goods, raw materials, and machinery (Unegbu & Ugwunna, 2024). Consequently, any disruption in transportation leads to significant imbalances between supply and demand. If logistics constraints prevent goods from reaching the market on time, the reduced supply pushes prices upward, even if monetary conditions remain stable. Policy inconsistencies, corruption, and a lack of coordination among institutions responsible for trade facilitation exacerbate these imbalances. Additionally, the structuralist perspective highlights the non-price mechanisms that distort market operations. Informal payments, multiple agency inspections, and erratic enforcement of port and other related transport regulations all create inefficiencies that act as hidden costs. These costs are deeply felt in real market prices. They function as friction in the economic system. The effect is increased transaction costs of doing business, which contribute to inflationary dynamics.

The Structuralist Inflation Theory also explains why conventional macroeconomic tools, such as interest rate hikes or tightening the money supply, often fail to contain inflation in Nigeria. These tools that are designed to curb demand prove ineffective when supply-side bottlenecks drive inflation. Raising interest rates to tackle inflation does little to fix the broken logistics chain that delays goods and increases costs. Instead, it may further suppress investment in infrastructure and logistics by increasing borrowing costs. From a policy standpoint, Structuralist theory suggests that countries must target the underlying structural inefficiencies in their economies to address inflation sustainably. In Nigeria, this means not only prioritising investments in logistics infrastructure like ports, roads, railways, and digital systems, but making the right choices that would help sustain the battle against inflation. For instance, there is the need to base the means of bulk cargo movement on rail rather than on road except of course the bulk cargo are mostly time-sensitive. The issue of the Lagos-Calabar coastal road construction is a case in point. Whilst the reason for this construction is mainly for evacuating goods from ports and manufacturing centres around the South-West of the country, it would invariably lead to higher unit cost of transportation to the hinterlands as against the use of rail. Reforming customs procedures rather than adjusting the fiscal policy, such as import duties and levies to match the exchange rates, and institutional coordination will also prove beneficial. Structural transformation is thus not merely about economic diversification but also about addressing the deep-seated inefficiencies that constrain supply.

6.2 Just-in-Case Inventory Management Strategy

The Just-in-Case (JIC) inventory management strategy represents a risk-averse approach to supply chain management. Firms using this strategy maintain higher inventory levels to safeguard against supply and demand uncertainties. Unlike the Just-in-Time (JIT) strategy, which aims to minimise inventory levels and reduce holding costs by relying on predictable and efficient supply chains, JIC prioritises resilience over efficiency. JIC has become prevalent due to the volatility associated with Nigeria. Businesses seeking to withstand the endemic challenges of port congestion, shipping delays, and unreliable inland transportation resort to JIC.

In a well-functioning logistics system and when interest rates are high, firms tend to adopt lean inventory systems that minimise waste and optimise cash flow. However, in Nigeria, firms face considerable risks when relying on timely deliveries. Importers and retailers often face cargo delays at ports, unforeseen customs holdups, and poor road conditions. These factors make it difficult to guarantee delivery dates and compel businesses to hold excess inventory to avoid stockouts and production halts. The JIC strategy is particularly prevalent among manufacturers who rely on imported raw materials or critical components. While this buffers against logistics failures, it also ties up capital, increases warehousing costs, and heightens the risk of inventory obsolescence or spoilage in the case of perishable goods. Retailers in Nigeria similarly rely on JIC practices, especially during high-demand seasons such as festive periods. Given the unpredictability of delivery timelines, many, import goods months in advance, using borrowed capital or internal reserves. This inflates operational costs and exposes businesses to currency and market risks. If exchange rates shift or demand falters, the high stock levels can lead to financial strain or losses.

From a macroeconomic perspective, widespread adoption of the JIC strategy contributes to inflation in multiple ways. First, the increased cost of storage and insurance is often passed on to consumers through higher retail prices. Similarly, when multiple firms adopt the same strategy, it creates artificial scarcity in the supply chain. Even if goods are available in warehouses, the perception of shortage is driven by firms through over-ordering and stockpiling. This phenomenon mirrors hoarding behaviour and adds volatility to pricing dynamics. Moreover, JIC reduces supply chain agility. When firms are burdened with large inventories, they become less responsive to market demand changes or consumer preference shifts. This rigidity often leads to overstocking of unpopular goods and understocking of in-demand items. This further disrupts the supply-demand equilibrium and contributes to inefficiencies in the broader economy.

The adoption of JIC in Nigeria also highlights the deeper issue of a lack of trust in institutional and infrastructural reliability. Businesses invest in excess stock not because it is the most efficient strategy, but because they have little faith in the systems meant to support their operations. This loss of confidence undermines private sector dynamism and discourages foreign investment. This is because investors view supply chain uncertainty as a significant risk factor. While JIC offers short-term risk mitigation, it is not sustainable as a long-term strategy. The additional costs erode profit margins and reduce competitiveness. This especially limits the growth potential of SMEs that lack the capital to stockpile effectively. In the long run, economies dominated by JIC practices experience lower productivity and higher inflation than those with agile and reliable supply chains.

To move beyond JIC dependence, it is important to address the root causes that make lean systems untenable. This includes investing in port modernization, improving customs efficiency, expanding rail and road networks, and enhancing digital integration across logistics platforms. As trust in the logistics system grows, firms will be better positioned to adopt hybrid inventory strategies that balance resilience with efficiency.

7. CONCLUSION

This chapter establishes a clear link between logistics inefficiencies and inflation in Nigeria. Port congestion and shipping delays are not isolated problems. They are symptoms of broader institutional and structural issues. These include inadequate infrastructure, poor governance, and weak regulatory frameworks. Through the lenses of Structuralist Inflation Theory and Just-in-Case inventory strategies, the analysis reveals that logistical challenges have macroeconomic consequences. They distort pricing, disrupt supply chains, and undermine business confidence. Without deliberate intervention, these challenges will continue to erode Nigeria's economic resilience and developmental prospects.

8. IMPLICATIONS FOR POLICY MAKERS AND INDUSTRY STAKEHOLDERS

This study recommends the following:

Infrastructure Modernisation: Investing in upgrading Nigeria's port facilities is pertinent. These upgrades will enhance loading and unloading capabilities, expand storage capacities, and improve safety measures. It is also important to increase investments in intermodal transport systems that seamlessly link rail, road, and sea networks to enhance smooth interconnectivity between ports and major highways. It is also important to establish what needs to be evacuated from cargo centers to distribution/consumer locations so as to determine what form of transport mode would be much cheaper and economical to construct. Haphazard transport infrastructure construction as witnessed the uncoordinated development of airports by state governments must be seriously discouraged.

Regulatory Reform: Regulatory bodies should simplify and streamline port operations. This can be done by consolidating the regulatory framework and reducing the number of agencies involved in port management and customs clearance. Implementing a robust digital documentation system to facilitate efficient cargo processing and reduce paperwork will also be instrumental in expediting the movement of goods through the ports.

Policy Stability: Clear and consistent transport and trade policies should be established and maintained. This will provide a stable environment for businesses and investors. This includes regular consultations with industry stakeholders to ensure policies reflect current market needs and promote long-term investments in the sector.

Capacity Building: The government should invest in extensive training and re-orientation programs for customs personnel and other agencies at the borders. This will ensure they are well-versed in modern logistics practices, including best practices in cargo handling, safety, and security. Furthermore, education on anti-corruption protocols should be provided to foster a transparent and ethical working environment.

Technological Adoption: Nigeria's logistics stakeholders should embrace cutting-edge technologies. This includes implementing AI-based cargo tracking systems that enhance visibility and accountability in cargo movement, utilizing blockchain technology for secure and immutable documentation processes, and applying predictive analytics to optimise planning, resource allocation, and inventory management.

Decentralisation of Trade: The government should strategically develop new ports and dry inland ports in various regions to alleviate the heavy reliance on Lagos as the primary trade hub. The existing ports also need to be rehabilitated to promote utilisation. This approach will help distribute trade activities evenly across the country, promoting regional economic development and reducing congestion at traditional gateways.

Improve Rail System: It is important to develop the rail system nationwide. This will offer alternative and more efficient means of inland cargo transportation. The rail system will offer more benefits in terms of increased speed of delivery and low costs.

REFERENCES

Aboyeji, O. J., & Aguda, A. S. (2024). Rural Transportation and its Impact on the Output and Income Generated from Cashew Production in Selected Rural Settlements in Kwara State, Nigeria. *Agricultural & Rural Studies,* 2(4), 0020.

Agbigbe, W. A. (2016). *The impact of transportation infrastructure on Nigeria's economic development*. Walden University.

Ahmodu, K. O., & Okeudo, J. N. (2021). Infrastructural development and service quality in the Nigerian ports. *British International Journal of Education and Social Sciences*, *8*(4), 1–12.

Baer, W., & Kerstenetzky, I. (Eds.). (1964). *Inflation and growth in Latin America.* Richard D. Irwin.

Central Bank of Nigeria. (2021). *2021 Annual Economic Report*. Central Bank of Nigeria. https://www.cbn.gov.ng/Out/2023/RSD/2021%20CBN%20ANNUAL%20ECONOMIC%20REPORT.a.pdf

Chinedum, O. (2018). Port congestion determinants and impacts on logistics and supply chain network of five African ports. *Journal of Sustainable Development of Transport and Logistics*, *3*(1 (4)), 70–82.

Coslett, B. G. (2022). Just-In-Time/Just-In-Case Inventory Management as an Influence on Supply Chain Disruption in Medical Systems Based in the Southeastern United States During the COVID-19 Pandemic.

Eddrgash, T. (2022). *Port congestion problem, causes and solutions* (Doctoral dissertation, Cardiff University).

Emenyonu, U. M., Onyema, H. K., Ahmodu, K. O., & Onyemechi, C. (2016). Econometric analysis of seaport development and its impact on the economic growth of Nigeria. *International Journal of Advanced Research*, *4*(2), 133–138.

Ihugba, O. A., Odii, A., & Njoku, A. C. (2014). Acute Logistic System: A Bane to Economic Growth and Development in Nigeria. *International Journal of Research in Arts and Social Sciences*, *7*(2), 236–247.

Ndalu, T. C., & Umennaihe, V. (2024). Port Infrastructure Quality and Economic Growth in Nigeria. *IIARD International Journal of Economics and Business Management*, *10*(9), 141–158.

Nwokedi, T. C., Nwachukwu, J. O., Eru, J. U., & Ogwo, N. E. (2022). Elongated Cargo Dwell Time in Nigeria Ports, the Root-Source and Economic Implications. *European Journal of Maritime Research, 1*(1), 11–18. DOI: 10.24018/maritime.2022.1.1.2

Ojadi, F. I., & Walters, J. (2015). Critical factors that impact on the efficiency of the Lagos seaports. *Journal of Transport and Supply Chain Management, 9*(1), 1–13. DOI: 10.4102/jtscm.v9i1.180

Oritse, G. & Bivbere, G. (2018, April). Persistent Apapa gridlock: Stakeholders blame NPA. *Vanguard Newspapers.*

Oyewole, F. O. (2019). Technology adoption and performance of Nigerian ports. *RSU Journal of Strategic and Internet Business, 4*(2), 714–746.

Thomas, A., Thomas, M. A. H., Turk, M. R. A., & Turk, R. (2023). *Food insecurity in Nigeria: Food supply matters.* International Monetary Fund.

Unegbu, P. I., & Ugwunna, O. T. (2024). Importation and manufacturing sector performance in Nigeria: An empirical analysis. *ANSU Journal of Arts and Social Sciences, 11*(2), 43–60.

Vidrova, Z. (2020). Supply chain management in the aspect of globalization. In *SHS Web of Conferences* (Vol. 74, p. 04031). EDP Sciences. DOI: 10.1051/shsconf/20207404031

World Bank. (2022). *Improving Transport Connectivity for Food Security in Africa: Strengthening Supply Chains.* World Bank. https://documents1.worldbank.org/curated/en/099013125143525383/pdf/P179933747174047835/P17993919896090b31b8c71d9df51feffc3.pdf

Yang, M., Fu, M., & Zhang, Z. (2021). The adoption of digital technologies in supply chains: Drivers, process and impact. *Technological Forecasting and Social Change, 169*, 120795. DOI: 10.1016/j.techfore.2021.120795

Ye, M., Si Mohammed, K., Tiwari, S., Ali Raza, S., & Chen, L. (2023). The effect of the global supply chain and oil prices on the inflation rates in advanced economies and emerging markets. *Geological Journal, 58*(7), 2805–2817. DOI: 10.1002/gj.4742

ENDNOTES

1 This citation, though old, is relevant in the context of the study

Chapter 6
Role of Technological Innovation in Supply Chain:
AI and Digital Twins as Tools for Improving Supply Chain Efficiency

Lalitha Bangalore Srinivasarao
https://orcid.org/0000-0002-9031-9415
Sivananda Sarma Memorial RV College, India

ABSTRACT

The combination of Artificial Intelligence (AI) and Digital Twins (DT) has transformed the entire supply chain management process. It has created dynamic, data driven virtual replica models of the physical systems. These technologies allow for accurate demand forecasting, risk mitigation and scenario preparation. Key challenges include fragmented data, reactive decision making and competencies by automating processes and enabling the forward thinking interventions. Applications are used in industries like manufacturing, logistics, energy, where DT replicates the workflows, optimize resource allocation and predict disturbance. Trendsetting companies have reported remarkable improvements in the forecast accuracy, cost reduction and operational agility in business. The author in this chapter has tried to focus upon the role of AI & DT in improving the supply chain efficiency of the business. Further the challenges of AI & DT are discussed, followed by the solutions and the recommendations.

DOI: 10.4018/979-8-3373-1982-7.ch006

INTRODUCTION:

The idea of Digital Twins (DT) looks innovative, but it was born decades ago. The Apollo 13 mission tragedy in 1970 did not stop the creators from doing further inventions. It inspired NASA to create simulators for its equipment and spacecraft in the 1980s. The development of the DT to gauge real-time survival options was prompted due to this disaster. The year 2003 marked a significant development when Michael Grieves phrased a new name, termed "digital twin," at the Product Life Cycle conference at the University of Michigan. (Grieves, 2023; Mohsen Attaran & Bilge Gokhan Celik,2023).

Industry 3.0 started with progress in manufacturing technology, the adoption of computers, and automation. The slightest change in the physical model is experienced in the digital model, and these changes help to make decisions for the future. The pandemic unveiled the supply chain's inability to work out a plan for the locations of essential commodities at multiple levels. Industry 4.0 has altered the entire manufacturing process itself (Syed Adeel Haneef Zaidi et al., 2024). It currently uses advanced technologies like block chain technology, the Internet of Things (IoT), cloud computing, and robotic technology. AI-based technologies have revolutionized the supply chain by augmenting productivity, addressing global labor shortages, and optimizing the transfer of goods. (Tao Cheng, 2018; Daqjang Guo & Soujanya Mantravadi, 2024). AI is adopted into every step of the supply chain, from the manufacturing floor to the final supply of the product .

One of the powerful tools is the Digital Twin (DT). DT are considered the virtual representations of the actual supply chain that help businesses anticipate interruptions, find weaknesses, and enhance productivity (Kraus et al., 2021). Using the supply chain networks, procedures, and inventory, business efficiency can be improved (Lambourdiere & Corbin, 2020). By 2026, the global Industry 4.0 market is expected to propagate $210 billion, impelled by the development of digital technology. AI & DT are essential for digital transformation in the manufacturing sector and are crucial to digital progression. These technologies advance customer satisfaction while simultaneously increasing operational effectiveness and profitability(Sullivan &Wamba, 2024) Cost reduction and innovation are the key pathways to applying artificial intelligence and enhancing a company's productivity. (Xiaohong Chen et al. 2025). The same has been confirmed by a recent survey by McKinsey and Company (McKinsey Report, 2024).

From basic simulation models to sophisticated AI-powered systems, DT have revolutionized supply chain management by enhancing visibility, optimizing efficiency, and enabling risk management. This has led to better decision-making and improved performance. Trends can be identified, possible issues are predicted, and procedures are optimized using AI algorithms. DT developed into intellectual systems that could simulate how individuals made decisions. AI can give solutions, from simple simulation models to practical problem-solving by analyzing data, identifying hazards, and recommending remedies. (Grieves, M.W., 2023). Intelligent systems are developed to imitate and generate new information and methods for making decisions in business.

COST-BENEFIT ANALYSIS OF INTEGRATION OF TECHNOLOGY INTO SUPPLY CHAIN MANAGEMENT:

Today's business environment is reshaping the supply chain operation, making it more swift, efficient, obvious, and responsive. The integration of AI into supply chain management is a necessity today to keep the companies more competitive. Technology has played an important role in business, from store management to demand forecasting and supplier coordination. Integration of technology like robotics, AI, and machine learning into the supply chain has eased various processes in the organization. Reduction in manual intervention and errors in the business has improved its efficiency. Faster operations have become possible due to the automation of business operations. Technology today helps in picking, sorting, and packing items with AI-powered robots and enables automated tracking systems to check the shipment status. Integration of these technologies helps the business to reduce costs, improve savings and delivery times, and increase supply chain performance. Further, frauds and errors are reduced, leaving no scope for alteration or manipulation of the data. Human errors are reduced due to smart contracts, and the overall accuracy and reliability of the business are improved.

The global digital twin market size is expected to increase to USD 110.1 billion by 2028, growing at a compound annual growth rate of 61.3% during the years 2023-2028. (Lee et al., 2020; Cho, Y. & Noh, S.D., 2024). According to a Bank of America report, AI could contribute up to USD$15.7 to the global economy by 2030 and has the potential to earn USD$3.2 trillion to USD$5.4 trillion in economic value. (BoFA Global Research Report, 2023).

THEORETICAL FRAMEWORK

TECHNOLOGY ACCEPTANCE MODEL (TAM): Several theoretical frameworks have been framed to examine the determinants and acceptance of information technology (Davis.et.al., 1989, Venkatesh.et.al. 2003). But out of all these models TAM is a theory that explains how people accept and use innovative technology and gained lot of prominence. The model is based on how the user believes the technology Previous literature and doctoral theses has revealed that actual use of a technology product is influenced by the behavioural objectives, attitude, perceived usefulness and perceived ease of use.(Akbari.et.al, 2020, Valid Parade Biranvad. et.al., 2015,Romeo Bandinelli.et.al, 2023). Trust plays an important role towards the customer's intention for information technology based products (Lalitha.B.S, & Dr.Ramanarayanan.C.S, 2016).

UNIFIED THEORY OF ACCEPTANCE AND USE OF TECHNOLOGY (UTAUT) is a model widely used to understand technology adoption in different contexts . Further moderating external factors influences the usage of technological services affects the relationship between the variables (Williams.et.al,2015, Cheng. et.al, 2022). Combining these two theories the researcher has tried to identify the research gap.

OBJECTIVES OF THE STUDY: AI & DT are expected to revolutionize the entire supply chain industry operations but businesses are still on the way to progress. This study aims to explore the research gaps in the literature and answer the following research questions:

a) What are the different kinds of integrated technology used in supply chain management? Will implementation of technology help the business grow?
b) What are the benefits derived from adoption of technology in supply chain management?
c) What are the challenges in adoption of technology and the probable solutions for supply chain industry ?

LEGAL POLICY FRAMEWORK: A robust framework for securing data across the field of supply chain management includes the establishment of specific guidelines and procedures for handling, storing, and distributing sensitive data across the different stages of the supply chain. The framework must also include third-party contracts, vendor contracts, encryption, and access controls on the implementation of the security measures. The following acts are applicable to supply chain management:

General Data Protection Regulation (GDPR)—It is a regulation from the European Law that governs how companies control the personal data of the residents, irrespective of the company's existence in the European Union. This framework was adopted in 2016 and has been effective from May 25, 2018. This act aims to protect the individual's fundamental rights and freedom, particularly on the protection of personal data.

Intellectual Property (IP): It refers to legally protected creations and covers inventions, literary and artistic works, paintings, music, designs, and symbols used in commerce. In supply chain management, intellectual property and copyrights are important for the protection of creativity in the business. These are the rights exclusively given to creations and bring in financial benefits to the creators. Patents, copyrights, trademarks or trade secrets are covered under this act.

DIGITAL TWINS (DT) TECHNOLOGIES:

Three main aspects of Digital Twins involve data acquisition, modeling, and application. DT uses four technologies to collect and store more real-time data, obtain information to provide valuable insights, and create a replica of the physical object. (Mohsen et al., 2023);(Mazhar Rathore, 2021). These technologies include the following:

Internet of Things (IoT): IoT has revolutionized supply chain management by embedding sensors, devices and the connectivity in the logistics network. This combination enables real time data collection, analysis and automation that can improve business-optimized operations and improve their bottom line. IoT with robotics and AI has automated the inventory picking, packing functions, improving operational performance, reduction in the manual errors and round the clock operations Predictive maintenance helps in reduction of unexpected downtime and expands the lifetime of the important assets. Real time inventory data helps maintain optimum stock levels, reduce overstocking .understocking .IoT sensors help maintain product quality to minimize defects and ensure consistency of products. Example: DHL uses IoT sensors to monitor shipment locations, best environments in goods in transit, Caterpillar has adopted IoT based predictive maintenance of equipment.

2. Cloud computing: Cloud computing is a transformative technology in supply chain activities. It enables all the stakeholders to access real time basis from anywhere, accessing visibility into inventory, shipments and demand forecasts. It improves decision making and reduce bottlenecks. Cloud based platforms helps in breaking down data silos and facilitate unified communication amongst the partners . Electronic data inter charge and vendor managed inventory reports help in automated reporting, communication and reduces delays and errors. Cloud solutions helps in scale up operations according to the need of the hour without heavy investment in the physical infrastructure. This dexterity is essential for market fluctuations, disruptions and the market growth. Cloud based solutions helps in detection of probable issues like inventory shortages, disruptions and support rapid mitigation strategies. Example: Fedex uses MS Azure to track delays and tricks on real time basis. Walmart uses Seller cloud software to help sellers maintain optimal inventory in stock keeping unit.

3. Artificial Intelligence (AI). AI is transforming supply chain process, improving decision process, and enriching supply chain efficiency and resilience. Using machine learning, predictive analytics and large language areas, AI helps companies to streamline operations, anticipate disruptions and respond to changing market conditions.AI tools optimize stock levels, reorder levels, minimize risks of overstocking and understocking. Machine learning automate tracking and documenting supply chain visibility. It helps in optimization of shipping routes, manages warehouse capacity, and tracks inventory leading to reduced fuel costs, delivery times and operative bottlenecks. AI systems help to identify risks and disurptions and allows companies to develop contingency plans and enhance resilience. Machine learning, expert systems, and deep learning assist the Digital twins in obtaining data and providing prized insights, making predictions on the outcomes, and obtaining suggestions for forthcoming problems. (Lyu et al., 2023)

4. Extended Reality (XR): XR encompasses augmented reality, virtual reality and mixed reality. XR technologies are modernizing rapidly the supply chain process by integrating digital tools from warehouse to logistics to training and visibility. AR equipped smart glasses overlay real time information such as item location, inventory levels, and optimal pick up for warehouse workers, reducing errors and productivity. Virtual reality enables remote walkthrough in the warehouses, helps business model and optimize delivery routes and improves both efficiency and sustainability. VR can be used for virtual tours and gives insight into supply chain processes and sustainability processes. AR dashboards displays the live metrics such as inventory levels, delivery levels and production bottlenecks enabling quick response for disruptions.

AI & DIGITAL TWINS IN SUPPLY CHAIN RESILIENCE

A supply chain digital twin is considered a replica or virtual simulation of a physical supply chain. It connects near-real-time data from different sources, such as Enterprise Resource Planning (ERP) data, factory outputs, inventory levels, vehicle locations, shipment schedules, and market dynamics, to give a complete solution to the supply chain. A digital twin helps businesses in the following manner:

- Changes in test supply chain designs
- Disclose bottlenecks, poor usage of inventory, and inefficient lanes
- Monitoring and identification of risks
- Streamline forecasting
- Categorize process improvements
- Improve collaboration between finance and procurement

A digital twin provides insights into its dynamics and forecasting outcomes. These imitation models utilize real-time data from sensors, IoT devices, and other sources to reflect what's happening in the real world. It has emerged as an effective tool for efficiency and agility.(Maria Teresa, et.al., 2024). Digital twins are creating new value and helping companies design, visualize, monitor, manage, and maintain assets more effectively. It also paves the way for new opportunities like the provision of advanced services and the generation of valuable insight from operational data. When integrated into smart manufacturing solutions, digital twins serve as a central point of analysis, combining real-time data from machines, inventory, supply chain, and logistics (Vitasek et al., 2005). This level of integration is essential for Industry 4.0 and digital twins, which focus on interconnectivity, automation, and data-driven decision-making in manufacturing environments.(Tavana.M.et.al., 2022).

Businesses can use data analytics and artificial intelligence to anticipate bottlenecks, disruptions, or problems even before they become apparent, and be proactive in their approach.(Kache et al., 2017) They can forecast future events, point out places that need rework, and assist in streamlining transfer routes and inventory levels. These factors aid in improving warehouse operations, transportation facilities, and inventory management, which will boost productivity and reduce waste. (Hrouga.M, & Sbihi.A, 2023). Digital twins also improve communication and cooperation amongst the suppliers, producers, distributors, and customers. Increased collaboration leads to better coordination, quicker decision-making, and leads to a continuous supply chain operation. Various scenarios and backup plans are tested along with digital twins that help businesses anticipate and handle crises.

The latest disruptive force in supply chain management is Artificial Intelligence, which improves operational effectiveness and decision-making (Rosen, R.et. al.,2015). By anticipating changes in the demand, spotting prospective interruptions and suggesting possible solutions, it assists businesses in streamlining their supply chain operations. AI-powered chatbots and virtual assistants improve real-time information on order status and shipment tracking. Integration of AI improves customer satisfaction and a better resilient supply chain. (Adama.H.et.al,2024) Digital twins allow business to revisit their supply chains and adopt changes to make them capable, effective, and resilient. These technologies allow companies to move from a steady supply chain to a swift one that evolves and adapts to business and market changes at a rapid pace. (Dr.Nagaraju Ellaturu et.al, 2024).

Artificial Intelligence (AI) and Digital Twins have become the most powerful technologies to transform, operate, and optimize supply chain management (Tao, Cheng. et.al.,2018). Resource allocation is based on the projects received. This enables the company to minimize costs and enhance operational efficiency. Customer service is improved as chatbots answer queries to automate routine tasks (Attaran.M,2020). Communication between suppliers, distributors, and customers is improved with the adoption of natural language processing. AI systems can improve by learning from new data. This is particularly useful in managing the supply chain environments where changes are going on continuously by learning from new data. It is used to manage the constant changes in the market, like fluctuating market demand and supply interruptions in the market.

Business scenarios are modeled and effects are evaluated for any disruptions (weather, strikes, or shortages of raw material) before they occur by constructing a digital twin of the entire supply chain. This helps companies in being tenacious to possible threats. Warehouse layouts and inventory levels can be improved with the use of digital twins, which forecast changes in demand and adjust supply accordingly. This improves stock management, lowers storage costs, and ensures on-time delivery. Digital twins provides a constant feedback on the supply chain performance. To ensure exceptional performance, companies monitor performance indicators via the lead time, overheads and product quality. With continuous information on different supply chain components digital twins helps the businesses evaluate the supply chain disruptions. Digital twins offer a favorable solution to these challenges by providing a real-time, powerful representation of a supply chain. Sensors, Radio Frequency Identification (RFID) tags, and advanced analytics are used by organizations to replicate the physical supply chain. (Zarbakhshnia & Karimi, 2024) For example, demand can be predicted for specific regions or segments, inventory tracking on individual stock keeping units or expected transport delays on explicit routes (Mageto, 2021).

AI & DT IN SMEs (Small and Medium Enterprises): AI has created a strong foothold in the field of the small scale and medium businesses also. Technology has paved way for the growth, cost reduction, increase in profits and efficiency (Nasscom Report, 2024). AI, with a combination of machine learning, predictive analysis, or natural language processing, helps in the growth of this sector. It helps in the development of these industries as it can work on large volumes of data and make well-informed decisions and obtain great insights, setting the ground to compete with big industrial corporations. Repetitive tasks, workflow efficiency, and effective usage of assets save time for the SMEs. Customer experience can be improved by anticipating customer needs and offering tailor made services. Market trends are identified, customer preferences are understood better and there is scope for better performance for the SMEs with the adoption of technology .

DT IN DEVELOPED AND DEVELOPING COUNTRIES AI-powered DT offers significant potential but differs in the implementation procedure due to infrastructure availability. Adoption of digital twins and simulation analysis in the developed countries improves business resilience and decision-making capacity and optimizes the operations via real-time monitoring and predictive ability. This helps in the adoption of preventive management and prepares the business for forthcoming challenges. In the developing countries it helps in better resource allocation in various sectors like agriculture and energy and paves the way for sustainable growth in the economy. But the challenges galore due to high installation costs, which outweigh the benefits. (Zali.N.et.al, 2024)

ROLE OF AI & DT AS TOOLS FOR IMPROVING SUPPLY CHAIN EFFICIENCY

Technological developments, business shifts, and leadership transitions have a profound effect on different ranges of industries. This has accelerated the adoption of DTs, which are replica setups of businesses. It can be a product, operational procedure, or entire supply chain of the business. Utilizing real-time data/images, a digital twin deals with a simulation model and increases the visibility of the product. This helps in the enhancement of the business and identification of any susceptibilities. Stakeholders can alter the virtual environment more quickly when compared to all features than the brick-and-mortar entities (Tao et al., 2019). These are the simpler, safer, and more effective ways to track performance and gain insights into various aspects of the organization. DT has existed over the years, but nowadays is used progressively in many sectors to achieve operational excellence. The market size of DT is estimated to reach $183 billion in sales by 2026, according to Gartner. A combination of artificial intelligence and creating process twins helps businesses in the simulation of real-world operations, analyze large data sets, find out business weaknesses and threats, and optimize workflows and processes. A business can improve operational agility and make data-driven decisions with the adoption of AI. (Chukwu, 2024).

DT have gained popularity of late due to a combination of advanced computer capabilities, the rise of the Internet of Things (IoT), and the cheaper availability of 5G networks. Whole prediction and operational inventiveness can be further unlocked with a combination of AI and machine learning. Implementation of the digital twin solutions may be hindered by poor data integrity or insufficient infrastructure allocation. Due to this, businesses need to approach them as essential systems and place a priority on data and resource availability, integrity, and confidentiality. Quick proliferation of the DT have caused businesses to adopt high fidelity model rather than remote models . (Shahadat, M. M. H., et al., 2023) They are now self-determining virtual systems capable of designing, simulating, validating, and optimizing plants, processes, and products due to AI and generative AI. Many organizations are understanding the benefits of improving organizational outcomes, increasing company value, and boosting competitiveness. Every aspect of the value chain is influenced and aids in the development of the next generation of goods and opens up novel sources of income.

With the creation of virtual representation of the physical system, digital twin technology is changing the facet of supply chain management. DT, when combined with machine learning, artificial intelligence provides unparalleled insights and growth opportunities. Due to these developments, real-time data on material flows, power consumption, process settings, and paraphernalia status by connecting devices on the shop floor. By processing and evaluating this data on a real-time basis, AI further improves this capability and helps take decisions more quickly and precisely. It can help forecast the production line bottlenecks or machine failures by analyzing the trends in power usage and equipment performance. This results in savings on maintenance expenses, augmented production efficiency, and less downtime. It helps in the estimation of goods and tracking the actual status of the goods in transit, providing a quick insight into the flow of goods. Based on the historical trends, machine learning can easily forecast estimated time of arrival with possible interruptions. The integration of DT into supply chain operations not only improves the competence but also builds the flexibility against disruptions. It is important that organizations need to adapt themselves to rapidly changing circumstances due to volatile markets, natural disasters, war between countries, or the pandemic. With the help of DT, companies can assess the scenarios in advance and plan their production schedules accordingly. This helps in long-term strategic planning and understanding the risks within the chain. It becomes easier to implement corrective measures and work towards sustained success in an ever-changing business environment .

CASE STUDIES: Based on the Grand View Research Report of 2024 on Digital Twin Market Size, Share and Trend Analysis for the years 2025-2030, USA and some of the Asian countries are considered as the largest, fastest growing segment in adoption of the DT. This report speaks on the various trends in the American and Asian markets. A SAP Insights Research report of 2023 also confirmed that DT will be the next game changer in various sectors across the world. Further a Capgemini insight report from the Capgemini Research Institute also have surveyed around 1000 organizations and conducted in depth interview to understand the impact of DT in the economy. The latest McKinsey Global Survey on AI have indicated that large companies are more swift in the adoption of technology and redesign of companies. Case studies were opted on the basis of these reports.

1.Case Study - Siemens

Siemens has a unique approach of combining the real and digital world with the Digital Twins. This technology helps in integration of production and product life cycle to make critical decision with confidence, optimize the performance of the organization and capitalize on the adversities. It continuously updates to reflects any change in the physical counterpart of the life cycle and allows for a feedback in the simulated environment. Companies are allowed to design, simulate, test, improve and validate them. DT for products including mechanics, electronics and software. Robust simulation tools are used to enhance the quality of final product while reducing the overall design cycle. DT in the production enables the design, and optimization of machines, production lines entire factories and plants in the digital world making it faster, efficient and sustainable. Technology used in this field paves way for improvement. From tracking processing orders, monitoring materials, or accurately measuring process times, including the utilization and optimization of material flow throughout the entire system. Siemens has combined DT with Siemens with Xcelerator has pulled the organizational into profitable mode. Users can obtain a direct feedback on their new actions and when new scenarios are created, this allows them to directly experience the impact of the changes adopted in real time.

2. Case Study BMW Group

BMW first built its DT in the year 2014 in its factory premises. This was developed in order to enable precise monitoring and optimization of the production processes. Adoption of technology minimized errors, enhanced quality and boosted efficiency of the company. It also helps in the simulation of innovative products and processes before the actual implementation. The production operations are recorded in a 3D scan and creates a digital twin where a person can virtually walk and have a glimpse of the different locations and time zones. Through this a new production line itself can be created with people and equipment. Employees can plunge themselves in the workplace with reality glasses and capturing and refining them digitally. It also enables the new vehicles to be included into the existing product line. This helps in focusing where action is still needed into the production network. Before the production of the electric version vehicles in 2021, the company rolled its fully operation virtual version at Regensberg, Bavaria factory. This can simulate production and scheduling of the work per each order. BMW uses the NVIDIA Omniverse Enterprise, which is a platform for building and operating 3D industrial metaverse applications to run real time digital simulations to optimize layouts, robotics and logistics systems virtually. The company has decided to extend the same technology across all product categories in the world. Implementation of virtualization and artificial intelligence are increasing the speed of planning in the organization. Due to this, the scattered teams across the world can work together on a real time basis and make decision faster, competent and helps in cost reduction.

By the end of 2022, BMW had installed virtual models of all its production across the globe. The company brought this under the " iFactory" initiative and noted that DT had reduced the production planning by roughly a third. For BMW this is an efficiency plan, supporting its sustainability projects and digital transformation goals. The iFactory initiative focusses on mainly three areas. viz., Lean, Green and Digital. With a customized application named as " BMW Factory Viewer", 15000 employees can access the application and use it for precise measurements, and collaborate for work across different location and time zones. This facility allows designers to create more competent layouts and connections across different shop floor process. Usage of data science provides the information on a real time basis and identify the root cause of problems to improve plant processes.

3.Case Study- Amazon

Amazon uses the digital twin technology, particularly through the AWS IoT Twinmaker, to improve its vast supply chain, including simulating warehouse management, optimizing warehouse design and flow . Amazon uses the DT to model different warehouse layouts and workflows allowing them to test the various picking and packing techniques to reduce logistics fulfilment time and improve the employees competence. Pre-trained robots are installed in warehouse to support the logistics function for enhanced productivity and efficiency. In 2019, Amazon had to face criticism for allowing fake products to be sold in their platform. Immediately the company had to embrace AI technology and stricter policies to combat the adverse effects of fake products .DT can predict machine maintenance, reducing downtime and overall efficiency. Shipments can be tracked easily along with product flow on real time basis, allowing for changing operations and achieving high levels of service . The twin maker service helps in building replica models of buildings, factories, industrial equipment and production lines. Integration of various data sources including IoT data, Computer Aided Designs (CAD) Models and Building Information Modelling (BIM) files helps to create digital twin visualizations. DT helps to do predictive analysis and optimize the operations .

4.Case Study- Tata Steel

Tata Steel is actively commercializing DT as a part of its wider digital transformation strategy, aiming to improve operational competence, sustainability and better consumer experience. Tata Steel has been spending money on innovative digital transformation technologies with an effort to become a more supple company that can acclimatize to shifting market conditions. Its efforts to quick decision making have increased from the pandemic era. By adopting DTa simulated digital reproduction of production using real time analytics- the organization has implemented digitization of projects. This has facilitated the development of analytics based smart factories. The company is designing new digital initiatives to boost key strategies . The company is implementing digitalization for both front end and back end operations on lines with business to consumer sector. This allows blue collar workers to achieve multiple aspects of factory operations away from the physical office premises. Tata Steel underlines the " YET-QP"(Yield, Energy, Throughput, Quality and Productivity)with respect to the Digital Twin. DT is used to improve key processes such as sintering. Tata Steel has come out with the world's first digital twin for the sintering process to exhaust emissions around 60% and enhance performance optimization. Controllab has generated a DT for Tata Steel's LK25 crane, supporting simulation based testing and revamp performance metrics. DT also helps in optimizing energy consumption and attaining sustainability goals by simulating and forecasting outcomes in real time. By crafting DT, Tata Steel has aligned with Industry 4.0 principles, with major focus on visualization, simulation, optimization and prediction to improve operational efficiency and responsiveness.

Benefits of Digital Twins (DT) in Supply Chain Efficiency:

Digital Twins(DT) are the replica models of physical supply chain, and are revolutionizing supply chain management by improving efficiency, resilience and decision making.(Gong.S, 2024). The benefits of adoption of these technologies are as follows:

1. **Real time visibility**- DT provides all inclusive real time insights into the various areas of supply chain operations like inventory level, production status and logistics. This transparency enables a quicker, informed decision making and improved overall operational efficiency.
2. **Predictive Analytics and Scenario Planning**- DT helps in simulating numerous scenarios such as demand shifts or supply disruptions . Organizations can predict risks and opportunities, optimize strategies and reduce the disruptions even before they occur.
3. **Inventory Optimization**- DT helps maintain the maximum inventory levels by analyzing real time data and forecasting the demand. This reduces over stocking and understocking, holding costs and improves customer satisfaction.

4. **Process Optimization**- Regular monitoring of supply chain processes allows DT to identify the inadequacies and bottlenecks. This leads to streamlined workflows, augmented space utilization in warehouse and enhanced resource allocation.
5. **Enhanced Collaboration**- DT has created a combined data sharing platform for different departments, fostering better collaboration and synchronized decision making. This promotes incessant up gradation in supply chain management .
6. **Resilience against disruptions**- By exploiting instantaneous data and predictive modelling, DTimprove the supply chain resilience against the disturbance caused by cross border tensions, natural disasters or demand fluctuations.
7. **Cost savings**-Companies using DT have reported reduction in the transportation costs, labour expenditure and capital expenditure. These savings are a result of the optimized operations and preemptive risk management.
8. **Sustainability**- DT contributes to sustainability in the organizations by reducing power consumption in the warehouse, minimizing packaging waste and enabling pre-emptive maintenance of the conveyance fleets.
9. **Competitive Advantage**: Adopting DT enhances customer service dependability and provides companies with an upper hand by enabling swift responses to market changes.

CHALLENGES OF DT IN SUPPLY CHAIN MANAGEMENT

Creation and execution of the DT involve complex processes in which all components of the system are interlinked and exchange information on a continuous basis. Different technologies are required to simulate a physical system within a virtual environment. The birth of Industry4.0 and advancements in key enabling technologies have opened up abundant opportunities to develop a unified platform with Digital Twins. DT is still in an infancy stage. Since it is embedded in each sub system or sub component, different systems are created for different supply chain processes to improve visualization and control in complex systems. Focussed technology can propound comprehensive insights and analysis for revamp integration with in the supply chain management network. It also helps in the design, testing and upgradation of each process into a broader system. DT sub systems presents numerous technical and organizational challenges and the practical aspects of implementation require further probe. Intricate nature of the DT infrastructure requires huge amount of data, continuous transmission and friendly technology integration while maintaining portability, managing high costs, utilizing resources efficiently and ensuring sustainability at both sub and network levels denote major hurdles. After gathering the real data to replicate the physical mode, a digital copy is created.

This connects every component of the system to achieve continuous connectivity and develop a consistent DT. This increases probing into cross department relationships and its interdependencies at every level of the design.

Some of the key obstacles in adoption of AI & DT are as follows:

1. **Impracticable expectations-** The capabilities of the DT are overestimated by companies and view it as an instant solution for their problems. But when the companies don't get the expected results its leads to disappointment. Disarranged expectations can stem from insufficient understanding of the operational mechanism of DT. A procedural learning process is essential for emotional realization.
2. **Data Complexity and Integration**: Data aggregation across multiple systems is tough due to the various levels and evolutions involved in supply chains. In order to pool business, sensor and contextual data while safeguarding data governance amongst shareholders. DT needs data models that are agreeable and shared. Incomplete data hoarding hampers vision and decision making, requiring responsive rather than proactive reactions to disruptions.
3. **Communication Gaps**- Planning departments and the IT teams struggle in the companies to effectively collaborate on projects. This gap may cause DT models to be unproductive and postpone their application. To close this breach, businesses need unified platforms for data sharing, a strong IT plan and consistent multi team collaborations
4. **External Cooperation and Supplier Trust**- Establishing reliability with suppliers and integrating information from other sources continues to be major hindrances. Establishing connections that allow for smooth information flow amidst companies is challenging but it is essential for successful adoption of DT. Majority of the company's supply chain operations trespass making data exchange and coordination more challenging.
5. **High Implementation costs:** Medium enterprises are limited with their capital investments. Such organizations find the initial investment in DT including sophisticated IT system, analytical tools and trained employees costly. Without transparent immediate advantages, businesses may not be able to invest on these technologies.
6. **User Engagement and Tool complexity**- Complicated tools frequently result in disengagement, forcing staff to adopt manual circumvent that impede communication and cooperation. Make more comprehensible tools and procedures to increase usability is essential for successful deployment.
7. **Limited Scalability**- DT is still in a nascent stage and have robustness in large scale supply chains with multiple intertwined activities such as fleet tracking, stock management and cold chain monitoring.

8. **Adaptability to disruptions** – DT helps in augmenting visibility and forecasting power, they are not impenetrable with black swan events or natural disasters or geopolitical unrest. DT must be used in combination with a more encompassing risk mitigating techniques.

SOLUTIONS AND RECOMMENDATIONS

Supply Chain efficiency is altered dramatically by AI & DT which make it possible for adaptive optimization, predictive analytics and instantaneous simulations. (Rosen R.et.al,(2015). But the stumbling blocks to their effective implementations calls for immediate solutions . Some of the key suggestions and recommendations are as follows:

1. **Security and Privacy of Data**: DT & AI algorithms rely heavily on huge amounts of data, including real time information from different sources which can act as a major source of cyber attacks. Further connecting with multiple vendors, systems and stakeholders increases the risk of data breach and leaks as large amounts of data pertaining to production processes, inventory levels and customer information also increases the risk. So companies, need to have a role based access system and cutting edge written in code to shield the private supply chain information . Block chain integration improves the efficiency by enabling translucent, secure and traceable process, which ultimately reduces the costs, improves collaboration and increasing trust amongst the shareholders. Further the usage of decentralized ledger technology augments the power of DT operations to advance the traceability and transparency of transactions. Frameworks such as General Data Protection Regulation (GDPR) needs to be adopted for cross border data flows, particularly with international transactions to ensure regulatory compliance. GDPR mandates that businesses collect and process the minimum amount of data only necessary which leads to streamlined management and reduced risk of breach.
2. **Complexity of Integration:** To improve supply chain efficiency, integrating businesses need to adopt API to interface scalable DT system with legacy, IoT and ERP system. API will determine what data what data DT will require from these technology based systems and what data it needs to provide to them. For a smooth data aggregation from varied sources cloud platforms like Amazon Web Services, or MS Azure can offer robust services for data storage, processing and further analysis. Companies choose a platform that handle large amount of data and growing customer base. In order to reduce customization costs, open source tools like prebuilt AI models and frameworks like Python, Open AI or

Hugging face, R are used by businesses. They adopt such open source tools as it is free to use, license and modify, thereby reducing the need for installation of expensive proprietary software.

3. **Interoperability and standardization** –To ensure continuous and efficient Internet of Things (IoT) implementation, collaboration with organizations like the Industrial Internet Consortium (IIC) is important for standardizing communication protocols and data formats. These standardized formats and protocols allows devices and system across different vendors to communicate and exchange data faultlessly. Further in order to increase the simulation accuracy, companies need to centralize the organized and the unstructured data.
4. **Difficulties in Operations** – In today's industrial world minimizing the downtime and increasing the equipment life has never been so important. Predictive maintenance technologies gives a revolutionary approach and helps companies to detect failures even before they occur. Advanced sensors, IoT connectivity and AI driven analytics systems are to the company's options to give predictive maintenance solutions. These predictive maintenance options have become a part of the standard maintenance practices and has delivered measurable returns to the business. DT helps in simulating different stock levels in the business such as fluctuations in demand, supply chain disruptions, or changes in the product life cycle to understand what is the potential impact on the inventory. Application of demand forecasting AI models, can reduce forecast mistakes to the tune of 15-30% on the basis of historical trends and extraneous variables.
5. **Readiness of the Organization**- Companies need to close the gap between the technical outputs and strategic choices. So there is an urgent need to upskill teams in AI interpretation and scenario planning. Companies need to adopt this replication first on a pilot basis and once it is successful, then the whole organization can be covered. Small scale and simple solutions such as warehouse congestion modelling need to be adopted on the first go and on a large scale later.
6. **Scalability and Cost:** In order to get early returns on their investments, companies need to give priority on high impact areas like supplier risk management and logistics bottlenecks. Supplier risk management helps in identifying and reducing potential issues with suppliers whereas logistics bottlenecks analyses slowdown or disruptions in the flow of goods. Companies need to implement systems to track inventory orders and shipments on a real time basis. Further usage of data and analytics to identify the root cause of bottlenecks and implementation of the solutions are also important.

7. **Securing and Retaining the talent**: Today AI in supply chain is not just appointment of staff but retaining the best talent in the organization. The success of the business largely depends upon who can blend the AI solutions with the supply chain.

FUTURE TRENDS AND DEVELOPMENTS IN AI & DT FOR SUPPLY CHAIN EFFICIENCY

Information Technology (IT) is the backbone of supply chain and adoption of AI will drive streamlined efficiency, clarity and innovation. IT practices will require up to date smooth incorporation of complex data streams from different origin. Things like cloud computing, Internet of Things(IoT), block chain technology that form the foundation of forecasting insights and real time tracking be a part of the continuously adapting system. IT infrastructure has to be strong and adaptive to ensure high end security and help minimize instances of fraudulent activities. Usage of AI & DT in supply chain management is not only gaining momentum with each passing day. Using its predictive analysis, AI is assisting companies to make more thoughtful decisions, mechanize processes and optimize efficiency or unheard of in the past.

Global supply chain is also growing into a complex ecosystem. Challenges galore global supply chains today. But AI and other developed technologies are offering the mandatory support to navigate these complexities. As more latest technologies comes into existence, the future of AI in supply chain is expected to make it more robust and more understandable.AI powered tools and platforms have already helped companies to reduce costs by one third, optimizing inventories, simplified operations and contribute in multiple ways to make supply chain reliable and precise. With the passing years, companies are making predictions based on the past trends, keeping in mind the challenges and considerations to make supply chains future ready with AI.

It is expected that in the forthcoming decade AI driven innovations are fundamentally going to change the field of supply chain management. AI will witness automated decision making and emerge as a game changer. These innovations have the capacity to re-evaluate the ways supply chain management operations will be carried on and decisions are taken. In the forthcoming years it is expected that AI will empower supply chains with precise demand forecasting and disturbing risk assessments. AI will develop different aspects of the supply chain from stock optimization to supplier selection, compliance monitoring, sustainable sourcing, increasing trust and transparency in the chain, reducing errors and improving safety to the next level. This will create supply chains that are more adaptive and intelligent. Automatically human errors will be reduced and work speed can be improved substantially. Sustainability practices will be adopted for resource optimization.

Some of these future trends in AI & DT in supply chain management are as follows:

1. **Adoption of advanced AI Technologies**

Gradually an increased trend of complex data analysis will be seen . Consequently decision making will implement AI system which is based on machine learning, deep learning and natural language processing (NLP). Machine Learning observes huge amounts of data and spot patterns that increases the insightful foresight for inventory requirements. Deep learning and machine learning approaches improve the capacity of Artificial Neural Network recognizing risks, integrating data, detecting irregularities, and evaluating pre-indicative maintenance requirements. Natural language processing will be predominant in facilitating augmented teamwork and employee machine communication which will increase workflow efficiency.

2. Better Integration with the Internet of Things (IoT)

Complex data analysis and better decision making is observed as more businesses implement advanced AI systems as they depend on machine learning, deep learning and natural language processing. Accuracy of the stock requires forecasting is expected to augment due to machine learning's capacity evaluate vast amounts of data and recognize trends. Artificial Neural Networks employ deep learning and machine learning techniques will more proficient at identifying risks, integrating data, detecting abnormalities, and evaluating projective maintenance requirements. Natural Language processing will be progressively important in upgrading team communication and employee machine interaction that increases workflow efficiency.

3. Autonomous Supply Chain and Robotics

The future will witness more automation in the supply chain field influenced by robotics and AI powered automation solutions. AI robots have the potential to picking, packing and sorting of goods. As the technology develops, order fulfillment now becomes much quicker and precise while utilizing less manpower and resources. It is estimated by Gartner that by 2027, 75% of the businesses will have implemented cyber physical automation in the warehouse automation. Companies like Amazon and other corporations which are at spearhead of using self navigating robots, is not affordable for other businesses. These robots can understand and move in the environment without being monitored by an operator or limited to a fixed or pre determined path (Tsang.Y.P.et.al.2024). But in the forthcoming decade there is every possibility that its popularity may grow and many companies may try to adopt it .

4. Block chain Technology

By securing safe and unaltered transaction records, block chain technology can assist businesses, in prevention of frauds and lowers counterfeiting. It enhances confidence amongst the supply chain companies in the future(Tiwari.S.et.al., 2023). Even though the usage of block technology is limited as of now, it has a bright future in the forthcoming years. Block chain technology can help businesses in making their supply chain more secure and traceable by adoption of cutting edge technologies like IoT, AI and smart contracts. For example, Capgemini India Pvt. Ltd., helps companies in staying innovative in their approach. Their advanced block chain technology solutions has helped out companies to adopt digital transformation in an innovative manner and venture into global markets. Fedex and Walmart use block chain technology to enhance food safety. Over the forthcoming years we can observe more number of businesses to implement technology in supply chain management to improve tracking and traceability.

5. AI Driven Hyper-personalization of Service

AI helps businesses to provide their clients with more customized experiences and suggestions. Today businesses are utilizing AI technology to tailor made services to serve customers. It also helps them to analyze client data and preferences. In the years to come, we may anticipate the surge in usage of block chain . Majority of the companies in the past used the one size fits for all strategy but today with the implementation of AI, it has opened the doors for hyper personalization and allows manufacturers to apply machine learning systems to improve autonomous manufacturing twists that increase the customer experience. Supply chains may also use analytics to reply to customer demand more quickly and efficiently when combined with other technologies such as AI driven forecasting . This can increase supply chain resilience by decreasing stocks by nearly a half.

Although AI has occupied a big chunk in the supply chain industry, businesses which want to stay and think ahead need to start implementation of aiOla. aiOla is an AI powered voice technology that exploits the power of speech and changes words into action. Supply chain managers today have automated majority of the areas of supply chain and obtain deep insights into data that would otherwise be lost with aiOla. By speaking informally, logistics staff can use aiOla to automate multiple operations like order processing and inspections. This will make employees to complete the task without much difficulty augmenting workers safety. aiOla enables speech data collection for teams, enabling businesses to take better decisions.. This speech recognition technology promotes better communication amongst workers and machines which reduces costs and likelihood of mistakes. Although some of them are still in the nascent stage, majority of the technologies that will take businesses on a ride in the future are already being used today. Companies need to have a basic understanding of how these systems function to suit their requirements .Companies which catch up the wave early can have a good advantage on their rivals. Since aiOla is a voice based pulpit, there is no learning curve and the organization can start optimizing its operations immediately.

CONCLUSION:

The previous decades, marked only the physical forms of maps and the adhoc nature of transport adopted to deliver the goods. So it was difficult to answer whether the inventory was sufficient to deliver the goods on time. From the smallest package to the largest one, supply chain planning is very much essential in logistics. The future of supply chain management is rational, with DT playing a prominent role. Implementing a reasoning supply chain technology foundation maybe multifaceted. Its key benefits include improved operational performance, reduced supply chain risk and enhanced adaptive strategy, make the journey worthwhile. As businesses grow continuously to traverse the different supply chain complexities across global markets, intellectual supply chains powered by technology will act as a differentiator. Supply chain DT acts as transformative technology that improves agility and efficiency in supply chain management. By creating virtual models that control real time data and advanced analytics, businesses can achieve ample visibility, optimize operative and pre-emptively address disruptions. Industrial giants like Cisco, Walmart, BMW have showcased the substantial gains in efficiency, cost cutting and improvement in customer satisfaction achievable via adoption of digital twin technology. Using advanced tools and platforms, revisiting the objectives to model validation and continuous optimization can be achieved. As more and more new versions of DT evolve, significant changes also come up. The biggest challenge DT face is the compatibility between different platforms and systems, data must flow flawlessly and securely amidst the physical and the digital world. Data privacy and security concerns are heightening apprehensions as the amount of collected and shared information upsurges. Despite the multiple challenges, future of DT is promising. Adoption of technology is expected to grow and this is driven by advancement in areas of Internet of Things (IoT), cloud computing and data analytics. With more companies adopting DT technology, the affordability and accessibility is likely to increase. Greater propagation of innovative applications in many industries is in store for the future. In conclusion, DT is carving a history by navigating between the industry's past, present and the future. It has transformed the way things are conceived, designed and operated in the global market. With their ability to assimilate data, simulate scenarios and take cognizant decisions, DT are leading the way towards a smarter, efficient and sustainable future.

REFERENCES:

Adama, H., Okeke, C., Akinoso, A., & Popoola, O., HenryA.Oladapo, AChukwuekem, DAbiodun, E. (2024). Economic Theory And Practical Impacts Of Digital Transformation In Supply Chain Optimization. *International Journal of Advanced Economics*, *6*(4), 95–107. DOI: 10.51594/ijae.v6i4.1072

Akbari, M., Khodayari, M., Danesh, M., Davari, A., & Padash, H. (2020). A bibliometric study of sustainable technology research. *Cogent Business & Management*, *7*(1), 1751906. https://www.tandfonline.com/doi/pdf/10.1080/23311975.2020.1751906. DOI: 10.1080/23311975.2020.1751906

Ananyi, S. O., & Somieari-Pepple, E. (2023). Cost Benefit Analysis of Artificial Intelligence in Education Management: Leadership perspectives. *International Journal of Economics, Environmental Development and Society*, *4*(3), 353–370.

Attaran, M. (2020). Digital technology enablers and their implications for supply chain management. Supply Chain Forum: An International Journal, 21(3), 158–172. DOI: 10.1080/16258312.2020.1751568

Attaran, M., & Celik, B. G. (2023)“ Digital Twin, Benefits, Use Cases, Challenges and Opportunities” Decision Analytics Journal 6 (2023)100165 https://www.sciencedirect.com/science/article/pii/S277266222300005X

Bandinelli, R., Scozzafava, G., Bindi, B., & Fani, V. (2023). Blockchain and Consumer Behaviour: Results of a Technology Acceptance Model in the ancient wheat sector. *Cleaner Logistics and Supply Chain*, *8*, 100117. DOI: 10.1016/j.clscn.2023.100117

Bank of America Global Research Report https://business.bofa.com/en-us/content/ai-trends-impact-report.html

Capgemini Research Report https://www.capgemini.com/wp-content/uploads/2022/05/Capgemini-Research-Institute_DigitalTwins_Web.pdf-

Cheng, T., & Chen, J. (2022). Calvin Kalun, FelixPoyin Lo(2022) “ Path Analysis of the roles of age, self efficacy, and TAM constructs in the acceptance of performing upper limb exercises through immersive virtual reality games. *International Journal of Industrial Ergonomics*,103360. https://www.sciencedirect.com/science/article/abs/pii/S0169814122001019. DOI: 10.1016/j.ergon.2022.103360

Chidozie, B., Ferreira, L. P., Ramos, A., & Ferreira, J. (2024). The Importance of Digital Transformation (5.0) in Supply Chain Optimization: An Empirical Study. *Production Engineering Archives*, *30*(1), 127–135. DOI: 10.30657/pea.2024.30.12

Cho, Y., & Noh, S. D. (2024). Design and Implementation of Digital Twin Factory Synchronized in Real-Time Using MQTT. *Machines (Basel), 12*(11), 759. DOI: 10.3390/machines12110759

Chukwu, N., Yufenyuy, S., Ejiofor, E., Ekweli, D., Ogunleye, O., Clement, T., Obunadike, C., Adeniji, S., Elom, E., & Obunadike, C. (2024). Resilient chain: Ai improved supply chain security and efficiency integration. *IJSMR*, *7*(3), 46–65. DOI: 10.37502/IJSMR.2024.7306

Daqjang Guo & Soujanya Mantravadi. (2024) " The role of DTin lean supply chain Management: Review and research directions" International Journal of Production Research DOI: , https://www.researchgate.net/publication/382250668_The_role_of_digital_twins_in_lean_supply_chain_management_review_and_research_directionsDOI: 10.1080/00207543.2024.2372655

Davis, F. D., Bagozi, R. P., & Warhsaw, R. P. (1989). User Acceptance of information technology: A comparison of two theoretical models. *Management Science*, *35*(8), 982–1003. DOI: 10.1287/mnsc.35.8.982

Dr. Nagaraju Ellaturu, Vandana. M., Naveena M, & M. Rajalakshmi, Dr. T. L. K., Dr. Shweta Bambuwala,. (2024). Ai-Driven Solutions for Supply Chain Management. Journal of Informatics Education and Research, 4(2). DOI: 10.52783/jier.v4i2.849

Gong, S. (2024). Digital transformation of supply chain management in retail and e-commerce. *International Journal of Retail & Distribution Management*, *53*(2), 1–19. DOI: 10.1108/IJRDM-02-2023-0076

Grand View Research https://www.grandviewresearch.com/industry-analysis/digital-twin-market-

Grieves, M. W. (2023) " Digital Twins, Past, Present and Future " In the Digital Twin. Edited by Noel Crespi, Adam.T. Drobot and Roberto Minerva 97-121, Cham: Springer International Publishing

Hakkak, V. P. B. M., & Nejad, O. N. (2015). Resistance to change in online banking and extension of Technology Acceptance Model(TAM). *Soobshcheniia Akademii Nauk Gruzinskoi SSR*, *9*(1)

Hrouga, M., & Sbihi, A. (2023). Logistics 4.0 for supply chain performance: Perspectives from a retailing case study. *Business Process Management Journal*, *29*(6), 1892–1919. DOI: 10.1108/BPMJ-03-2023-0183

In Data Labs. https://indatalabs.com/blog/ai-cost-reduction#:~:text=The%20sectors%20that%20seem%20to,reductions%20of%2010%20to%2019%25.-

Kache, F., & Seuring, S. (2017). Challenges and opportunities of digital information at the intersection of Big Data Analytics and supply chain management. *International Journal of Operations & Production Management*, *37*(1), 10–36. DOI: 10.1108/IJOPM-02-2015-0078

Kinsey Report, Mc. The State of AI: How organizations are requiring to capture value https://www.mckinsey.com/capabilities/quantumblack/our-insights/the-state-of-ai

Kraus, S., Jones, P., Kailer, N., Weinmann, A., Chaparro-Banegas, N., & Roig-Tierno, N. (2021) Digital transformation: An overview of the current stateof the art of research. Sage Open, 11(3), 21582440211047576. *(PDF) The Importance of Digital Transformation (5.0) in Supply Chain Optimization: An Empirical Study-* https://www.researchgate.net/publication/378427870_The_Importance_of_Digital_Transformation_50_in_Supply_Chain_Optimization_An_Empirical_Study [accessed Apr 20 2025].

Lalitha.B.S & Ramanarayan.C.S (2016) "Effectiveness of Innovative Retail Banking Services in Karnataka "https://shodhganga.inflibnet.ac.in/handle/10603/219112#

Lambourdiere, E., & Corbin, E. (2020). Blockchain and maritime supply-chain performance: Dynamic capabilities perspective. *Worldwide Hospitality and Tourism Themes*, *12*(1), 24–34. DOI: 10.1108/WHATT-10-2019-0069

Lee, J., Siahpour, S., Singh, J., & Azamfar, M. (2020). Integration of digital twin and deep learning in cyber-physical systems: Towards smart manufacturing. *IET Collaborative Intelligent Manufacturing*, *2*(1), 34–36. DOI: 10.1049/iet-cim.2020.0009

Lyu, J., He, Y., & Zhou, F. (2023). Digital Technique-Enabled Container Logistics Supply Chain Sustainability Achievement. *Sustainability (Basel)*, *15*(22), 16014. DOI: 10.3390/su152216014

Mageto, J. (2021). Big Data Analytics in Sustainable Supply Chain Management: A Focus on Manufacturing Supply Chains. *Sustainability (Basel)*, *13*(13), 7101. DOI: 10.3390/su13137101

Maria Teresa Espinosa Jaramilo, Manuel Enrique Chenet Zuta, Chaitanya Koneti, Jayasundar, S, Soledad Del Rosario Olivares, Z, Flor Marina Carvajal Ordonez (2024)" DTin Supply Chain Operations Bridging the Physical and Digital Worlds using AI", Journal of Electrical Systems 20-10s1764-1764-1774. .DOI: 10.52783/jes.5434

Onma Enyejo, J., Peter Fajana, O., Sele Jok, I., Judith Ihejirika, C., Olusola Awotiwon, B., & Motilola Olola, T. (2024). Digital Twin Technology, Predictive Analytics, and Sustainable Project Management in Global Supply Chains for Risk Mitigation, Optimization, and Carbon Footprint Reduction through Green Initiatives. International Journal of Innovative Science and Research Technology (IJISRT), 609–630. DOI: 10.38124/ijisrt/IJISRT24NOV1344

Rathore, M. M., Shah, S. A., Shukla, D., Bentafat, E., & Bakiras, S. (2021). The role of AI Machine Learning and Big Data in Digital Twinning:A systematic Literature Review, Challenge and Opportunities. *IEEE Access : Practical Innovations, Open Solutions*, *9*, 32030–32052. https://www.researchgate.net/publication/349508978_The_Role_of_AI_Machine_Learning_and_Big_Data_in_Digital_Twinning_A_Systematic_Literature_Review_Challenges_and_Opportunities. DOI: 10.1109/ACCESS.2021.3060863

Report, N. (2024) Role of AI in SMEs- https://community.nasscom.in/communities/ai/role-ai-smes-

Rosen, R., Von Wichert, G., Lo, G., & Bettenhausen, K. D. (2015). About the importance of autonomy and DTfor the future of manufacturing. *IFAC-PapersOnLine*, *28*(3), 567–572. DOI: 10.1016/j.ifacol.2015.06.141

SAP Insights Research Center-https. www.sap.com/india/blogs/digital-twins-at-work-

Shahadat, M., Nathan, R., Chowdhury, A., & Fekete-Farkas, M. (2023). Digital Technologies for Firms' Competitive Advantage and Improved Supply Chain Performance. *Journal of Risk and Financial Management*, *16*(2), 94. DOI: 10.3390/jrfm16020094

Sullivan, Y., & Wamba, S. F. (2024). Artificial Intelligence and adaptive response to market changes: A strategy to enhance firm performance and innovation. *Journal of Business Research*, *174*, 114500. DOI: 10.1016/j.jbusres.2024.114500

Syed, A. H. Z., Khan, S. A., & Chaabane, A. (2024)" Unlocking the potential of DTin supply chains: A systematic review,"Supply Chain Analytics, Volume 7, 100075, ISSN 2949-8635, . (https://www.sciencedirect.com/science/article/pii/S2949863524000189)DOI: 10.1016/j.sca.2024.100075

Tao, F., Cheng, J., Qi, Q., Zhang, M., Zhang, H., & Sui, F. (2018). Digital Twin-Driven Product Design, Manufacturing and Service with Big Data. *International Journal of Advanced Manufacturing Technology*, *94*(9-12), 3563–3576. DOI: 10.1007/s00170-017-0233-1

Tao, F., Zhang, H., Liu, A., & Nee, A. Y. (2019). Digital twin in industry: State-of-the-art. *IEEE Transactions on Industrial Informatics*, *15*(4), 2405–2415. DOI: 10.1109/TII.2018.2873186

Tavana, M., Raeesi Vanani, I., Kumar Gangadhari, R., & Shaabani, A. (2022). A Review of Digital Transformation on Supply Chain Process Management Using Text Mining. *Processes (Basel, Switzerland)*, *10*(5), 842. DOI: 10.3390/pr10050842

Tiwari, S., Sharma, P., Choi, T.-M., & Lim, A. (2023). Blockchain and third-party logistics for global supply chain operations: Stakeholders' perspectives and decision roadmap. *Transportation Research Part E, Logistics and Transportation Review*, *170*, 103012. DOI: 10.1016/j.tre.2022.103012

Tsang, Y. P., Tang, V., Wu, C. H., & Li, F. (2024). Unlocking the Potential of Robotic Process Automation for Digital Transformation in Logistics and Supply Chain Management. *Journal of Global Information Management*, *32*(1), 1–24. DOI: 10.4018/JGIM.361710

Venkatesh, V., Gordon, B. D., & Fred, D. D. (2003). User Acceptance of information technology, towards a unified view. *Management Information Systems Quarterly*, *27*(3), 425–478. DOI: 10.2307/30036540

Vitasek, K. L., Manrodt, K. B., & Abbott, J. (2005). What makes a Lean Supply chain. *Supply Chain Management Review*, *9*(7), 39–45.

Williams, M. D., Rana, N. P., & Dwivedi, Y. K. (2015). The Unified Theory of Acceptance and usage of technology (UTAUT): A literature review. *Journal of Enterprise Information Management*, *28*(3), 443–488. DOI: 10.1108/JEIM-09-2014-0088

XiaohongChen, Liu Liu, Dayuan Li, Yangfan Han XialiangLiu (2025) " The impact of Artificial Intelligence on the new quality productive forces of enterprise", Volume 1, Article 3, Journal of Digital Management https://link.springer.com/article/10.1007/s44362-024-00002-1

Zali.N, Soltani.A, Najafi.P., Ebadi Qajari & Mehrju.M(2024) DTfor Smarter Iranian Cities: A future studies perspective, Computational Urban Science, 4(1), Article 43, https://pure.tue.nl/ws/portalfiles/portal/347098619/s43762-024-00155-9.pdfDOI: 10.1007/s43762-024-00155-9

Zarbakhshnia, N., & Karimi, A. (2024). Enhancing third-party logistics providers partnerships: An approach through the D.L.A.R.C.S supply chain paradigm. *Resources, Conservation and Recycling*, *202*, 107406. DOI: 10.1016/j.resconrec.2023.107406

Key Terms and Definitions

Artificial Intelligence: AI refers to the ability of machines to mimic human intelligence processes such as learning, reasoning, problem solving and decision making.

Internet of Things(IoT): IoT refers to those physical devices, vehicles or any other devices which can gather and exchange data .

Extended Reality: It is an umbrella term and comprises the technologies that combine the physical and digital world.

Cloud computing: It is on demand delivery of IT services via the internet and includes the servers, storage, databases, software, analytics and artificial intelligence.

Digital Twins: A digital twin is a virtual representation of the object, system or process. The entire life cycle of the asset is updated from real data with the usage of simulation, machine learning and reasoning to take better decisions.

Supply Chain Management: It is a process that includes the conversion of raw materials into finished goods and delivers it to final user.

Supply chain efficiency: It refers to the ability of the business to optimize resources, processes and technology to delivers products and services cost effectively and efficiently. It includes streamlining processes, waste reduction and maximize resource utilization to deliver products on time

Resilience: Resilience in the supply chain management refers to the supply chain to expect adapt, and recover from disasters, disruptions and confirming business continuity.

Digital maturity: This term in supply chain management refers to the company's usage level of digital technology and data to improve efficiency, visibility and swiftness in the supply chain.

Chapter 7
Green and Costly Decarbonizing Supply Chains in an Inflationary Era

L. B. Muralidhar
https://orcid.org/0000-0003-3453-613X
Jain University, India

V. Lavakumar
https://orcid.org/0000-0002-3539-9280
GITAM School of Business, GITAM University, India

N. Sathyanarayana
https://orcid.org/0000-0002-4185-7751
Jain University, India

Varanasi Rahul
https://orcid.org/0000-0003-2407-7654
Jain University, India

R. Arun
https://orcid.org/0009-0001-1571-3201
Jain University, India

ABSTRACT

Decarbonizing supply chains is crucial for sustainability but is economically daunting, especially in a period of inflation. Rising costs for renewable energy, sustainable materials, and carbon pricing contribute to companies' cost burdens. Cost-efficiency

DOI: 10.4018/979-8-3373-1982-7.ch007

vs. sustainability is highlighted in theoretical frameworks like Triple Bottom Line and Dynamic Capabilities. AI-based logistics, blockchain transparency, and circular economy strategies are adopted to mitigate inflationary pressures. Business strategies are shaped by policy measures like the EU's CBAM and the U.S. Inflation Reduction Act. Cost-effective decarbonization is realized through technological innovation, policy alignment, and economic incentives to enhance resilience in the long term.

1. INTRODUCTION

Decarbonisation in supply chains is a strategic imperative aligned with the Sustainable Development Goals (SDGs) and the Paris Agreement, creating long-term business resilience. Pressure from inflation, however, poses severe challenges to cost efficiencies, and companies must reconcile economic constraints with sustainability objectives. Underpinning theories such as the Triple Bottom Line (Elkington, 1997) emphasise economic, environmental, and social sustainability. Stakeholder Theory (Freeman, 1984) and Institutional Theory (DiMaggio & Powell, 1983) point to regulation and consumers as drivers of sustainable supply chain behavior. The Resource-Based View (Barney, 1991) emphasises further the competitive strengths of differentiated capabilities such as green logistics. Dynamic Capabilities Theory (Teece, Pisano, & Shuen, 1997) emphasises adapting to environmental regulations and economic constraints.

Various sustainability models, such as carbon footprint analysis and circular economy models (Ellen MacArthur Foundation, 2013), incorporate frameworks for emission reduction and resource optimisation. Likewise, Life Cycle Assessment (Guinée et al., 2011) evaluates environmental impacts across phases in a supply chain to encourage overall measures for sustainability. Nonetheless, traditional efficiency-based models such as Just-in-Time (JIT) logistics are a deterrent to processes of decarbonisation due to their high carbon footprint (Christopher & Peck, 2004), while Resilient Supply Chain Model has risk management integrated in measures for sustainability to encourage stability in economic shock times (Sheffi, 2005).

One of the most significant challenges in decarbonization is to mitigate inflationary pressures in procurement, logistics, and energy consumption, particularly as the added cost of green transport, renewable energy, and sustainable raw materials burdens companies, most prominently in developing economies (World Bank, 2023). Furthermore, inflation reduces purchasing power and, thus, demand for sustainable products. Mitigating all such economic constraints, companies are resorting to carbon pricing schemes (Nordhaus, 2019), AI-based route optimisation in logistics, blockchain for end-to-end visibility in the supply chain, and digital twins for carbon footprint simulation (Gao et al., 2021). Supplier diversification strategies reduce cost risks, making companies financially sustainable (Gereffi & Lee, 2016).

Despite all such developments, cost efficiency and balance in decarbonisation is still a fundamental challenge. Government policies play a crucial role in driving supply chain decarbonisation through regulations, incentive programs, and international collaboration. Carbon-intensive imports are taxed in the Carbon Border Adjustment Mechanism (CBAM) in the European Union, compelling companies to integrate sustainability (European Commission, 2022). The United States' Inflation Reduction Act of 2022 provides subsidies for investments in clean energy. China's Dual Carbon Goals (2021) have an impact on international supply chain strategies. Cross-border sustainability is promoted by international agencies such as the United Nations Framework Convention on Climate Change (UNFCCC) and the World Economic Forum's Clean Skies for Tomorrow Initiative (WEF, 2023). However, fragmentation in regulations between jurisdictions introduces complexity in compliance for international companies, requiring harmonised policy interventions.

Front-runner firms, such as Tesla, Unilever, and Maersk, demonstrate scalable sustainability programs, ranging from renewable energy consumption to biofuel-powered shipping and sustainable procurement (Tesla, 2022; Unilever, 2023; Maersk, 2023). However, intensive investment, unavailability of standardised carbon reporting structures, and technological gaps in developing economies remain hurdles. Geopolitical tensions and supply chain disruptions add complexity to the issues, necessitating agile policy responses and interindustry coordination (IMF, 2023). Decarbonising the supply chain will require a delicate balance of short-term economic imperatives and long-term sustainability goals. Future research should explore AI-driven efficiencies, analyse robust policy frameworks, and analyse the means by which green transition can unlock long-term economic potential, building resilience and profitability in a rapidly evolving world.

Background

Supply chain decarbonisation is now a non-negotiable imperative, part of fulfilling global climate commitments. But as inflation steepens the cost of green alternatives—such as low-emission technologies, renewable energy, and recycled materials—firms find themselves caught in a tightrope of fiscal restraint and environmental responsibility. The potential of AI and blockchain for maximising emissions transparency and operational efficiency is accelerating, but remains untapped, hindered by patchy regulation and fragmented international cooperation. Without coordinated policy reform and transnational action, progress will be piecemeal. To firms, the future demands no compromise but strategic alignment—where green goals become not external prescriptions but deep-seated drivers of resilience, ingenuity, and long-term economic resilience.

Main Focus

The supply chain decarbonisation under the pressure of inflation poses a stark paradox: the most vital transition technologies remain financially out of reach for many, particularly those less-resourced parts of the world. High-capital assets such as solar equipment, electric vehicle fleets, and bio-based inputs strain the fiscal limits of already volatile firms. Budgetary retrenchment tends to push decision-makers toward unsustainable short-term options, perpetuating environmental inertia. Compounding this is the insidious rise of greenwashing—when reputation rewards take precedence over real impact, eroding stakeholder trust and weakening enforcement systems. The lack of standard carbon accounting methods further atomises global accountability, making performance data unreliable and comparisons across borders questionable. In this splintered system, ambition is not enough; integrity, accuracy, and equitable access must be the future.

2. DECARBONISATION STRATEGIES FOR SUPPLY CHAINS

Supply chain decarbonisation is a strategic imperative for businesses to achieve global climate goals and reduce their carbon footprint. With supply chains accounting for 60% or more of GHG emissions in specific sectors, businesses need to take comprehensive end-to-end actions, such as supply chain mapping, supplier engagement, integration with renewable energy sources, adoption of the circular economy, and digitalisation, to reduce emissions (World Economic Forum, 2021). Emission hotspots and Scope 3 emissions, measured using carbon accounting software, enable businesses to realise emission savings effectively. Supplier collaboration also improves value chain sustainability (CDP, 2020; Gold & Heikkurinen, 2018).

Besides, adopting renewable energy resources like solar, wind, and biofuels in production and logistics minimises emissions (IRENA, 2020). Circular economy measures, such as product design for recyclability, take-back schemes, and use of sustainable materials, enhance supply chain sustainability (Ellen MacArthur Foundation, 2019). Technological advancements, such as AI, blockchain, and IoT, contribute to real-time emission tracking, enhanced operating efficiency, and increased transparency in the supply chain (Saberi et al., 2019). AI-based logistics optimise transport routes, reducing fuel consumption, while sustainable mobility technologies such as zero-emission vehicles (ZEVs), hydrogen fuel cells, and intermodal freight transport reduce emissions from distribution networks (McKinnon, 2018; Li, Chen, & Wang, 2022).

Industry leaders like Amazon are making a standard with 100,000 electrified delivery trucks to be deployed by 2030 and more investments in hydrogen-powered freight trucks, which save CO_2 emissions to the tune of 80% (Amazon, 2021; Li, Chen, & Wang, 2022). Nestlé and Unilever are also pioneering sustainable packaging innovations, including biodegradable packaging and reusable designs, to reduce plastic waste (González et al., 2023; Unilever, 2020; Zhu et al., 2022). Tesla and Walmart have further stepped up decarbonisation with solar-powered distribution centers, and microgrids and ultra-fast EV charging stations further enhance sustainability in logistics centers (Green & Martin, 2023).

Besides technology, encouragement from regulations in the form of subsidies and a carbon tax accelerates the adoption of clean energy, and green process production compels industries to embrace solar, wind, and green hydrogen (World Resources Institute, 2021; Schmidt, Brown, & Green, 2023). Priority is being given to responsible sourcing through the use of low-carbon and recycled materials, as well as making environmental and ethical demands on suppliers (Apple, 2021). Credibility is given through Fairtrade, FSC, and Cradle-to-Cradle (C2C) certifications, and blockchain-based supply tracking ensures transparency and accountability (Lewis, 2019; World Economic Forum, 2020). An industry-wide commitment to sustainability is evident in large-scale initiatives, such as Walmart's Project Gigaton, which aims to reduce one gigaton of emissions by 2030 (Walmart, 2021).

Although initial investments in clean energy, digital optimisation, and sustainable sourcing can be costly, the long-term benefits, operating efficiencies, and investor appeal typically offset these investments (IRENA, 2020). Renewable energy reduces electricity costs, AI-based logistics optimises fuel efficiency, and energy-efficient production reduces waste, all of which improve profitability (Accenture, 2021). Government financing, in the form of subsidies, tax credits, and grants, also supports the transformation, as seen in initiatives such as the U.S. Inflation Reduction Act and the EU Green Deal, which promote clean energy investments and sustainable purchasing (EPA, 2020). Pressure to net-zero supply chains complements corporate sustainability initiatives, with companies such as Apple, Microsoft, and IKEA committing to using renewable energy and sustainable materials in operations (IKEA, 2021). Green building certifications such as LEED and BREEAM promote energy-efficient operations, complementing sustainability initiatives (World Resources Institute, 2020).

In addition, AI and blockchain technologies enable real-time emission tracking and supply chain optimisation to address shifting sustainability regulations (Saberi et al., 2019). Decarbonisation is not merely a requirement from an environmental point of view but a driver of business competitiveness, reducing emissions while enhancing cost efficiency, regulation compliance, and brand reputation. Resilient and sustainable supply chains can be built for businesses by combining renewable energy, responsible material acquisition, digitalisation, and circular economy principles. As industries transition to net-zero operations, companies that proactively move towards decarbonisation will be able to position themselves to lead in environmental stewardship and long-term profitability, ultimately achieving a competitive advantage in a transforming world market.

3 ECONOMIC CHALLENGES OF DECARBONIZATION

Decarbonisation is essential to achieve international climate targets but is a significant economic challenge, with high costs for green technologies and sustainable materials for SMEs. While renewable energy systems, EVs, and energy-efficient appliances save costs in the long term, their high initial costs deter investment, especially in resource-constrained developing economies (IRENA, 2020; World Bank, 2020). Additionally, sustainable materials such as recycled plastic, biodegradable packaging, and low-carbon steel remain expensive due to limited supply and high processing costs, which deter mass adoption (Ellen MacArthur Foundation, 2019; Lewis, 2019). However, delaying decarbonisation is dangerous as consumers and investors increasingly prioritise sustainability, making it a strategic imperative (CDP, 2020).

Governments provide low-interest loans and grants, as well as issue tax credits, to offset financing barriers. For example, the U.S. Inflation Reduction Act subsidises investment in clean energy (White House, 2022). Shared business relationships among firms, suppliers, and industry peers facilitate collective investment in clean energy systems, thereby reducing cost burdens (World Resources Institute, 2020). New financing instruments, such as green bonds and sustainability-linked loans, enable firms to raise capital on favorable terms contingent upon their sustainability performance (Climate Bonds Initiative, 2021). Operational efficiencies such as lean production and waste reduction further offset costs through lower overall expenditure (EPA, 2020).

Furthermore, with the increasing demand for green solutions, economies of scale will facilitate access to green technologies and materials (Ellen MacArthur Foundation, 2019). However, economic insecurity and inflation exacerbate economic barriers, as high costs for green technologies such as solar panels, wind turbines, and energy-efficient appliances reduce their feasibility for resource-poor companies (Uddin & Rahman, 2023; Avazkhodjaev et al., 2023). Higher rates further restrict access to capital, discouraging long-term investments in sustainability (Haider, 2015).

Additionally, inflation increases the cost of essential raw materials, such as lithium for electric vehicle (EV) batteries and rare earth elements for renewable energy systems, further escalating costs (Avazkhodjaev et al., 2023). Economic recession contributes to policy uncertainty, discouraging extensive decarbonisation due to concerns about regulatory risks (Olasehinde-Williams et al., 2023; Hassan & Xia, 2023). Financial crises lead firms to prioritize short-term survival over long-term investment in sustainability, hindering progress toward net-zero emissions and green projects (Patankar & Jenkins, 2023). Market volatility further discourages investment in sustainability, as inflation reduces purchasing power and consumers prefer low-priced, low-sustainability products, making green products unprofitable (Farooq, 2023). Limited access to green finance in economic crises worsens the problem, and firms cannot access funds for financing decarbonisation (Konte & Ndiaye, 2017).

Additionally, added costs burden government budgets, reducing green incentives and shifting economic burdens to firms (Patankar & Jenkins, 2023). To counteract such obstacles, firms must reconcile economic constraints with sustainability objectives through cost-effective interventions—such as energy efficiency gains, waste minimisation, and circular economy interventions—to facilitate decarbonization without economic disruption (Arfaoui et al., 2023). Leveraging government subsidies and tax credits further eases economic pressure, facilitating a low-cost transition to renewable energy (Patankar & Jenkins, 2023).

Diversification in supply chains and investment in circular economy models—e.g., utilising recycled material or purchasing from local sources—can mitigate the inflationary pressure on raw material costs (Olasehinde-Williams et al., 2023). Enhanced public-private partnerships (PPPs) enable firms to access funds and share green investment risks, thereby enhancing long-term financial sustainability (Hassan & Xia, 2023). Transparent communication about the long-term economic value of sustainability is crucial for attracting investors and maintaining customer confidence as consumers continue to offer support amid economic turbulence (Farooq, 2023). Decarbonization in a cost-effective manner requires firms to balance environmental ambitions and economic limitations.

Although upfront investments in process improvements, energy efficiency, and renewable energy pose a cost challenge, they ultimately provide long-term cost savings and a competitive edge. For example, a report on OCP Group, a large phosphate company, concluded that installing solar panels and batteries can reduce carbon emissions by 70% and provide significant cost savings over twenty years (Lavigne & Tankov, 2023). Nevertheless, policy ambiguity is a significant deterrent, as uncertain changes in regulations can erode the profitability of investments in sustainability (França et al., 2023).

In order to manage such risks, firms have to integrate decarbonisation into strategic planning in a way consistent with long-term profitability and market positioning. Technological innovation and operating flexibility contribute to feasibility, with AI-based energy management, predictive analytics, and automation maximising energy use and reducing inefficiency and economic unviability (Fleschutz et al., 2023). Additionally, demand flexibility—where firms adjust energy use in line with real-time pricing—reduces cost and increases efficiency. Open sustainability reporting builds confidence and ensures long-term investment in green projects (Council on Sustainability Transformation, 2023). Cost-effective and high-impact measures, such as emissions tracking, supply chain optimisation, and energy-efficient production, must be prioritised to achieve maximum environmental benefits with minimal economic risks (Bertrand Piccard's Solar Impulse Foundation, 2023).

In the end, cost-effective decarbonisation is a question of investment versus future economic benefits, using government incentives, integrating sustainability into business strategies, employing cutting-edge technologies, and engaging stakeholders. Regardless of economic and regulatory limitations, companies that advance with sustainability will be able to outcompete, save costs, and be more resilient in a green economy. With increasingly stringent international climate regulations and shifting market demands for sustainability, companies that accept decarbonisation will be well-positioned for long-term success.

4. TECHNOLOGICAL INNOVATIONS ENABLING DECARBONIZATION

Supply chains are being transformed using AI and ML, with emissions tracked in real time, logistics streamlined to minimise fuel consumption, and demand forecasting to mitigate emissions due to waste (Hasan, 2025; Rane et al., 2023). Supplier selection is optimised using AI, with environmental performance factors considered, and ML simulations help firms decide on the best-fit strategies for reducing carbon emissions (Mehendale, 2020).

Additionally, blockchain and IoT enhance transparency, accountability, and efficiency, as blockchain ensures product authenticity and IoT sensors monitor emissions and resource usage to optimise energy consumption (Kamble et al., 2021; Mastos et al., 2021). Their integration optimises order management, creates supply chain resilience, and facilitates circular economy initiatives through product lifecycle tracking and promoting resource efficiency (Bechtsis et al., 2021). Blockchain smart contracts also automate finance and compliance, removing administrative inefficiencies and ensuring greater sustainability (Kamble et al., 2021).

Conversely, net-zero emissions are promoted through hydrogen energy, biofuels, and carbon capture technologies in sectors such as heavy industry and long-distance transportation, where electrification is not feasible. Green hydrogen, produced through renewable energy electrolysis, is a viable alternative to fossil fuels but is costly to manufacture and faces infrastructural challenges (Shafiee et al., 2023). Hydrogen enhances integration with renewable energy, but infrastructural repurposing is costly (Cebon et al., 2023; Hofmann et al., 2024).

Similarly, biofuels in the form of sustainable aviation fuel (SAF) lower transport emissions but are still expensive and in short supply, accounting for only 0.2% of jet fuel consumption in 2023 (Author(s), 2020). Carbon capture and storage (CCS) in biofuel production enhances climate benefits, but its effectiveness depends on carbon pricing, technological innovation, and policy action (IRENA, 2023; Goodarzi & Li, 2023). However, economic considerations like inflation, rising costs for renewable energy systems, and raw material price volatility in lithium and rare earth elements complicate investment in decarbonisation (Uddin & Rahman, 2023).

High interest rates further restrict access to capital, discouraging investments in long-term sustainability (Haider, 2015; Avazkhodjaev et al., 2023). Additionally, shifting policy frameworks create uncertainty, deterring firms from making significant investments in green projects (Olasehinde-Williams et al., 2023). Financial crises exacerbate such issues, as inflation reduces consumers' purchasing power, decreases demand for green products, and lowers profitability for green firms (Patankar & Jenkins, 2023; Farooq, 2023). Governments with tight budgets cannot sustain green subsidies either, shifting the cost burden to firms (Patankar & Jenkins, 2023).

To navigate these barriers, firms must introduce cost-reduction measures, such as energy efficiency gains, waste minimisation, and circular economy measures, to save on costs and facilitate decarbonisation (Arfaoui et al., 2023). Leveraging government subsidies and tax credits further lowers costs, making adoption more affordable (Patankar & Jenkins, 2023). Supply chain diversification and the utilisation of recyclable materials from within reduce inflationary pressure on raw material costs and enhance business resilience (Olasehinde-Williams et al., 2023). Increasing public-private partnerships (PPPs) provides firms with access to green finance and shared risks in decarbonisation (Hassan & Xia, 2023).

Adequate transparency in sustainability fosters investor and customer confidence and trust, thereby gaining market support in uncertain economic times (Farooq, 2023). Although investments in clean energy, AI optimisation, and energy-efficient processes initially have cost issues, in the long run, they offer cost advantages and a competitive edge. For instance, a study in the OCP Group revealed that investing in solar panels and battery storage could reduce carbon emissions by 70% and save substantial funds over twenty years (Lavigne & Tankov, 2023).

However, unpredictable policy changes serve as a deterrent, as changing policies can render investment viability null and void (França et al., 2023). To mitigate such risks, businesses need to integrate sustainability into their business strategies, associating green investments with long-term profitability and market positioning. AI-based energy management, predictive analytics, and automation complement decarbonisation, optimising energy consumption, reducing inefficiencies, and making economic viability more attainable (Fleschutz et al., 2023).

Real-time adjustment of energy consumption, such as tuning for optimal sound quality, is a delicate balance between cost management and operational efficiency. Open sustainability disclosure, such as a window into the soul of a firm, generates long-term trust (Council on Sustainability Transformation, 2023). Focusing on low-risk, high-gain activities—such as emissions monitoring or lean manufacturing—enables companies to navigate the complex terrain of environmental responsibility while insulating themselves from economic pitfalls(Bertrand Piccard's Solar Impulse Foundation, 2023).

All three unite like a symphony, with AI orchestrating low-emissions logistics, blockchain serving as the ledger of integrity, and IoT fine-tuning resource usage. They are the unsung heroes of supply chain decarbonisation—transforming untidy, energy-intensive systems into streamlined, open, and green ones, like polishing a draft into a masterpiece of efficiency and accountability(Saberi et al., 2019; Kamble et al., 2021).

Cheap decarbonisation is akin to taking the scenic route—exchanging upfront costs for the promise of a future payoff. Investment in green technologies, combined with policy stimulus and collective action, is the fuel driving organisations toward competitive success. As the green economy grows, those that embed sustainability into their core activities will not only survive but also thrive. Ultimately, carbon reduction is not just about compliance—it is about establishing a foothold in a sustainable, future-proof marketplace.

5. REGULATORY AND POLICY FRAMEWORKS

The Paris Agreement (2015) has significantly influenced global supply chains, compelling companies and governments to introduce stringent decarbonisation measures to limit the global temperature increase to 1.5–2° C above pre-industrial levels. The signatory states must present Nationally Determined Contributions

(NDCs) that impose emission reduction responsibilities on manufacturing, logistics, and energy-intensive sectors (Berkhout & Smith, 2021).

However, firms operating in multiple jurisdictions find it challenging to adapt to the varied NDCs, sectoral regulations, and carbon pricing schemes. Schemes like the Carbon Border Adjustment Mechanism (CBAM) in the EU impose levies on high-carbon imports, prompting international producers to reduce their emissions. Meanwhile, the U.S. Inflation Reduction Act (IRA) incentivises clean energy consumption and discourages high-carbon foreign supplies. Similarly, cap-and-trade schemes like the EU Emissions Trading Scheme (EU ETS) and China's National Carbon Market push firms to invest in clean energy, carbon capture technologies, and sustainable sourcing, exerting cost pressures (Clark & Tilman, 2021). Complying with such regulations requires substantial capital investments, which are particularly challenging during periods of economic instability and inflation.

Firms are also tasked with navigating inconsistent regulatory frameworks that require varying disclosure demands for greater transparency, efficient data collection systems, and third-party audits, which add to costs and operational burdens. Governments provide relief from financial burdens through tax credits, subsidies, and grants for investments in low-emission technologies. Programs such as the U.S. IRA, the EU Green Deal Industrial Plan, and India's PLI Scheme provide companies with incentives to transition to low-emission technologies; however, accessing these programs requires navigating intricate regulatory frameworks and demonstrating verifiable emission reductions (Fankhauser & Hepburn, 2020).

Additionally, regulations such as the EU Corporate Sustainability Reporting Directive (CSRD) and the U.S. SEC Climate Disclosure Rule require investments in emission tracking and compliance systems. China's Dual Carbon Goals (carbon peaking in 2030, carbon neutrality in 2060) impose stringent limits on high-emission sectors, and the International Maritime Organization's (IMO) Carbon Intensity Indicator (CII) compels international shipping companies to use cleaner fuels and optimise fleet efficiency.

Even as such policies deliver long-term environmental benefits, they impose economic and operational burdens, most significantly on capital-intensive sectors such as steel, cement, automotive, and aviation (Gielen & Boshell, 2022). Inflation, disruptions in the supply chain, and geopolitical conflicts contribute to difficulties in adhering to them since low-carbon operations require costly investments in clean energy, electrified fleets, and circular economy measures. Rising costs for critical materials, such as lithium, cobalt, and nickel, which are required for EV batteries and green buildings, as well as green building codes and ESG reporting, contribute to economic strains (Brown & Green, 2023). SMEs face difficulty in incorporating compliance tracking technologies, and variations in sustainability reporting frameworks like Global Reporting Initiative (GRI), Task Force on Climate-Related

Financial Disclosures (TCFD), and International Sustainability Standards Board (ISSB) raise audit costs and introduce inconsistencies in corporate adoption of sustainability (Gopalakrishnan & Matthews, 2023).

Additionally, carbon pricing has other implications for financial planning, as firms in high-taxation economies, such as the EU, are competitively disadvantaged compared to firms in low-regulation economies. Volatility in the price of carbon credits renders financial planning difficult for businesses that invest in offsets, and additional compliance costs from within their supply chains contribute to inflation in end-consumer goods. However, firms can employ strategic interventions to mitigate such difficulties and maintain stability in their economies. Green finance products, such as green bonds, sustainability-linked loans, and carbon trading, serve as alternative financing avenues for investment in decarbonisation. ESG investors are increasingly favoring companies with firm sustainability commitments, making green finance products a crucial driver for financing low-carbon transformation.

New regulatory frameworks, such as the EU's Carbon Border Adjustment Mechanism (CBAM), the US Inflation Reduction Act, and China's carbon goals, are shaping the future of decarbonised supply chains. However, the fragmented nature of global regulations presents challenges for multinational companies trying to comply with various emission reduction policies. Policies that require greater transparency and stricter emission standards increase costs for firms but also create opportunities for those adopting green practices (Berkhout & Smith, 2021; Gielen & Boshell, 2022).

AI-driven carbon monitoring and traceability with the help of blockchain technology are not only efficiency tools—they are new accountability tools, redefining the relationship of firms with evolving regulatory regimes. Technology is only part of the solution, however; constructive collaborations with the state, civil society, and sectoral groupings are required for the development of effective, sector-appropriate decarbonisation frameworks. Circular economy approaches—remanufacturing and waste valorisation—have the twin dividend of smoothing cost volatility and locking in low-carbon standards. Off-grid renewable energy and power purchase arrangements provide a hedge against shocks and lock in environmental standards. Incorporating these approaches into the core business design makes compliance a strategic enabler, not a constraint, insulating firms from volatility and steering them toward organised, climate-convergent growth (Mishra & Sharma, 2022).

6. CONSUMER DEMAND FOR SUSTAINABLE SUPPLY CHAINS

Growing environmental consciousness has altered consumer expectations, prompting companies to integrate sustainability into their purchasing and supply chain practices. Ethical production is no longer a competitive advantage but the norm. As the environmental crisis deepens, a group of consumers increasingly associate environmental integrity with product value, prompting behind-the-curve companies toward reform or lose competitive position in a market increasingly driven by climatic consumption habits (Anderson & Tushman, 2021).

Customers nowadays evaluate products based on their social and environmental responsibility, and companies are responding with more sustainable supply chains that have a smaller carbon footprint, reduced waste, and fair working conditions. Businesses are adopting sustainable raw material acquisition, fair-trade alliances, and energy-efficient logistics. They are implementing circular economy strategies, such as recycling, remanufacturing, and product life extension, which enhances brand loyalty and provides companies with a competitive edge in a more eco-friendly marketplace (Anderson & Tushman, 2021).

The rise of digital marketplaces and e-commerce has heightened consumers' expectations regarding sustainability, as online marketplaces provide greater transparency into product origins and corporate responsibility programs. Social media activism has further heightened scrutiny of business operations and, hence, reputational risks for companies that fail to have sustainable programs in place. Therefore, businesses must integrate sustainability into their supply chains and communicate such programs through campaigns, sustainability reports, and third-party certifications (Sarkis & Zhu, 2020).

Independent certification schemes, such as Fair Trade, FSC, LEED, and ISO 14001, guarantee consumers that sustainability practices are followed, fostering confidence and differentiating companies in competitive markets (Carboni & Kumar, 2021). However, with an increasing number of cases of greenwashing—where firms exaggerate or mislead about their sustainability credentials—there has been a greater need for rigorous third-party audits and enforcement to ensure that certified companies meet high standards of sustainability. Certifications such as the Marine Stewardship Council (MSC) for sustainable seafood and the Global Organic Textile Standard (GOTS) for organic textiles further enhance transparency, thereby fostering consumers' confidence and brand loyalty in the long term (Barbosa & Santos, 2020).

Besides consumer confidence, certification for sustainability is crucial in business-to-business relationships, as large retailers and multinational firms increasingly require ESG conformity from their suppliers. Such companies without approved certifications may be precluded from procurement contracts, and banks and investors are increasingly incorporating sustainability credentials into their loan and investment decisions (Chen & Zhao, 2022). Certification is challenging to achieve and maintain, with conformity audits, data collection, and changing regulations adding to cost and administrative burdens, most significantly for resource-limited SMEs. With regulators increasingly enforcing stricter sustainability rules, certification is becoming a conformity requirement and a key differentiator in the competition.

Consumer preferences are increasingly influencing businesses to adopt more sustainable practices. Consumers are demanding more eco-friendly products, leading companies to optimise their supply chains for lower emissions, waste reduction, and ethical sourcing. This shift is also being supported by social media activism and heightened transparency, as consumers scrutinise companies' environmental impact more than ever before (Anderson & Tushman, 2021; Ritchie & Roser, 2021).

Patagonia, Tesla, and Unilever represent the strategic power of incorporating sustainability into supply chains beyond compliance. Patagonia's emphasis on durability, rather than disposability—captured by its "Worn Wear" program—remakes value creation by aligning consumer participation with environmental responsibility. By creating purpose-driven participation, the strategy generates loyalty and quietly upends the fast-fashion paradigm. Tesla's redefinition of supply networks—through renewable incorporation, battery recycling, and regionalised sourcing—exemplifies a systems-thinking approach that mitigates geopolitical and environmental risks. Its vertical alignment of clean technologies with emerging mobility standards is more than innovative; it is a purposeful break from fossil-fueled dependencies. These cases suggest that real sustainability, when incorporated structurally, not only insulates a reputation but also enhances operational resilience and market differentiation (Baldwin & Freeman, 2022).

Conversely, Unilever's Sustainable Living Plan has established challenging targets for waste reduction, emission management, supply chain transparency, responsible palm oil and cocoa sourcing, and promoting sustainable agriculture among smallholder farmers. By incorporating sustainability into their business strategy, companies have seen an increase in customer confidence, improved control over compliance, and enhanced business performance. Sustainability has proven to be a driver for profitability and resilience in the long term (Dahlmann & Branicki, 2022).

The above examples demonstrate that businesses that meet consumers' sustainability demands have increased brand loyalty, reduced regulatory risks, and enhanced competitiveness. With sustainability becoming a market imperative rather than a choice, businesses that fail to incorporate sustainable measures risk losing consumers' confidence, market access, and growth opportunities in a rapidly transforming world economy where environmental responsibility is a key driver of business success (Dahlmann & Branicki, 2022).

Recent developments have led to a growing demand for supply chain sustainability among consumers, with firms such as Patagonia and Unilever adopting circular economy strategies and fair labor practices in response to increasing pressures for ethical consumption (Baldwin & Freeman, 2022; Dahlmann & Branicki, 2022). Social media and online platforms have also facilitated consumer mobilisation and demands for transparency and accountability, compelling firms to pursue legitimate sustainability labels and preventing greenwashing (Sarkis & Zhu, 2020; Carboni

& Kumar, 2021). Meanwhile, geopolitical tensions—such as EU investigations on Chinese solar panels and U.S. tariffs on clean tech imports—have disrupted the trade in green technologies and raw materials, increasing costs and complicating decarbonisation strategies (Nygaard, 2022; Schäpe, 2024). Supply chain risk interruptions induced by resource nationalism among cobalt- and lithium-rich nations have also forced businesses to adopt supply chain diversification and responsible sourcing practices that comply with Fairtrade standards (Zabelin & Dongen, 2024; Nsude et al., 2024). Together, all these trends imply the imperative of aligning supply chain decarbonization with not only environmental and financial objectives but also with consumer pressure and geopolitical necessities.

7. FINANCIAL INSTRUMENTS AND INCENTIVES FOR DECARBONIZATION

The finance community is no longer a passive spectator of the sustainability agenda—it is now a key driver of the low-carbon transition. Mechanisms like green bonds redefine capital deployment by linking investment with quantifiable environmental performance. These vehicles, often incentivised by preferential tax treatment and concessional terms, re-balance risk-return calculations for the benefit of climate-compatible investments. By investing capital into renewable infrastructure, low-carbon logistics, and green production, they reframe environmental accountability as a source of assets rather than a cost. Support from multilateral institutions like the World Bank further legitimises their credibility, suggesting that finance, when directed strategically, can engineer systemic environmental change beyond rhetorical endorsement (Dauvergne, 2020).

Sustainability-linked loans (SLLs) serve as a reward mechanism, where firms earn lower interest payments for achieving sustainability objectives, such as reducing emissions or enhancing energy efficiency. Unlike green bonds, which fund specific projects, SLLs provide firms with the flexibility to integrate sustainability into their overall strategy. Thus, they represent the best solution for firms that wish not only to finance but also integrate environmental responsibility into their core activity—transforming sustainability from a project into a core philosophy.

Venture capital also finances green start-ups that create new sustainable technologies. Venture capital funds have invested in sustainable product start-ups, clean energy, carbon capture, and electric vehicles; thus, there is greater financial interest in sustainability. Venture capital investments encourage start-ups to innovate while also scaling up sustainable solutions commercially, thus promoting global decarbonization (Doyle & McKinley, 2023).

Governments and financial institutions have implemented various policies to encourage companies to reduce emissions and adopt a low-carbon economy. Some of the most effective policies to encourage emission reductions are carbon pricing through a carbon tax and cap-and-trade systems. By assigning a cost to carbon emissions, these policies encourage companies to adopt cleaner production processes, invest in energy-efficient technologies, and use alternative sources of energy. (Walker & Jones, 2023).

Another strong incentive is to provide tax credits and grants to corporations that invest in green infrastructure and low-emission technology. The US Investment Tax Credit (ITC) and Production Tax Credit (PTC) for alternative energy plants generously reward corporations for installing solar, wind, and other renewable energy sources. Subsidies for electric vehicle, battery energy storage, and carbon capture equipment manufacturing equally promote the decarbonisation of polluting industries (Evans & Fang, 2021).

Mechanisms like carbon markets and Renewable Energy Credits reframe sustainability as a commodity, monetising reductions, as it were. RECs underpin the development of renewable capacity by creating economic value for clean energy, while carbon offsets—through reforestation, for example, or the suppression of methane—enable firms to externalise the responsibilities of mitigation, with ethical considerations surrounding accountability versus convenience. Financialisation of environmental stewardship spurs action but also the possibility of commodifying responsibility. Public-private partnerships, meanwhile, redefine the boundaries of green infrastructure investment. These collaborative arrangements extend beyond transactional financing, distributing capital risk while enabling scale, speed, and innovation for ventures that align with the climate. Far from symbolic, such partnerships make operational the decarbonisation of the system, bridging fiscal resilience with ecological integrity. The stakes extend beyond compliance—they involve the economics of tomorrow's legitimacy (Kim & Lee, 2021).

Economic systems of carbon pricing, like cap-and-trade or carbon taxation, serve as the compass for firms toward decarbonisation. Green bonds, in particular, serve as a bridge between finance capital and green accountability. They offer firms the opportunity to reduce their carbon footprint with the added benefits of lower interest payments and tax incentives—a fiscal win-win, much like sowing the seeds of a green future with both environmental and economic returns (Dauvergne, 2020; Evans & Fang, 2021).

Sustainability-linked supply chain financing serves as a moral compass for firms, encouraging suppliers to adopt green behaviors in exchange for preferential credit terms. Large players, such as Walmart and Unilever, are leading the charge with programs that reward suppliers of low-emission technology. Impact investing, a growing force for change in the finance world, aligns financial returns with tangible social and environmental impacts, fostering a new generation of sustainable start-ups and energy-efficient businesses. The new trend is akin to sowing seeds in a receptive market, allowing start-ups driven by the circular economy to scale up. These collective finance tools not only fund sustainability—they prove that profitability and green can go hand-in-hand, creating a low-carbon, resilient supply chain for the future (Ritchie & Roser, 2021).

8. GEOPOLITICAL AND SOCIAL DIMENSIONS

The transition to a green economy is fraught with challenges as it navigates complex geopolitical dynamics and social equity concerns that impact international supply chains. Geopolitical risks such as resource nationalism and trade tensions affect access to important minerals for green technologies since over 70% of cobalt and other essential resources are concentrated in highly corrupt states, and hence there are issues concerning supply stability (Zabelin & Dongen, 2024; Nygaard, 2022). Disruptions in international supply chains are increased due to resource nationalism since states with abundant reserves of lithium and cobalt prefer indigenous industries and restrict exports, affecting international flows of trade.

At the same time, ongoing trade disputes—e.g., U.S. tariffs on Chinese green goods and EU investigations into Chinese electric vehicles and solar panels—raise costs, making clean technologies more expensive and slowing down the clean energy revolution (Schäpe, 2024). These disputes should be tackled with green transition strategies that balance geopolitical risks with making green technologies affordable and accessible. Beyond geopolitical considerations, a fair transformation calls for social equity considerations to be incorporated in all steps in the value chain, from raw material extraction to distribution. Decarbonisation strategies usually fail when they enhance social inequalities, calling for companies to move beyond measures for compliance (Karaosman et al., 2024).

Ethical and fair working practices and responsible sourcing are paramount, requiring diversification of geographies for sourcing and compliance with Fairtrade principles to avoid reliance on exploitative labour. Investments in workers' education and training allow for skills to be developed in local communities to participate in a green economy, and fair remuneration and good working conditions improve economic and social resilience (SGSCAR, 2023). Marginalised groups and developing economies disproportionately bear green transition costs, with measures like the Carbon Border Adjustment Mechanism (CBAM) in the European Union creating a trade barrier for high-carbon imports, penalising resource-poor economies that cannot quickly decarbonise. Such economic growth barriers necessitate policies that balance economic inclusion with environmental ends. Technological transfers, funding, and capacity building are important for developing countries to adopt sustainable approaches without sacrificing economic gains (Crespy & Munta, 2023).

Global cooperation is crucial in bridging social and geopolitical challenges in decarbonising supply chains. Fairtrade certification ensures transparency in the production of Clean Energy Technology materials, such as nickel, cobalt, and lithium, from Global South nations, promoting ethical processing and extraction (Nsude et al., 2024). Global cooperation ensures sustainable progress, with bodies like the World Economic Forum advocating for policy collaboration and coordination. One environmental regulation helps prevent leakage, and internationally standardised labor standards protect workers along supply chains. Financial and technological assistance to developing nations ensures easy implementation of sustainable processes without economic destabilisation.

Additionally, supply chain transparency and traceability enable consumers and businesses to make informed decisions, promoting ethical business practices across various industries. Academic research also contributes to enhancing the social aspects of the green transition, preventing the displacement of workers, and minimising economic insecurity. Emission reduction as a priority, without addressing social imbalances, is achieved at the expense of disadvantaged groups, particularly in high-carbon industries. Business policy must incorporate programs to support workers, economic development initiatives for affected areas, and policies to prevent offshoring in vulnerable industries (Crespy & Munta, 2023).

Geopolitical conflicts and economic instability, including inflation and raw material costs, pose significant threats to global supply chains. The need for rare earth metals in electric vehicles and renewable energy technologies amid inflationary pressures complicates the ability of companies to balance sustainability goals with economic demands. These issues are also exacerbated by political unrest and trade wars, which destabilise supply chains and pose additional barriers to decarbonisation (Nygaard, 2022; Zabelin & Dongen, 2024).

SMEs making forays into the sea of decarbonisation are like small boats contending with turbulent oceans—exposed to the high up-front investment for green technology with no capacity to weather the storm. In emerging economies, fiscal constraints and economic volatility discourage investment in sustainability. Political tensions, such as resource nationalism and trade disputes, create unexpected waves, disrupting supply chains and driving up the prices of key materials. The volatility leaves SMEs exposed as they struggle with establishing a clear direction toward sustainable practice with the economic and financial barriers that thwart their ability to grow into a low-carbon economy.

The green transition, although necessary, tends to deepen social divides, especially in the developing world, with the most vulnerable populations bearing the greatest brunt. It is like asking the most vulnerable limbs of the tree to bear the load of growth.

Realising these social and economic imbalances provides a better understanding of the challenges firms face when decarbonising, especially against the backdrop of increasing inflation. Navigating the delicate balance between environmental sustainability and social equity is a reflection of the broader global aspirations for equity and the necessity of a just and equitable green future.

While the technological and economic aspects of supply chain decarbonisation are the focus, we should not overlook the social side, particularly for small and medium-sized enterprises (SMEs). SMEs exist as tightrope walkers, balancing survival with sustainability with little buffer and funds for green technologies (Gopalakrishnan & Matthews, 2023). In developing economies, the grip is further tightened due to inflationary pressure, and the green transition remains a distant dream (Uddin & Rahman, 2023). The answer is not just making environmental changes—it is ensuring that sustainability does not leave vulnerable SMEs behind, building a just and robust future.

The social effects of decarbonisation will be secondary, but the green transition mustn't further marginalise vulnerable groups. Think of a balance scale—when the weight of sustainability is imposed on SMEs, the entire system is likely to collapse (Karaosman et al., 2024). A fair decarbonisation strategy should be a safety net for such firms, with the injection of funds, access to green technology, and capacity building (Crespy & Munta, 2023). Sustainability will be economically viable and socially viable only if this scenario prevails. Growth will then be accessible to everyone, not a privilege reserved for the few.

Recent history, such as the Ukraine - Russia conflict, indicates the impact of geopolitical risks on energy supply chains, influencing investment and accelerating the imperative for diversified clean energy alternatives. It is akin to riding a storm—while the winds of geopolitical tensions whip up unpredictability, well-crafted environmental rules and innovation act as the anchor, stabilising the progress(Wang et al., 2024). A just transition requires more than just technology; it necessitates a balance of economic competitiveness, social justice, and global stability. By prioritising decent work, responsible sourcing, and international cooperation, we can make the energy transition work toward a green economy that is not only sustainable but also equitable for all.

9. RESILIENCE AND RISK MANAGEMENT IN DECARBONIZED SUPPLY CHAINS

Decarbonisation reimagines supply chain resilience, demanding fluency across ecological volatility, unpredictability driven by inflation, and geopolitical fragmentation. Foresight, redefined as strategic risk management, begins not with reaction but with careful diagnostics—Life Cycle Assessments and predictive modeling identify fault lines before disruption cascades. Digital infrastructure—blockchain for provenance, cloud for responsiveness, and analytics for scenario planning—translates these insights into operational intelligence. Technical expertise, however, is insufficient. Structural flexibility through supplier diversification and contingency frameworks offers insulation from systemic exposure(Hajarath & Vummadi, 2024). A decarbonised supply chain is no longer a linear optimisation problem; it is a dynamic architecture—immune from rupture by embedding anticipation, decentralisation, and real-time responsiveness at its core.

Enduring supply relationships act as strategic ballast against the destabilising forces of environmental turbulence and inflation(Stone, 2022). As input prices for green materials fluctuate, shared investment plans and responsive payment systems serve as a stabilising force, distributing fiscal pressure along the supply chain. What marks agile firms is not insulation from volatility but the precision with which they read it. Industry 4.0 technologies—above all, AI-powered forecasting, real-time supply chain visibility, and process automation—decode noise into actionable foresight. These technologies rewire operational reflexes, enabling firms to pivot with low friction. In a world of disruption, resilience is founded on relational depth and digital acuity, not reactive cost-cutting(Weber et al., 2023).

The application of IoT-driven predictive analytics across supply networks redefines responsiveness as ongoing recalibration rather than reactive adjustment. Real-time synchronisation of demand signals, inventory flows, and sustainability considerations is facilitated (Al-Talib et al., 2022). Inflation renders the economics of decarbonisation challenging, but short-term cost aversion typically obscures longer-term efficiency savings. The Total Cost of Ownership approach addresses this short-termism by revealing embedded value—lower energy loads, leaner resource cycles, and lower emissions. When firms co-finance low-carbon technologies and decentralised logistics, cost is a strategic lever, not a limiting factor. The repositioning rethinks supply chains not as liabilities to be managed, but as orchestrated systems that can compound resilience and environmental return concurrently (Dai et al., 2021).

Additionally, institutional pressures and regulatory mandates encourage sustainable supply chain management with a focus on the integration of technological innovations and governance structures to facilitate decarbonisation. Financial sustainability in attaining sustainability requires businesses to adopt cost-reduction models such as lean manufacturing, green logistics, and circular economy principles. A circular economy enables recycling of materials, minimisation of waste, and resource efficiency, with cost as well as environmental benefits. AI-powered demand forecasting and blockchain-enabled track and trace optimise inventory management, reduce waste, and enhance profitability, particularly in food and FMCG supply chains (Adewale et al., 2024).

Collaborative supply chain investments yield significant cost and environmental benefits, as demonstrated by Migros Trading Joint Stock Company, which achieved a balance between cost management and sustainability efforts to attain long-term profitability (Karcıoğlu & Öztürk, 2022). Sustainable procurement agreements also facilitate a crucial balance between cost reduction and risk mitigation, as companies must negotiate agreements that provide a hedge against economic risk while still fulfilling their sustainability commitments. Cost-benefit trade-off models and contract analysis enable companies to strengthen supplier alliances while mitigating exposure to economic risks. Data-oriented procurement models facilitate long-term sustainability partnerships among original equipment manufacturers (OEMs), suppliers, and retail partners, aiming to deliver greater stability to the supply chain (Dubey et al., 2018).

Additionally, mathematical programming models integrate cost control and logistics operations with environmental considerations, optimising transportation systems by minimising energy consumption, inventory costs, and carbon emissions, and potentially achieving cost savings of €25 million and reduced environmental impacts (Egami, 2024). Decarbonised supply chains, however, require an integrated approach to risk management in a trade-off between economic stability and sustainability factors. Decarbonisation can be achieved in organisational contexts through the adoption of early risk identification measures, the development of adequate contingency plans, and the establishment of cost-effective models that link investments in sustainability to long-term economic gains. Digitalisation, circular economy concepts, and collaboration with suppliers enable resilience in supply chains by reducing vulnerabilities and improving the capacity to adapt. With volatile market conditions prevailing in a rapidly changing business environment, firms that adopt sustainability-based strategies in risk management will achieve long-term stability, competitiveness, and economic sustainability.

10. FUTURE TRENDS AND OPPORTUNITIES

Technological innovations for energy and emissions management are quietly redefining the horizons of global supply chains, not just as compliance levers but as drivers of strategic change. Once a laboratory curiosity, green hydrogen is now carving out its niche in industrial decarbonisation—not just as a source of energy but as a replacement for carbon-intensive feedstocks for steel and cement production (Noussan et al., 2020). It is like a molecular diplomat, bridging the gaps of energy needs and environmental requirements. Intelligent grids, choreographed by 5G-enabled IoT infrastructures, operate with the precision of a surgeon—dispensing energy, predicting demand, and eliminating systemic inefficiencies that had previously eluded detection (Adenekan et al., 2024). Carbon capture is no longer on the fringes of environmental policy; technologies such as direct air capture and oceanic sequestration have become engineered ecosystems, merging the sensitivity of the natural world with the rigour of the industrial world (Esiri et al., 2024; Hari et al., 2020).

Energy storage technologies—whether solid-state batteries or 3D electrode systems—are time vaults, storing today's renewable energy for the uncertainties of the future, stabilising the grid in a world growing increasingly allergic to fossil dependency (Falkowski et al., 2024). The emerging replacement of lithium-ion materials with bio-based carbon represents a metaphorical reboot, turning back to nature to balance the excesses of extraction (Lin et al., 2024). The circular economy is no longer a niche dream; it is a self-healing loop where waste serves as input and the supply chain achieves metabolic efficiency (Falkowski et al., 2024).

Insetting, as opposed to offsetting, embeds carbon reduction into the operational bloodstream of firms, making green action a line item no longer but instead an ethos (Kakodkar et al., 2024). Not only does Blockchain record such changes—it consecrates them, making them visible, verifiable, and valuable (Zhang et al., 2024). As the unpredictability of geopolitics and the pressures of the natural world intersect, such technologies are not only interventions—rather, they represent the infrastructure of resilience, rewriting the logic upon which commerce and carbon exist.

11. METAFRAMEWORK

The decarbonisation model presents a web of dependencies, with economic pressure, regulation, technology, customer demand, and finance intersecting to shape sustainable supply chains. Inflation forces firms, especially small and medium-sized enterprises (SMEs), to make their processes leaner through AI-driven logistics, automation, and the principles of the circular economy, such as optimising the efficiency of a machine's components. Regulation is a source of challenge and stimulus, with compliance costs on the one side and emissions reduction on the other. Technology, from the transparency of blockchain to the traceability of IoT and renewable energy, sharpens the resilience of the supply chain. Customer demand is the compass guiding firms toward green investments. Financial tools, such as green bonds and public-private partnerships, open the door to cost-saving decarbonisation, making firms more resilient against economic shocks.

12. CONCLUSION

Decarbonising supply chains under conditions of inflation calls for a delicate balance—where economic demands don't take precedence from environmental needs. Regulation systems must be flexible, nudging low-carbon take-up rather than triggering lockdown. Firms, on the other hand, must embed cost-saving sustainability into core processes, not as an afterthought but as inherent reasoning. Consumers' demand is dynamic, insistent, and continuously reshaping market aspirations. In such a scenario, awareness is revolutionary—not as a slogan, but as a driver that reshapes preferences and behaviors. It is only with active participation and systemic alignment that supply chains become conduits of environmental integrity, rather than conduits of displaced responsibility.

Resilience, grounded on strategic foresight, enables firms to realign during disruption without compromise on sustainability or fiscal prudence. Technology is no longer adjunct—it is the structural backbone. AI investments for predictive precision, blockchain for the integrity of transactions, and decentralised renewable energy as buffers against inflation reframe operational agility. No firm, however, exists in isolation. Coherence across regulatory systems, real corporate accountability, and long-term consumer advocacy constitute a triadic power force driving systemic change. As volatility accumulates, the principles of the circular economy and cross-sector partnerships offer no escape routes, but calculated entry points into future-proof, economically sound, and ecologically integrated supply chain systems.

REFERENCES

Accenture. (2021). How AI Can Enable a Sustainable Future. https://www.accenture.com

Adenekan, N, Ezeigweneme, N., & Chukwurah, N. (2024). Driving innovation in energy and telecommunications: Next-generation energy storage and 5G technology for enhanced connectivity and energy solutions. *International Journal of Management & Entrepreneurship Research*, *6*(5), 1581–1597. DOI: 10.51594/ijmer.v6i5.1124

Adewale, T., Nsisong, *., Eyo-Udo, L., Toromade, A., & Ngochindo, A. (2024). Integrating sustainability and cost-effectiveness in food and FMCG supply chains: A comprehensive model. *Comprehensive Research and Reviews Journal.*

Al-Talib, M., Anosike, A., Arturo, J., Nadeem, S., & Melhem, W. (2022). Utilising IoT to attain resilience across supply chains. *Proceedings of the International Conference on Industrial Engineering and Operations Management.*

Amazon. (2021). Amazon's commitment to sustainability. https://www.aboutamazon.com

Anderson, B., & Tushman, M. (2021). The role of sustainability in global supply chains: A decarbonization perspective. *The Journal of Supply Chain Management*, *57*(2), 89–105.

Apple. (2021). Apple's environmental progress report. https://www.apple.com

Arfaoui, N., Chaâbane, N., Gaies, B., & Messaoud, J. (2023). Are sustainable investments interdependent? The international evidence. *Journal of Sustainable Finance & Investment*, *13*(1), 1–25.

Avazkhodjaev, S., Mamasobirov, D., & Ganiev, A. A. G. (2023). Inflation, inflation uncertainty and output growth: Empirical evidence from transition economies in southeastern Europe. *Economic Analysis and Policy*, *77*, 123–134.

Ayad, H., Abbas, S., Nakhli, M. S., Jibir, A., & Shahzad, U. (2023). Industrial growth, health care policy uncertainty and carbon emissions: Do trade and tax policy uncertainties matter for sustainable development in the USA? *Structural Change and Economic Dynamics*, *66*, 151–160. DOI: 10.1016/j.strueco.2023.04.005

Baldwin, R., & Freeman, R. (2022). Carbon pricing and supply chain adaptation: A review of global mechanisms. *Energy Policy*, *158*, 112345.

Barbosa, L. C., & Santos, M. R. (2020). The effectiveness of carbon border adjustment mechanisms in reducing emissions. *Environmental Science & Policy*, *107*, 28–36.

Barney, J. (1991). Firm resources and sustained competitive advantage. *Journal of Management, 17*(1), 99–120. DOI: 10.1177/014920639101700108

Berkhout, F., & Smith, A. (2021). Climate regulations and firm strategy: A case study analysis. *Business Strategy and the Environment, 30*(3), 1430–1448.

Bertsimas, D., Cory-Wright, R., & Digalakis, V., Jr. (2022). Decarbonizing OCP. *arXiv preprint arXiv:2209.06341*.https://arxiv.org/abs/2209.06341

Brown, T., & Green, J. (2023). ESG disclosures and corporate sustainability: Policy implications for supply chains. *Journal of Business Ethics, 180*, 103–122.

Carboni, J., & Kumar, P. (2021). The economic impact of carbon trading schemes: A global review. *Climate Policy, 21*(5), 670–689.

CDP. (2020). Global supply chain report 2020. https://www.cdp.net

Chen, H., & Zhao, W. (2022). Decarbonization policies in the logistics sector: An empirical assessment. *Transportation Research Part D, Transport and Environment, 105*, 103233.

Christopher, M., & Peck, H. (2004). Building the resilient supply chain. *International Journal of Logistics Management, 15*(2), 1–14. DOI: 10.1108/09574090410700275

Clark, M., & Tilman, D. (2021). Sustainability in supply chains: The role of eco-friendly consumer preferences. *Nature Sustainability, 4*(6), 456–462.

Climate Bonds Initiative. (2021). Green bonds and sustainable finance. https://www.climatebonds.net

Crespy, A., & Munta, M. (2023). Lost in transition? Social justice and the politics of the EU green transition. *Transfer: European Review of Labour and Research, 29*(2), 235–251. DOI: 10.1177/10242589231173072

Dahlmann, F., & Branicki, L. (2022). The role of corporate green bonds in financing decarbonization. *Journal of Sustainable Finance & Investment, 12*(2), 178–198.

Dai, J., Xie, L., & Chu, Z. (2021). Developing sustainable supply chain management: The interplay of institutional pressures and sustainability capabilities. *Sustainable Production and Consumption, 28*, 254–268. DOI: 10.1016/j.spc.2021.04.017

Dauvergne, P. (2020). The green economy illusion: Corporate sustainability and environmental harm. *Global Environmental Politics, 20*(1), 87–105.

de Lange, R., & Jackson-Moore, W. (2024). From trade-offs to payoffs: CEOs on creating value with climate action. *PwC*.https://www.pwc.com/gx/en/issues/esg/ceos-creating-value-climate-action.html

DHL. (2020). DHL's sustainability initiatives. https://www.dhl.com

Doyle, M., & McKinley, J. (2023). Carbon neutrality and business resilience: The impact of regulatory frameworks. *Sustainable Development*, *31*(1), 55–72.

Dubey, V., Chavas, J., & Veeramani, D. (2018). Analytical framework for sustainable supply-chain contract management. *International Journal of Production Economics*, *200*, 240–261. DOI: 10.1016/j.ijpe.2018.03.003

Egami, R. (2024). Mathematical programming model for cost-optimized and environmentally sustainable supply chain design. *AIP Advances*, *14*(2), 025230. DOI: 10.1063/5.0192256

Ellen MacArthur Foundation. (2019). Circular economy in cities: Project guide. https://www.ellenmacarthurfoundation.org

EPA. (2020). Lean manufacturing and the environment. https://www.epa.gov

Esiri, N. E., Jambol, N. D. D., & Ozowe, N. C. (2024). Best practices and innovations in carbon capture and storage (CCS) for effective CO2 storage. *International Journal of Applied Research in Social Sciences*, *6*(6), 1227–1243. DOI: 10.51594/ijarss.v6i6.1212

European Commission. (2022). Carbon Border Adjustment Mechanism. https://ec.europa.eu

Evans, J., & Fang, X. (2021). Green finance: The effectiveness of sustainability-linked loans. *Finance Research Letters*, *42*, 101867.

Falkowski, V., Reinhold, C., Rist, U., Sterzl, Y., & Pfleging, W. (2024). Next-Generation Batteries through Advanced 3D Electrode and Material Concepts. *ECS Meeting Abstracts*.

Fankhauser, S., & Hepburn, C. (2020). The role of carbon taxation in a just transition. *Oxford Review of Economic Policy*, *36*(2), 285–304.

Farah, A., Wu, J., & Zhang, J. (2024). Co-optimizing cost and CO_2 emissions for green hydrogen production in grid-connected renewable energy systems. *arXiv preprint arXiv:2404.11995*.https://arxiv.org/abs/2404.11995

Farooq, U. (2023). Economic growth, foreign investment, tourism, and electricity production as determinants of economic performance. *Journal of Economic Studies (Glasgow, Scotland)*, *50*(2), 1–15.

Fleschutz, M., Bohlayer, M., Braun, M., & Murphy, M. D. (2023). From prosumer to flexumer: Case study on the value of flexibility in decarbonizing the multi-energy system of a manufacturing company. *arXiv preprint arXiv:2301.07997*.https://arxiv.org/abs/2301.07997

França, A., López-Manuel, L., Sartal, A., & Vázquez, X. H. (2023). Adapting corporations to climate change: How decarbonization impacts the business strategy–performance nexus. *Business Strategy and the Environment*, *32*(8), 5615–5632. DOI: 10.1002/bse.3439

Freeman, R. E. (1984). *Strategic management: A stakeholder approach*. Pitman.

Gielen, D., & Boshell, F. (2022). Renewable energy and decarbonization in global industries. *Energy Strategy Reviews*, *42*, 100884.

Gold, S., & Heikkurinen, P. (2018). Transparency fallacy: Unintended consequences of stakeholder claims on responsibility in supply chains. *Accounting, Auditing & Accountability Journal*, *31*(1), 318–337. DOI: 10.1108/AAAJ-06-2015-2088

Goodarzi, S., & Li, L. (2023). Economic viability of the energy-water-hydrogen nexus for power system decarbonization. *arXiv preprint arXiv:2311.07891*.https://arxiv.org/abs/2311.07891

Gopalakrishnan, B., & Matthews, D. (2023). The impact of government subsidies on sustainable technology adoption. *Energy Economics*, *119*, 105381.

Haider, A. (2015). Impact of immigration on economic growth in Canada and in its smaller provinces. *International Migration (Geneva, Switzerland)*, *53*(2), 1–21.

Hajarath, K., & Vummadi, J. (2024). Analysing Different Risk Management Approaches and Their Effectiveness in Enhancing Supply Chain Resilience. *International Journal of Supply Chain Management*.

Hari, R., Balaji, P., & Karunamurthy, K. (2020). Carbon Capture and Storage Using Renewable Energy Sources: A Review. *IOP Conference Series. Earth and Environmental Science*, 573.

Hassan, S. T., & Xia, E. (2023). How do green energy investment, economic policy uncertainty, and natural resources affect greenhouse gas emissions? *Environmental Science and Pollution Research International*.

Hofmann, F., Böing, F., & Bertsch, V. (2024). Hydrogen and CO_2 network strategies for the European energy system. *Nature Communications*, *15*(1), 1–14. PMID: 38169466

IKEA. (2021). IKEA's renewable energy goals. Retrieved from https://www.ikea.com

IRENA. (2021). Capturing Carbon: Exploring the Role of Carbon Capture and Storage. Abu Dhabi: IRENA. https://www.irena.org/-/media/Irena/Files/Technical-papers/IRENA_Capturing_Carbon_2021.pdf

Jerbi, A., Jribi, H., Aljuaid, A., Hachicha, W., & Masmoudi, F. (2022). Design of Supply Chain Transportation Pooling Strategy for Reducing CO2 Emissions Using a Simulation-Based Methodology: A Case Study. *Sustainability*.

Kakodkar, R., Allen, R., Demirhan, C., Fu, X., Pappas, I., Mutlu, M., & Pistikopoulos, E. (2024). Multiperiod Modeling and Optimization of Hydrogen-Based Dense Energy Carrier Supply Chains. *Processes (Basel, Switzerland)*, *12*(3), 469. DOI: 10.3390/pr12030469

Kamble, S. S., Gunasekaran, A., & Dhone, N. C. (2021). Blockchain technology for sustainable supply chain management. *International Journal of Production Research*, *59*(8), 2350–2381.

Karaosman, H., Marshall, D., & Ward, I. (2024). *For the many not the few: introducing just transition for supply chain management.*

Karcıoğlu, R., & Öztürk, S. (2022). Sustainable cost management in the supply chain: A case analysis. *HOLISTIC ECONOMICS*, *1*(1), 49–64. DOI: 10.55094/hoec.1.1.05

Kim, E., & Lee, Y. (2021). The role of blockchain in sustainable supply chains: Enhancing transparency and accountability. *Technological Forecasting and Social Change*, *170*, 120892.

Lin, W., Zhao, S., Lu, B., Jiang, F., Lu, Z., & Xu, Z. (2024). Structures, performances and applications of green biomass derived carbon in lithium-ion batteries. *Energy Materials*, *4*(5). DOI: 10.20517/energymater.2024.09

McKinsey & Company. (2021). The economic challenges of decarbonization. https://www.mckinsey.com

Mishra, P., & Sharma, R. (2022). Green bonds and investor behavior: Trends and challenges. *Journal of Environmental Management*, *316*, 115315.

Noussan, M., Raimondi, P., Scita, R., & Hafner, M. (2020). The Role of Green and Blue Hydrogen in the Energy Transition—A Technological and Geopolitical Perspective. *Sustainability (Basel)*, *13*(1), 298. DOI: 10.3390/su13010298

Nsude, C. C., Loraamm, R., Wimhurst, J. J., Chukwuonye, G. N., & Debnath, R. (2024). Renewables but unjust? Critical restoration geography as a framework for addressing global renewable energy injustice. *Energy Research & Social Science*, *114*, 103609. DOI: 10.1016/j.erss.2024.103609

Nygaard, A. (2022). The Geopolitical Risk and Strategic Uncertainty of Green Growth after the Ukraine Invasion: How the Circular Economy Can Decrease the Market Power of and Resource Dependency on Critical Minerals. *Circular Economy and Sustainability*, *3*(2), 1099–1126. DOI: 10.1007/s43615-022-00181-x

OECD. (2021). Economic implications of decarbonization. https://www.oecd.org

Quarton, C., & Samsatli, S. (2020). The value of hydrogen and carbon capture, storage and utilisation in decarbonising energy: Insights from integrated value chain optimisation. *Applied Energy*, *257*, 113936. DOI: 10.1016/j.apenergy.2019.113936

Research Network Sustainable Global Supply Chains. (2023). *Sustainable global supply chains in times of geopolitical crises: Annual report 2023*. Stiftung Wissenschaft und Politik (SWP).

Ritchie, H., & Roser, M. (2021). The impact of consumer preferences on supply chain sustainability. *Environmental Research Letters*, *16*(4), 045012.

Saberi, S., Kouhizadeh, M., & Sarkis, J. (2019). Blockchain technology and the sustainable supply chain: A review. *International Journal of Production Research*, *57*(7), 2092–2110. DOI: 10.1080/00207543.2018.1533261

Sarkis, J., & Zhu, Q. (2020). Environmental sustainability and supply chain resilience. *Journal of Cleaner Production*, *258*, 120774.

Sarkis, J., & Zhu, Q. (2020). Environmental sustainability and supply chain resilience. *Journal of Cleaner Production*, *258*, 120774.

Stone, M. (2022, July 13). Decarbonized supply chains are resilient supply chains. *McKinsey & Company*. https://www.mckinsey.com/~/media/mckinsey/email/rethink/2022/07/2022-07-13d.html

Tesla. (2021). Tesla's sustainability report. https://www.tesla.com

Uddin, G., & Rahman, M. (2023). Inflation, inflation uncertainty and output growth: Empirical evidence from transition economies in southeastern Europe. *Economic Analysis and Policy*, *77*, 123–134.

Unilever. (2023). Sustainability Report. https://unilever.com

Walker, H., & Jones, N. (2023). Circular economy practices in sustainable supply chains. *Resources, Conservation and Recycling*, *192*, 106828.

Wang, Q., Wang, X., & Li, R. (2024). Geopolitical risks and energy transition: The impact of environmental regulation and green innovation. *Humanities & Social Sciences Communications*, *11*(1), 1272. DOI: 10.1057/s41599-024-03770-3

Weber, M., Franke, P., & Aumueller, U. (2023). POSSIBILITIES AND LIMITS OF DIGITALIZATION TO INCREASE SUPPLY CHAIN RESILIENCE. *Beykent Üniversitesi Fen ve Mühendislik Bilimleri Dergisi*.

WEF. (2023). Clean Skies for Tomorrow Initiative. https://weforum.org

World Bank. (2023). Global Economic Prospects. https://worldbank.org

World Economic Forum. (2020). The future of supply chain decarbonization. https://www.weforum.org

Zhang, C., Xu, Y., & Zheng, Y. (2024). Blockchain Traceability Adoption in Low-Carbon Supply Chains: An Evolutionary Game Analysis. *Sustainability (Basel)*, *16*(5), 1817. DOI: 10.3390/su16051817

Chapter 8
The Rise of Circular Supply Chains:
Recycling and Closed-Loop Systems Could Mitigate Inflationary Pressures

Md Mehedi Hasan Emon
https://orcid.org/0000-0002-6224-9552
American International University-Bangladesh, Bangladesh

Tahsina Khan
https://orcid.org/0000-0001-8032-3376
Bangladesh University of Professionals, Bangladesh

ABSTRACT

The circular economy (CE) provides a transformational strategy for alleviating inflationary pressures via resource dependence reduction, supply chain optimization, and waste minimization. The contributions of circular business models, technical developments, and changing consumer behavior to economic stability are investigated in this chapter. Blockchain for supply chain transparency, predictive analytics powered by artificial intelligence, and IoT-enabled resource efficiency are among the fundamental technologies. Furthermore, helping to reduce price volatility and stabilize production costs are remanufacturing, recycling, and second-hand markets. Businesses may increase supply chain resilience, lower running costs, and provide consumers with reasonably priced, environmentally friendly choices by using circular economy concepts. The importance of using circular solutions to solve inflationary issues and promote long-term economic sustainability is underlined in this chapter.

DOI: 10.4018/979-8-3373-1982-7.ch008

OVERVIEW OF THE CHAPTER

The effectiveness of circular supply networks in deflating inflationary pressures and building supply chain resilience is examined in this chapter. Raw material scarcity, geo-political push towards greater disruption in global supply networks, and economic instability are making the traditional linear model of the supply chain increasingly unworkable. The chapter exposes the idea of circular economies by highlighting key ideas such waste reduction, resource recovery and closed-loop systems. This explains how integration of circular economy (CE) concepts to supply chain management may increase efficiency of resources, reduce dependency on unconsolidated material sources and enable long term economic stability. The chapter emphasizes how technological progress such as blockchain, IoT and AI through better traceability, transparency and working efficiency can support the strengthening of circular supply chain. Examining customer behavior shows how the demand for sustainable products influences company decision making, should help companies to develop circular processes.

This chapter is filled with real world cases from a variety of disciplines which demonstrate how the CE concepts are applied and how they influence cost control and inflation reduction. In addition, it makes policy recommendations to businesses and governments highlighting the requirement of technological investment, stakeholder involvement and regulatory support to enhance such expansions of circular supply chains. This chapter makes the case that changing to a CE is not only an environmental requirement but also a cash alternative to enhance stability and resilience in a growing turbulent global market.

RETHINKING SUPPLY CHAINS IN AN ERA OF DISRUPTIONS

Geopolitical wars, pandemics as well as missing raw materials and laws aimed at environmental sustainability have made hitherto unheard-of challenges for the world supply chains. These upheavals have generated inflationary pressures, increased cost of production and transportation etc. which have increased the prices of goods and services. Conventional supply chains exist mostly in the linear "take-make-dispose" model, and are fast becoming unsustainable because of the high dependence on a few resources and inadequate waste management (Emon & Khan, 2024b; Kirchherr et al., 2023).

The CE provides a paradigm shift by prioritizing the issues of sustainability, resource economies and waste reduction. Via the use of closed-loop systems and re-manufacturing and recycling, firms may lessen dependence on raw materials, harden their resilience to supply disruptions, and in the long term offer stable costs via which. The de-inflationary consequence of this move is hinged on this because companies with circular supply chains enjoy lower material costs, better operating efficiency, and lower-price volatility. In addition technical innovations such as artificial intelligence (AI), blockchain, the Internet of Things (IoT) are extremely important in enabling circular supply chains more scalable and efficient as these technologies drive traceability, the allocation of resources and waste management practices (Emon et al., 2025; Seyyedi et al., 2024).

UNDERSTANDING CIRCULAR ECONOMIES: A SUSTAINABLE SHIFT IN SUPPLY CHAINS

Circular economics (CE) represents a turning point from the traditional linear supply chain model involving "take-make-dispose" approach to a closed-loop model that is premised on sustainability, efficiency, and perpetual economic sustainability (Kirchherr et al., 2023). Whereas linear models that are dependent on finite resources and waste a great deal but ensure constant utilization of resources, CE's put waste minimization, resource recovery and product lifecycle management of paramount importance. As world trade is discussing issues of environmental concern, changing prices of basic supplies, and scarcity of resources, this method is gradually becoming increasingly important.

Key Principles of Circular Economies

1. Waste Reduction: Minimizing Environmental Impact

The main objective of CE is waste reduction through creating objects which are reusable, refurbish able, or recyclable. This idea supports the use of ecologically friendly manufacturing techniques like modular designs that enable component re-placement and repair and biodegradable materials. Companies like Apple and IKEA have led waste reduction projects involving circular practices using take-back programs and the manufacturing of items using recyclable or reused materials. Moreover, businesses are increasingly using industrial symbiosis where waste from one activity provides a raw supply for another. Leftovers from steel production including blast furnace slag are utilized as raw materials in the cement sector, therefore reducing waste and the need for virgin resources (Falsafi & Fornasiero, 2022).

2. Resource Recovery: Maximizing Material Efficiency

Resource recovery is a crucial component of the CE, emphasizing the extraction of value from used materials to diminish reliance on virgin resources. By means of advanced recycling and material recovery strategies, companies may lessen their reliance on scarce or expensive raw resources, thus strengthening supply chain resilience and so mitigating cost volatility. By recovering valuable metals including gold, silver, and palladium from outdated electrical devices, the electronics industry best shows resource recovery. Companies like Dell and HP have started recycling programs to collect and reinterpret important materials from outdated products, therefore reducing the environmental effects of mining and manufacturing costs. Moreover, recovery of biological resources is increasingly common in fields like energy and agriculture. A sustainable energy source, biogas synthesis from organic waste simultaneously addresses waste management problems (Dhanya et al., 2020; Khan et al., 2024).

3. Product Lifecycle Management: Extending Product Utility

Product lifecycle management (PLM) seeks to prolong the utility of products via repair, remanufacturing, and repurposing, therefore guaranteeing that items stay operational for an extended duration prior to disposal. This approach makes goods more affordable and sustainable as it lowers environmental effects and consumer costs. Remanufacturing—that is, rebuilding and improving vehicle components rather than producing new ones has been embraced by the automotive sector Remanufacturing projects started by companies like Bosch and Caterpillar revitalize old components to a condition like new, therefore reducing material waste and energy consumption. Circular models best shown by companies like Patagonia and H&M, who have started resale and repair programs to extend the life of clothing are being embraced by the fashion industry more and more. This benefits consumers as well as helps to reduce the environmental effects of fast fashion, a major contributor to world waste (Cesarina Mason et al., 2022).

The Economic and Environmental Benefits of Circular Economies

The shift to circular supply networks has substantial economic and ecological benefits. Companies may lower manufacturing costs, increase efficiency, and build long-lasting resilience against inflationary pressures by reducing dependency on raw materials, improving waste management, and extending product lifetimes (Glavič, 2021). CE's line up with world sustainability goals, particularly the United Nations Sustainable Development Goals (SDGs), which support ethical consumption and manufacturing. Guaranteeing resource security, cost stability, and long-term company sustainability, the CE is both an environmental need and an economic need (Emon & Khan, 2024a).

DIFFERENCES BETWEEN LINEAR AND CIRCULAR SUPPLY CHAINS

Traditionally, supply chains followed a linear model wherein resources were obtained, transformed into items, consumed, and finally disposed away. For decades, this approach has dominated industrial production, producing significant waste creation, resource depletion, and environmental degradation. Conversely, circular supply chains aim to create a closed-loop system that lowers waste, improves resource economy, and includes sustainability into the production process.

Companies and governments striving to reduce supply chain disruptions, save costs, and address climate change concerns that is, from linear to circular supply chains increasingly depend on this move from linear to circular supply networks (Park et al., 2022). The main differences between linear and circular supply chains throughout various aspects are shown in the table below:

Table 1.

Aspect	Linear Supply Chains	Circular Supply Chains
Resource Utilization	Extractive and wasteful	Regenerative and efficient
Waste Management	Disposal at end-of-life	Reuse, recycling, remanufacturing
Cost Implications	High due to new material acquisition	Reduced through material recovery
Environmental Impact	High carbon footprint	Lower emissions and pollution

1. Resource Utilization: Extractive vs. Regenerative Approaches

Linear supply chains depend on an extractive framework that involves the continual harvesting, processing, and disposal of natural resources, resulting in resource depletion and heightened production costs. Industries dependent on limited resources face pricing volatility and supply uncertainty as the world's demand for raw materials rises. Rare earth metals, which are both restricted in supply and impacted by geopolitics and export restrictions, are much relied upon in the electronics industry. Regenerative methods are given top priority in circular supply chains, thereby ensuring that resources and commodities are employed for maximum lifetime. By means of recycling, repair, and remanufacturing, businesses may drastically reduce their need for virgin resources. Remanufacturing techniques for engine components have been utilized by automakers like Renault and BMW, therefore lowering material consumption and production costs (Sarfraz et al., 2021).

2. Waste Management: Disposal vs. Recovery

Linear supply chains substantially contribute to waste generation owing to its "take-make-dispose" methodology. With a significant amount originating from industrial production and packaging waste, the (Sharma & Jain, 2020) forecasts that global solid waste output would reach 3.4 billion tons by 2050. Reusability of resources and waste recovery come first in circular supply chains. This covers methods include remanufacturing, upcycling, and product take-back campaigns, thereby ensuring that items are reintegrated into the supply chain rather being thrown away. Nike's Reuse A Shoe project reduces waste and the need of raw material by collecting and reusing old shoes to form new sports surfaces.

3. Cost Implications: High Expenditure vs. Cost Optimization

Linear supply chains tend to spend more incurring increased costs, which is because of dependence on fresh material purchase, disposal costs, and energy-intensive manufacturing mechanisms. Commodity price fluctuations worsen the financial strain businesses are under. The rising cost of crude oil instantly affects the plastics and packaging industries, hence raising running costs (Ncube et al., 2020). By means of material recovery optimization and waste reduction, circular supply networks provide significant financial advantages. Closed-loop system users have lowered landfill costs, lowered raw material prices, and improved energy efficiency. The firms, Dell and HP, have used efficient circular strategies by reusing various parts from outdated devices to reduce manufacturing costs and e-waste disposal costs.

4. Environmental Impact: High Carbon Footprint vs. Sustainability

The environmental effects of linear chains are far reaching, causing an increased level of greenhouse gas (GHG) emissions and pollution whilst reducing biodiversity. Fashion industry produces about 10% of world carbon emissions largely as a result rapid fashion manufacture, textile waste and water pollution. However, circular supply networks offer a viable solution to cut environmental destruction and carbon emissions. Given the effort put in place, recycling, eco-design, and usage of renewable energy sources – that all combined will help considerably reduce the environmental burden on the environment. Patagonia Worn Wear project promotes repairing and reuse of clothing thus reducing textile waste and energy use (Khan et al., 2020).

Economic and Strategic Benefits of Transitioning to Circular Supply Chains

Several strategic and financial benefits are evident by the transition from linear to circular supply chains include:

- **Cost Savings:** Through recycling and remanufacturing and thus lightening the dependency on expensive raw materials.
- **Supply Chain Resilience:** By distributing input sources, minimizing supply chain interferences may enhance resource security.
- **Regulatory Compliance:** After the world sustainability frameworks like the UN SDGs United Nations, 2022 and the EU Green Deal.
- **Competitive Advantage:** The market uniqueness and enhanced brand recognition are what companies using the circular models get.

Initially the dominant strategy, linear supply chains are becoming unsustainable due to resource depletion, rising pricing, and environmental damage. A sustainable alternative that increases resource efficiency, reduces waste, and strengthens supply chain resilience is circular supply networks. The move towards closed-loop systems will be crucial in relieving inflationary pressures, ensuring long-term sustainability, and therefore meeting global climate goals as businesses and governments recognize the economic and environmental advantages of circularity.

CASE STUDIES: SUCCESSFUL CIRCULAR ECONOMY IMPLEMENTATIONS

As global supply chains rapidly shift towards sustainability, several businesses are adopting CE ideas to augment resource efficiency, minimize waste, and bolster overall resilience. Emphasizing good use of CE ideas, this part features five case studies from various sectors. These cases show how companies using creative ideas are simultaneously solving environmental issues and obtaining financial benefits.

Case Study 1. Automotive Industry: Renault's Circular Supply Chain Model

Renowned automaton Renault has made significant progress in implementing circular economic concepts with their business practices. Resource constraints and rising carbon emissions provide serious problems for the automotive industry; so, companies like Renault need to rethink their supply chain approach.

Remanufacturing, recycling, and modular design are placed at a very high priority in the enormous circular supply chain architecture Renault has developed. This strategy is based on their remanufacturing plant in Flins, France; where the engine, gearbox, and electrical system components are rebuilt to the quality standards as that of the new parts (Pérez et al., 2025). Apart from remanufacturing, Renault pays attention to the element recycling from retired vehicles. The company cooperates with recycling companies to find precious resources such as plastics and metals for reuse during the production process. This minimizes the waste output and the need for raw materials too. Renaults commitment to modular design enables easy maintenance and replacement of many components on vehicles leading to a prolonged life for vehicles all in all. This design concept reduces reliance on resources and reduces the need for additional components.

The use of circular processes has therefore made Renault have much lower carbon emissions, and production cost. The company's activities in component remanufacturing and recycling have reduced resource usage significantly. According to Renault's sustainability report, remanufacturing reduces CO2 emissions by up to 70% compared with manufacturing new items from raw material (Albertsen et al., 2021). This holistic approach positions Renault as a leader in the market for automotive businesses and illustrates the potential way in which concepts from the CE might offer financial and environmental advantage.

Case Study 2. Consumer Electronics: Dell's Closed-Loop Recycling Program

E-waste is one of the fastest-growing waste sources globally and the consumer electronics sector has a great conundrum with electronic trash. Dell, an advanced technology company, has overcome this challenge through using a closed-loop recycling scheme that incorporates CE concepts.

Dell's closed-loop-recycling initiative makes it possible for the recovery of resources from old devices for a reuse process in new good manufacturing. Customers are encouraged to return unwanted gadgets through Dell's take back program, they provide easy and convenient way for proper disposal of equipment (Radtke et al., 2022). When the devices are returned, Dell recovers the precious components such as copper, aluminum and plastics from the materials. These materials can be then applied for the production of new Dell goods providing thus the closing of the loop and decreasing the dependence on the virgin resources. Dell prioritizes the creation of goods with environmental considerations, including recycled materials into their gadgets. For example, the company's XPS laptops use recycled carbon fiber and polymers, underscoring Dell's dedication to reducing its environmental impact.

The closed-loop recycling program has produced substantial outcomes for Dell. In 2022, Dell reported the collection of nearly 2 billion pounds of discarded electronics worldwide, successfully diverting these items from landfills (Wilson & Goffnett, 2022).

Case Study 3. Fashion Industry: Patagonia's Worn Wear Program

The fashion industry is notorious for its negative effects on the environment, which result in a lot of garbage and pollution. With its Worn Wear campaign, which models CE ideas, outdoor clothing company Patagonia has become well-known for sustainable design. The Worn Wear program of Patagonia encourages the recycling, resale, or repair of used clothing. The company offers clothes repair services, therefore promoting sustainability and reducing the need for new purchases by helping to fix damaged goods. Consumers may trade their worn Patagonia products for store credit, which is then fixed and resold for lessened prices. The effort emphasizes the need to extend product lifetime and lower textile waste. Patagonia works to change customer behavior toward sustainability by encouraging clothing repair and reuse. The Worn Wear program of Patagonia has demonstrated financial benefits. Within one year, the company claimed, sales of its refurbished goods provided by the Worn Wear program totaled $10 million (Tewary & Upadhyay, 2025).

Case Study 4. Retail Sector: IKEA's Circular Business Model

Renowned furniture retailer IKEA has admitted the necessity of using CE ideas to solve environmental problems and improve sustainability in its activities. Significant waste generation in the retail sector, especially from furniture and packaging, characterizes it and calls for a change to more sustainable approaches.

IKEA started many circularity-oriented programs including furniture take-back and resale initiatives. Consumers may bring unwanted furniture back to IKEA, where it is refurbished and then resold for lessened rates. This program not only reduces waste but also improves consumer access to sustainable furniture options. Apart from running take-back programs, IKEA is investing in renewable energy and creating products for maximum disassembly and recycling. By 2030 the company wants to use only recyclable and renewable resources in its goods, therefore drastically lowering its environmental impact (Cudjoe et al., 2021). IKEA has pledged to eliminate single use plastics from its product line and calls for sustainability in packaging. The firm is exploring new packaging solutions that conserve waste while at the same time increasing product protection.

The circular operations of IKEA have been receiving positive results as the company states that thousands of tons of furniture have been successfully moved from landfills through their take-back and resale activities. By supporting reuse, the IKEA is helping to counteract the effects of the swings in prices and limited raw materials as it brings in consumers looking for green substitutes. This circular business template apart from ramping IKEA up as ethical store, this strategic strategy makes the company prepared to be successful in a competitive arena for the long run (Vadakkepatt et al., 2021).

Case Study 5. Food and Beverage Industry: Loop's Reusable Packaging Initiative

The food and beverage industry plays a major role in increasing packaging waste, and therefore innovative ideas for better sustainability are very much required. Loop, a global circulation packaging platform, has become an industry leader in solving this problem via a reusing packaging initiative, Loop.

To offer its consumers durable and returnable containers for their products, Loop collaborates with established companies including Nestlé and Unilever. Consumers buy reusable packaging, which can then be returned to the Loop for cleaning and refilling aimed at dramatically reducing single use wastes (Coelho et al., 2020). The idea establishes a circular flow of products with the reduced effect of packing on the environment. Loop's strategy encourages corporate entities to design packaging that would be long-lived such that they can be part of the CE and promote environmentally friendly consumption.

Customers' positive response to the reuseable packaging movement taken up by Loop has improved brand image and created loyalty from the consumer. Loop provides green alternatives for single-use packaging to satisfy increasing consumer demand for green products from companies (Diprose et al., 2023). In addition, one can reuse the reusable containers several rather than throw away after one use, thus cutting packaging cost for the consumers and for the companies in the long run.

These case studies reveal the areas of application of the concepts of CE. Companies in the automotive, fashion, technology, retail, food and beverages, using innovative methods, are effectively integrating sustainability into the supply chain. These companies not only decrease their environmental footprint but also enhanced resilience, best use of resources, and increased economic return through the use of circular approaches. The transition to sustainable practices will continue to impact on the world's supply chains while helping to establish a sustainable future for all as more businesses come to understand the value of circularity.

TECHNOLOGICAL INNOVATION AND CIRCULAR ECONOMIES

Technological advancements are reshaping CE concepts' application through increased efficiency, transparency and their sustainability in supply chains. Innovative technological solutions are required to translate from conventionally linear models, which are defined in terms of exploration, usage, and discarding, to circular ones, which emphasize reuse, recycling, and remanufacturing. Emerging technologies like blockchain, the IoT, and AI are critically cardinal in facilitating ready improvement in resource utilization, transparency improvement, and waste reduction (Emon et al., 2024).

Blockchain for Supply Chain Transparency

The unchangeable, distributed ledger system provided by blockchain technology brings more traceability and openness to circular supply chains. Ensuring the authenticity of recycled goods and monitoring the lifetime of recycled goods is crucial to minimization of fraud and contribution to consumer trust in a CE. Starting from the purchase of raw materials to disposing or reuse after the goods, blockchain delivers smooth records of every deal; hence develops a verifiable digital record. Blockchain's ability to allow material passport systems tracking of the composition, source, and history of materials used in manufacture is a main advantage. Blockchain is being used by fashion and electronics companies to confirm the authenticity of recycled goods. This ensures conformity to environmental standards and strengthens brand trust (Waris et al., 2024).

Reverse logistics are a necessary part of circular supply chains also enhanced by blockchain technology. By using a transparent monitoring system, blockchain enables effective remanufacturing, refurbishments, and returns of products. By tracking food supply chains thanks to IBM's Food Trust blockchain technology, companies like Nestlé and Walmart help to reduce food waste and improve safety (Sharma & Singh, 2022). Using blockchain technology to track returned diamonds and electronics, companies like Ever ledger ensure ethical recycling practices and responsible procurement. Blockchain has challenges like large energy consumption and integration issues even with its advantages. Green blockchain technologies and hybrid models combining blockchain with IoT are helping to reduce these restrictions, therefore enabling a possible tool for circular supply chains (Emon, 2025).

Internet of Things (IoT) for Resource Optimization

IoT is revolutionizing circular economies via real-time monitoring and data acquisition, enhancing resource efficiency, and minimizing waste. IoT technologies which include RFID tags and smart sensors help businesses track product usage, monitor environmental conditions, and project maintenance needs, thereby extending the lifetime of products and improving efficiency. Predictive maintenance of consumer electronics is one obvious IoT use. IoT-enabled sensors find equipment and component degradation in areas like manufacturing and transportation, therefore enabling early repairs before failure. By prolonging product use, this reduces downtime, prevents wasteful replacements, and promotes sustainability. For its aviation engines, Rolls-Royce uses IoT-driven predictive maintenance, for example, thereby improving fuel efficiency and reducing waste.

Product-as-a-service (PaaS) business models are made possible by IoT, in which companies retain ownership of objects and provide them as services rather than directly sold ones. With IoT sensors to track use, Philips provides lighting-as-a-service, therefore optimizing energy consumption and reducing electrical waste (Kandpal et al., 2024). Likewise, tire companies like Michelin provide tires as a service, tracking wear and performance using IoT to thus guarantee quick replacements and minimize material waste.

Artificial Intelligence (AI) for Predictive Analytics

Data-driven decision-making, improved inventory control, and targeted waste reduction strategies are helping AI change circular economies. Predictive analytics enabled by AI help businesses to forecast demand, maximize manufacturing, and reduce excess inventory, thereby improving the effectiveness of closed-loop supply chains. Material sorting and recycling in the CE makes a major application for AI (Emon & Khan, 2025a). Many times, conventional recycling techniques run into inefficiencies resulting from contamination and poor sorting. Showcased as AMP Robotics, AI-powered robotic devices employ machine learning to accurately identify and separate different materials, hence improving recycling rates and lowering landfill trash. These technologies advance circular supply network sustainability and help to recover resources.

Design of circular products depends much on AI. AI is used in generative design algorithms to create objects with less raw materials, faster disassembly, and extended lifetime that need less manufacturing. By use of AI and 3D printing, Adidas's Future craft Loop project produces completely recyclable shoes, therefore reducing environmental effect and encouraging circularity in the fashion industry (Khan & Hasan Emon, 2024; Maguire & Robson, 2023). Moreover, by means of automated customer engagement and sustainable consumption analysis, AI helps to create circular businesses. AI-driven chatbots and recommendation systems are used by companies to let consumers know about choices for product recycling and support environmentally friendly buying behavior (Sinha et al., 2024). Using AI-generated insights, companies might improve pricing policies, reduce excess production, and coordinate their activities with ideas from the CE.

Digital Twin Technology for Circular Manufacturing

In circular economies, digital twin technology which creates virtual copies of real objects and processes be sure that it cues ever more important. By means of the modeling of real-world processes, digital twins help manufacturers in testing and optimizing circular procedures, thereby reducing trial-and- error costs and resource depletion. Companies like BMW and Tesla in the automotive industry develop automobiles with modular components using digital twin simulations, therefore easing repairs and remanufacturing in the sector. This approach not only increases supply chain resilience to raw material shortages but also extends product lifecycles. Digital twins monitor product performance and project end-of-life events, therefore enabling closed-loop production systems. By use of digital twin models, Siemens improves wind turbine maintenance, hence optimizing efficiency and reducing material waste (Singh et al., 2022). Through better resource efficiency and the support of sustainable manufacturing techniques, these programs help to strengthen the CE.

3D Printing for Sustainable Production

By allowing on-demand manufacture, reducing material waste, and improving product personalization, 3D printing also known as additive manufacturing is revolutionizing circular economies. Unlike traditional subtractive manufacturing, which generates significant waste, 3D printing builds objects progressively using only the necessary materials. 3D printing has great use in the CE, mostly in the creation of spare components. Companies like Volkswagen and Airbus make replacement components when required using 3D printing, therefore reducing inventory costs and preventing resource waste. For industries with lengthy product lifecycles, including aerospace and automotive, where the availability of replacement parts may extend product capability, this is particularly beneficial. By including recycled plastics, metals, and bio-based compounds into the production process, 3D printing also helps to enable resource recycling. Nike uses 3D printing to produce environmentally friendly footwear components from recycled materials, therefore lowering its environmental effect (Bianchi et al., 2022). Local product manufacture using recycled materials considerably enhances supply chain sustainability.

By optimizing resource usage, increasing transparency, and lowering waste, technological developments are very essential in hastening the change to circular economies. Blockchain technology reduces fraud, assures supply chain openness, and helps to track recycled resources. IoT-powered resource optimization by means of intelligent waste management systems and predictive maintenance extend product lifecycles. AI driven analytics enhance demand projection, recycling efficiency, and circulation product design. At the same time, 3D printing and digital twin technologies allow us to achieve sustainable manufacturing while decreasing material waste and practicing closed-loop production.

Businesses are likely to experience better environmental sustainability and cost effectiveness, as well as resilience, if industries involve more of such technologies. Bridging new technology with circular supply chains is not only useful in the reduction of resource depletion but also encourages world competitiveness that is based on innovation. If we are to fully leverage circular economies, politicians, businesses and consumers need to come together to develop regulatory frameworks, invest and scale infrastructure investment and public awareness campaign. Concrete usage of technology may turn the companies through circular economies and may reduce the environmental impact to allow people to live in a more sustainable future.

CONSUMER BEHAVIOR AND CIRCULAR PRACTICES

The behavior of customers has a significant impact upon CE ideas' implementation because having their attitudes toward sustainability change, the companies must restructure their supply networks. Customers select products & services based on their values when they get to be more environmentally conscious, which is therefore driving the companies to incorporate circular ideas into their operations. The transition to sustainability has created an increased need for eco-friendly products, increasing interest in being a part of circular process and focus on transparency on what material-sourcing and recycling techniques are used. This portion examines the influence of consumer behavior on the move towards circular economies, the impacts of sustainable purchasing trends, and what businesses can gain from such behavioral transitions to improve their circular supply chains.

Growing Demand for Sustainable Products

Increasing awareness of environmental problems and ethical consumption beliefs has tremendously increased consumer demand for eco-friendly products in the last few years. Research indicates that consumers are increasingly seeking products produced from recycled materials, raw materials supplied in a sustainable manner, as well as packaging in a friendly manner to the environment. This trend has made companies push circular concepts into their supply chains to remain competitive and increase brand loyalty. Most of this change is being driven by the increasing environmental consciousness of younger groups. Research reveals that the Millennials and the Generation Zs consumers are likely to give sustainability priority when making purchases compared to others (Brand et al., 2022; Khan et al., 2024b). These consumers are individuals who actively look for environmentally friendly products and would be willing to pay more prices for the same with lesser negative impacts on the surrounding. The number of such companies as Patagonia or IKEA, which speak about circular business models and sustainable sourcing demonstrates how well companies align the consumer preferences of sustainability can help the market.

Willingness to Participate in Circular Initiatives

Aside from buying eco-friendly products, consumers are also contributing to the CE through second-hand markets, repair plans, and product take-back schemes. Through such actions companies can cut waste, lengthen the lifetimes of products and decrease manufacturing costs thereby promoting more environmentally friendly corporate models. One obvious manifestation of consumer participation in circular initiatives is the increase in the number of clothing resale websites including ThredUp and Depop. Sustained by consumers who favor off-the-peg clothing because of the environmental and monetary improvements it brings, the international second-hand fashion market will outgrow fast fashion in terms of size by 2030 (Papamichael et al., 2024). Such companies as Levi's and H&M are also running take-back campaigns in which customers can return their old clothes in return for a discount to store, with the end aim of encouraging circularity in the fashion industry.

Similarly, repair and reconstruction projects are spreading throughout many other fields. Companies such as Apple and Dell provide device repair and refurbishment services, therefore reducing electronic waste and extending gadget life. This lines up with consumer expectations for increased item longevity and reparability. By requiring manufacturers to provide spare parts and repair services, therefore fostering a culture of reuse over waste, the European Union's "Right to Repair" laws strengthen consumer rights. Moreover, consumer preparedness to embrace furniture rental companies and car-sharing programs helps to improve the CE. Platforms like

Zipcar and Rent the Runway show the shift from traditional ownership models to access-based consumption, therefore reducing resource depletion and providing consumers with flexible and reasonably priced choices (Kumar, 2024). Companies that use these consumer behaviors might improve their circular supply chain plans while maintaining profitability and market relevance.

The Role of Brand Trust and Transparency

The success of CE initiatives depends much on consumer confidence. Customer opinions and purchase decisions are highly influenced by openness in sustainability commitments, production techniques, and material procurement. Companies that effectively present their CE projects improve brand equity, build customer loyalty, and set themselves apart in cutthroat markets. One of the main concerns of consumers purchasing sustainable products is the possibility of greenwashing false claims about the environmental benefits of a good. Research shows that consumers of companies that provide certifications, blockchain monitoring, and third-party audits verifiable data on their sustainability efforts tend to trust them. Transparency policies of Unilever, which include thorough information on production and procurement, have strengthened brand reputation and consumer confidence.

Moreover, companies that use digital technology to enhance openness have experienced higher consumer interaction. Blockchain technology helps companies to provide consumers real-time data on product lifecycles, therefore ensuring authenticity and ethical origins (Emon & Khan, 2025b). Blockchain technology is used by platforms such as Provenance and IBM's Food Trust to track and validate sustainable sourcing practices, therefore arming consumers with validated data before decisions on purchases. Consumer demand for sustainability reporting has led to a multiplication of Environmental, Social, and Governance (ESG) disclosures. Companies that open freely about their developments in ethical labor standards, low carbon footprint, and CE initiatives build consumer trust and attract to investors that are ecologically sensitive (Fortunati et al., 2020). Companies which overlook the necessity of transparency compromise their brand and decrease consumer trust, thereby stressing the importance of honest and transparent sustainability communication.

Psychological and Social Drivers of Circular Consumption

Adoption of CE activities by consumers affects psychological and social factors as well as environmental ones. Research shows that sustainable consumption habits are much influenced by personal beliefs, society norms, and apparent behavioral control. One basic psychological motivator is the concept of self-perception. Those who identify as environmentally concerned are more likely to engage in circular behaviors include recycling, buying second-hand goods, and starting repair projects (Pretner et al., 2021). By aligning sustainability with personal beliefs, marketing strategies that support sustainable identities—best shown by Patagonia's "Don't Buy This Jacket"— significantly influence customer decision-making.

Circular consumption is highly influenced by social context. When sustainable methods seem like socially acceptable behavior, consumers are more likely to adopt them. Circular techniques might be widely adopted thanks in part to peer influence, social media trends, and celebrity sponsorships (Nicolaou, 2022). Millions of consumers have been inspired to adopt waste-reducing strategies by zero-waste lifestyle influencers, therefore highlighting the need of social proof in environmental projects. Furthermore, affecting user involvement in circular initiatives are perceived simplicity and financial incentives. While some consumers show that they are ready to adopt sustainable practices, challenges like high pricing, limited availability, and inconvenience usually prevent adoption. By means of financial incentives, simplification of take-back programs, and improved access to sustainable products, companies may help to overcome these challenges. Adoption of CE ideas depends much on consumer behavior. Rising demand for sustainable products, openness to participate in circular initiatives, and emphasis on brand trust and transparency points on the importance of matching business strategy with evolving customer expectations. Organizations who explicitly communicate about its sustainability commitments and incorporates CE concepts into its activities can boost customer loyalty, strengthen positioning in the market, and hence promote environmental sustainability. Companies should respond to sustainable consumption patterns, employ digital technologies for openness and address underlying psychological and social factors shaping circular conduct elicited by increasing consumer expectations. By promoting customer involvement in circular operations companies could meet the requirements of conscious customers to the environment and create a stronger and more sustainable economy.

MITIGATING INFLATIONARY PRESSURES THROUGH CIRCULAR ECONOMY PRACTICES

For businesses and for consumers, inflationary pressures develop serious challenges concerning the overall strength of the whole economy, efficiencies of supply chains, and prices of manufacturing. The CE provides effective means to eliminate these restraints by decreasing dependency on raw resources and increasing resource efficiency as well as reducing running expenditures. Cyclic business models can address waste, streamline supply chains and not be dependent upon fluctuating commodity prices which much helps in countering the inflation. Called to address these issues of resource efficiency, cost management, supply chain resilience and long-term economic viability, this section looks at how CE strategies may be able to mitigate inflationary pressures.

Resource Efficiency and Cost Savings

The CE relieves inflationary pressure to a large extent by optimizing resource use. Traditional linear economic models make one more sensitive to price up- and downs of raw material since it depends on the extraction, manufacturing and discarding of commodities. Circular models propose reiterating reuse, recycling, and remanufacturing to reduce dependence on virgin resources and stabilize costs through this. The recycling of materials in the production process may benefit some industries by reducing price volatility associated with commodities markets. The construction sector is a shining example of this: employing recycled steel, recovered wood, and sustainable cement substitutes helps businesses save procurement costs and protects them from price swings brought on by inflation. Remanufacturing and component reusing help the electronics industry to lower manufacturing costs while maintaining product quality.

Apart from cost savings based on materials, energy efficiency is also essential in lowering consumption. Circular business models that combine renewable energy sources with energy-efficient manufacturing techniques help businesses to reduce running costs and lessen the effect of inflation-driven energy price hikes (Kreutzer, 2024). Companies that make investments in sustainable energy solutions such as solar-powered manufacturing facilities have long-term cost stability and reduced dependency on the markets for fossil fuels.

Waste Reduction and Cost Control

A basic concept of the CE, waste reduction helps companies control costs in inflationary times. Companies may save material input costs and production waste by designing products with durability, repairability, and recyclability first priorities. To extend product life and reduce waste disposal costs, companies ranging from consumer electronics to fashion have embraced take-back and refurbishment programs. Apple's trade-in program lets consumers return their devices for resale and refurbishment, therefore lowering e-waste and creating additional revenue sources. Remanufacturing components has become more important to the automotive sector, which helps to reduce the need for expensive new materials and lowers client vehicle maintenance costs. Another area in which CE ideas help to reduce inflationary pressures is the drop in food waste. Restaurants and stores that use surplus food redistribution programs save waste disposal costs and provide reasonably priced food options for consumers facing rising prices. Efforts like Too Good To Go, a portal matching consumers with leftover food at discounted rates, show how circular solutions may simultaneously address inflation and environmental concerns (Chakraborty & Mattila, 2024).

Supply Chain Resilience and Inflation Mitigation

Rising production costs and pricing volatility might follow from disruptions in the supply chain brought on by inflation and world economic swings. By lowering dependency on a few resources and expanding sourcing options, CE approaches improve supply chain resilience.

Closed-loop supply chains where materials and components are recovered and reintegrated into production can help businesses reduce exposure to inflation-induced supply chain interruptions, for example. The COVID-19 epidemic revealed the flaws in linear supply chains, leading to shortages of materials that raised prices. Companies that used circular practices local sourcing and material recovery among other things were better in controlling supply chain interruptions and maintaining cost stability. Moreover, IoT-enabled supply chain monitoring and blockchain technologies improve openness and efficiency, hence reducing waste and improving demand forecasting. AI-driven predictive analytics help companies to improve inventory control, thereby lowering excess manufacturing costs and reducing inflationary risks connected to supply-demand differences (Song et al., 2025).

Consumer Affordability and Economic Sustainability

The CE lowers the cost of required goods and services, therefore giving consumers instant benefits. Inflation reduces purchasing power, thereby making it more difficult for individuals to get fresh goods. Economic substitutes for traditional purchasing include circular consumption models including the sharing economy, rental services, second-hand markets, and second-hand markets. Resale sites for clothing like ThredUp and The RealReal provide consumers access to high-quality second-hand fashion at discounted prices, therefore helping them to control expenses in inflationary times. Similarly, refurbished electronics markets allow consumers to get durable technological products at less rates than new models. These strategies not only reduce environmental impact but also provide consumers whose rising living expenditures need real financial assistance (Yang et al., 2023).

Furthermore, companies that use circular business models generally find cost savings, which helps them to maintain competitive pricing without passing expenditures resulting from inflation to consumers. In inflationary environments, businesses may maintain profitability by streamlining production processes, cutting waste, and employing alternative resources. This can help to stabilize pricing. Although inflationary pressures cause financial problems for businesses and people, CE concepts propose workable alternatives to reduce these consequences. Circular B2B models enhance resource efficiency, reduce waste, help build supply chain resilience, and give customers affordable options. So, these will help to stabilize the prices and support long term sustainability in the economy.

Companies employing circular ideas would be better placed to master inflationary uncertainties affecting world economies that inflow the rising prices but at the same time maintain profitability and customer satisfaction. Policymakers and corporate heads have to encourage circular concepts by incentive, regulatory mechanisms and sustainable technology investments to lead to greater acceptance. Aside from a strategic effort to deliver a level of economic rationality in inflationary boundary, the change to a CE is an ecological necessity.

POLICY IMPLICATIONS AND RECOMMENDATIONS

Improved circular supply chains need governments, businesses, and international organizations to act in concert to establish principles that promote sustainable behavior. To achieve meaningful circularity; aggressive policy frameworks may incentivize businesses, regulate policies, and promote an industry-wide collaboration. A CE transition is a strategical necessity to boost the resilience of economy, alleviate restrictions on resources, and deliver long-term sustainability and environmental necessity. The effects of governmental policies, legal framework and business activities on the accelerated uptake of circular supply chains are explored in this section.

Government Incentives for Circular Practices

Through incentives that encourage businesses to be sustainable, the government ensures circular supply chains are advanced. Among the economic tools that will possibly make circular business models to become financially viable, there are tax incentives, subsidies and grants that can help in pushing down the barriers against such models. (Salvador et al., 2022).

Tax Incentives and Subsidies

Governments may give tax breaks for enterprises that use concepts from the CE. Some of the tax credits to businesses operating waste reduction, resource-efficient manufacturing and renewable energy could bring about sustainable transformation. In some countries, it is now easier to obtain supplies of circular goods because some countries have managed to reduce the value-added tax (VAT) rates on repair services and reconditioned goods. Circularity can be enhanced through grants for sustainable product innovation, secondary raw material recycling and recycling infrastructure. European Union' s CE Action Plan (CEAP) supports circular business initiatives, therefore assisting sectors to evolve from a linear to a CE (Pinyol Alberich et al., 2023).

Investment in Recycling Infrastructure

Stout markets for secondary goods and recycling materials are prerequisites for a CE. Governments should allocate the money for modern recycling plants, high technology of material recycling and waste-to-energy ones in order to improve resource efficiency. Public-private partnerships (PPPs) may enable large investments in circular infrastructure, hence ensuring businesses have premium recycled material at reasonable prices.

Public Procurement Policies

CE acceptance may be induced by governments by harnessing public procurement. Highlighting the type of goods and services that are sustainable can go a long way in enhancing demand for circular products and this becomes a model for the business sector. The Green Public Procurement (GPP) framework established in the EU promotes environmental friendly products, which, in turn, will minimize the environmental impact and will be promoting the circular innovation (Sönnichsen & Clement, 2020).

Regulatory Frameworks for Sustainable Supply Chains

Corporate commitment to CE ideas requires regulatory action. Circularity in sectors is required to be driven by governments if explicit waste management rules, extended producer responsibility (EPR), and eco-design have to be applied.

Waste Management Regulations

Tighter regulations around waste management and use of landfills may motivate the businesses to switch to circular approaches. Countries like Sweden and Germany have enacted landfill bans for recyclable and biodegradable garbage; thus, companies need other waste management modalities, such as the use of material recovery and product reuse. Moreover, mandatory recycling targets could help the sector to use circular supply chains. In Japan the Home Appliance Recycling Law requires collection and recycling of old devices, thereby improving material recovery rates, and decreasing e-waste (Emon, 2025; Rene et al., 2021).

Extended Producer Responsibility (EPR)

EPR laws mandate that manufacturers are responsible for the full lifetime of their products including disposal of post-consumer waste. Using initiatives such as Extended Producer Responsibility (EPR), Governments may in turn encourage firms to manufacture products that are durable, repairable and recyclable. The Waste Electrical and Electronic Equipment (WEEE) directive of the EU requires all electronics manufacturers to cover disposal, recycling, and collection of their products. Similar policies in Canada and South Korea have enhanced circularity in such industry areas as electronics and automobile manufacture (Herrador et al., 2020).

Eco-Design Standards

Stricter eco-design rules contribute to producing items of lifetime, recyclability, and energy economy. The Eco-design Directive of the EU sets environmental performance standards for products, therefore reducing material waste throughout multiple sectors and significant energy savings. Regulatory policies need to mandate the manufacture of recycled goods. Setting minimum recycled material requirements in textiles, electronics, and packaging will help to create stable markets for secondary materials, hence lowering dependency on virgin resources (Patti et al., 2020).

Business Strategies for Circular Integration

Although government policies provide the foundation for the application of a CE, businesses must actively include circular concepts into their supply chains. Circular approach companies see lower costs, better brand recognition, and more resilience to resource shortages (Borms et al., 2023).

Material Innovation

Establishing circular supply chains requires funding biodegradable and recyclable materials. Businesses must give the creation of substitute materials that reduce environmental impact priority, maintaining product effectiveness. Sustainable alternatives to conventional plastics and metals include bioplastics, mycelium-based packaging, and recycled composite materials (Teeraphantuvat et al., 2024). Companies in the fashion industry such Patagonia and Adidas have successfully included sustainable fabrics and recycled fibers into their products, therefore lowering their reliance on virgin resources and waste generation.

Reverse Logistics and Product Lifecycle Management

In circular supply chains, reverse logistics is crucial as it helps things be returned, refurbished, and resale able. To extend product life and reduce waste, companies must use take-back systems, repair projects, and remanufacturing processes. Remanufacturing projects for automotive components by companies like Renault and BMW help to reduce the need for fresh raw materials and provide consumers with affordable repair choices and so minimizing the need for new raw materials and thus minimizing the requirement of automotive manufacturers. By means of furniture buy-back and resale programs, retailers such as IKEA have encouraged circular consumption and therefore reduced landfill trash (Lučić & Uzelac, 2024).

Cross-Industry Collaboration

Establishing closed-loop ecosystems calls for inter-industry cooperation. Companies must build circular value chains by working with suppliers, recyclers, and technology companies. Industrial symbiosis whereby one company's waste becomes a resource for another may significantly increase resource efficiency and provide cost benefits. To provide sustainable packaging solutions, Unilever works with recycling firms and plastic waste collectors, therefore reducing plastic waste and guaranteeing a continuous supply of recycled materials. By turning demolition waste into new building materials, the construction industry has embraced cross-industry collaboration, therefore promoting circular building techniques (Ossio et al., 2023).

CONCLUSION: EMBRACING CIRCULAR SUPPLY CHAINS FOR ECONOMIC AND ENVIRONMENTAL RESILIENCE

The shift to circular supply chains marks a basic change in the perspective of businesses and governments toward resource management. The growing relevance of recycling and closed-loop systems in reducing inflationary pressures, enhancing sustainability, and therefore promoting long-term economic stability has been investigated in this chapter. Raw material shortages, geopolitical uncertainty, and climate change are causing more disruptions to global supply networks that call for the adoption of circular processes as a practical substitute to reduce dependency on virgin resources, stabilize pricing, and improve supply chain resilience. This conversation reveals, among other important things, that circular supply networks provide many more advantages than traditional linear models. CE's provide resource recovery, product lifetime extension, and waste minimization top priority above the linear "take-make- disposal" paradigm. Existing case study reports on successful work in various industries indicate that companies can realize environmental sustainability side by side with the attainment of competitive advantage, cost saving, and loyalty of brand through circular movements. Moreover, the most important to facilitate smart waste management, predictive maintenance, and effective reverse logistics are technological innovations including AI, blockchain and the Internet of things.

Much of the change to a CE is based on consumer behavior. Individuals are moving to using sustainable products and circular activities such as secondhand markets and take back products slowly as awareness of environmental problems grows. Sustainable, brand-integrity-focused, and open companies are in a better position to attract and keep customers environmentally conscious. Circular supply networks offer more than just basic cost savings; they have economic benefits. By using recycling, remanufacturing and refurbished products, circular models stabilize production costs, alleviate raw material price volatility and offer new profit streams. Reaching a totally CE calls for coordinated actions among consumers, businesses, and governments. Policymakers must provide supportive policies to encourage circular business practices like extended producer responsibility (EPR) programs, eco-design criteria, and financial incentives. Investing in secondary material markets, recycling infrastructure, and inter-industry alliances might help to speed the shift to a CE.

REFERENCES

Albertsen, L., Richter, J. L., Peck, P., Dalhammar, C., & Plepys, A. (2021). Circular business models for electric vehicle lithium-ion batteries: An analysis of current practices of vehicle manufacturers and policies in the EU. *Resources, Conservation and Recycling*, *172*, 105658. DOI: 10.1016/j.resconrec.2021.105658

Bianchi, I., Forcellese, A., Simoncini, M., Vita, A., Castorani, V., Arganese, M., & De Luca, C. (2022). Life cycle impact assessment of safety shoes toe caps realized with reclaimed composite materials. *Journal of Cleaner Production*, *347*, 131321. DOI: 10.1016/j.jclepro.2022.131321

Borms, L., Brusselaers, J., Vrancken, K. C., Deckmyn, S., & Marynissen, P. (2023). Toward resilient organizations after COVID-19: An analysis of circular and less circular companies. *Resources, Conservation and Recycling*, *188*, 106681. DOI: 10.1016/j.resconrec.2022.106681 PMID: 36160477

Brand, B. M., Rausch, T. M., & Brandel, J. (2022). The Importance of Sustainability Aspects When Purchasing Online: Comparing Generation X and Generation Z. *Sustainability (Basel)*, *14*(9), 5689. DOI: 10.3390/su14095689

Cesarina Mason, M., Pauluzzo, R., & Muhammad Umar, R. (2022). Recycling habits and environmental responses to fast-fashion consumption: Enhancing the theory of planned behavior to predict Generation Y consumers' purchase decisions. *Waste Management (New York, N.Y.)*, *139*, 146–157. DOI: 10.1016/j.wasman.2021.12.012 PMID: 34971902

Chakraborty, D., & Mattila, A. S. (2024). The effect of self-conscious emotions of guilt and regret on consumers' intentions to reduce food waste. *Journal of Sustainable Tourism*, 1–19. DOI: 10.1080/09669582.2024.2406532

Coelho, P. M., Corona, B., ten Klooster, R., & Worrell, E. (2020). Sustainability of reusable packaging–Current situation and trends. *Resources, Conservation and Recycling. X*, *6*, 100037. DOI: 10.1016/j.rcrx.2020.100037

Cudjoe, D., Zhu, B., Nketiah, E., Wang, H., Chen, W., & Qianqian, Y. (2021). The potential energy and environmental benefits of global recyclable resources. *The Science of the Total Environment*, *798*, 149258. DOI: 10.1016/j.scitotenv.2021.149258 PMID: 34332393

Dhanya, B. S., Mishra, A., Chandel, A. K., & Verma, M. L. (2020). Development of sustainable approaches for converting the organic waste to bioenergy. *The Science of the Total Environment*, *723*, 138109. DOI: 10.1016/j.scitotenv.2020.138109 PMID: 32229385

Diprose, G., Lee, L., Blumhardt, H., Walton, S., & Greenaway, A. (2023). Reducing single use packaging and moving up the waste hierarchy. *Kotuitui, 18*(3), 268–289. DOI: 10.1080/1177083X.2022.2154230

Emon, M. M. H. (2025). The Mediating Role of Supply Chain Responsiveness in the Relationship Between Key Supply Chain Drivers and Performance: Evidence from the FMCG Industry. *Brazilian Journal of Operations & Production Management, 22*(1), 2580. DOI: 10.14488/BJOPM.2580.2025

Emon, M. M. H., & Khan, T. (2024a). A Systematic Literature Review on Sustainability Integration and Marketing Intelligence in the Era of Artificial Intelligence. *Review of Business and Economics Studies, 12*(4), 6–28. DOI: 10.26794/2308-944X-2024-12-4-6-28

Emon, M. M. H., & Khan, T. (2024b). Unlocking Sustainability through Supply Chain Visibility: Insights from the Manufacturing Sector of Bangladesh. *Brazilian Journal of Operations & Production Management, 21*(4), 2194. DOI: 10.14488/BJOPM.2194.2024

Emon, M. M. H., & Khan, T. (2025a). The mediating role of attitude towards the technology in shaping artificial intelligence usage among professionals. *Telematics and Informatics Reports, 17*, 100188. DOI: 10.1016/j.teler.2025.100188

Emon, M. M. H., & Khan, T. (2025b). The transformative role of Industry 4.0 in supply chains: Exploring digital integration and innovation in the manufacturing enterprises. *Journal of Open Innovation, 11*(2), 100516. DOI: 10.1016/j.joitmc.2025.100516

Emon, M. M. H., Khan, T., Rahman, M. A., Hamid, A. B. A., & Yaakub, N. I. (2025). GreenTech Revolution: Navigating Challenges and Seizing Opportunities. In *AI and Green Technology Applications in Society* (p. 63–90). IGI Global Scientific Publishing. DOI: 10.4018/979-8-3693-9879-1.ch003

Emon, M. M. H., Khan, T., Rahman, M. A., & Siam, S. A. J. (2024). Factors Influencing the Usage of Artificial Intelligence among Bangladeshi Professionals: Mediating role of Attitude Towards the Technology. *2024 IEEE International Conference on Computing, Applications and Systems (COMPAS)*, 1–7. DOI: 10.1109/COMPAS60761.2024.10796110

Falsafi, M., & Fornasiero, R. (2022). Explorative Multiple-Case Research on the Scrap-Based Steel Slag Value Chain: Opportunities for Circular Economy. *Sustainability (Basel), 14*(4), 2284. DOI: 10.3390/su14042284

Fortunati, S., Martiniello, L., & Morea, D. (2020). The Strategic Role of the Corporate Social Responsibility and Circular Economy in the Cosmetic Industry. *Sustainability (Basel), 12*(12), 5120. DOI: 10.3390/su12125120

Glavič, P. (2021). Evolution and Current Challenges of Sustainable Consumption and Production. *Sustainability (Basel), 13*(16), 9379. DOI: 10.3390/su13169379

Herrador, M., Cho, Y., & Park, P. H. (2020). Latest circular economy policy and direction in the Republic of Korea: Room for enhancements. *Journal of Cleaner Production, 269*, 122336. DOI: 10.1016/j.jclepro.2020.122336

Kandpal, V., Jaswal, A., Santibanez Gonzalez, E. D. R., & Agarwal, N. (2024). *Sustainable Energy Transition.* Circular Economy, and ESG Practices., DOI: 10.1007/978-3-031-52943-6

Khan, T., Emon, M. M. H., & Rahman, M. A. (2024a). A systematic review on exploring the influence of Industry 4.0 technologies to enhance supply chain visibility and operational efficiency. *Review of Business and Economics Studies, 12*(3), 6–27. DOI: 10.26794/2308-944X-2024-12-3-6-27

Khan, T., Emon, M. M. H., & Rahman, S. (2024b). Marketing Strategy Innovation via AI Adoption: A Study on Bangladeshi SMEs in the Context of Industry 5.0. *2024 6th International Conference on Sustainable Technologies for Industry 5.0 (STI)*, 1–6. DOI: 10.1109/STI64222.2024.10951050

Khan, T., & Hasan Emon, M. M. (2024). Determinants of AI Image Generator Adoption Among Marketing Agencies: The Mediating Effects of Perceived Usefulness. *2024 IEEE 3rd International Conference on Robotics, Automation, Artificial-Intelligence and Internet-of-Things (RAAICON)*, 177–182. DOI: 10.1109/RAAICON64172.2024.10928548

Khan, T., Rahman, S. M., & Hasan, M. M. (2020). Barriers to Growth of Renewable Energy Technology in Bangladesh. *Proceedings of the International Conference on Computing Advancements*, 1–6. DOI: 10.1145/3377049.3377086

Kirchherr, J., Yang, N.-H. N., Schulze-Spüntrup, F., Heerink, M. J., & Hartley, K. (2023). Conceptualizing the Circular Economy (Revisited): An Analysis of 221 Definitions. *Resources, Conservation and Recycling, 194*, 107001. DOI: 10.1016/j.resconrec.2023.107001

Kreutzer, R. T. (2024). Sustainability in Corporate Governance and on the Customer Side. In *The Path to Sustainable Corporate Management* (p. 1–59). Springer Fachmedien Wiesbaden., DOI: 10.1007/978-3-658-43974-3_1

Kumar, J. (2024). Psychological mechanisms behind access-based luxury brand consumption: Empirical investigation from the lens of new ownership paradigm. *Journal of Business Research, 175*, 114539. DOI: 10.1016/j.jbusres.2024.114539

Lučić, A., & Uzelac, M. (2024). Addressing global overconsumption: Positioning the anti-consumption through communication appeals. *Corporate Communications, 29*(2), 187–205. DOI: 10.1108/CCIJ-08-2023-0114

Maguire, S., & Robson, I. (2023). Business Innovation and Change for Circular Economy. In *Sustainable Development Through Global Circular Economy Practices* (p. 113–132). Emerald Publishing Limited., DOI: 10.1108/978-1-83753-590-320231005

Ncube, L. K., Ude, A. U., Ogunmuyiwa, E. N., Zulkifli, R., & Beas, I. N. (2020). Environmental Impact of Food Packaging Materials: A Review of Contemporary Development from Conventional Plastics to Polylactic Acid Based Materials. *Materials (Basel), 13*(21), 4994. DOI: 10.3390/ma13214994 PMID: 33171895

Nicolaou, C. (2022). Generations and Branded Content from and through the Internet and Social Media: Modern Communication Strategic Techniques and Practices for Brand Sustainability—The Greek Case Study of LACTA Chocolate. *Sustainability (Basel), 15*(1), 584. DOI: 10.3390/su15010584

Ossio, F., Salinas, C., & Hernández, H. (2023). Circular economy in the built environment: A systematic literature review and definition of the circular construction concept. *Journal of Cleaner Production, 414*, 137738. DOI: 10.1016/j.jclepro.2023.137738

Papamichael, I., Voukkali, I., Economou, F., Liscio, M. C., Sospiro, P., Naddeo, V., & Zorpas, A. A. (2024). Investigation of customer behavior regarding circular fashion. *Sustainable Chemistry and Pharmacy, 41*, 101675. DOI: 10.1016/j.scp.2024.101675

Park, Y. W., Blackhurst, J., Paul, C., & Scheibe, K. P. (2022). An analysis of the ripple effect for disruptions occurring in circular flows of a supply chain network*. *International Journal of Production Research, 60*(15), 4693–4711. DOI: 10.1080/00207543.2021.1934745

Patti, A., Cicala, G., & Acierno, D. (2020). Eco-Sustainability of the Textile Production: Waste Recovery and Current Recycling in the Composites World. *Polymers, 13*(1), 134. DOI: 10.3390/polym13010134 PMID: 33396936

Pérez, M., Lieder, M., Jeong, Y., & Asif, F. M. A. (2025). A simulation-based decision support tool for circular manufacturing systems in the automotive industry using electric machines as a remanufacturing case study. *International Journal of Production Research*, 1–20. DOI: 10.1080/00207543.2025.2464912

Pinyol Alberich, J., Pansera, M., & Hartley, S. (2023). Understanding the EU's circular economy policies through futures of circularity. *Journal of Cleaner Production, 385*, 135723. DOI: 10.1016/j.jclepro.2022.135723

Pretner, G., Darnall, N., Testa, F., & Iraldo, F. (2021). Are consumers willing to pay for circular products? The role of recycled and second-hand attributes, messaging, and third-party certification. *Resources, Conservation and Recycling, 175*, 105888. DOI: 10.1016/j.resconrec.2021.105888

Radtke, M. L., de Almeida, S. O., & Espartel, L. B. (2022). What Brought Me Here? Different Consumer Journeys for Practices of Sustainable Disposal through Take-back Programmes. *Sustainability (Basel), 14*(9), 5003. DOI: 10.3390/su14095003

Rene, E. R., Sethurajan, M., Kumar Ponnusamy, V., Kumar, G., Bao Dung, T. N., Brindhadevi, K., & Pugazhendhi, A. (2021). Electronic waste generation, recycling and resource recovery: Technological perspectives and trends. *Journal of Hazardous Materials, 416*, 125664. DOI: 10.1016/j.jhazmat.2021.125664 PMID: 33838506

Salvador, R., Barros, M. V., Donner, M., Brito, P., Halog, A., & De Francisco, A. C. (2022). How to advance regional circular bioeconomy systems? Identifying barriers, challenges, drivers, and opportunities. *Sustainable Production and Consumption, 32*, 248–269. DOI: 10.1016/j.spc.2022.04.025

Sarfraz, M. S., Hong, H., & Kim, S. S. (2021). Recent developments in the manufacturing technologies of composite components and their cost-effectiveness in the automotive industry: A review study. *Composite Structures, 266*, 113864. DOI: 10.1016/j.compstruct.2021.113864

Seyyedi, S. R., Kowsari, E., Gheibi, M., Chinnappan, A., & Ramakrishna, S. (2024). A comprehensive review integration of digitalization and circular economy in waste management by adopting artificial intelligence approaches: Towards a simulation model. *Journal of Cleaner Production, 460*, 142584. DOI: 10.1016/j.jclepro.2024.142584

Sharma, K. D., & Jain, S. (2020). Municipal solid waste generation, composition, and management: The global scenario. *Social Responsibility Journal, 16*(6), 917–948. DOI: 10.1108/SRJ-06-2019-0210

Sharma, S. K., & Singh, V. (2022). Digitization of the food industry enabled by Internet of Things, blockchain, and artificial intelligence. In *Current Developments in Biotechnology and Bioengineering* (p. 421–445). Elsevier., DOI: 10.1016/B978-0-323-91158-0.00013-2

Singh, M., Srivastava, R., Fuenmayor, E., Kuts, V., Qiao, Y., Murray, N., & Devine, D. (2022). Applications of Digital Twin across Industries: A Review. *Applied Sciences (Basel, Switzerland), 12*(11), 5727. DOI: 10.3390/app12115727

Sinha, P., Sharma, M., & Agrawal, R. (2024). AI enabled business decisions that enhance sustainability impact of an apparel and fashion supply chain. *Technology Analysis and Strategic Management*, 1–18. DOI: 10.1080/09537325.2024.2424428

Song, Y., Yu, W., Jacobs, M. A., & Chavez, R. (2025). Pandemic-related inventory management practices and financial performance: Exploring the roles of pandemic-related production uncertainty and big data analytics capability. *International Journal of Production Research*, 1–20. DOI: 10.1080/00207543.2025.2470990

Sönnichsen, S. D., & Clement, J. (2020). Review of green and sustainable public procurement: Towards circular public procurement. *Journal of Cleaner Production, 245*, 118901. DOI: 10.1016/j.jclepro.2019.118901

Teeraphantuvat, T., Jatuwong, K., Jinanukul, P., Thamjaree, W., Lumyong, S., & Aiduang, W. (2024). Improving the Physical and Mechanical Properties of Mycelium-Based Green Composites Using Paper Waste. *Polymers, 16*(2), 262. DOI: 10.3390/polym16020262 PMID: 38257061

Tewary, A., & Upadhyay, P. (2025). Proposing a 6R framework promoting circular strategies for platform organizations. *Digital Policy. Regulation & Governance, 27*(2), 145–174. DOI: 10.1108/DPRG-11-2023-0169

Vadakkepatt, G. G., Winterich, K. P., Mittal, V., Zinn, W., Beitelspacher, L., Aloysius, J., Ginger, J., & Reilman, J. (2021). Sustainable Retailing. *Journal of Retailing, 97*(1), 62–80. DOI: 10.1016/j.jretai.2020.10.008

Waris, I., Suki, N. M., Ahmed, A., & Barkat, W. (2024). Environmental corporate social responsibility initiatives and green customer citizenship behavior in tourism industry: The mediating roles of green trust, customer-company identification and green corporate image. *Social Responsibility Journal, 20*(6), 1138–1156. DOI: 10.1108/SRJ-07-2023-0378

Wilson, M., & Goffnett, S. (2022). Reverse logistics: Understanding end-of-life product management. *Business Horizons, 65*(5), 643–655. DOI: 10.1016/j.bushor.2021.10.005

Yang, M., Chen, L., Wang, J., Msigwa, G., Osman, A. I., Fawzy, S., Rooney, D. W., & Yap, P.-S. (2023). Circular economy strategies for combating climate change and other environmental issues. *Environmental Chemistry Letters, 21*(1), 55–80. DOI: 10.1007/s10311-022-01499-6

KEY TERMS AND DEFINITIONS

Circular Economy (CE): – By encouraging recycling, remanufacturing, and waste reduction to build a closed-loop system and therefore minimize environmental damage and economic inefficiencies, a sustainable economic model that emphasizes resource efficiency gains priority.

Closed-Loop Supply Chain: – Integrating product reuse, recycling, and remanufacturing into a supply chain guarantees that resources and goods are always in use instead of thrown away after a single use.

Supply Chain Resilience: – The capacity of a supply chain to resist interruptions, adjust to changing market circumstances, and recover effectively by means of flexible, sustainable, and economic policies.

Technological Innovation in Circularity: – Using blockchain, IoT, and artificial intelligence to improve traceability, resource optimization, and efficiency in circular supply chains.

Remanufacturing: – A method of extending the lifetime of worn-out or used goods by means of repair, refurbishing, or component replacement thereby restoring their original state.

Consumer Circular Behavior: – Consumers that support sustainable practices including product reuse, involvement in recycling programs, and choice of environmentally friendly products have different buying and use patterns.

Inflationary Pressures in Supply Chains: – Circular economy solutions help to offset economic elements causing supply chain costs to rise, including resource constraints, increasing manufacturing costs, and disturbance of equilibrium.

Chapter 9
Economic Nationalism and De-Globalization:
How Reshoring and Protectionist Policies Are Reshaping Supply Chains and Inflation

Zerihun Kinde Alemu
https://orcid.org/0000-0002-8546-2882
Ethiopian Civil Service University, Ethiopia

Shashi Kant
https://orcid.org/0000-0003-4722-5736
Bule Hora University, Ethiopia

ABSTRACT

Emphasizing the intricacies and debates surrounding economic nationalism, particularly with regard to job creation, manufacturing prices, and supply chain resilience. This paper investigates the revival of reshoring as well as protectionist policies. The study shows that although reshoring has the possibility to create employment, it struggles with notable issues like increased domestic manufacturing prices and skill shortages when examined qualitatively using case studies from the United States, Germany, and China, as well as industry report data. Along with protectionist policies can result in higher consumer prices and trade reprisals, so undermining their intended advantages. The results underline the importance of a balanced strategy taking into account all three of these elements. Future paths include putting sustainable practices in reshoring initiatives into action as well as enhancing workforce development and encouraging business-education cooperation to close skill shortages.

DOI: 10.4018/979-8-3373-1982-7.ch009

INTRODUCTION

Economic nationalism along with de-globalization has become major topics influencing world trade dynamics in recent years (Ghazalian, 2025). The trend of reshoring—returning manufacturing to home shores—has picked up as countries rethink their dependence on worldwide supply networks (Guillén & Torres, 2025). This change demonstrates deeper sociopolitical currents that give national interest priority over global interdependence, not only an economic reaction (Mariotti, 2024). Though its roots are in the late 20th century, the COVID-19 epidemic and geopolitical tensions have brought this idea back into focus as they revealed weaknesses in global supply systems (D'Ambrosio & Lavoratori, 2025). The Reshoring Initiative claimed 350,000 jobs came back to the U.S. in 2021; this number could exaggerate results. Many jobs are concentrated within low-wage industries consisting of manufacturing, where automation lowers net employment increases. The total effect on industrial production as well as the long-term viability of jobs still stays unknown, too. (Dedej & Medici, 2024). Studies based on actual data show that businesses are more and more driven by customer preferences for locally produced products, the need for more supply chain resilience, and growing labor costs in emerging nations (Clark et al., 2025). A Deloitte poll, for instance, revealed that 63% of industrial leaders feel the epidemic has caused companies to reconsider their supply chain plans (Rahimjonovich, 2025).

Cross-country factual comparisons show the different effects of economic nationalism as well as de-globalization across developing countries (Guillén & Torres, 2025). In this regard, India's "Make in India" program sought to increase domestic manufacturing but caused a 6-8% rise in consumer prices as the consequence of higher production expenses (Kant et al., 2025). Protectionist policies through Brazil during the 2010s caused a 1.5% annual decline in GDP growth and inflation rates to rise by about 3% (Rahimjonovich, 2025). On the other hand, even with global disruptions, Vietnam's strategic integration into world supply chains maintains inflation fairly stable, enabling it to keep a 6.3% annual increase in GDP in 2021 (D'Ambrosio & Lavoratori, 2025). These cases show that while some nations experience inflationary stresses from reshoring along with protectionism, other individuals succeed in balancing domestic production alongside global supply chain integration, therefore highlighting the complicated interaction between national policies as well as economic results in the Global South (Anlauf & Schmalz, 2025). But, there are difficulties with this change. Businesses have practical challenges include increased local manufacturing expenses, restricted supply of trained labor, and the requirement for major infrastructural investment (Anlauf & Schmalz, 2025). Along with, there is a significant study vacuum on the long-term effects of these measures on inflation rates and economic stability. Many current researches emphasize short-term results, which leaves us without knowledge on the larger consequences of protectionist policies and reshoring. The chapter goals for a conversation on protectionism and reshoring are:

1. Examine the Trends: To investigate the present trends in reshoring and protectionist policies, stressing the driving forces behind these changes in the world economic scene.
2. To evaluate the effects of reshoring on local economies—including job creation, economic resiliency, and shifts in consumer behaviour—while also weighing the possible downsides.
3. To investigate pertinent theoretical frameworks that clarify the reasons and consequences of reshoring as well as protectionism, hence laying a basis for comprehending these events.
4. To highlight the difficulties businesses have putting reshoring plans into practice, especially those related to worker skills, increased operating expenses, and infrastructural constraints.
5. Talk About Policy Implications: To examine the effects of protectionist measures on domestic industry and international trade relations, thereby considering the short-term advantages as well as the long-term repercussions.
6. To underline excellent practices for companies thinking about reshoring, including techniques for labor development, technological integration, as well as sustainable practices.
7. To suggest future study paths that fill holes in the present literature, hence promoting more investigation of the intricacies of reshoring and protectionist.

Therefore, this chapter intends to fill up these voids by offering a thorough examination of how reshoring and protectionism are changing supply chains and impacting inflation. We will examine the interaction of national policies with worldwide economic trends, hence providing ideas for future academics and legislators. The main issue driving this research is: How do reshoring and protectionist policies interact to change supply chains, and what are their consequences for future economic stability and inflation? Examining this issue will help us to highlight paths for more efficient policy frameworks and plans able to negotiate the complexity of a fast changing world scene.

BACKGROUND OF STUDY

Many nations have been compelled to reevaluate their manufacturing policies as a result of the return of economic nationalism as well as de-globalization, which has led to an increased emphasis on reshoring (Mariotti, 2024). This change is not only a theoretical concept; rather, it is demonstrated via a variety of case studies that emphasize the real obstacles that governments confront when attempting to undertake reshoring programs (Rahimjonovich, 2025). A significant illustration of this phenomenon is the United States of America, where the tendency of reshoring has been driven by both economic as well as political considerations (Dedej & Medici, 2024). In order to encourage businesses to bring manufacturing back to the United States, the government of the United States has created incentives (Guillén & Torres, 2025). Despite this, difficulties still exist (Clark et al., 2025). When it comes to skilled crafts in particular, many businesses are experiencing substantial labor shortages, which cause delays in the process of scaling up production (D'Ambrosio & Lavoratori, 2025). For example, General Motors encountered challenges in its efforts to reshore the manufacture of electric car batteries owing to a shortage of trained personnel (Canteri et al., 2024). This highlights the necessity of workforce development in conjunction with reshoring regulations (Ghazalian, 2025).

Reshoring is a concept that has been adopted by a number of European nations, including Germany and France, with the intention of bolstering domestic economies and decreasing reliance on supply chains that originate from other countries (Ghauri et al., 2024). However, in comparison to emerging markets, these countries have relatively high labor costs, which makes the practicality of reshoring from an economic standpoint more difficult (Anlauf & Schmalz, 2025). The French textile sector is the subject of a case study that indicates that although some businesses have been able to effectively relocate manufacturing back to France, many others continue to struggle with the increased operational expenses and restricted scalability that might impair competitiveness in the face of cheaper imports (Bai, 2025). Economic nationalism as well as de-globalization are dramatically changing supply networks and affecting inflationary tendencies (Csaba, 2025). A Peterson Institute for International Economics research concluded that, mostly because of rising labor and operational costs in wealthy nations, reshoring may raise manufacturing costs by 20 to 30% (Popov, 2025). This change could help to keep inflation going; for example, U.S. reshoring initiatives have been connected to a long-term rise in consumer prices of 1 to 2% (Ghazalian, 2025). Furthermore, protectionist measures, such as tariffs, can interfere with global supply networks, resulting to diminished efficiency and increased pricing for raw commodities (Rahimjonovich, 2025). Rising protectionism, according to the World Bank, would reduce world GDP by 1.5% over the next ten years, hence stressing the macroeconomic consequences of such policies

(D'Ambrosio & Lavoratori, 2025). Overall, while reshoring can increase local job growth, its inflationary pressures alongside the larger economic repercussions of protectionism provide substantial hurdles for policymakers (Guillén & Torres, 2025).

In a similar manner, the government of Japan has advocated for reshoring as a component of a more comprehensive economic strategy to improve the state of domestic manufacturing (Ying-Jun, 2025). Although these attempts have been made, businesses such as Sony have discovered that it is difficult to strike a balance between the advantages of local manufacturing and the reality of global supply networks (Csaba, 2025). As an illustration of the complexity involved in completely committing to reshoring, consider the fact that although some components are now made in Japan, others continue to be acquired from nations with lower manufacturing prices. This is done in order to keep overall production costs acceptable (Popov, 2025). Along with, emerging economies are not exempt from the tendency of reshoring their production (Kant & Ashuro, 2025). Countries such as India have witnessed an increase in the number of businesses that are aiming to create local production in order to reduce the risks that are connected with interruptions in global supply (Kant et al., 2025). Nevertheless, considerable obstacles have been presented in the form of infrastructural deficiencies and bureaucratic roadblocks. This is demonstrated by a case study of the Indian electronics industry, which reveals that although some companies have made significant progress in localizing production, there are still challenges that continue to inhibit growth, such as unstable supply chains and regulatory inefficiencies (Guillén & Torres, 2025).

The aforementioned examples highlight the myriad of problems that are involved in the implementation of reshoring policies in a variety of different scenarios. As nations attempt to strike a balance between their own national interests and the reality of the global economy, the purpose of this research is to examine the practical experiences that have been gained in order to give insights into successful solutions that might solve the inherent challenges that include reshoring. It is essential for entrepreneurs and politicians who are attempting to adjust to the changing economic landscape to have a solid understanding of these problems.

STATEMENT OF PROBLEM

There is a difficult challenge that is characterized by an ideal condition of robust, concentrated supply chains that promote national economic resilience. This problem is presented by the trend toward reshoring and protectionist measures (Dedej & Medici, 2024). On the other hand, this vision is frequently contradicted by reality, which draws attention to a number of gaps that make the execution of these tactics more difficult (Ghazalian, 2025). The empirical data demonstrates that although reshoring has the potential to assist in the strengthening of local economies, the actual outcomes have been inconsistent, with many efforts failing to meet the expectations that were presented (Clark et al., 2025). Numerous businesses, for instance, have reported continuous difficulties with labor shortages, increased production costs, along with supply chain inefficiencies, which has led to mixed results about the long-term advantages of this technique. This is despite the fact that large expenditures have been made in reshoring (D'Ambrosio & Lavoratori, 2025). The discussion around reshoring is made much more complicated by the existence of theoretical gaps. The dynamic interplay that exists between global trade policy and local economic realities is frequently not captured by the frameworks that are already in place (Mariotti, 2024). A great number of studies concentrate solely on the short-term effects on the economy, without effectively addressing the more far-reaching consequences for inflation, supply chain stability, and consumer behavior (Anlauf & Schmalz, 2025). Because of this neglect, there is a knowledge vacuum, since policymakers do not have full insights into the possible long-term repercussions of protectionist policies and reshoring activities (Rahimjonovich, 2025).

In addition, contextual gaps appear when one takes into consideration the various economic landscapes that exist in different nations (Nam, 2024). Due to the fact that different countries have different labor markets, regulatory frameworks, and industrial capacity, what is successful in one country might not be relevant in another (Kant et al., 2025). It is possible, for instance, that the United States of America might reap the benefits of reshoring in high-tech industries, but developing nations such as India could have difficulty replicating this success due to the difficulties associated with infrastructure and bureaucracy (Guillén & Torres, 2025). The high operational expenses, the restricted availability of competent personnel, and the requirement for major investments in infrastructure and technological developments are all physical manifestations of the practical issues that are occurring (Festing & Proff, 2024). When businesses are trying to strike a balance between the competitive pressures of globalization and the demands of local manufacturing, they frequently find themselves stuck in a loop that causes them to be unable to make decisions on their strategic planning (Wong et al., 2024).

Particularly with the growth of platform economies and remote employment, the interdependencies across reshoring as well as digital globalization are becoming more intricate (Rahimjonovich, 2025). Digital technologies provide more efficiency and connection when businesses move production back home, hence enabling enterprises to keep worldwide reach despite localised manufacturing (Anlauf & Schmalz, 2025). Consumer opinions, however, are rather important; many people are more attracted to goods marked "locally made" inspired by patriotic trade stories and a want to assist local industries (Clark et al., 2025). Though it brings up issues concerning price and quality, this behavioral change might increase demand for reshored products (Nam, 2024). The difficulty is in striking a balance between customer expectations alongside the reality of manufacturing expenses. Furthermore, while remote labor grows common, businesses may find it simpler to run reshored operations; nonetheless, industry along with regional economic circumstances will determine how well this approach works (Wong et al., 2024). Eventually, companies negotiating the changing economic scene must grasp these dynamics if they are to survive (Kant et al., 2025).

By offering a complete examination of how reshoring and protectionist policies interact with current economic frameworks and supply chain dynamics, the purpose of this study is to address the gaps that have been identified with regard to these topics. Identifying optimal practices and frequent hazards will be accomplished via the examination of case studies originating from a variety of nations and industries. Along with, the purpose of this research is to investigate the long-term effects that these policies will have on inflation and economic stability. The findings gained from this investigation will provide significant insights for policymakers and future academics. The purpose of this study is to create a clearer roadmap for navigating the obstacles of a fast expanding global economy. This will eventually contribute to better informed decision-making and strategic planning in the area. This will be accomplished by exposing the intricacies and interdependencies of reshoring.

THEORETICAL FOUNDATION

Theory of Comparative Advantage

Economist David Ricardo's theory of comparative advantage holds that nations should concentrate on producing commodities and services for which they have the least opportunity cost (Kant et al., 2025). Traditionally, this idea advocates free trade and globalization by urging countries to concentrate on their strengths and import products that can be manufactured more effectively elsewhere. But, in the context of reshoring, this idea comes under fire as businesses more and more assess the hidden costs of long-distance supply chains, including ethical concerns about labor abuses overseas and hazards of disruption. The importance of comparative advantage is being questioned as these elements take center stage, hence stressing the requirement of a complex knowledge of competitiveness in a worldwide society (D'Ambrosio & Lavoratori, 2025).

Porter's Diamond Model

Diamond by Michael Porter Model of national advantage offers a tool for grasping how particular sectors inside a nation might attain competitive success. The model stresses four main drivers: factor conditions, demand circumstances, linked and supporting industries, and company strategy, structure, and competition. Because it emphasizes the need of local circumstances in supporting competitive businesses, this theory is especially helpful for examining reshoring. Strong demand for locally manufactured products, together with encouraging government policies, can improve the success of reshoring projects, for example. The model, however, shows the difficulties of reshoring in countries without the required infrastructure and qualified workforce (Ghazalian, 2025).

Theory of Institutions

Institutional theory emphasizes how institutions shape organizational behavior and the systems under which they run. Relevant to reshoring, this theory investigates how regulatory settings, cultural standards, and social expectations shape business decision-making. For example, companies could decide to reshore not just for financial considerations but also to fit with increasing customer need for ethical manufacturing and sustainability. Bureaucratic inefficiencies and uneven laws, however, might undermine the efficacy of reshoring strategies, hence highlighting the need of a supporting institutional environment in attaining favorable results (Rahimjonovich, 2025).

Resource-Based Perspective (RBV)

According to the Resource-Based View, a company's competitive advantage is mostly determined by its own resources and skills. This theory holds that businesses thinking about reshoring have to evaluate their own strengths—such as technology, qualified labor, and creative capacity—to decide the viability and possible advantages of bringing manufacturing back to home shores. Using these tools, businesses may add value and stand out in the market. On the other hand, the RBV suggests that insufficient fundamental resources might seriously hinder effective reshoring and call for investments in new technology and workforce development (Mariotti, 2024).

The Resource-Based View (RBV) will be the main theoretical framework for this paper. The main reason for this decision is the fundamental influence a company's own resources and skills have on the outcome of reshoring projects. The RBV offers a complete framework for examining the practical issues and strategic factors natural in the reshoring process by emphasizing how businesses may use their own strengths to negotiate the complexity involved. This point of view will help to better understand how companies may efficiently react to the demands of economic nationalism by maximizing their operational capacity in a shifting world scene.

The theories of Comparative Advantage, Porter's Diamond Model, Institutional Theory, along with the Resource-Based View (RBV) are interrelated in ways that highlight the intricacies of reshoring and its consequences for competitive advantage. David Ricardo's Comparative Advantage usually supports free trade by saying that countries should focus on making products with the least opportunity cost. But, in terms of reshoring, this idea runs into problems when businesses give long-distance supply chains' hidden expenses, including ethical concerns and disruption risks, more and more attention. This change emphasizes the requirement of a complex knowledge of competitiveness that transcends simple economic efficiency to include more general society elements (Guillén & Torres, 2025). .

By offering a framework for knowing how particular industries inside a country might attain competitive success, Porter's Diamond Model deepens this conversation even further. The model stresses four main drivers: factor circumstances, demand conditions, connected with supporting industries, as well firm strategy (Dedej & Medici, 2024). These factors are especially important for reshoring as robust local demand for locally manufactured products and encouraging government regulations may greatly improve the viability of returning production back home (Nam, 2024). The model, however, highlights the difficulties experienced by nations without the required infrastructure and qualified labor, hence stressing the need of local circumstances in helping competitive enterprises (Clark et al., 2025). By emphasizing how regulatory frameworks, cultural norms, along with social expectations impact organizational behavior, Institutional Theory supports these viewpoints. Reshoring may inspire businesses not just financially but also by increasing customer desire for ethical production and sustainability. Emphasizing the requirement of a supporting institutional framework to get favorable results, this theory shows that bureaucratic inefficiencies and conflicting rules might compromise the efficacy of reshoring initiatives.

Examining the internal capacities of companies thinking about reshoring using the Resource-Based View (RBV) is therefore essential. This concept holds that a company's own resources and abilities mostly decide its competitive advantage. To assess the feasibility of returning manufacturing to their home nations, companies have to consider their strengths including technology, qualified labor, and creative capacity. Though outside influences are important, the RBV underlines that a company's internal resources are more important for effectively negotiating the complexity of reshoring.

A complete knowledge of reshoring results from including ideas from these theories. The RBV emphasizes how internal strengths and weaknesses shape a company's capacity to react to outside pressures and market needs under its general framework. These ideas taken together reveal the several dimensions of reshoring and indicate that businesses have to think about a mix of economic, local, institutional, as well as internal elements to properly control their reshoring plans in a changing worldwide environment. This comprehensive strategy lets companies optimize their operational capability even if economic nationalism and shifting customer expectations present difficulties. The combination of Comparative Advantage, the Porter's Diamond Model, Institutional Theory, as well as Resource-driven View (RBV) in a de-globalized setting post-COVID shows both tensions and harmonies. Although Comparative Advantage stresses cost reductions through worldwide commerce, Porter's Diamond emphasizes local competitiveness, implying a conflict between global sourcing along with local output. Institutional Theory emphasizes the impact of local laws and customs, which might impede RBV's emphasis on using particular internal resources. Strategic decision-making is made more difficult by this difference as companies have to negotiate nationalistic policies and adjust to changing customer tastes for local products, hence undermining conventional competitive regulations in a fragmented economic environment.

DEFINITION AND ORIGIN OF TERMS

Reshoring: It is the process of returning manufacturing and production operations to a company's home nation from foreign sites. Companies started to reevaluate their worldwide supply networks in the early 21st century, especially in view of issues like increasing labor expenses overseas, geopolitical concerns, and supply chain interruptions. This phrase originated then. The COVID-19 epidemic, which exposed weaknesses in worldwide logistics and drove companies to rethink the hazards connected with offshore, helped the idea to gain notable momentum. Reshoring's goals are to strengthen local economic development, increase supply chain resilience, and boost domestic job generation (Rahimjonovich, 2025).

Economic Nationalism: Political and economic theory called economic nationalism gives a nation's economy first priority over world concerns. As governments tried to shield their sectors from foreign competition via tariffs, subsidies, and other protectionist policies, this phrase became more popular in the late 19th and early 20th centuries. Discontent with globalization, which many believe has caused job losses and economic inequalities, has driven the growth of economic nationalism in recent years. This philosophy supports measures encouraging sustainable economic development inside national boundaries, protection of local jobs, and policies fostering domestic production (Ghazalian, 2025).

De-globalization

Often by means of trade restrictions, tariffs, and protectionist measures, de-globalization is the process of lowering interconnectedness and integration between national economies. The phrase developed in response to globalization, which characterizes the growing interconnection of economies and cultures all around. Economic crises, political changes, and social movements supporting localism among other things have all contributed to de-globalization's growing prominence. This tendency emphasizes the need for more self-sufficiency and resilience in home economies, hence underlining a rising doubt about the advantages of globalization (D'Ambrosio & Lavoratori, 2025).

Protectingism

An economic strategy meant to protect a nation's own industries from foreign competition by use of tariffs, quotas, and other trade restrictions, protectionism is Originating in the mercantilist policies of the 16th to 18th centuries, the phrase describes countries' desire to boost exports and limit imports in order to bolster their economies. Especially in times of economic crisis, the necessity to save local jobs and businesses helps to justify protectionist policies. Though, even if protectionism can provide immediate advantages, it might also cause trade wars, increased consumer prices, and strained international relations, hence calling into doubt its long-term effectiveness (Guillén & Torres, 2025).

Analyzing modern developments in global trade and economic policy requires an understanding of these words—reshoring, economic nationalism, de-globalization, and protectionism. Every word captures a reaction to the complexity of a fast changing economic scene where countries are struggling with the consequences of globalization and looking for ways to strengthen their local economies. These ideas still significantly influence the conversation on economic policy and international commerce as they change.

EMPIRICAL LITERATURE REVIEW

The empirical studies on reshoring, economic nationalism, de-globalization, and protectionist policies show a rich tapestry of motives, results, and obstacles (Mariotti, 2024). Particularly in the aftermath of the COVID-19 epidemic, which revealed weaknesses in global supply networks, several studies have recorded the rising tendency of reshoring across many sectors. A report from the Reshoring Initiative, for example, revealed that 350,000 positions were created in the U.S. manufacturing industry in 2021, hence highlighting the possibility of reshoring to improve domestic employment and economic stability (Rahimjonovich, 2025). Studies show that growing labor costs in developing nations, supply chain interruptions, and customer desire for locally sourced goods are driving businesses more and more to reshore. Many industrial leaders in a Deloitte poll said the epidemic has led them to reconsider their supply chain plans; 63% of them said they were thinking about reshoring as a realistic choice. Particularly in the technology industry, where companies like Apple have started to spread their manufacturing sites to reduce risks related to trade conflicts and geopolitical concerns, this change is clear (Ghazalian, 2025). Empirical research may be strengthened by using statistics databases as the World Bank, which claims trade policies have a 3% GDP growth effect, and OECD data revealing a 25% increase in reshoring-related employment (Clark et al., 2025).. Trade organization statistics also show that in impacted industries, tariffs raised consumer prices by 1.5%, hence offering important information Guillén & Torres, 2025).

Notwithstanding these encouraging developments, empirical research nevertheless highlights notable difficulties linked to reshoring. Research has indicated that although reshoring may result in employment growth, high operating expenses, lack of qualified workers, and poor infrastructure frequently impede the process. Research on the U.S. automotive sector, for instance, underlined how General Motors struggled to locate enough workers to assist its reshoring efforts, hence postponing the ramp-up of domestic output (Clark et al., 2025). Along with, the studies show disagreement on the long-term economic effects of protectionist measures (Mariotti, 2024). Although some research indicates that these policies might offer temporary respite for domestic businesses, others warn that they could provoke responses from trading partners, hence starting trade wars that could damage general economic development (Nam, 2024). A thorough study by the National Bureau of Economic Research revealed that protectionist measures can cause higher consumer costs and lower product availability, hence calling into question their efficacy in promoting sustainable economic development (Guillén & Torres, 2025). The literature also lacks information on the interaction between reshoring and other general economic developments including inflation. Especially in light of increasing input prices and supply chain changes, few studies have carefully investigated how returning production to home shores may affect inflationary pressures. This disparity draws attention to the necessity of more research on the long-term effects of reshoring as well as protectionist policies, particularly as nations negotiate post-pandemic economic issues (Dedej & Medici, 2024).

After examining, the empirical research emphasizes the several dimensions of reshoring and its effects on economic policy. Although more studies are showing the advantages of reshoring, major obstacles still exist that have to be handled to guarantee effective execution. Future studies should seek to increase knowledge of these processes by investigating the possibilities and challenges reshoring offers in the framework of an ever more nationalistic and protectionist world scene.

ISSUES, CONTROVERSIES, PROBLEMS

The revival of reshoring as well as protectionist measures has certainly generated a variety of problems and debates that cloud the discussion on economic nationalism (Clark et al., 2025). The conflict between the wish for local job development and the reality of increased production costs connected with domestic manufacturing is one main concern. Although many businesses struggle financially when moving operations, reshoring is sometimes praised for its possible employment creation. For example, labor expenses in rich nations are usually more than those in developing ones, which creates a paradox whereby the expected advantages of reshoring could not come true if businesses cannot stay price competitive. This scenario calls into question the viability of reshoring as a long-term strategy for generating jobs (D'Ambrosio & Lavoratori, 2025). A significant case study is the U.S. manufacturing sector, which has shown a slow rise in reshoring efforts since 2010 (Ghazalian, 2025). A Boston Consulting Group analysis found that approximately 1 million manufacturing jobs were gained in the U.S. across 2010 and 2018, in part due to General Electric and Apple returning some production to the U.S. The same report, however, underlined how difficult it is for many companies to maintain this drive given high personnel expenses and the necessity for sophisticated automation systems. For instance, investments in automation balanced GE's choice to move certain appliance manufacturing back to the United States, which called into question the net job creation advantages of reshoring (Rahimjonovich, 2025).

The study of reshoring in developing countries, especially with regard to SMEs and labor demographics including women, young people, along with migrant workers, shows notable consequences (Clark et al., 2025). Often lacking the means to change fast, SMEs might alienate underprivileged populations. While women and young people could gain from increased employment prospects, society standards or skill mismatches could prevent them from reaching these positions (Mariotti, 2024). Essential for many industries, migrant workers might find employment uncertainty if domestic recruiting takes top priority (Rahimjonovich, 2025). But to really grasp the whole dynamics of reshoring, one must include the viewpoints of labor unions, NGOs, as well as indigenous people who fight for fair labor conditions along with social justice (D'Ambrosio & Lavoratori, 2025). The efficacy of protectionist policies is another major debate. Advocates say that such policies preserve local businesses and jobs, while opponents say that protectionism could raise consumer costs and limit market options (Mariotti, 2024). A great example is the trade conflicts between the U.S. and China, where tariffs placed on Chinese products have raised consumer costs. A University of California, Berkeley analysis found that the tariffs on $250 billion worth of Chinese goods produced an average rise of $1,277 per year for American families. Particularly when retaliatory actions intensify into trade wars, this scenario has spurred debates about the general effectiveness of protectionism in promoting economic development (Clark et al., 2025). The question of supply chain resilience has also become more important, especially in relation to worldwide disturbances as the COVID-19 epidemic. The epidemic drew attention to weaknesses in just-in-time supply chains, which led many businesses to question their dependence on foreign manufacturing. A McKinsey poll indicated that 93% of supply chain executives said the epidemic caused interruptions that caused them to seriously rethink their sourcing policies. Automakers such as Ford and General Motors, for example, have started to localize their supply chains; yet, building additional domestic manufacturing capacity presents difficulties. For the semiconductor sector, the U.S. government has started programs to fund local chip production as it understands that depending on foreign supply networks exposes weaknesses (Mariotti, 2024).

In industries like technology and engineering, where there is increasing need for specialised skills, the issue of workforce development is most noticeable. The revival of reshoring projects in the automobile industry in Germany, for instance, has drawn attention to the demand for qualified workers in modern manufacturing. A study from the German Economic Institute showed that about 60% of industrial sector businesses struggle to locate suitable personnel. This need has pushed companies to work with vocational colleges and universities to provide training courses suited to industry demands, therefore highlighting the need of coordinated efforts between companies and educational institutions (Rahimjonovich, 2025). Finally, the environmental effects of reshoring and protectionism are more and more under question. Although bringing manufacturing back home can lower transportation emissions, the whole environmental effect relies on how domestic businesses run. Rapid development in China has sometimes come at the cost of environmental damage (Dedej & Medici, 2024). Businesses thinking on reshoring have to evaluate if domestic manufacturing can be run sustainably as well. For example, a report from the International Energy Agency indicated that if businesses used cleaner technology, the move to local production in the textiles sector may reduce carbon emissions. A whole strategy to reshoring that takes into account not just economic considerations but also environmental sustainability will help to address this complexity (Guillén

& Torres, 2025). After examining, the challenges, debates, and controversies surrounding reshoring and protectionist policies underline the importance of a complex knowledge of these processes.

Sectoral studies reveal that the technology and automotive sectors lead reshoring initiatives, hence greatly affecting local economies and supply networks (D'Ambrosio & Lavoratori, 2025). Though less obviously, other industries including farming, medical care, and service sectors are also impacted (Rahimjonovich, 2025). For example, whereas healthcare industries could gain from localised manufacture of necessary items, reshoring in agriculture might improve food security (Mariotti, 2024). By promoting collaboration and commerce among member nations, regional trade agreements such as RCEP and AfCFTA help to offset nationalistic tendencies (Ghazalian, 2025). These agreements can enable a more integrated approach regarding regional economic resilience by helping to smooth supply chains while decreasing the negative consequences of protectionism. Case studies from nations such the United States, Germany, and China show the many consequences of these policies. Job creation, economic resilience, and environmental sustainability objectives must be balanced as nations negotiate the difficulties of economic nationalism. For politicians and companies trying to carry out successful reshoring projects in an ever more linked globe, tackling these problems will be very vital.

SOLUTIONS

A multifarious strategy is required to handle the difficulties related to reshoring and protectionist legislation. Above all, improving worker development is absolutely vital (Mariotti, 2024). Training programs that provide workers with the skills required for contemporary industry should be developed by governments as well as educational institutions working together (Dedej & Medici, 2024). Programs include vocational training, apprenticeships, and business collaborations can assist to close the skills gap. Programs such to Germany's dual education system, which integrates classroom learning with practical experience, may be used, for example, to guarantee a consistent flow of qualified personnel. Investing in workforce development helps countries to better assist businesses trying to reshore and boost local economies (D'Ambrosio & Lavoratori, 2025). Encouraging reshoring depends on another significant solution: promoting a favorable regulatory environment. Policymakers ought to think about providing businesses that return manufacturing jobs back home tax benefits, grants, and subsidies as incentives (Ghazalian, 2025). These incentives can assist balance the increased operating expenses related to local production, hence enabling reshoring for companies. Streamlining regulatory procedures also helps to eliminate administrative obstacles and enable faster changes for businesses hoping to set up or grow domestic operations (Clark et al., 2025). Attracting investment and supporting sustained economic development depend on the creation of a good business environment (Bu, 2024). Successful reshoring projects also depend on infrastructural development. To assist local manufacturing, governments have to give transportation, energy, and digital infrastructure development top priority. Improved infrastructure not only increases logistical efficiency but also draws companies by lowering operating delays and expenses. Creating a favorable environment for reshoring, for instance, would be facilitated by building industrial parks with access to consistent utilities and transportation systems (Mariotti, 2024). Along with, investing in cutting-edge technology like automation and robotics may improve competitiveness and production, hence increasing the appeal of local manufacturing (Rahimjonovich, 2025).

Another important approach is to encourage cooperation between companies and local communities. Interacting with stakeholders—including local governments, business groups, and community organizations—can assist one find particular needs and difficulties linked to reshoring. Cooperative initiatives can produce customized answers for local labor demands, infrastructural needs, and community issues. Encouraging a culture of innovation in local businesses also helps to guarantee long-term success for reshored companies by driving ongoing improvement and market change adaption. Ultimately, tackling the environmental effect of reshoring calls for a dedication to sustainable methods. To reduce their environmental impact, businesses should use green manufacturing practices and fund renewable energy sources. Policymakers may assist this change by offering incentives for sustainable habits and promoting clean technology research and development. Countries that coordinate their reshoring initiatives with environmental sustainability will be able to compete in the worldwide market and handle climate change issues (D'Ambrosio & Lavoratori, 2025).

DISCUSSION

The main results of this study on protectionist measures, de-globalization, economic nationalism, and reshoring show a complex scene characterized by both possibilities and obstacles. One notable result is the rising tendency of reshoring as businesses try to reduce risks connected with global supply chains, especially in light of COVID-19-related disturbances. Many companies have come to understand the need of local production for strengthening supply chain resilience, which has led to a remarkable rise in domestic manufacturing employment. Though this change has some advantages, it also draws attention to the difficulties of rising operating expenses and the demand for a qualified labor. The intricacy of protectionist measures is another important discovery. Although many people defend these policies as required to protect local businesses and jobs, studies show they could raise consumer costs and provoke responses from trade partners, hence aggravating trade conflicts. The study shows that whereas protectionism could offer temporary comfort for some industries, it could negatively affect consumer welfare and economic growth in the long run.

The chapter also emphasizes how crucial workforce development is for enabling effective reshoring projects. Many businesses find major talent shortages when they try to move operations back to home shores. The results imply that the possibility of reshoring to generate employment might be compromised without focused training courses and educational alliances. This underlines the requirement of a concerted effort between companies and educational institutions to create a workforce competent to satisfy the needs of contemporary manufacturing. Along with, the results underline the vital part infrastructure plays in helping to support reshoring initiatives. Improving logistical efficiency and lowering operating costs depend on investments in digital infrastructure, energy, and transportation. The study shows that well-developed infrastructure not only draws companies but also helps their long-term viability in a competitive worldwide market. Ultimately, the main results of this study show the several aspects of reshoring and protectionist.

CONCLUSION

The intricate interaction between reshoring, economic nationalism, de-globalization, as well as protectionist measures has been thoroughly explored in this chapter. Establishing a basic knowledge of the present economic scene, we started by defining important words and following their roots. We next looked into actual studies stressing the reasons for reshoring, the advantages it may offer, and the major obstacles businesses have in putting it into effect. By means of many case studies, we showed the actual consequences of these tendencies and found important holes in the current knowledge. The debate over problems and difficulties around reshoring exposed the several sides of the subject. Although the possibility of job creation and economic resilience is clear, the reality usually entails increased operating expenses, lack of qualified workers, and supply chain transformation complexity. These difficulties highlight the need of efficient solutions, which we thoroughly discussed. We found practical ideas for businesses and politicians by stressing worker development, building encouraging regulatory environments, funding infrastructure, encouraging community cooperation, and stressing environmental sustainability. This chapter underlines in conclusion that whereas reshoring along with protectionist policies provide both possibilities and difficulties, long-term success depends on a balanced strategy. Understanding the complexities of these ideas will be vital as nations negotiate the changing economic scene. Future academics and legislators are urged to investigate these dynamics more closely, bearing in mind the interaction between local and global elements to support a robust and sustainable manufacturing industry.

MANAGERIAL IMPLICATIONS

The results of this study on protectionist measures and reshoring have numerous significant management consequences for companies negotiating the complexity of the current economic scene. In the beginning, leaders have to see the strategic importance of reshoring as a way to improve supply chain resilience. Companies can reduce risks connected with global disturbances by means of thorough analysis of their manufacturing procedures and consideration of the advantages of local sourcing. This proactive strategy not only preserves operational continuity but also fits with rising customer desire for locally manufactured products. Along with, the focus on workforce development highlights the need for managers to make investments in training and skill development for their staff members. The presence of a qualified staff becomes vital when businesses move activities back to domestic sites. To create customized training programs that target certain skills deficits, managers should give educational institutions top priority in their relationships. Businesses may guarantee their competitiveness and ability to change with industrial technology by promoting a culture of ongoing learning and growth. Managers should use technology for efficiency, invest in staff training, along with creating industry-specific policies giving local sourcing first priority. In industries like healthcare, building alliances with local suppliers can improve resilience. In the automobile sector, automated processes and sustainable practices help to simplify manufacturing; ongoing market research guides adaptive tactics in changing conditions. The need of infrastructure investment also highlights a management need to work with local governments and business leaders in support of better infrastructure. Managers should be proactive in spotting infrastructure issues affecting their operations and work with community leaders to promote projects improving logistics and connectivity. This involvement helps the business as well as the general economic health of the area. At last, the results underline the need for businesses to embrace sustainable practices as they change their manufacturing strategy.

PRACTICAL IMPLICATIONS

For companies trying to negotiate the changing economic scene, the practical consequences of reshoring as well as protectionist measures are considerable. One of the most obvious consequences is the requirement for businesses to review their supply chain policies. Companies thinking in reshoring have to do comprehensive cost-benefit studies to grasp the financial and operational consequences of relocating production nearer to home. This involves assessing not just direct labor expenses but additional considerations like logistics, transportation, and possible tariffs. Understanding these components clearly will help businesses to create educated choices in line with their long-term strategic objectives. Another useful consequence is the need for improved cooperation between educational institutions and companies. Practical alliances can close the skills gap as manpower shortages turn more important in reshoring initiatives. To create training programs directly in line with business demands, businesses should actively interact with local vocational schools and universities. Ensuring the workforce is prepared with the required skills to flourish in contemporary industrial settings, this cooperation can be in the form of internships, apprenticeships, alongside curriculum development. Investing in local talent helps businesses not only guarantee a qualified staff but also support community growth.

Along with, businesses have to include infrastructure into their operational strategy as it is crucial. This means not just assessing current infrastructure but also supporting changes that would increase efficiency. To emphasize infrastructure requirements such transportation systems, energy supply, and digital connection, businesses should engage in dialogue with local governments. Participating in these discussions helps businesses to influence regulations that enable more seamless operations and lower supply chain management and logistics expenses. For companies involved in reshoring, sustainability also comes up as a sensible issue. Companies have to include sustainability into their manufacturing processes as customers push more eco-friendly practices. This can mean using clean technology, cutting waste, and procuring resources sensibly. Doing so helps businesses not only fulfill legal standards but also improve their brand image and attract eco-conscious customers

THEORETICAL IMPLICATIONS

The theoretical consequences of reshoring along with protectionist measures provide insightful analysis of the changing dynamics of world trade as well as economic strategy. One important theoretical consequence is the challenge to conventional globalization ideas, which usually stress the advantages of global supply networks and comparative gains This change motivates academics to investigate new frameworks considering the complexity of contemporary manufacturing and the interaction between local and worldwide economic elements. Another theoretical consequence relates to the knowledge of economic nationalism and its influence on trade policy formation. The reasons for protectionist policies ought to be carefully investigated as more nations implement them. The growth of economic nationalism pushes academics to look into the underlying socio-political elements propelling these changes as it questions conventional wisdom supporting free trade and open markets. This study can help to clarify how national identity, security issues, and internal economic constraints affect policy choices, hence changing the scene of international commerce.

The junction of sustainability and economic policy also offers a great field for theoretical investigation. Integrating sustainability into company operations becomes very vital when companies carry out reshoring projects. This begs the issue of how theories of environmental economics and corporate social responsibility may guide governmental policy and company behavior. Theoretical frameworks have to change to handle the balance between environmental stewardship and economic development, thereby investigating how businesses may gain competitiveness while simultaneously supporting sustainable development. Along with, when reshoring changes employment patterns, the consequences for labor market theories are important. The return to home manufacturing brings up issues with labor relations, skill needs, and workforce dynamics. The particular difficulties brought on by reshoring might call for a rethinking of theories on labor market segmentation and skill mismatches.

RECOMMENDATIONS

Policymakers, companies, and educational institutions need to follow many guidelines if they are to properly handle the problems and debates surrounding protectionist policies and reshoring. A main advice is to strengthen programs for developing the workforce. Governments should work with business leaders to provide focused training courses emphasizing the abilities required for contemporary manufacturing. This calls for funding vocational training, apprenticeships, and technical education in line with industry requirements. Partnerships between educational institutions and businesses helps to shape curriculum so that they provide workers with the necessary skills. Promoting the fields of STEM education at younger levels also helps to motivate future generations to choose jobs in manufacturing, so guaranteeing a strong talent pipeline. Another important advice is to carry out encouraging programs and incentives. By means of tax incentives, grants, and subsidies for businesses dedicated to returning manufacturing to home beaches, policymakers have to foster an atmosphere supporting reshoring. Easier transitions can result from streamlining the regulatory procedure for building and expanding manufacturing plants. Working with industry players to pinpoint particular obstacles and simplify rules would guarantee that companies can run effectively and help local economies. This cooperative strategy can improve the general business environment and promote domestic manufacturing investment. Supporting reshoring initiatives depends on investment in infrastructure. Governments should give transportation, energy, and digital infrastructure development that enables effective manufacturing operations top priority. While dependable energy supplies can lower operational costs for companies, upgrading roads, trains, and ports can improve logistical efficiency. Investing in digital infrastructure also helps businesses to use cutting-edge technology including automation and IoT (Internet of Things), hence increasing production and competitiveness. A well-developed infrastructure guarantees that companies can function properly in a worldwide market and also draws them.

Examining the connections between nationalism, reshoring, inflation, as well as labor markets in a post-pandemic setting uncovers a rich web of interactions. Often nationalistic policies push reshoring initiatives as governments want to safeguard local businesses and strengthen economic resiliency. But, as businesses have more running costs, this change might result in greater manufacturing prices, which would cause inflation. Inflation, then, reduces consumer buying power, which may therefore impair demand for reshored goods. Reshoring also affects labor markets by providing chances for local people while maybe marginalizing those in worldwide supply networks. This dynamic calls for a thorough framework to chart these causal links so that enterprises and governments can negotiate the changing economic scene. Such a model would clarify how various components interact, hence assisting in the resolution of issues and the exploitation of possibilities in a fast changing environment. Addressing the particular demands connected with reshoring requires encouraging cooperation between companies and local communities. Working with community stakeholders—including local governments and business groups—will help one find issues and possibilities connected to local workforce development and infrastructure needs.

FUTURE DIRECTIONS

As the world economic scene changes, future directions in the research of reshoring as well as protectionist policies are set to tackle various important issues. Examining sophisticated manufacturing technologies and their influence on reshoring choices is one hopeful path. Researchers should look at how automation, artificial intelligence, alongside additive manufacturing among other advances affect cost structures, productivity, and the general viability of domestic manufacturing as they become more common. Knowing the interaction between technical developments and reshoring might help one to see how businesses can use these tools to improve competitiveness and handle labor issues as well. The study of the socio-political elements fueling economic nationalism and protectionism is another crucial field for future research. Scholars should emphasize the reasons behind changing trade policies as nations struggle with the consequences of globalization, looking at how these patterns are shaped by public opinion, political ideas, and economic circumstances. This study can reveal the fundamental causes of protectionism and guide legislators on possible ways to strike a balance between national interests and worldwide economic integration.

Examining questions of environmental sustainability uncovers trade-offs in home industry, where more local output could raise carbon footprints. Protectionist policies by countries create trade retaliation concerns that call WTO compliance and world trade standards into question. Significant trends also include techno-nationalism and data sovereignty, which drive nations to give local tech businesses and data security first priority, hence changing global cooperation alongside affecting economic policies in a post-pandemic society. The junction of reshoring and environmentally friendly practices offers a great path for investigation as well. Examining the influence of corporate social responsibility on manufacturing choices, future research could investigate how businesses may harmonize their reshoring initiatives with environmental objectives. Research may concentrate on best practices for including sustainable practices into reshoring plans as well as the long-term advantages of such integration for companies and communities. Knowing the link between sustainability and reshoring will enable businesses to present themselves as leaders in ethical manufacturing.

LIMITATIONS

The chapter outlines certain shortcomings that have to be recognized in order to offer a fair view on the debate of reshoring as well as protectionist policies. The dependence on current literature and empirical investigations, which could not completely reflect the fast changing dynamics of global commerce and manufacturing, is one major drawback. New events might make certain results out of date or less relevant as the economic scene changes. This time constraint emphasizes the importance of continuous research to match the evolving environment and include new trends not yet seen in the present corpus of knowledge. Sourcing information could also be biased as most research could concentrate on particular sectors or areas. This can result in a partial knowledge of the consequences of reshoring in various industries and geographical settings. For example, whereas manufacturing could be well covered, other industries like services or agriculture would get less focus, which would distort the overall effect of reshoring along with protectionism. Future studies should aim for a more thorough approach including a wider spectrum of sectors and geographical locations to offer a more complex knowledge of these events. The chapter could also fall short in sufficiently covering the intricacies of the interaction between global supply chains and reshoring. Although the emphasis is on the advantages and difficulties of reshoring, it is crucial to think about how local choices are still affected by worldwide interconnections. Supplier connections, international treaties, and market needs might all restrict companies' capacity to completely reshore operations. A more complete picture of the reshoring phenomena and its consequences might come from a closer look at these intricacies. Along with, the chapter focuses mostly on the economic side of reshoring as well as protectionism, maybe neglecting other important angles including cultural, social, as well as ethical ones. These elements can greatly affect company decisions as well as public opinion. A thorough study requires an awareness of the larger social consequences of reshoring, including ethical sourcing and community effects. Finally, the emphasis on management and theoretical consequences in the chapter can create a lack of practical uses for smaller companies or startups. Because of their resources and power, larger companies may overshadow conversations on reshoring, which might not reflect the realities of smaller businesses

REFERENCES

Anlauf, A., & Schmalz, S. (2025). The Grand Delusions of Globalization. *Critical Sociology*, 08969205251334983. DOI: 10.1177/08969205251334983

Bai, B. (2025). (De) Globalization, the Global Imaginary, and Religious Narratives: A Theoretical Framework and the East Asia Litmus Test. *Religions*, *16*(1), 75. DOI: 10.3390/rel16010075

Bu, Q. (2024). Can de-risking avert supply chain precarity in the face of China-US geopolitical tensions? From sanctions to semiconductor resilience and national security. *International Cybersecurity Law Review*, *5*(3), 413–442. DOI: 10.1365/s43439-024-00125-1

Canteri, I., Capoani, L., Efremov, S., & Viapiana, A. (2024). Is the World Preparing for More Resilient Economies? *L'industria*, *45*(4), 607–641.

Clark, R., Kreps, S., & Rao, A. (2025). The political economy of reshoring: Evidence from the semiconductor industry. *PLoS One*, *20*(2), e0316473. DOI: 10.1371/journal.pone.0316473 PMID: 39951419

Csaba, L. (2025). Globalization and European Integration: A Central European Perspective. *Journal of Risk and Financial Management*, *18*(2), 53. DOI: 10.3390/jrfm18020053

D'Ambrosio, A., & Lavoratori, K. (2025). Reshoring to survive? The other side of de-globalization. *Economia e Politica Industriale*, 1–23. DOI: 10.1007/s40812-025-00342-7

Dedej, A., & Medici, L. (2024). Is Globalization Over? *Interdisciplinary Journal of Research and Development*, *11*(1), 7–7. DOI: 10.56345/ijrdv11n102

Festing, C., & Proff, H. (2024). Mediating the Paradoxes of (De-) Internationalization through Digital Platforms. *International Journal of Business Science and Applied Management*, *19*(2), 35–56. DOI: 10.69864/ijbsam.19-2.187

Ghauri, P. N., Oxelheim, L., & Randøy, T. (2024). The changed geopolitical map: implications for international business policy in a sustainable finance perspective. In *Handbook of International Business Policy* (p. 170–189). Edward Elgar Publishing. DOI: 10.4337/9781035308682.00018

Ghazalian, P. L. (2025). Globalization and the Fallout of the COVID-19 Pandemic. *WORLD (Oakland, Calif.)*, *6*(1), 4. DOI: 10.3390/world6010004

Guillén, A., & Torres, I. C. (2025). Changes in the World Geopolitical Order and the Reconfiguration of Productive Systems: The Mexican Case. *Agrarian South - the Journal of Political Economy*, *14*(1), 22779760241313169. DOI: 10.1177/22779760241313169

Kant, S., Adula, M., & Alemu, G. M. (2025). Effect of Green Supply Chain Management Practice on Firm Performance With Mediation of Green Innovation in Ethiopia. In *Eco-Logistics and Sustainable Supply Chain Innovations* (p. 61–84). IGI Global Scientific Publishing.

Kant, S., Adula, M., & Duloma, H. (2025). The Rise of Product-as-a-Service Models in the Digital Era Redesigning Business Models for Circular Innovation in the Horn of Africa. In *Innovating Sustainability Through Digital Circular Economy* (p. 133–160). IGI Global Scientific Publishing.

Kant, S., & Ashuro, T. (2025). Effect of Eco-Logistics Practices on Organizational Performance With Mediating Role of MSE Competitiveness in Ethiopia. In *Eco-Logistics and Sustainable Supply Chain Innovations* (p. 39–60). IGI Global Scientific Publishing.

Kant, S., Niguse, T., Terefe, A., & Adula, M. (2025). Emerging Trends and Innovations: Effect on Social Sustainability in Manufacturing Supply Chains by Shifts in Consumer Behavior in the Horn of Africa. *Enhancing Social Sustainability in Manufacturing Supply Chains*, 135-162.

Mariotti, S. (2024). "Open strategic autonomy" as an industrial policy compass for the EU competitiveness and growth: The good, the bad, or the ugly? *Economia e Politica Industriale*, 1–26.

Mariotti, S. (2024). "Win-lose" globalization and the weaponization of economic policies by nation-states. *Critical Perspectives on International Business*, *20*(5), 638–659. DOI: 10.1108/cpoib-09-2023-0089

Nam, K. (2024). Digital Transformation and Inter-Regional Dynamics: Accelerating Chinese Multinationals' Internationalization in the De-globalization Era. *Global Business & Finance Review*, *29*(8), 31–45. DOI: 10.17549/gbfr.2024.29.8.31

Popov, V. (2025). Is Globalization Coming to an End Due to the Rise in Income Inequality? *Journal of Risk and Financial Management*, *18*(3), 138. DOI: 10.3390/jrfm18030138

Rahimjonovich, M. S. (2025). THE RISE OF DEGLOBALIZATION: IS THE WORLD MOVING AWAY FROM FREE TRADE? *Web of Humanities: Journal of Social Science and Humanitarian Research*, *3*(4), 80–89.

Wong, C. Y., Yeung, H. W. C., Huang, S., Song, J., & Lee, K. (2024). Geopolitics and the changing landscape of global value chains and competition in the global semiconductor industry: Rivalry and catch-up in chip manufacturing in East Asia. *Technological Forecasting and Social Change*, *209*, 123749. DOI: 10.1016/j.techfore.2024.123749

Ying-Jun, L. I. N. (2025). Changing Orders in International Economic Law Volume 1: A Japanese Perspective *Asian Journal of International Law*, 1-2, p. 223

KEY TERMS WITH DEFINITIONS

1. **Reshoring:** Bringing the production and manufacturing operations back to a company's home nation from foreign sites. This approach seeks to improve supply chain resilience, save transportation costs, and react to customer preferences for locally manufactured products.
2. **Protectionism:** Economic policies meant to protect home businesses from foreign competition by means of tariffs, quotas, and other forms of trade restrictions. Though they could result in greater consumer costs and trade conflicts, protectionist policies are meant to encourage local employment as well as economic stability.
3. **Economic Nationalism:** A philosophy emphasizing the needs of the nation-state over global trade and collaboration. Particularly in times of economic instability, it frequently shows up in laws meant to safeguard local businesses and encourage home manufacturing.
4. **Supply Chain Resilience:** A supply chain's capacity to predict, plan for, and react to disturbances while preserving operational continuity. Particularly in reaction to world events, reshoring initiatives are driven by a desire to strengthen supply chain resilience.
5. **Corporate Social Responsibility (CSR):** A business strategy that includes social and environmental issues into a company's operations as well as stakeholder relationships. Often impacting choices about reshoring, CSR programs emphasize ethical sourcing, sustainability, along with community involvement.
6. **Labor Market Dynamics:** The patterns and developments defining jobs, pay, and educational qualifications in a particular labor market. Companies thinking on reshoring must grasp labor market dynamics as it affects the supply of qualified people and general operational expenses.
7. **Global Supply Chain:** A global network of suppliers, producers, and distributors supporting the creation and dissemination of commodities. Because global supply networks are sometimes complicated and interrelated, companies find it especially difficult to make reshoring choices.

Chapter 10
Preparing for the Next Disruption:
Lessons Learned From Past Crises and Building a Playbook for Future Supply Chain Shocks

Tahsina Khan
https://orcid.org/0000-0001-8032-3376
Bangladesh University of Professionals, Bangladesh

Md Mehedi Hasan Emon
https://orcid.org/0000-0002-6224-9552
American International University-Bangladesh, Bangladesh

ABSTRACT

This chapter, titled "Preparing for the Next Disruption: Lessons Learned from Past Crises and Building a Playbook for Future Supply Chain Shocks," offers a critical examination of historical supply chain disruptions and the strategic lessons they impart for enhancing future resilience. It systematically traces the chronology of major global crises, analyzing their economic and inflationary consequences, and draws on illustrative case studies that highlight effective organizational responses. The chapter further investigates the transformative role of digitalization and artificial intelligence in the early detection and mitigation of supply chain risks, while exploring how sustainable branding practices can foster long-term consumer trust. A structured framework for developing a proactive disruption response playbook is proposed, alongside targeted policy recommendations aimed at strengthening both national and global supply chain resilience. The chapter concludes by outlining key avenues for future scholarly inquiry in this increasingly vital domain.

DOI: 10.4018/979-8-3373-1982-7.ch010

CHAPTER OVERVIEW

In a world growing ever more uncontrollable, global supply chains have come to be both essential and extremely fragile. In the last two decades, a wave of disrupting events such as the COVID-19 pandemic, Russia-Ukraine war, climate driven calamities, and absolute resource shortages have unveiled a high level of vulnerability in the way the world's supply network is organized, operated, and defended. Such were not only the impediments to production delivery systems but have also rippled through to global prices, directly fuelling inflationary pressures and economic instability. The compounding effect of these disruptions has highlighted the pressing need to move from reactive crisis control to proactive continuity building in supply chain systems.

This chapter, *"Preparing for the Next Disruption: Lessons Learned from Past Crises and Building a Playbook for Future Supply Chain Shocks,"* is an attempt to put together a strategic framework built based on historical analysis, theoretical foundation and digital innovation. Although every disruption is different, there are patterns in response and in recovery that have important implications for business, governments and multilateral institutions. By analyzing certain case studies e.g. global supply constraints of the COVID-19 era, ripple effect of geopolitical instability on food energy supply chains, applying long tail consequences of semiconductor shortages, we extract practical lessons that could help to create a repeatable and adaptable playbook for future disruptions.

MAPPING HISTORICAL DISRUPTIONS: A CHRONOLOGICAL PERSPECTIVE

The full comprehension of the weakest spots in supply chains and a protection strategy is based on careful consideration of the significant disruptive events that influence worldwide supply networks. All notable supply chain disruptions are critical learning opportunities revealing what a supply chain does when stressed and knowledge for developing resilient sustainable supply chain system in the future.

The COVID-19 Pandemic: Global Supply Chains in Paralysis

When COVID-19 first appeared towards the end of 2019 before mass global distribution began early in 2020, it became the largest supply chain disruption of this period. The pandemic caused immediate heavy ceasing over all locations of manufacturing centers together with transportation services and sources of labor due to lockdown and quarantine needs and regulations on health safety. Shutdowns that took place across the globe contributed to unprecedented delays in leading ports while provoking extensive shipping backlog and the sudden rise of the prices of transportation. The pandemic caused organizations to reassess their dependency on a single supplier in East Asian regions. The heavy Chinese manufacturing centers, starting with Wuhan, produced severe supply constraints for businesses that maintained their operations there. The collapse in supply chains became an obstacle because non-diverse supplier strategies created complete production stoppages. The supply chain disruptions caused the business world to quickly shift their attention toward nearshoring practices and dual sourcing strategies while they began adopting digital supply chain tracking solutions (van Hoek & Dobrzykowski, 2021). The pandemic-driven impact on business operations will eventually establish buffer inventory management and enhanced local manufacturing capabilities together with digitalized supply chain processes as lasting business practices.

The Russia-Ukraine Conflict: Geopolitical Risks Revisited

The Russia-Ukraine war initiated in early 2022 delivered yet another serious blow to global supply networks which had partially recovered from the pandemic. The war disrupted essential market flows of wheat, corn, fertilizers and oil and natural gas which fuel global agricultural production together with manufacturing operations. Before the war Russia and Ukraine provided approximately 30% of all wheat exports to the world but the trade interruptions because of sanctions caused major disturbances in global food prices. During the war the energy supply dependencies of Europe became apparent particularly since the continent depended on Russian gas imports for its energy needs. The entire energy market experienced substantial price surges because of the conflict which negatively touched both residential customers as well as major industrial companies including chemicals manufacturers and car manufacturers and heavy manufacturing facilities (Gollakota & Shu, 2023). The spreading economic waves produced significant inflation that put additional strain on the post-COVID economic growth. The conflict pushed European governments to find essential supplies more quickly while they worked on both energy source variety and supplier network adjustments for geopolitical independence.

Semiconductor Shortages: A Case of High-Tech Fragility

The worldwide shortage of semiconductor components became one of the longest and most intricate industrial disturbances that started during the pandemic and persisted into 2023 and beyond. The rapid increase in semiconductor demand for automobiles and other electronics as well as medical devices and industrial equipment occurred because of digital transformation alongside remote work requirements.

According to Ling et al. (2021), the COVID-related shutdowns of manufacturing sites in Taiwan and South Korea and Malaysia exposed the dangers of geographical concentration.

The chip crisis showed that high-tech component supply chain disruptions create a chain reaction which stops production throughout entire industrial sectors. Ford and General Motors joined numerous automotive firms when they suspended production while electronics companies experienced delays in their rolling out of new products. The export restrictions together with investment barriers created by China and Taiwan because of their geopolitics tensions with the U.S. worsened the situation. Many countries established ground-breaking semiconductor self-sufficiency measures after the U.S. CHIPS Act and European Chips Act were implemented for enhancing national supply chain protection (Santiago et al., 2024).

Other Recent Disruptions: Climate and Logistics Shocks

Multiple climate-related and logistical disruptions have greatly compounded supply chain stress despite the major disruptions mentioned independently. Extremely severe weather has repeatedly destroyed infrastructure networks through events including German floods alongside wildfires in California from 2020 to 2022 and Southeast Asian typhoon occurrences. The blockade of the Suez Canal by Ever Given in 2021 demonstrated how one maritime bottleneck could capture valuable cargo worth billions for weeks. Supply chain design needs to integrate environmental and logistical risks assessment due to the importance these factors have on producing resilient supply systems. Organizations are improving shock absorption through their implementation of climate resilience features combined with route flexibility capabilities alongside smart port technology deployments (Fekete & Sandholz, 2021).

Learning from History: Toward Resilient Supply Chains

Every disruption shares four primary characteristics: lean inventory management, insufficient real-time monitoring, supplier clusters in specific regions and minimal risk management strategies. Organization resilience has transformed from a beneficial feature into an essential requirement in our present times. Tele-digital twins combined with real-time tracking together with artificial intelligence-based prediction technology and multi-source supply chain management (SCM) allowed businesses to survive these disruptions. Supply chain leaders must learn from past experiences to develop flexible transparent and responsive supply chain systems because of the threats from cyberattacks, and pandemics and climate change continue to grow. Stakeholders who grasp these events in their proper sequence acquire vital knowledge to forecast vulnerabilities so better disruptions can be anticipated.

UNDERSTANDING THE INFLATIONARY IMPACT OF SUPPLY CHAIN SHOCKS

The crucial relationship between supply chain interruptions and inflationary pressure has become a central focus for economists since the pandemic outbreak as well as geopolitical tensions and natural disasters. The economic principle in force throughout this relationship states that limited supply combined with constant or rising demand will result in higher prices. The basic relationship between supply constraints and constant demand leading to rising prices becomes substantially challenging to understand through the analysis of global supply chains because such networks cause lagged effects to spread inflation across multiple sectors and through sequential network connections.

The Mechanisms Linking Supply Chains and Inflation

Normal supply chain operations face disruptions through supply chain shocks that produce shortages in essential components as well as finished products. Price levels have increased because supply cannot keep up with the existing market demand. The COVID-19 pandemic demonstrated one of the most noticeable expressions of this phenomenon through its creation of severe congestion in worldwide shipping networks. During port closures and restrictions on movement and container shortages international shipping prices surged to as much as 500% above normal in selected routes. Consumer price increases for all goods such as electronics and food and medical supplies emerged after logistics costs soared.

Impediments to raw material and energy deliveries intensify inflationary outcomes in many different industries. Numerous shutdowns among mining and refining companies due to the pandemic caused essential metal prices such as copper lithium and aluminum to soar uncontrollably. The Russia-Ukraine war caused oil and gas prices to rise thus creating global inflation through higher production and transportation expenses (Meng & Yu, 2023). The cases demonstrate that breakages within upstream supply chain create progressive price increases that flow down the chain.

Sectoral Vulnerabilities and Asymmetric Inflationary Impacts

The responsiveness of economic sectors to supply chain disruptions creates an imbalance in which sectors experience asymmetrical rises in prices. The automotive industry together with electronics production and pharmaceuticals manufacturing and agricultural supply operations show maximum sensitivity due to their strict requirements for raw materials and essential intermediate goods. Production delays alongside unprecedented climbing vehicle prices became evident in 2021 because of the semiconductor shortage that started during 2020. This shortage especially affected automobile manufacturing across the U.S. resulting in used car prices that surged over 40%. Supply chain interruptions concerning both fertilizers and grain exports have severely damaged the agriculture market. Russia along with Ukraine provide vital fertilizer and grain exports to the world but the conflict emerging from their nations reduced supply which triggered major food price increases. Food prices reached their most elevated level in ten years according to the FAO, Food Price Index during 2022 because of the regional conflicts spreading worldwide inflationary effects (Sohag et al., 2023). The transmission of price shocks across international trade networks among different parts of the world is known as imported inflation.

Causal Feedback Loops and Inflation Persistence

The disruptions within supply chains produce self-perpetuating feedback mechanisms which extend inflation into more extended timeframes. The permanent rise in input prices following disruptions makes firms modify their pricing approaches because they expect ongoing market fluctuations and regulatory reforms. According to Choi et al. (2023), Businesses that operated with just-in-time inventory approaches transition to sustainable yet more expensive supply chain models featuring buffer inventories and several supplier networks. Production processes transformations enact cost increases that persist in the market and become difficult to reverse. The anticipation of ongoing inflation drives the continuation of price increases in the market. Price expectations for future time periods cause businesses and consumers to modify their decisions by asking workers for higher pay and anticipating cost increases through higher pricing and central banks implementing restrictive monetary measures. Rational economic actions by individuals end up sustaining the inflationary cycle. Supply chain interruptions generate both short-term operational disruptions and economic forces which both extend and intensify inflationary situations.

Supply Chain Reconfiguration and Inflationary Trade-offs

Supply chain resilience enhancement through reshoring production and supplier base regionalization and inventory growth creates price rises across the board. These vulnerability reduction strategies create higher production expenses which will persist during short to medium-sized time periods. The labor expenses in developed territories surpass the rates found in offshore producing centers thus resulting in higher manufacturing costs for operations returning from offshore locations (Emon, 2023). The process creates problems for policy experts because they must decide how to protect supply chain stability against rising prices. Supplies chains become more sustainable due to environmental and regulatory pressure which produces cost-push inflation. The green supply chain adoption necessitates financial resources for cleaner technology infrastructure coupled with traceability systems together with regulatory compliance frameworks to achieve sustainable economic conditions. Additional expenses from improved security will increase consumer prices unless productivity benefits exceed these costs.

CASE STUDIES: WHAT WORKED AND WHAT DIDN'T

Success within global supply chain operations depends heavily on an organization's ability to adapt to disruptions in the current transforming industry environment. The examination of international corporations and businesses categorized as SMEs demonstrates key approaches which organizations should take when managing crises and developing resilience. Multiple celebrated cases within this section demonstrate supply chain response methods which succeeded and failed respectively.

Successful Case Studies

Unilever: Agility and Digital Transformation

As a global consumer goods corporation Unilever shows how digital transformation together with agility strengthens supply chain resilience. The COVID-19 pandemic started in early 2020 to create major difficulties for Unilever because its supply systems became interrupted while customer buying patterns changed. Unilever adapted its business by using digital technology with analytics capabilities to monitor supply chain performance. Unilever put forward sophisticated predictive models based on current operational data to forecast changing consumer demand patterns. The company successfully optimized production planning because of this capability which helped in resource distribution. Unilever accelerated production in their factories to meet soaring personal care product demand following the increase of hygiene awareness while managing missing materials supply. Unilever chose e-commerce as one of its core strategic thrusts to deliver products directly to consumers. The organization enhanced its virtual operations by spending on electronic advertising campaigns along with establishing deals with electronic commerce platforms. Unilever succeeded at keeping its sales intact because of this strategic move which let the company obtain new market segments that transitioned their business operations to online platforms (Emon, 2025).

Procter & Gamble: Supply Chain Diversification

Procter & Gamble (P&G) as one of the major consumer goods companies highlighted the value of supply chain diversification throughout the pandemic period. The supply chain disruptions and manufacturing problems led P&G to conduct swift evaluations of its supplier system to discover at-risk areas. P&G built a dual-sourcing plan that added multiple suppliers for specific materials including plastics and chemicals to reduce operational risks. The organization could keep its production steady even when a single supplier experienced disruptions because of this system. According to Meghrajani & Shah (2022) P&G shifted to different suppliers for its hygiene products during the initial pandemic months which retained essential product availability for end consumers. P&G spent resources on developing essential supplier relationships that reinforced collaborative development for innovation. The partnership between P&G and its suppliers enabled co-development through which both parties generated solutions that improved efficiency and improved response speed. Scheduled meetings between P&G executives and suppliers became essential during the pandemic because they allowed the company to find solutions to evolving market conditions and customer demands.

Tesla: Vertical Integration and Resilience

Tesla, the EV manufacturer, has boosted supply chain resilience through vertical integration of its operations. The pandemic caused semiconductor supply shortages to hit Tesla resulting in delays for both manufacturing and delivery times. Through vertical integration of essential components such as batteries Tesla managed to lessen some negative effects from disruptions in its external supply network. The integration of battery production facilities at its facilities enhanced Tesla's ability to manage production independently from outside suppliers and gave it better supply chain control. The strategy enabled better target production achievement and provided Tesla with fast innovation capabilities. Relieving semiconductor shortages in automotive produced by Tesla became possible when the company developed custom hardware elements for its vehicles (Mahdavian et al., 2021). The ability of Tesla to adapt efficiently to supply chain challenges became clear through its swift changes in response to changing consumer preferences. The rapid increase in EV market demand triggered Tesla to increase production while expanding facilities that allowed it to maintain solid sales results across industry disturbances.

Unsuccessful Case Studies

Boeing: Challenges with Supply Chain Complexity

Boeing as a global aerospace leader exposed itself to severe marketplace obstacles throughout the COVID-19 crisis which demonstrated the weaknesses of elaborate supply chain relationships. Business operations became vulnerable to global shutdowns due to Boeing's extensive network of suppliers. The Boeing 737 Max program showcases in a harsh way the SCM problems faced by organizations. Flight tragedies and two airline disasters forced temporary aircraft bans and stopped production on the program. The pandemic increased Boeing's supply chain problems which resulted in delayed aircraft production together with delayed delivery times. The company encountered problems in supply chain coordination because many of its multiple suppliers experienced independent obstacles (Luthra et al., 2022). Boeing experienced substantial financial loss because it could not properly handle its complex supply chain operations as market stakeholders lost their confidence in the company. The experience showed Boeing that its distributed supply network created limitations in supply chain agility thus demonstrating clear priority for direct supply chain optimization.

General Motors: Struggles with Supplier Relationships

The semiconductor shortage of 2020 tested General Motors (GM) by exposing problems in their supplier relationships together with their crisis management abilities. The increase in vehicle demand created a problem for GM because it faced challenges when acquiring sufficient semiconductor chips which are vital components for modern automobiles. General Motors did not take proactive action because they expected a semiconductor shortage despite already being prevalent. Its shortage of suppliers became a critical issue because the company depended on minimal supplier numbers to provide semiconductor products while failing to properly expand its supply base network. The absence of proper planning about semiconductors cost GM multiple financial setbacks when it had to reduce production and suspend operations at multiple factories (Ammar et al., 2022). GM suffered considerably from the semiconductor crisis because its competitors mobilized their supply chains faster while the company demonstrated weaknesses in both supplier relationships and supply chain flexibility. The business struggles from poor supplier strategy exemplify why organizations must not undervalue the need for diverse suppliers and strategic alliances throughout crisis situations.

Hertz: Failure to Adapt to Changing Market Conditions

The pandemic forced Hertz, the car rental giant, to face significant market challenges which revealed weaknesses in SCM as well as its ability to adapt to changes. When travel restrictions were hit, and rental car demand dropped drastically Hertz obtained too many vehicles combined with insufficient funding to operate its business. Its basic business structure coupled with delayed adaptive measures caused the company to face financial trouble. The crisis made Hertz fail to control its vehicle inventory effectively resulting in surplus cars that remained unrented. The market transformations were too quick for Hertz to respond since they lacked supply chain flexibility as a strategy. The Company has plunged into bankruptcy in May 2020 due to its inflexible supply chain structure (Kaur et al., 2023). Businesses must meet agile and responsive operations to suit market dynamics since Hertz's experience proves this necessity in emergencies. Poor adaptation of the market and consumer preferences take established companies to the brink of destruction.

Lessons Learned and Best Practices

The case studies give great insight into the different ways in which organizations can develop supply chain resilience and different mistakes to avoid. Successful firms, Unilever and Procter & Gamble, exhibited their success in terms of agility with digital transformations and the supplier diversification for managing disruptions. By observing these firms, we learn that organizations need to spend money on real-time analytics along with creating flexible supply connection networks with digital systems that are useful in improving monitoring as well as adaptability. Boeing in collaboration with General Motors and Hertz faced challenges because of complex supply chains and poor supplier diversity and rigid company response capabilities. Such organizations show that the strict supply chain setups act as barriers to efficient crisis response and the spill over of the disruption effects.

Key Best Practices for Resilient Supply Chains

Diversification of Suppliers: Organizations need to remove their focus on a single source supplier and opt for a dual sourcing strategy to safeguard against disruption risks.

Investment in Digital Tools: Maximum use of data analytics coupled with digital technologies can improve supply chain visibility and hence prepare the organizations to respond to historical disruption proactively.

Agility and Flexibility: Supply chains should be flexible enough to adjust to the changed market conditions and consumer choice and thus, the company should be able to move faster during a crisis.

Strengthening Supplier Relationships: Prospective relationships with suppliers may contribute to cooperation and innovation which may strengthen the supply chain.

Scenario Planning and Risk Assessment: Continuous evaluation of possible risks and the preparation of plans to cope with if they occur prepare organizations for different disruption scenarios.

THE ROLE OF DIGITALIZATION AND AI IN EARLY DISRUPTION DETECTION

Supply chain resilience established itself as a primary organizational objective because organizations worldwide are navigating complex unpredictable global environments. Early detection systems linked to proactive responses in SCM became essential after the COVID-19 outbreak together with the Russia-Ukraine conflict and climate emergencies and semiconductor scarcity. Digital technologies, especially AI alongside the Internet of Things (IoT), blockchain and predictive analytics show great promise in SCM because they help organizations detect threats early while also allowing for rapid responses (Sodhi et al., 2022).

The Rise of AI and Predictive Analytics in Disruption Management

Through AI and predictive analytics businesses obtain unmatched abilities to handle data and detect patterns and generate strategic choices. AI systems process vast data sets consisting of structured and unstructured data which include supplier records, weather patterns, news feeds and social media and they detect anomalous patterns to provide early warnings about impending disruptions. Machine learning algorithms recognize lead time disorders and supplier delivery disruptions that trigger companies to perform early investigations before issues worsen. Predictive analytics which operate as an AI subset utilize historical data, real-time recorded information and generate future outcome forecasts. Predictive tools based on regression analysis and time-series modeling and neural networks estimate the probability of supply chain events including demand surges and transportation delays and raw material shortages as they recommend corrective actions. Organizations use this capability to act ahead of situations instead of merely responding to them. IBM together with DHL use real-time monitoring capabilities of their AI-powered risk management platforms to track global events and supply chain nodes throughout their operating hours. By analyzing news reports and supplier performance metrics and political instability indices this system produces alerts for possible disruptions. Through this analysis businesses receive actionable information which they can employ in their scenario planning tools to speed up response strategy development (Niu et al., 2021).

Digital Twins and Real-Time Visibility

The supply chain obtains a digital twin representation using real-time integrated information from multiple sources to model its physical form. This technological solution enables supply chain managers to see and test how disorder events will affect their operations before actual disruptions happen. Through digital twin's managers can detect supply chain blockages while analyzing changing factors and suggesting instant supply chain performance improvements (Emon & Khan, 2024b). The implementation of digital twin models by companies exactly when COVID-19 struck allowed them to forecast multiple supply chain disruption scenarios and their effects on inventory management and delivery routes and business partner networks. Through complete visibility into operations companies could redirect shipments while they adjusted production times to prevent major financial losses.

Building an Early Warning System: The Digital Playbook

Developing an effective early disruption detection system requires a cohesive digital strategy or playbook that integrates various technologies across the supply chain. The key components of this digital playbook include:

1. **Data Integration and Centralization**: Centralizing supply chain data from suppliers; logistics partners, market indicators and external data is vital for monitoring. Cloud based platforms allow for easy sharing and working in departments as well as geographies.

2. **AI-Driven Risk Scoring**: Machine learning models can then assign risk scores to suppliers, regions and products based on previous performance, and emerging threats. These risk scores are useful to prioritize monitoring and allocation of resources.
3. **Real-Time Dashboards and Alerts**: Interactive dashboards that are run by AI provide supply chain leaders with an all-around view of performance parameters, disruptions, as well as risk hotspots. Such tools can trigger real time alerts thereby allowing prompt informed decision making.
4. **Scenario Planning and Simulation**: Advanced analytics and digital twins enable organizations to model the effect of different disruption scenarios. This sustains contingency planning and stress testing of supply chains' strategies.
5. **Blockchain for Transparency**: Blockchain technology will make the supply chain transparent and trackable thus it will be easier to trace movement of goods and validate supply chain events. It also minimizes the risk of fraud and increased trust among stakeholders.

Real-World Applications and Business Transformation

The multinational companies Nestlé Siemens and Maersk have moved to place AI-driven platforms to monitor and address disruptions taking place in its operations. The AI tools employed by Nestlé observe agricultural outputs and climate changes which affect cocoa and coffee supply in the market. The company achieves better procurement choices through its supplier relationship enhancement by making informed decisions. The logistics business leader Maersk devoted significant funding to develop AI and IoT systems for obtaining instant shipping operation data. Predictive maintenance algorithms from the company track container conditions as well as vessel performance while decreasing unexpected breakdowns which enhances delivery reliability. Cloud-based AI tools give small and medium enterprises the opportunity to access scalable and price-friendly AI solutions. Microsoft Dynamics 365 and Oracle NetSuite allow smaller firms to use their predictive analytics modules for inventory demand forecasting and demand pattern detection at affordable costs through their cloud-based platforms (Jimenez et al., 2020).

Challenges and Considerations

Several obstacles stand in the way of implementing AI and digitalization even though they hold great promise. The quality issues along with restricted data access present the main obstacle for implementation. AI systems need extensive data collections that are also free from any errors to achieve reliable predictive outcomes. When data shows inconsistencies and fragmentation it produces unreliable forecast predictions along with incorrect decision-making. Supplemental changes within an organization need proper evaluation as a vital step. Organizations must train their personnel for digital tools application and implement data-focused systems while handling resistance to transformational change in SCM. The use of digital technologies requires a solution for security threats and data privacy ethical matters to guarantee safe and responsible operations. The high investment costs related to digital infrastructure pose challenges for SMEs since large enterprises can afford such expenses. Early disruption detection technologies gain wider accessibility through government funds together with industry developed training programs and shared digital platforms which industry associations should provide (Dhirani et al., 2023).

SUSTAINABLE BRANDING AND CONSUMER TRUST IN DISRUPTED ECONOMIES

Brands today face recognition because customers look past their products and services to see their declared values and sustainable practices. Consumer trust assumes supremacy in emergencies such as global pandemics, natural catastrophes and economic downturns. Interruptions in the supply systems pose huge threats to a company reputation, hence the need for organizations to adopt sustainable branding to protect consumer confidence. The interplay between sustainable branding and disruption management is the subject of this section in which organizations learn how to protect their brand values in disruptive situations.

The Importance of Sustainable Branding in Times of Crisis

Sustainable branding is one that brings into play social alongside ethical and environmental aspects of how a brand lays claim to itself while conveying messages to its audience. In times of sever crisis, customers select brands that are committed to sustainability combined with transparent ethics. According to Vredenburg et al. (2020) consumer support for brands increases if their values are similar to the brands when the challenging times come. By using sustainable practices brands can mitigate consumer trust losses and establish long term stability and operational strength throughout a supply chain disruption.

1. **Transparency**: complete openness is the necessary core element of sustainable branding. The current consumers ought to understand the production place as well as the production process and ethical production process used. When issues arise companies, which actively educate their stakeholders on problems and their intended solutions, develop greater stakeholder trust with the customers.

A brand that unveils supply chain methods along with sustainability specific ethical sourcing practice enables customers to have trust in their sustainable actions.

2. **Ethical Sourcing**: A responsible sourcing approach conducts businesses with moral procurement practices by inspecting workplace standards concurrently with environmental sustainability and fair market operations. Upholding the ethical standards in sourcing operations help companies to be socially responsible even in disruption times to their customers. The ethical sourcing platform embraced by Patagonia as well as its environmental sustainability promises has seen the firm sustain consumer trust in tough market times.
3. **Environmental Responsibility**: Brands must reduce their environmental affectations as customers demand sustainable businesses from their favorite's brands. Organizations which implement sustainable practices towards waste reduction and use of renewable resources based on circular economic principles will be building up its brands reputation. Large brands and the like examples of brands. During covid 19 dedicated its operation to sustainability by producing environmentally friendly packaging while cutting carbon emission to serve environmentally concerned consumers.

Case Studies of Brands Upholding Consumer Trust

Unilever: Commitment to Sustainability During the Pandemic

As a major multinational consumer goods business Unilever has maintained sustainability as a central component of its brand quality since its inception. Unilever engaged in active steps throughout the COVID-19 pandemic to maintain its commitments thus building trust with consumers who remained loyal to the company. The organization started community support programs by providing free hygiene items for medical staff and by expanding essential items distribution to pockets of need. Unilever observed "Sustainable Living" brands like Dove Knorr and Lipton gaining increased market sales throughout the pandemic period thus showing sustainable branding meets consumer preferences better in crisis situations. Unilever built stronger consumer trust while improving its brand image by giving clear details about sustainability practices and ethical sourcing methods which solidified its status as sustainability leadership (Strand, 2024).

Ben & Jerry's: Advocacy for Social Justice

Ben & Jerry's serves as an exceptional brand which managed to retain customer trust through disruptions through its dual focus on environmental sustainability and social justice. Ben & Jerry's dedicated its focus to climate change advocacy and racial justice awareness programs starting from COVID-19 through various social justice movements. Using its platform Ben & Jerry's promotes vital social issues which connects its brand identity to broader societal awareness. Ben & Jerry's maintains dedicated customer loyalty by both sharing its customers' values and taking a stand for constructive change. According to Chu et al. (2023) consumer motivation to buy from cause-supporting brands stands at 70%. The meaningful social engagement of Ben & Jerry's demonstrates how purposeful involvement creates trustworthy relationships with consumers.

IKEA: Sustainable Practices and Community Support

IKEA established substantial progress in building its sustainable brand image across global markets during the pandemic era. IKEA has set a goal to transition into a circular business by 2030 in which all materials used in products will be either renewable or recycled. IKEA demonstrated its environmentally focused approach by readjusting its supply network to decrease sustainability pressure. IKEA started various community support programs where they donated furniture together with resources to medical hospitals and marginalized neighborhood areas. IKEA protected customer loyalty through open sustainability reporting and community support programs that reinforced its position as a remarkable brand (Elf et al., 2021).

Strategies for Enhancing Brand Resilience and Promoting Sustainability

To foster consumer trust in disrupted economies, organizations can implement several key strategies that align with sustainable branding principles:

1. **Crisis Communication**: Organizations should create an effective communication system focused on open dialogue and truthfulness throughout disruptions. Present all challenges with transparency together with all actions to solve them alongside sustainable commitments for the future. Brands that articulate their ideas neatly eventually gain on client trust as well as showing organizational responsibility.

2. **Invest in Sustainable Practices**: SCM has to make sustainability central to its identity by ethical sourcing practice and waste reduction and environmental stewardship. Sustainable practice investment makes brands acquire market segmentation opportunities while wooing environmentally minded customers.
3. **Engage with Stakeholders**: Promote real engagement with consumers, employees and communities. The company should stakeholder involvement in sustainability projects but be reaching out for brand value feedback from these people. This partnership activity between brands and stakeholders enhances brand reliability and develops loyal jobs in customer relations.
4. **Leverage Technology for Transparency**: Blockchain among other digitally based technology should be deployed to introduce transparency in SCM practices. Transparency allows brands to give the access of production process information to customers both product sourcing and manufacturing so they can raise their sustainable commitment and build trust as well.
5. **Align with Social Causes**: A company should take up social initiatives that attract its target clients. Other customers rely on brands that actively engage in social issues because it proves they have real effort to achieve positive changes without having fraud representations.

FRAMEWORK FOR BUILDING A DISRUPTION RESPONSE PLAYBOOK

The current VUCA environment demands that organizations must come up with effective responses to disruptions which threaten their supply chains. The COVID-19 pandemic together with geopolitical tensions and natural disasters have solidified the business need to create complete disruption response playbook systems. Businesses need the disruption response playbook to contain risk evaluation procedures and crisis messaging techniques and alternate strategies with adequate stakeholder involvement for proactive supply chain administration. The following section introduces a step-by-step guide for developing a disruption response playbook that focuses on building organizational resistance against coming disruptions.

Risk Assessment

Identifying Vulnerabilities

All disruption response playbooks require a detailed risk assessment as their initial foundation for development. Businesses need to detect and assess weak points that exist throughout their supply chain infrastructure. Organizations perform internal and external factors analysis through operations risk assessment to identify elements that may affect supply chain performance including supplier reliability along with geopolitical risks and environmental and market stability. A complete risk assessment practice permits businesses to grasp the fundamental characteristics of their vulnerabilities while creating better risk management plans as described by the Global Supply Chain Institute (Gurtu & Johny, 2021).

Tools for Risk Assessment

To effectively assess risks, organizations can leverage various tools and methodologies, including:

- **Risk Mapping**: Supply chain risk contemplation enables businesses to identify vulnerable zones and organize their response activities correctly. Risk mapping supplies a visual tool for vulnerable spaces to further enlightened leadership decisions.
- **Scenario Analysis**: Potential disruption scenario development is used by organizations to identify different plausible outcomes and to their resulting effects in addition. Scenario analysis allows team members to understand the ways by which different components integrate when crisis arises hence producing important knowledge for organization planning.
- **Supplier Risk Ratings**: Organizations need to come up with supplier risk rating systems to determine supplier stability and reliability. To measure suppliers' organizations, we need to examine financial performance along with historical performance and geographical factors.

Crisis Communication

Establishing Clear Channels

An organization should therefore be concerned with effective crisis communications because this will ensure stakeholder trust and coordinated responses. Companies require specific routes through which information will be disseminated both inside and outside the company. The organization should constitute an intervention group that controls both message handling and update distribution and response to queries.

Developing a Communication Plan

A crisis communication plan should be clearly described:

- **Key Messages**: Organizations must develop a uniform communication which should explain what type of disruption and operational impacts are, in addition to risk reduction measures. Organizations must uphold clear precise communication to prevent the creation of wrong information by their stakeholders.
- **Audience Segmentation**: When special communication strategies are generated for different categories of people among them staff members and suppliers and customers and investors, it makes it possible to deliver critical data to every recipient properly. In order to achieve trust-building, one needs to be aware of the specific needs/ issues of each target group.
- **Regular Updates**: Organizations need to deliver ongoing updates as a disturbance continues. The organization demonstrates its commitment to resolving the issue through frequent communication which aids transparency maintenance.

Contingency Planning

Developing Contingency Plans

Every disruption response playbook must contain backup strategies which present alternative methods to preserve operations during emergencies. Firms can develop contingency plans through strategic decision-making that identifies essential functions together with backup operational resources before defining alternate methods to continue operations during emergency situations (Ambrogio et al., 2022).

Key Components of Contingency Planning

Effective contingency plans should encompass the following components:

- **Resource Allocation**: Organizations need to identify their critical resources like workforce members as well as tools and stock then devise distribution plans for these elements during disruptions.
- **Alternative Suppliers**: Organizations can improve their resilience by developing relationships with supplier networks ahead of time. Companies need to find substitute suppliers ahead of time to evaluate both their performance ability and reliability.
- **Flexibility in Operations**: Organizations gain the ability to adjust rapidly to new situations when operations include adaptable capabilities. Organizations build operational flexibility by training employees in multiple roles and using different transport methods and expanding their product varieties.

Stakeholder Engagement

Building Relationships

An organization needs to actively connect with their key stakeholders starting from suppliers to customers to employees to communities for developing resilience. Organizations experience better challenge responses when their solid relationships enable both better collaboration and information sharing throughout disruptions.

Strategies for Stakeholder Engagement

To build meaningful relationships with stakeholders, organizations can implement the following strategies:

- **Regular Communication**: Regular stakeholder communication provides organizations with an opportunity to share their activities and plans along with their current challenges with their stakeholders. The practice establishes trust while guaranteeing stakeholders feel recognized and play an active part in organizational decision-making activities.
- **Collaborative Problem-Solving**: Optimal results from disruptions emerge through stakeholder collaboration in problem-solving sessions. Organizations should include their suppliers along with customers and employees in dialogue to benefit from various talents and viewpoints.
- **Corporate Social Responsibility (CSR) Initiatives**: An organization builds stronger relationships with stakeholders through CSR activities which deliver value to nearby communities. The involvement in local initiatives together with contributions to social causes during disruptions reflects organizational commitment to social responsibility while earning community goodwill.

Continuous Improvement and Learning

Implementing a Learning Culture

To support organizational learning the disruption response playbook needs to develop an environment of continuous improvement. The effectiveness of response must be evaluated using thorough post-incident reviews once disruptions are concluded to identify better ways and strategies for future incidents (Alzoubi & Aziz, 2021).

Key Steps for Continuous Improvement

To foster continuous improvement, organizations can implement the following steps:

- **Debriefing Sessions**: Key stakeholders need to participate in debriefing sessions following disruptions to examine both achievements and facing obstacles and gaining learning points. Open dialog becomes possible through this procedure which enhances organizational transparency.
- **Feedback Mechanisms**: Organizations can build feedback systems such as surveys and focus groups to receive information from their employees' customers and suppliers. Organizations use the obtained feedback to design the future and make strategic decisions.
- **Benchmarking and Best Practices**: Industry monitoring combined with peer benchmarking and adoption of leading disruption response practices should be permanent organizational practices. Organizations who monitor emerging technologies and methodologies will experience improved performance of their response strategies.

Policy Recommendations for National and Global Resilience

The vulnerabilities of world-connected systems become apparent through supply chain interruptions which result from pandemics and geopolitical tensions and climate shifts and technical malfunctions. These events starting with COVID-19 followed by the Russia-Ukraine war disrupted manufacturing along with logistics and trade which worsened inflation levels while endangering the living standards of people. The successful prevention of risks to supply chain resilience and development of strong resistance requires national governments together with international bodies to work jointly with private sector organizations on thorough policy implementation. Integrated policies across multiple levels allow national strategies to connect with corporate approaches to develop resilient supply chain networks.

Establishing National Supply Chain Resilience Strategies

National authorities must accept supply chain resilience as an essential element of economic national security. The United States together with Japan along with Australia and the European Union have established basic strategic frameworks for their critical supply chains.

Policies should prioritize:

- **Identifying Critical Supply Chains**: The government needs to establish ongoing reservoirs of crucial items and conduct supplier-dependence assessments for medical supplies as well as food and semiconductors and rare earth elements.
- **Mapping Supply Chain Dependencies**: National policies should initiate efforts to detect single vulnerability points by tracking supply chain dependencies from source to end destination. Identification of single points of failure becomes more effective because of this approach.

Fostering Regional Diversification and Friend-Shoring

The excessive reliance on several global hubs especially China for raw materials and intermediate goods has raised risk vulnerability for companies. Public officials should create programs that promote friendly sourcing where industry relationships shift directly towards nations with geopolitical stability and friendly political alignment.

- **Trade Policy Tools**: Trade agreements need modifications which will promote business diversity. According to Páez, (2024), New trade partnerships emerge from regional agreements such as Comprehensive and Progressive Agreement for Trans-Pacific Partnership and African Continental Free Trade Area.
- **Investment Support**: Businesses obtain financial backing through public funds alongside tax benefits to set up production facilities outside industrial concentrations. The Japanese government supports enterprises by offering financial aid to relocate their operations from China into Southeast Asian regions.

Strengthening Public-Private Collaboration

Day-to-day supply chain issues require public-private collaboration because governments operate alone, they cannot solve these problems effectively. Strong public-private partnerships (PPPs) through policies must establish cooperative responsibilities in forecasting risks and sharing data as well as responding to emergencies.

- **Joint Risk Assessment Platforms**: Governments should collaborate with networking stakeholders for implementing AI-powered and big data-enabled supply chain risk observatories which identify disruptions as they happen.
- **Emergency Response Protocols**: National emergency protocols must establish official positions for large-scale logistics and manufacturing businesses

to perform. Both FedEx and DHL acted as key distribution partners of vaccines throughout the COVID-19 pandemic.

- **Information Sharing Standards**: Policymakers need to develop standardized security-enabled systems for sharing supply chain information. A strategic response plan requires real-time monitoring throughout supply chain levels.

Incentivizing Technological Adoption for Resilience

Governments should enable Industry 4.0 technology implementations by establishing financial programs which guarantee support and proper regulatory frameworks that encourage their adoption (Emon & Khan, 2025b; Khan et al., 2024a).

- **Subsidies and Grants**: SMEs should receive financial help for digital transformation and SCM software adoption through official support programs.
- **Public Digital Infrastructure**: National logistics platforms that receive funding along with digital customs systems will improve the efficiency of trade and increase system stability.
- **Cybersecurity Regulations**: Governments need to apply minimum digital security requirements for both vital data protection and supply chain operational continuity in this digital era.

Promoting Sustainability and Circular Economy Principles

Sustainability needs to be included in resilient supply chain development. Growth in environmental events including floods and droughts together with wildfires has started to disrupt manufacturing sector operations and logistics networks. Universally accepted policies need to make sustainability and resilience intersect by advancing sustainable circular systems and eco-friendly freight handling methods (Liu et al., 2023).

- **Eco-Incentives**: The implementation of national regulations provides incentives to companies that accomplish renewable energy integration as well as material recycling and supply chain emission reduction.
- **Green Logistics Corridors**: Governments need to invest their resources into building environmentally friendly transportation infrastructure that includes electric vehicle corridors and multimodal hubs for decreasing environmental impact.

- **Mandatory ESG Reporting**: Organizations that enforce ESG disclosure in supply chain operations both hold themselves accountable and direct corporate strategies toward national sustainability targets.

FUTURE OF SUPPLY CHAINS: NAVIGATING CHALLENGES AND OPPORTUNITIES

The forthcoming industry shift of worldwide supply chains develops through technological evolution in addition to changing consumer behavior patterns and environmental demands and geopolitical developments. Modern supply chains create obstacles alongside new opportunities for corporate organizations and governmental agencies and purchasing customers. The analysis examines supply chain growth by studying major market trends, technological solutions, sustainable practices, together with geopolitical alterations in the market.

Key Trends Shaping the Future of Supply Chains

Increased Digitalization and Automation

The transformation of supply chain operations through digital techniques presently changes supply chain operations which show signs of accelerating growth moving forward. The SCM approach of modern companies has started to change dramatically through applications of artificial intelligence (AI) along with machine learning and IoT and blockchain technologies. Supply chain executive data in a recent Miceli et al. (2021) indicate that 84% of survey respondents believe organization digitalization is essential for enhanced resilience combined with better efficiency. The major aspect of this transformation revolves around automation technologies. The logistics industry currently adopts automated warehouses together with autonomous vehicles and drone technology in its everyday operations. Amazon uses robotics systems in its fulfillment centers to create higher operational speed and efficiency (Emon & Khan, 2025a). The new technology streamlines operations while it addresses workforce deficits and minimizes operational expenses.

Shift Towards Resilient Supply Chains

Traditional supply chains revealed their weaknesses when the COVID-19 pandemic along with contemporary geopolitical conflicts occurred. Businesses now replace their efficiency-based leadership approach with resilience-focused strategies because of the recent crisis events. Successful supply chain resilience demands multiple suppliers, elevated product stockpiles along with backups within supply chain structures. Executive leaders surveyed by Shishodia et al. (2023) indicated that their plans for supply chain resilience include comprehensive risk management framework implementation to boost their supply chain resilience. To maintain business operation continuity during disruptions businesses should dedicate investments toward flexible sourcing and establish regional production hubs and strengthen supplier relationships.

Sustainability as a Core Value

Organizations from all industries now treat sustainability as a primary organizational value that determines their business management approach. People who value environmental responsibility have made companies reorganize their supply chain structures to prioritize sustainability. Organizations must decrease their carbon footprints and cut down waste together with applying circular economy models. Ran et al. (2022) showed that 66% of consumers would increase their product cost when choosing sustainable options. Due to these changes companies now assess their supply chain activities while investing in clean energy and building environmentally friendly packaging solutions. Unilever strives to eliminate all emissions from its value chain throughout a 2039 timeframe.

Geopolitical Dynamics and Regionalization

Supply chain strategies must adapt to worldwide tensions between countries and economic conflicts and shifts within global power structures. Companies reassess their production and sourcing dependencies, so they shift to regionalization as a new business strategy. Businesses are moving their production facilities towards their primary markets as part of a risk reduction strategy in response to global disruptions. Many businesses become "friend-shore" operators by moving their production bases into stable countries that share the same set of values. Companies from electronics and pharmaceutical industries demonstrate this trend by moving their supply bases out of China to establish operations in Vietnam India and Mexico (Jakovljevic et al., 2021).

EMERGING TECHNOLOGIES FOR SUPPLY CHAIN INNOVATION

Artificial Intelligence and Machine Learning

AI together with machine learning technologies brings substantial changes to SCM. Technology platforms powered by AI inspect enormous data reservoirs which lead to identification of valuable patterns and help maximize inventory control and upgrade forecast predictions. Companies can use AI technologies to improve their market reaction capabilities while monitoring customer preferences as they happen. AI technology built into the IBM Watson Supply Chain platform helps companies gain insights about operational disruptions and make strategic recommendation decisions (Emon & Khan, 2024a).

Blockchain for Transparency and Security

The supply chain sector benefits from growing use of blockchain technology to achieve better authentication and safety through decentralized ledgers. The decentralized secure ledger characteristics of blockchain allow organizations to track products throughout their supply route so they can validate authenticity as well as ethical sourcing practices. The diamond company De Beers employs blockchain technology to verify diamond origins which proves to customers purchases come from conflict-free sources (Khan & Hasan Emon, 2024). Blockchains will be crucial for developing trust and supply chain transparency because consumers continue to show rising concern for ethical sourcing.

Internet of Things (IoT) for Real-Time Monitoring

SCM experiences a groundbreaking revolution through the Internet of Things because real-time monitoring powers asset tracking throughout entire supply chain operations. Through IoT devices that include sensors along with RFID tags companies gain beneficial data about temperature and humidity values as well as location information to follow product movement and protect product quality. Companies in the food and beverage sector implement IoT technology for perishable goods temperature monitoring thus reducing waste and improving food safety (Khan et al., 2024b). Having immediate access to real-time information supports better decisions which enable faster responses that drive supply chain durability.

Implications of Geopolitical Shifts

The political world continues to change thus companies need to handle sophisticated international trading requirements together with import tariffs and legal frameworks. Nationalistic trends together with protectionist measures in various countries currently create more trade obstacles which disrupt global supply chain operations. Companies must develop flexible strategic plans to handle the emerging perils that come from changing geopolitical situations.

Strengthening Supply Chain Security

The protection of supply chains demands organizations to enhance risk management practices to reinforce supply chain security. Organizations need to perform complete risk assessments as they establish several supply chain partners and establish strong cybersecurity systems which defend sensitive data and operational processes from cyberattacks (Emon et al., 2024).

Building Collaborative Relationships

For resilient supply chains to develop business entities must collaborate with governmental authorities alongside industry associations. The exchange of knowledge along with proven methods and available assets enables stakeholders to tackle the problems arising from geopolitical shifts alongside the market uncertainties together. Through public-private partnerships the infrastructure along with technologies and logistics systems receive innovation-backed investment that makes supply chains more resilient. Governments need to collaborate with industrial leaders to establish laws that endorse partnership work and information sharing between all stakeholders.

CHAPTER INSIGHTS AT A GLANCE

A significant transformation of supply chain operations emerges from technological improvements together with changing customer demands and environmental constraints and international market changes. Organizational supply chains require equal strategic importance to operational needs because business environments grow intricate and unpredictable. Four main trends will greatly influence supply chain futures in terms of digitalization expansion and sustainability movement as well as regional supply chain distribution and international political confusions. Adopting digital evolution based on AI together with IoT and blockchain should be positive for organizations to embrace the same to adapt with market evolution. Such technologies allow producers to obtain crucial operational solutions, increasing transparency and optimization efficiency, as well as enable immediate decision making. Companies can identify impending disruptions in their supply chain by taking the use of automated analytical tools into consideration in order to allow them to take effective measures to maintain their supply chain functions. Developments of a supply chain strategy must make sustainable practice an integral aspect. Businesses that devote themselves to sustainable operations, through ethical sourcing and waste reduction, while controlling their carbon footprints bring in consumer customers and ensure the longevity of the current business. Organizations understand that sustainability pioneers are supported competitively for their eco-friendly invention, and this drives them further from the basic compliance requirements. Geopolitical occurrences serve as a major factor which will determine SCM in the future. Countries will buttress relationships with regional suppliers for a reduction of reliance on isolated sources due to trade relations assessments. Some of the features of this change necessitate business to form effective regional partnerships, which in turn enhances their supply chain resistance. Business success in future challenges depends on developing full disruption response plans that will involve risk assessments, crisis message as well as crisis contingency design with interested stakeholders while their interest is nurtured all along. Businesses improve resilient supply chain networks by aligning their strategic plans with national policies which keep them fit and enable them to endure market disruptions and change their environment.

REFERENCES

Alzoubi, H. M., & Aziz, R. (2021). Does emotional intelligence contribute to quality of strategic decisions? The mediating role of open innovation. *Journal of Open Innovation, 7*(2), 130. DOI: 10.3390/joitmc7020130

Ambrogio, G., Filice, L., Longo, F., & Padovano, A. (2022). Workforce and supply chain disruption as a digital and technological innovation opportunity for resilient manufacturing systems in the COVID-19 pandemic. *Computers & Industrial Engineering, 169*, 108158. DOI: 10.1016/j.cie.2022.108158 PMID: 35431410

Ammar, M., Haleem, A., Javaid, M., Bahl, S., & Verma, A. S. (2022). Implementing Industry 4.0 technologies in self-healing materials and digitally managing the quality of manufacturing. *Materials Today: Proceedings, 52*, 2285–2294. DOI: 10.1016/j.matpr.2021.09.248

Choi, T. Y., Netland, T. H., Sanders, N., Sodhi, M. S., & Wagner, S. M. (2023). Just-in-time for supply chains in turbulent times. *Production and Operations Management, 32*(7), 2331–2340. DOI: 10.1111/poms.13979

Chu, S.-C., Kim, H., & Kim, Y. (2023). When brands get real: The role of authenticity and electronic word-of-mouth in shaping consumer response to brands taking a stand. *International Journal of Advertising, 42*(6), 1037–1064. DOI: 10.1080/02650487.2022.2138057

Dhirani, L. L., Mukhtiar, N., Chowdhry, B. S., & Newe, T. (2023). Ethical Dilemmas and Privacy Issues in Emerging Technologies: A Review. *Sensors (Basel), 23*(3), 1151. DOI: 10.3390/s23031151 PMID: 36772190

Elf, P., Isham, A., & Gatersleben, B. (2021). Above and beyond? How businesses can drive sustainable development by promoting lasting pro-environmental behaviour change: An examination of the IKEA Live Lagom project. *Business Strategy and the Environment, 30*(2), 1037–1050. DOI: 10.1002/bse.2668

Emon, M. M. H. (2023). A Systematic Review of the Causes and Consequences of Price Hikes in Bangladesh. *Review of Business and Economics Studies, 11*(2), 49–58. DOI: 10.26794/2308-944X-2023-11-2-49-58

Emon, M. M. H. (2025). The Mediating Role of Supply Chain Responsiveness in the Relationship Between Key Supply Chain Drivers and Performance: Evidence from the FMCG Industry. *Brazilian Journal of Operations & Production Management, 22*(1), 2580. DOI: 10.14488/BJOPM.2580.2025

Emon, M. M. H., & Khan, T. (2024a). A Systematic Literature Review on Sustainability Integration and Marketing Intelligence in the Era of Artificial Intelligence. *Review of Business and Economics Studies, 12*(4), 6–28. DOI: 10.26794/2308-944X-2024-12-4-6-28

Emon, M. M. H., & Khan, T. (2024b). Unlocking Sustainability through Supply Chain Visibility: Insights from the Manufacturing Sector of Bangladesh. *Brazilian Journal of Operations & Production Management, 21*(4), 2194. DOI: 10.14488/BJOPM.2194.2024

Emon, M. M. H., & Khan, T. (2025a). The mediating role of attitude towards the technology in shaping artificial intelligence usage among professionals. *Telematics and Informatics Reports, 17*, 100188. DOI: 10.1016/j.teler.2025.100188

Emon, M. M. H., & Khan, T. (2025b). The transformative role of Industry 4.0 in supply chains: Exploring digital integration and innovation in the manufacturing enterprises. *Journal of Open Innovation, 11*(2), 100516. DOI: 10.1016/j.joitmc.2025.100516

Emon, M. M. H., Khan, T., Rahman, M. A., & Siam, S. A. J. (2024). Factors Influencing the Usage of Artificial Intelligence among Bangladeshi Professionals: Mediating role of Attitude Towards the Technology. *2024 IEEE International Conference on Computing, Applications and Systems (COMPAS)*, 1–7. DOI: 10.1109/COMPAS60761.2024.10796110

Fekete, A., & Sandholz, S. (2021). Here Comes the Flood, but Not Failure? Lessons to Learn after the Heavy Rain and Pluvial Floods in Germany 2021. *Water (Basel), 13*(21), 3016. DOI: 10.3390/w13213016

Gollakota, A. R. K., & Shu, C.-M. (2023). Covid-19 and energy sector: Unique opportunity for switching to clean energy. *Gondwana Research, 114*, 93–116. DOI: 10.1016/j.gr.2022.01.014 PMID: 35136377

Gurtu, A., & Johny, J. (2021). Supply Chain Risk Management: Literature Review. *Risks, 9*(1), 16. DOI: 10.3390/risks9010016

Jakovljevic, M., Wu, W., Merrick, J., Cerda, A., Varjacic, M., & Sugahara, T. (2021). Asian innovation in pharmaceutical and medical device industry – beyond tomorrow. *Journal of Medical Economics, 24*(sup1), 42–50. DOI: 10.1080/13696998.2021.2013675

Jimenez, V. J., Bouhmala, N., & Gausdal, A. H. (2020). Developing a predictive maintenance model for vessel machinery. *Journal of Ocean Engineering and Science, 5*(4), 358–386. DOI: 10.1016/j.joes.2020.03.003

Kaur, J., Kumar, S., & Joshi, R. (2023). Is supply chain finance an antidote to SMEs in the economic crisis? - A qualitative inquiry. *International Journal of Logistics Management, 34*(6), 1890–1910. DOI: 10.1108/IJLM-10-2021-0496

Khan, T., Emon, M. M. H., & Rahman, M. A. (2024a). A systematic review on exploring the influence of Industry 4.0 technologies to enhance supply chain visibility and operational efficiency. *Review of Business and Economics Studies, 12*(3), 6–27. DOI: 10.26794/2308-944X-2024-12-3-6-27

Khan, T., Emon, M. M. H., & Rahman, S. (2024b). Marketing Strategy Innovation via AI Adoption: A Study on Bangladeshi SMEs in the Context of Industry 5.0. *2024 6th International Conference on Sustainable Technologies for Industry 5.0 (STI)*, 1–6. DOI: 10.1109/STI64222.2024.10951050

Khan, T., & Hasan Emon, M. M. (2024). Determinants of AI Image Generator Adoption Among Marketing Agencies: The Mediating Effects of Perceived Usefulness. *2024 IEEE 3rd International Conference on Robotics, Automation, Artificial-Intelligence and Internet-of-Things (RAAICON)*, 177–182. DOI: 10.1109/RAAICON64172.2024.10928548

Ling, G. H. T., Md Suhud, N. A., Leng, P. C., Yeo, L. B., Cheng, C. T., Ahmad, M. H. H., & Ak Matusin, A. M. R. (1704). binti Md Suhud, N. A., Leng, P. C., Yeo, L. B., Cheng, C. T., Ahmad, M. H. H., & Ak Matusin, A. M. R. (2021). Factors Influencing Asia-Pacific Countries' Success Level in Curbing COVID-19: A Review Using a Social–Ecological System (SES) Framework. *International Journal of Environmental Research and Public Health, 18*(4), 1704 DOI: 10.3390/ijerph18041704 PMID: 33578829

Liu, H., Shi, Y., Yang, X., & Zhang, W. (2023). The Role of Business Environment and Digital Government in Mitigating Supply Chain Vulnerability—Evidence from the COVID-19 Shock. *Sustainability (Basel), 15*(3), 2323. DOI: 10.3390/su15032323

Luthra, S., Sharma, M., Kumar, A., Joshi, S., Collins, E., & Mangla, S. (2022). Overcoming barriers to cross-sector collaboration in circular supply chain management: A multi-method approach. *Transportation Research Part E, Logistics and Transportation Review, 157*, 102582. DOI: 10.1016/j.tre.2021.102582

Mahdavian, A., Shojaei, A., Mccormick, S., Papandreou, T., Eluru, N., & Oloufa, A. A. (2021). Drivers and barriers to implementation of connected, automated, shared, and electric vehicles: An agenda for future research. *IEEE Access : Practical Innovations, Open Solutions, 9*, 22195–22213. DOI: 10.1109/ACCESS.2021.3056025

Meghrajani, I., & Shah, S. (2022). Product extension or channel extension – a case of Cronos Industries Pvt Ltd. *Emerald Emerging Markets Case Studies*, *12*(4), 1–28. DOI: 10.1108/EEMCS-10-2021-0350

Meng, X., & Yu, Y. (2023). Does the Russia-Ukraine conflict affect gasoline prices? *Energy Economics*, *128*, 107113. DOI: 10.1016/j.eneco.2023.107113

Miceli, A., Hagen, B., Riccardi, M. P., Sotti, F., & Settembre-Blundo, D. (2021). Thriving, Not Just Surviving in Changing Times: How Sustainability, Agility and Digitalization Intertwine with Organizational Resilience. *Sustainability (Basel)*, *13*(4), 2052. DOI: 10.3390/su13042052

Niu, Y., Ying, L., Yang, J., Bao, M., & Sivaparthipan, C. B. (2021). Organizational business intelligence and decision making using big data analytics. *Information Processing & Management*, *58*(6), 102725. DOI: 10.1016/j.ipm.2021.102725

Páez, L. (2024). The Political Economy of Preferential Trade in the Global Economy: Why Africa Needs to Refrain from Mega-regionals and Other FTAs with Third Parties. In *The African Continental Free Trade Area* (p. 241–284). Springer Nature Switzerland. DOI: 10.1007/978-3-031-66605-6_8

Ran, Y., Nilsson Lewis, A., Dawkins, E., Grah, R., Vanhuyse, F., Engström, E., & Lambe, F. (2022). Information as an enabler of sustainable food choices: A behavioural approach to understanding consumer decision-making. *Sustainable Production and Consumption*, *31*, 642–656. DOI: 10.1016/j.spc.2022.03.026

Santiago, F., Haraguchi, N., & Lavopa, A. (2024). Global Trends and World Order: Implications for New Industrial Policies in Developing Countries. *Journal of Industry, Competition and Trade*, *24*(1), 5. DOI: 10.1007/s10842-024-00419-4

Shishodia, A., Sharma, R., Rajesh, R., & Munim, Z. H. (2023). Supply chain resilience: A review, conceptual framework and future research. *International Journal of Logistics Management*, *34*(4), 879–908. DOI: 10.1108/IJLM-03-2021-0169

Sodhi, M. S., Seyedghorban, Z., Tahernejad, H., & Samson, D. (2022). Why emerging supply chain technologies initially disappoint: Blockchain, IoT, and AI. *Production and Operations Management*, *31*(6), 2517–2537. DOI: 10.1111/poms.13694

Sohag, K., Islam, M. M., Tomas Žiković, I., & Mansour, H. (2023). Food inflation and geopolitical risks: Analyzing European regions amid the Russia-Ukraine war. *British Food Journal*, *125*(7), 2368–2391. DOI: 10.1108/BFJ-09-2022-0793

Strand, R. (2024). Global Sustainability Frontrunners: Lessons from the Nordics. *California Management Review*, *66*(3), 5–26. DOI: 10.1177/00081256241234709 van Hoek, R., & Dobrzykowski, D. (2021). Towards more balanced sourcing strategies – are supply chain risks caused by the COVID-19 pandemic driving reshoring considerations? *Supply Chain Management*, *26*(6), 689–701. DOI: 10.1108/SCM-09-2020-0498

Vredenburg, J., Kapitan, S., Spry, A., & Kemper, J. A. (2020). Brands Taking a Stand: Authentic Brand Activism or Woke Washing? *Journal of Public Policy & Marketing*, *39*(4), 444–460. DOI: 10.1177/0743915620947359

KEY TERMS AND DEFINITION

Supply Chain Disruption: A shocking incident which hampers the normal flow of goods and materials at the nodes of the supply chain resulting in delays or shortages or costly delays. These are examples such as pandemics and geopolitical conflicts and natural disasters.

Resilience: The capacity of a supply chain to look ahead, prepare for, react to and rebound from disruptions while preserving essential activities and adapting to prolonged, permanent changes.

Just-in-Time (JIT): A supply chain inventory technique that reduces inventory levels by only taking in goods whenever they are required for production or sales. Although effective, JIT is very much susceptible to disruptions.

Digital Supply Chain: A supply chain that is improved through digital technologies such as Artificial Intelligence (AI), the Internet of Things (IoT), blockchain, and cloud computing to increase visibility, speed and decision making.

Sustainable Branding: A brand strategy focused on the foundations of environment, society, and ethics addressing a growing need for trust from a consumer perspective in the era of disruption.

Inflationary Pressure: The upward pressure on prices due to supply shortage, increased production cost, or demand-supply imbalance, quite frequently set off or aggravated by supply chain shock.

Disruption Response Playbook: A framework available in a structured and proactive form describing procedures, communication mechanisms, and emergency plans that organizations can use in case of supply chain crisis.

Compilation of References

Aboyeji, O. J., & Aguda, A. S. (2024). Rural Transportation and its Impact on the Output and Income Generated from Cashew Production in Selected Rural Settlements in Kwara State, Nigeria. *Agricultural & Rural Studies, 2*(4), 0020.

Accenture. (2021). How AI Can Enable a Sustainable Future. https://www.accenture.com

Adama, H., Okeke, C., Akinoso, A., & Popoola, O., HenryA.Oladapo, AChukwuekem, DAbiodun, E. (2024). Economic Theory And Practical Impacts Of Digital Transformation In Supply Chain Optimization. *International Journal of Advanced Economics*, *6*(4), 95–107. DOI: 10.51594/ijae.v6i4.1072

Adenekan, N, Ezeigweneme, N., & Chukwurah, N. (2024). Driving innovation in energy and telecommunications: Next-generation energy storage and 5G technology for enhanced connectivity and energy solutions. *International Journal of Management & Entrepreneurship Research*, *6*(5), 1581–1597. DOI: 10.51594/ijmer.v6i5.1124

Adewale, T., Nsisong, *., Eyo-Udo, L., Toromade, A., & Ngochindo, A. (2024). Integrating sustainability and cost-effectiveness in food and FMCG supply chains: A comprehensive model. *Comprehensive Research and Reviews Journal.*

Agbigbe, W. A. (2016). *The impact of transportation infrastructure on Nigeria's economic development*. Walden University.

Ahmodu, K. O., & Okeudo, J. N. (2021). Infrastructural development and service quality in the Nigerian ports. *British International Journal of Education and Social Sciences*, *8*(4), 1–12.

Aimer, N. M. M. (2017). The effects of oil price volatility on the economic sectors of Libya. *International Journal of Business and Social Research*, *6*(12), 13. DOI: 10.18533/ijbsr.v6i12.1017

Akbari, M., Khodayari, M., Danesh, M., Davari, A., & Padash, H. (2020). A bibliometric study of sustainable technology research. *Cogent Business & Management, 7*(1), 1751906. https://www.tandfonline.com/doi/pdf/10.1080/23311975.2020.1751906. DOI: 10.1080/23311975.2020.1751906

Aladwani, J. (2024). Oil volatility uncertainty: Impact on fundamental macroeconomics and the stock index. *Economies, 12*(6), 140. DOI: 10.3390/economies12060140

Albertsen, L., Richter, J. L., Peck, P., Dalhammar, C., & Plepys, A. (2021). Circular business models for electric vehicle lithium-ion batteries: An analysis of current practices of vehicle manufacturers and policies in the EU. *Resources, Conservation and Recycling, 172*, 105658. DOI: 10.1016/j.resconrec.2021.105658

Allison, G. (2017). *Destined for war: Can America and China escape Thucydides's trap?* Houghton Mifflin Harcourt.

Al-Talib, M., Anosike, A., Arturo, J., Nadeem, S., & Melhem, W. (2022). Utilising IoT to attain resilience across supply chains. *Proceedings of the International Conference on Industrial Engineering and Operations Management.*

Alzoubi, H. M., & Aziz, R. (2021). Does emotional intelligence contribute to quality of strategic decisions? The mediating role of open innovation. *Journal of Open Innovation, 7*(2), 130. DOI: 10.3390/joitmc7020130

Amazon. (2021). Amazon's commitment to sustainability. https://www.aboutamazon.com

Ambrogio, G., Filice, L., Longo, F., & Padovano, A. (2022). Workforce and supply chain disruption as a digital and technological innovation opportunity for resilient manufacturing systems in the COVID-19 pandemic. *Computers & Industrial Engineering, 169*, 108158. DOI: 10.1016/j.cie.2022.108158 PMID: 35431410

Ammar, M., Haleem, A., Javaid, M., Bahl, S., & Verma, A. S. (2022). Implementing Industry 4.0 technologies in self-healing materials and digitally managing the quality of manufacturing. *Materials Today: Proceedings, 52*, 2285–2294. DOI: 10.1016/j.matpr.2021.09.248

Ananyi, S. O., & Somieari-Pepple, E. (2023). Cost Benefit Analysis of Artificial Intelligence in Education Management: Leadership perspectives. *International Journal of Economics, Environmental Development and Society, 4*(3), 353–370.

Anderson, B., & Tushman, M. (2021). The role of sustainability in global supply chains: A decarbonization perspective. *The Journal of Supply Chain Management, 57*(2), 89–105.

Anlauf, A., & Schmalz, S. (2025). The Grand Delusions of Globalization. *Critical Sociology*, 08969205251334983. DOI: 10.1177/08969205251334983

Antonova, N. (2024, Nov 12). *Sympower*. Retrieved January 22, 2025, from https://sympower.net/articles/what-are-energy-markets#understanding-Energy-markets

Apple. (2021). Apple's environmental progress report. https://www.apple.com

Arfaoui, N., Chaâbane, N., Gaies, B., & Messaoud, J. (2023). Are sustainable investments interdependent? The international evidence. *Journal of Sustainable Finance & Investment*, *13*(1), 1–25.

Asadollah, O., Carmy, L. S., Hoque, M. R., & Yilmazkuday, H. (2024). Geopolitical risk, supply chains, and global inflation. *World Economy*, *47*(8), 3450–3486. DOI: 10.1111/twec.13585

Ascari, G., Bonam, D., & Smadu, A. (2024a). Global supply chain pressures, inflation, and implications for monetary policy. *Journal of International Money and Finance*, *142*, 103029. DOI: 10.1016/j.jimonfin.2024.103029

Attaran, M. (2020). Digital technology enablers and their implications for supply chain management. Supply Chain Forum: An International Journal, 21(3), 158–172. DOI: 10.1080/16258312.2020.1751568

Attaran, M., & Celik, B. G. (2023)" Digital Twin, Benefits, Use Cases, Challenges and Opportunities" Decision Analytics Journal 6 (2023)100165 https://www.sciencedirect.com/science/article/pii/S277266222300005X

Avazkhodjaev, S., Mamasobirov, D., & Ganiev, A. A. G. (2023). Inflation, inflation uncertainty and output growth: Empirical evidence from transition economies in southeastern Europe. *Economic Analysis and Policy*, *77*, 123–134.

Ayad, H., Abbas, S., Nakhli, M. S., Jibir, A., & Shahzad, U. (2023). Industrial growth, health care policy uncertainty and carbon emissions: Do trade and tax policy uncertainties matter for sustainable development in the USA? *Structural Change and Economic Dynamics*, *66*, 151–160. DOI: 10.1016/j.strueco.2023.04.005

Baer, W., & Kerstenetzky, I. (Eds.). (1964). *Inflation and growth in Latin America*. Richard D. Irwin.

Bai, B. (2025). (De) Globalization, the Global Imaginary, and Religious Narratives: A Theoretical Framework and the East Asia Litmus Test. *Religions*, *16*(1), 75. DOI: 10.3390/rel16010075

Baldwin, R. (2021). *The great convergence: Information technology and the new globalization*. Harvard University Press.

Baldwin, R., & di Mauro, B. W. (2020). *Economics in the Time of COVID-19*. CEPR Press.

Baldwin, R., & Freeman, R. (2022). Carbon pricing and supply chain adaptation: A review of global mechanisms. *Energy Policy, 158*, 112345.

Bandinelli, R., Scozzafava, G., Bindi, B., & Fani, V. (2023). Blockchain and Consumer Behaviour: Results of a Technology Acceptance Model in the ancient wheat sector. *Cleaner Logistics and Supply Chain, 8*, 100117. DOI: 10.1016/j.clscn.2023.100117

Bank of America Global Research Report https://business.bofa.com/en-us/content/ai-trends-impact-report.html

Barbosa, L. C., & Santos, M. R. (2020). The effectiveness of carbon border adjustment mechanisms in reducing emissions. *Environmental Science & Policy, 107*, 28–36.

Barney, J. (1991). Firm resources and sustained competitive advantage. *Journal of Management, 17*(1), 99–120. DOI: 10.1177/014920639101700108

Berkhout, F., & Smith, A. (2021). Climate regulations and firm strategy: A case study analysis. *Business Strategy and the Environment, 30*(3), 1430–1448.

Bertsimas, D., Cory-Wright, R., & Digalakis, V., Jr. (2022). Decarbonizing OCP. *arXiv preprint arXiv:2209.06341*.https://arxiv.org/abs/2209.06341

Bianchi, I., Forcellese, A., Simoncini, M., Vita, A., Castorani, V., Arganese, M., & De Luca, C. (2022). Life cycle impact assessment of safety shoes toe caps realized with reclaimed composite materials. *Journal of Cleaner Production, 347*, 131321. DOI: 10.1016/j.jclepro.2022.131321

Bordo, M. D., & Levin, A. T. (2020). [*Pandemic and the Economic Response: A Global Perspective*. NBER.]. *COVID*, 19.

Borms, L., Brusselaers, J., Vrancken, K. C., Deckmyn, S., & Marynissen, P. (2023). Toward resilient organizations after COVID-19: An analysis of circular and less circular companies. *Resources, Conservation and Recycling, 188*, 106681. DOI: 10.1016/j.resconrec.2022.106681 PMID: 36160477

Brand, B. M., Rausch, T. M., & Brandel, J. (2022). The Importance of Sustainability Aspects When Purchasing Online: Comparing Generation X and Generation Z. *Sustainability (Basel), 14*(9), 5689. DOI: 10.3390/su14095689

Brown, T., & Green, J. (2023). ESG disclosures and corporate sustainability: Policy implications for supply chains. *Journal of Business Ethics, 180*, 103–122.

Bu, Q. (2024). Can de-risking avert supply chain precarity in the face of China-US geopolitical tensions? From sanctions to semiconductor resilience and national security. *International Cybersecurity Law Review*, *5*(3), 413–442. DOI: 10.1365/s43439-024-00125-1

Canteri, I., Capoani, L., Efremov, S., & Viapiana, A. (2024). Is the World Preparing for More Resilient Economies? *L'industria*, *45*(4), 607–641.

Capgemini Research Report https://www.capgemini.com/wp-content/uploads/2022/05/Capgemini-Research-Institute_DigitalTwins_Web.pdf-

Carboni, J., & Kumar, P. (2021). The economic impact of carbon trading schemes: A global review. *Climate Policy*, *21*(5), 670–689.

CDP. (2020). Global supply chain report 2020. https://www.cdp.net

Central Bank of Nigeria. (2021). *2021 Annual Economic Report*. Central Bank of Nigeria. https://www.cbn.gov.ng/Out/2023/RSD/2021%20CBN%20ANNUAL%20ECONOMIC%20REPORT.a.pdf

Cesarina Mason, M., Pauluzzo, R., & Muhammad Umar, R. (2022). Recycling habits and environmental responses to fast-fashion consumption: Enhancing the theory of planned behavior to predict Generation Y consumers' purchase decisions. *Waste Management (New York, N.Y.)*, *139*, 146–157. DOI: 10.1016/j.wasman.2021.12.012 PMID: 34971902

Chakraborty, D., & Mattila, A. S. (2024). The effect of self-conscious emotions of guilt and regret on consumers' intentions to reduce food waste. *Journal of Sustainable Tourism*, 1–19. DOI: 10.1080/09669582.2024.2406532

Cheng, T., & Chen, J. (2022). Calvin Kalun, FelixPoyin Lo(2022) " Path Analysis of the roles of age, self efficacy, and TAM constructs in the acceptance of performing upper limb exercises through immersive virtual reality games. *International Journal of Industrial Ergonomics*,103360. https://www.sciencedirect.com/science/article/abs/pii/S0169814122001019. DOI: 10.1016/j.ergon.2022.103360

Chen, H., & Zhao, W. (2022). Decarbonization policies in the logistics sector: An empirical assessment. *Transportation Research Part D, Transport and Environment*, *105*, 103233.

Chidozie, B., Ferreira, L. P., Ramos, A., & Ferreira, J. (2024). The Importance of Digital Transformation (5.0) in Supply Chain Optimization: An Empirical Study. *Production Engineering Archives*, *30*(1), 127–135. DOI: 10.30657/pea.2024.30.12

Chinedum, O. (2018). Port congestion determinants and impacts on logistics and supply chain network of five African ports. *Journal of Sustainable Development of Transport and Logistics*, *3*(1 (4)), 70–82.

Choi, T. Y., Netland, T. H., Sanders, N., Sodhi, M. S., & Wagner, S. M. (2023). Just-in-time for supply chains in turbulent times. *Production and Operations Management*, *32*(7), 2331–2340. DOI: 10.1111/poms.13979

Cho, Y., & Noh, S. D. (2024). Design and Implementation of Digital Twin Factory Synchronized in Real-Time Using MQTT. *Machines (Basel)*, *12*(11), 759. DOI: 10.3390/machines12110759

Christopher, M., & Peck, H. (2004). Building the resilient supply chain. *International Journal of Logistics Management*, *15*(2), 1–14. DOI: 10.1108/09574090410700275

Christopher, M., & Peck, H. (2020). Building the Resilient Supply Chain. *International Journal of Logistics Management*, *31*(3), 389–409.

Chukwu, N., Yufenyuy, S., Ejiofor, E., Ekweli, D., Ogunleye, O., Clement, T., Obunadike, C., Adeniji, S., Elom, E., & Obunadike, C. (2024). Resilient chain: Ai improved supply chain security and efficiency integration. *IJSMR*, *7*(3), 46–65. DOI: 10.37502/IJSMR.2024.7306

Chu, S.-C., Kim, H., & Kim, Y. (2023). When brands get real: The role of authenticity and electronic word-of-mouth in shaping consumer response to brands taking a stand. *International Journal of Advertising*, *42*(6), 1037–1064. DOI: 10.1080/02650487.2022.2138057

Clark, M., & Tilman, D. (2021). Sustainability in supply chains: The role of eco-friendly consumer preferences. *Nature Sustainability*, *4*(6), 456–462.

Clark, R., Kreps, S., & Rao, A. (2025). The political economy of reshoring: Evidence from the semiconductor industry. *PLoS One*, *20*(2), e0316473. DOI: 10.1371/journal.pone.0316473 PMID: 39951419

Climate Bonds Initiative. (2021). Green bonds and sustainable finance. https://www.climatebonds.net

Coelho, P. M., Corona, B., ten Klooster, R., & Worrell, E. (2020). Sustainability of reusable packaging–Current situation and trends. *Resources, Conservation and Recycling. X*, *6*, 100037. DOI: 10.1016/j.rcrx.2020.100037

Coibion, O., Gorodnichenko, Y., & Weber, M. (2020). *The Impact of COVID-19 on Consumer Behavior: Evidence from the US*. NBER.

Coslett, B. G. (2022). Just-In-Time/Just-In-Case Inventory Management as an Influence on Supply Chain Disruption in Medical Systems Based in the Southeastern United States During the COVID-19 Pandemic.

Crespy, A., & Munta, M. (2023). Lost in transition? Social justice and the politics of the EU green transition. *Transfer: European Review of Labour and Research*, *29*(2), 235–251. DOI: 10.1177/10242589231173072

Csaba, L. (2025). Globalization and European Integration: A Central European Perspective. *Journal of Risk and Financial Management*, *18*(2), 53. DOI: 10.3390/jrfm18020053

Cudjoe, D., Zhu, B., Nketiah, E., Wang, H., Chen, W., & Qianqian, Y. (2021). The potential energy and environmental benefits of global recyclable resources. *The Science of the Total Environment*, *798*, 149258. DOI: 10.1016/j.scitotenv.2021.149258 PMID: 34332393

D'Ambrosio, A., & Lavoratori, K. (2025). Reshoring to survive? The other side of de-globalization. *Economia e Politica Industriale*, 1–23. DOI: 10.1007/s40812-025-00342-7

Dahlmann, F., & Branicki, L. (2022). The role of corporate green bonds in financing decarbonization. *Journal of Sustainable Finance & Investment*, *12*(2), 178–198.

Dai, J., Xie, L., & Chu, Z. (2021). Developing sustainable supply chain management: The interplay of institutional pressures and sustainability capabilities. *Sustainable Production and Consumption*, *28*, 254–268. DOI: 10.1016/j.spc.2021.04.017

Daqjang Guo & Soujanya Mantravadi. (2024) " The role of DTin lean supply chain Management: Review and research directions" International Journal of Production Research DOI: , https://www.researchgate.net/publication/382250668_The_role_of_digital_twins_in_lean_supply_chain_management_review_and_research_directionsDOI: 10.1080/00207543.2024.2372655

Dauvergne, P. (2020). The green economy illusion: Corporate sustainability and environmental harm. *Global Environmental Politics*, *20*(1), 87–105.

Davis, F. D., Bagozi, R. P., & Warhsaw, R. P. (1989). User Acceptance of information technology: A comparison of two theoretical models. *Management Science*, *35*(8), 982–1003. DOI: 10.1287/mnsc.35.8.982

de Lange, R., & Jackson-Moore, W. (2024). From trade-offs to payoffs: CEOs on creating value with climate action. *PwC*.https://www.pwc.com/gx/en/issues/esg/ceos-creating-value-climate-action.html

Dedej, A., & Medici, L. (2024). Is Globalization Over? *Interdisciplinary Journal of Research and Development, 11*(1), 7–7. DOI: 10.56345/ijrdv11n102

Del Rio-Chanona, R. M., Mealy, P., Pichler, A., Lafond, F., & Farmer, J. D. (2020). Supply and demand shocks in the COVID-19 pandemic: An industry and occupation perspective. *Oxford Review of Economic Policy, 36*(Supplement_1), S94–S137. DOI: 10.1093/oxrep/graa033

Detmers, G., Ho, S., & Karagedikli, Ö. (2022). Understanding Consumer Inflation Expectations during the COVID-19 Pandemic. *The Australian Economic Review, 55*(1), 141–154. DOI: 10.1111/1467-8462.12460 PMID: 35601136

Dhanya, B. S., Mishra, A., Chandel, A. K., & Verma, M. L. (2020). Development of sustainable approaches for converting the organic waste to bioenergy. *The Science of the Total Environment, 723*, 138109. DOI: 10.1016/j.scitotenv.2020.138109 PMID: 32229385

Dhirani, L. L., Mukhtiar, N., Chowdhry, B. S., & Newe, T. (2023). Ethical Dilemmas and Privacy Issues in Emerging Technologies: A Review. *Sensors (Basel), 23*(3), 1151. DOI: 10.3390/s23031151 PMID: 36772190

DHL. (2020). DHL's sustainability initiatives. https://www.dhl.com

Diaz, E. M., Cunado, J., & De Gracia, F. P. (2024). Global drivers of inflation: The role of supply chain disruptions and commodity price shocks. *Economic Modelling, 140*, 106860. DOI: 10.1016/j.econmod.2024.106860

Diprose, G., Lee, L., Blumhardt, H., Walton, S., & Greenaway, A. (2023). Reducing single use packaging and moving up the waste hierarchy. *Kotuitui, 18*(3), 268–289. DOI: 10.1080/1177083X.2022.2154230

Doyle, M., & McKinley, J. (2023). Carbon neutrality and business resilience: The impact of regulatory frameworks. *Sustainable Development, 31*(1), 55–72.

Dr. Nagaraju Ellaturu, Vandana. M., Naveena M, & M. Rajalakshmi, Dr. T. L. K., Dr. Shweta Bambuwala,. (2024). Ai-Driven Solutions for Supply Chain Management. Journal of Informatics Education and Research, 4(2). DOI: 10.52783/jier.v4i2.849

Drezner, D. W. (2019). *The sanctions paradox: Economic statecraft and international relations*. Cambridge University Press.

Dubey, V., Chavas, J., & Veeramani, D. (2018). Analytical framework for sustainable supply-chain contract management. *International Journal of Production Economics, 200*, 240–261. DOI: 10.1016/j.ijpe.2018.03.003

Dulam, R., Furuta, K., & Kanno, T. (2021). Consumer panic buying: Realizing its consequences and repercussions on the supply chain. *Sustainability (Basel), 13*(8), 4370. DOI: 10.3390/su13084370

Eddrgash, T. (2022). *Port congestion problem, causes and solutions* (Doctoral dissertation, Cardiff University).

Egami, R. (2024). Mathematical programming model for cost-optimized and environmentally sustainable supply chain design. *AIP Advances, 14*(2), 025230. DOI: 10.1063/5.0192256

Elf, P., Isham, A., & Gatersleben, B. (2021). Above and beyond? How businesses can drive sustainable development by promoting lasting pro-environmental behaviour change: An examination of the IKEA Live Lagom project. *Business Strategy and the Environment, 30*(2), 1037–1050. DOI: 10.1002/bse.2668

Ellen MacArthur Foundation. (2019). Circular economy in cities: Project guide. https://www.ellenmacarthurfoundation.org

Emenyonu, U. M., Onyema, H. K., Ahmodu, K. O., & Onyemechi, C. (2016). Econometric analysis of seaport development and its impact on the economic growth of Nigeria. *International Journal of Advanced Research, 4*(2), 133–138.

Emon, M. M. H., Khan, T., Rahman, M. A., Hamid, A. B. A., & Yaakub, N. I. (2025). GreenTech Revolution: Navigating Challenges and Seizing Opportunities. In *AI and Green Technology Applications in Society* (p. 63–90). IGI Global Scientific Publishing. DOI: 10.4018/979-8-3693-9879-1.ch003

Emon, M. M. H. (2023). A Systematic Review of the Causes and Consequences of Price Hikes in Bangladesh. *Review of Business and Economics Studies, 11*(2), 49–58. DOI: 10.26794/2308-944X-2023-11-2-49-58

Emon, M. M. H. (2025). The Mediating Role of Supply Chain Responsiveness in the Relationship Between Key Supply Chain Drivers and Performance: Evidence from the FMCG Industry. *Brazilian Journal of Operations & Production Management, 22*(1), 2580. DOI: 10.14488/BJOPM.2580.2025

Emon, M. M. H., & Khan, T. (2024a). A Systematic Literature Review on Sustainability Integration and Marketing Intelligence in the Era of Artificial Intelligence. *Review of Business and Economics Studies, 12*(4), 6–28. DOI: 10.26794/2308-944X-2024-12-4-6-28

Emon, M. M. H., & Khan, T. (2024b). Unlocking Sustainability through Supply Chain Visibility: Insights from the Manufacturing Sector of Bangladesh. *Brazilian Journal of Operations & Production Management, 21*(4), 2194. DOI: 10.14488/BJOPM.2194.2024

Emon, M. M. H., & Khan, T. (2025a). The mediating role of attitude towards the technology in shaping artificial intelligence usage among professionals. *Telematics and Informatics Reports, 17*, 100188. DOI: 10.1016/j.teler.2025.100188

Emon, M. M. H., & Khan, T. (2025b). The transformative role of Industry 4.0 in supply chains: Exploring digital integration and innovation in the manufacturing enterprises. *Journal of Open Innovation, 11*(2), 100516. DOI: 10.1016/j.joitmc.2025.100516

Emon, M. M. H., Khan, T., Rahman, M. A., & Siam, S. A. J. (2024). Factors Influencing the Usage of Artificial Intelligence among Bangladeshi Professionals: Mediating role of Attitude Towards the Technology. *2024 IEEE International Conference on Computing, Applications and Systems (COMPAS)*, 1–7. DOI: 10.1109/COMPAS60761.2024.10796110

EPA. (2020). Lean manufacturing and the environment. https://www.epa.gov

Esiri, N. E., Jambol, N. D. D., & Ozowe, N. C. (2024). Best practices and innovations in carbon capture and storage (CCS) for effective CO2 storage. *International Journal of Applied Research in Social Sciences, 6*(6), 1227–1243. DOI: 10.51594/ijarss.v6i6.1212

European Commission. (2022). Carbon Border Adjustment Mechanism. https://ec.europa.eu

Evans, J., & Fang, X. (2021). Green finance: The effectiveness of sustainability-linked loans. *Finance Research Letters, 42*, 101867.

Falkowski, V., Reinhold, C., Rist, U., Sterzl, Y., & Pfleging, W. (2024). Next-Generation Batteries through Advanced 3D Electrode and Material Concepts. *ECS Meeting Abstracts.*

Falsafi, M., & Fornasiero, R. (2022). Explorative Multiple-Case Research on the Scrap-Based Steel Slag Value Chain: Opportunities for Circular Economy. *Sustainability (Basel), 14*(4), 2284. DOI: 10.3390/su14042284

Fankhauser, S., & Hepburn, C. (2020). The role of carbon taxation in a just transition. *Oxford Review of Economic Policy, 36*(2), 285–304.

Farah, A., Wu, J., & Zhang, J. (2024). Co-optimizing cost and CO_2 emissions for green hydrogen production in grid-connected renewable energy systems. *arXiv preprint arXiv:2404.11995*.https://arxiv.org/abs/2404.11995

Farooq, U. (2023). Economic growth, foreign investment, tourism, and electricity production as determinants of economic performance. *Journal of Economic Studies (Glasgow, Scotland), 50*(2), 1–15.

Fekete, A., & Sandholz, S. (2021). Here Comes the Flood, but Not Failure? Lessons to Learn after the Heavy Rain and Pluvial Floods in Germany 2021. *Water (Basel), 13*(21), 3016. DOI: 10.3390/w13213016

Ferguson, N. M., et al. (2020). *Impact of Non-Pharmaceutical Interventions (NPIs) to Reduce COVID-19 Mortality and Healthcare Demand.* Nature.

Festing, C., & Proff, H. (2024). Mediating the Paradoxes of (De-) Internationalization through Digital Platforms. *International Journal of Business Science and Applied Management, 19*(2), 35–56. DOI: 10.69864/ijbsam.19-2.187

Fleschutz, M., Bohlayer, M., Braun, M., & Murphy, M. D. (2023). From prosumer to flexumer: Case study on the value of flexibility in decarbonizing the multi-energy system of a manufacturing company. *arXiv preprint arXiv:2301.07997*.https://arxiv.org/abs/2301.07997

Foroutan, P., & Lahmiri, S. (2024). Deep learning systems for forecasting the prices of crude oil and precious metals. *Financial Innovation, 10*(1), 111. Advance online publication. DOI: 10.1186/s40854-024-00637-z

Fortunati, S., Martiniello, L., & Morea, D. (2020). The Strategic Role of the Corporate Social Responsibility and Circular Economy in the Cosmetic Industry. *Sustainability (Basel), 12*(12), 5120. DOI: 10.3390/su12125120

França, A., López-Manuel, L., Sartal, A., & Vázquez, X. H. (2023). Adapting corporations to climate change: How decarbonization impacts the business strategy–performance nexus. *Business Strategy and the Environment, 32*(8), 5615–5632. DOI: 10.1002/bse.3439

Franzoni, F. A., Giannetti, M., & Tubaldi, R. (2023). Supply chain shortages, large firms' market power, and inflation. SSRN *Electronic Journal.* DOI: 10.2139/ssrn.4586302

Freeman, R. E. (1984). *Strategic management: A stakeholder approach.* Pitman.

Friedman, T. L. (2021). *The world is flat: A brief history of the twenty-first century.* Farrar, Straus and Giroux.

Gafurdjan, Z. (2024). Inflation and its Effects on Consumer Behavior and Economic Policies. *Deleted Journal, 10*(10), 3–6. DOI: 10.54613/ku.v10i10.895

Gates, B. (2020). *The Case for COVID-19 Vaccines and Global Health Equity*. Gates Foundation.

Ghauri, P. N., Oxelheim, L., & Randøy, T. (2024). The changed geopolitical map: implications for international business policy in a sustainable finance perspective. In *Handbook of International Business Policy* (p. 170–189). Edward Elgar Publishing. DOI: 10.4337/9781035308682.00018

Ghazalian, P. L. (2025). Globalization and the Fallout of the COVID-19 Pandemic. *WORLD (Oakland, Calif.), 6*(1), 4. DOI: 10.3390/world6010004

Ghosh, S. (2022). COVID-19, clean energy stock market, interest rate, oil prices, volatility index, geopolitical risk nexus: Evidence from quantile regression. *Journal of Economic Development, 24*(4), 329–344. DOI: 10.1108/JED-04-2022-0073

Gielen, D., & Boshell, F. (2022). Renewable energy and decarbonization in global industries. *Energy Strategy Reviews, 42*, 100884.

Gkikas, D. C., & Theodoridis, P. K. (2021). AI in Consumer Behavior. In *Learning and analytics in intelligent systems* (pp. 147–176). DOI: 10.1007/978-3-030-80571-5_10

Glavič, P. (2021). Evolution and Current Challenges of Sustainable Consumption and Production. *Sustainability (Basel), 13*(16), 9379. DOI: 10.3390/su13169379

Gold, S., & Heikkurinen, P. (2018). Transparency fallacy: Unintended consequences of stakeholder claims on responsibility in supply chains. *Accounting, Auditing & Accountability Journal, 31*(1), 318–337. DOI: 10.1108/AAAJ-06-2015-2088

Goldstein, A. (2020). *China's rise to power: Conceptions of state governance and global influence*. Stanford University Press.

Gollakota, A. R. K., & Shu, C.-M. (2023). Covid-19 and energy sector: Unique opportunity for switching to clean energy. *Gondwana Research, 114*, 93–116. DOI: 10.1016/j.gr.2022.01.014 PMID: 35136377

Gollust, S. E., Nagler, R. H., & Fowler, E. F. (2020). *The Influence of COVID-19 News Coverage on U.S. Public Opinion*. Journal of Health Politics, Policy, and Law.

Gong, S. (2024). Digital transformation of supply chain management in retail and e-commerce. *International Journal of Retail & Distribution Management, 53*(2), 1–19. DOI: 10.1108/IJRDM-02-2023-0076

Goodarzi, S., & Li, L. (2023). Economic viability of the energy-water-hydrogen nexus for power system decarbonization. *arXiv preprint arXiv:2311.07891*.https://arxiv.org/abs/2311.07891

Gopalakrishnan, B., & Matthews, D. (2023). The impact of government subsidies on sustainable technology adoption. *Energy Economics*, *119*, 105381.

Gostin, L. O. (2016). Global Health Security and the WHO: Assessing the International Health Regulations 2005. *Journal of the American Medical Association*, *315*(10), 1039–1040. PMID: 27623457

Gould-Davies, N. (2022). Economic sanctions and international power struggles. *International Affairs*, *98*(2), 305–321.

Grand View Research https://www.grandviewresearch.com/industry-analysis/digital-twin-market-

Grieves, M. W. (2023) " Digital Twins, Past, Present and Future " In the Digital Twin. Edited by Noel Crespi, Adam.T. Drobot and Roberto Minerva 97-121, Cham: Springer International Publishing

Guan, Y., (2020). Zoonotic origins of human coronavirus infections. *Journal of Clinical Virology*, *127*, 104406.

Guillén, A., & Torres, I. C. (2025). Changes in the World Geopolitical Order and the Reconfiguration of Productive Systems: The Mexican Case. *Agrarian South - the Journal of Political Economy*, *14*(1), 22779760241313169. DOI: 10.1177/22779760241313169

Gurtu, A., & Johny, J. (2021). Supply Chain Risk Management: Literature Review. *Risks*, *9*(1), 16. DOI: 10.3390/risks9010016

Haider, A. (2015). Impact of immigration on economic growth in Canada and in its smaller provinces. *International Migration (Geneva, Switzerland)*, *53*(2), 1–21.

Ha, J., Kose, M. A., Ohnsorge, F., & Yilmazkuday, H. (2023). Understanding the global drivers of inflation: How important are oil prices? *Energy Economics*, *127*, 107096. DOI: 10.1016/j.eneco.2023.107096

Hajarath, K., & Vummadi, J. (2024). Analysing Different Risk Management Approaches and Their Effectiveness in Enhancing Supply Chain Resilience. *International Journal of Supply Chain Management*.

Hakkak, V. P. B. M., & Nejad, O. N. (2015). Resistance to change in online banking and extension of Technology Acceptance Model(TAM). *Soobshcheniia Akademii Nauk Gruzinskoi SSR*, *9*(1)

Hamid, M., & Ganne, A. (2023). Artificial Intelligence in energy markets and power system. *International Research Journal of Modernization in Engineering Technology and Science*. Advance online publication. DOI: 10.56726/IRJMETS35943

Hari, R., Balaji, P., & Karunamurthy, K. (2020). Carbon Capture and Storage Using Renewable Energy Sources: A Review. *IOP Conference Series. Earth and Environmental Science*, 573.

Harrison, A., & Watson, P. (2020). *COVID-19 and Supply Chain Disruption: Lessons Learned and Strategies for Future Resilience*. McKinsey & Company.

Hassan, S. T., & Xia, E. (2023). How do green energy investment, economic policy uncertainty, and natural resources affect greenhouse gas emissions? *Environmental Science and Pollution Research International.*

Herrador, M., Cho, Y., & Park, P. H. (2020). Latest circular economy policy and direction in the Republic of Korea: Room for enhancements. *Journal of Cleaner Production, 269*, 122336. DOI: 10.1016/j.jclepro.2020.122336

Hesary, F. T., Rasoulinezhad, E., & Kobayashi, Y. (2015). Oil price fluctuations and oil consuming Sectors: An Empirical analysis of Japan. SSRN *Electronic Journal.* DOI: 10.2139/ssrn.2670444

Heymann, D. L. (2020). Pandemic Preparedness and Response: The Role of International Cooperation. *Lancet.*

Hoda, S., Singh, A., Rao, A., Ural, R., & Hodson, N. (2020). Consumer demand modeling during COVID-19 pandemic. *2021 IEEE International Conference on Bioinformatics and Biomedicine (BIBM)*, 2282–2289. DOI: 10.1109/BIBM49941.2020.9313281

Hofmann, F., Böing, F., & Bertsch, V. (2024). Hydrogen and CO_2 network strategies for the European energy system. *Nature Communications, 15*(1), 1–14. PMID: 38169466

Hrouga, M., & Sbihi, A. (2023). Logistics 4.0 for supply chain performance: Perspectives from a retailing case study. *Business Process Management Journal, 29*(6), 1892–1919. DOI: 10.1108/BPMJ-03-2023-0183

Huang, Y. (2020). Geopolitics of COVID-19: An Overview of China's Political and Economic Response. *Asian Perspective, 44*(4), 561–577.

Hu, Z. (2022). Consumer behavior prediction based on machine learning scenarios. In *Proceedings of the 2022 International Conference on Bigdata Blockchain and Economy Management (ICBBEM 2022)* (pp. 410–419). DOI: 10.2991/978-94-6463-030-5_43

Ihugba, O. A., Odii, A., & Njoku, A. C. (2014). Acute Logistic System: A Bane to Economic Growth and Development in Nigeria. *International Journal of Research in Arts and Social Sciences*, 7(2), 236–247.

IKEA. (2021). IKEA's renewable energy goals. Retrieved from https://www.ikea.com

IMF. (2021). *World Economic Outlook: Managing Divergent Recoveries*. IMF.

In Data Labs. https://indatalabs.com/blog/ai-cost-reduction#:~:text=The%20sectors%20that%20seem%20to,reductions%20of%2010%20to%2019%25.-

IRENA. (2021). Capturing Carbon: Exploring the Role of Carbon Capture and Storage. Abu Dhabi: IRENA. https://www.irena.org/-/media/Irena/Files/Technical-papers/IRENA_Capturing_Carbon_2021.pdf

Irwin, D. A. (2020). *Clashing over commerce: A history of U.S. trade policy*. University of Chicago Press.

Jahanshahi, H., Uzun, S., Kaçar, S., Yao, Q., & Alassafi, M. O. (2022). Artificial Intelligence-Based Prediction of Crude Oil Prices Using Multiple Features under the Effect of Russia–Ukraine War and COVID-19 Pandemic. *Mathematics*, *10*(22), 4361. DOI: 10.3390/math10224361

Jakovljevic, M., Wu, W., Merrick, J., Cerda, A., Varjacic, M., & Sugahara, T. (2021). Asian innovation in pharmaceutical and medical device industry – beyond tomorrow. *Journal of Medical Economics, 24*(sup1), 42–50. DOI: 10.1080/13696998.2021.2013675

Jama, I. (2024). Understanding the consumer: AI-Driven predictive analytics and the transformation of purchasing behavior. *Proceeding of International Student Conference on Business, Education, Economics, Accounting, and Management.*, *2*(1), 2174–2190. DOI: 10.21009/ISC-BEAM.012.157

Jasanoff, S. (2020). The COVID-19 Pandemic: A Global Crisis of Trust. *Science*, *368*(6497), 1431–1432.

Jerbi, A., Jribi, H., Aljuaid, A., Hachicha, W., & Masmoudi, F. (2022). Design of Supply Chain Transportation Pooling Strategy for Reducing CO2 Emissions Using a Simulation-Based Methodology: A Case Study. *Sustainability*.

Jimenez, V. J., Bouhmala, N., & Gausdal, A. H. (2020). Developing a predictive maintenance model for vessel machinery. *Journal of Ocean Engineering and Science*, *5*(4), 358–386. DOI: 10.1016/j.joes.2020.03.003

Jones, K. E.. (2020). Global Trends in Emerging Infectious Diseases. *Nature*. PMID: 18288193

Kache, F., & Seuring, S. (2017). Challenges and opportunities of digital information at the intersection of Big Data Analytics and supply chain management. *International Journal of Operations & Production Management*, *37*(1), 10–36. DOI: 10.1108/IJOPM-02-2015-0078

Kakodkar, R., Allen, R., Demirhan, C., Fu, X., Pappas, I., Mutlu, M., & Pistikopoulos, E. (2024). Multiperiod Modeling and Optimization of Hydrogen-Based Dense Energy Carrier Supply Chains. *Processes (Basel, Switzerland)*, *12*(3), 469. DOI: 10.3390/pr12030469

Kamble, S. S., Gunasekaran, A., & Dhone, N. C. (2021). Blockchain technology for sustainable supply chain management. *International Journal of Production Research*, *59*(8), 2350–2381.

Kandpal, V., Jaswal, A., Santibanez Gonzalez, E. D. R., & Agarwal, N. (2024). *Sustainable Energy Transition*. Circular Economy, and ESG Practices., DOI: 10.1007/978-3-031-52943-6

Kant, S., Niguse, T., Terefe, A., & Adula, M. (2025). Emerging Trends and Innovations: Effect on Social Sustainability in Manufacturing Supply Chains by Shifts in Consumer Behavior in the Horn of Africa. *Enhancing Social Sustainability in Manufacturing Supply Chains*, 135-162.

Kant, S., Adula, M., & Alemu, G. M. (2025). Effect of Green Supply Chain Management Practice on Firm Performance With Mediation of Green Innovation in Ethiopia. In *Eco-Logistics and Sustainable Supply Chain Innovations* (p. 61–84). IGI Global Scientific Publishing.

Kant, S., Adula, M., & Duloma, H. (2025). The Rise of Product-as-a-Service Models in the Digital Era Redesigning Business Models for Circular Innovation in the Horn of Africa. In *Innovating Sustainability Through Digital Circular Economy* (p. 133–160). IGI Global Scientific Publishing.

Kaplan, R. D. (2014). *Asia's Cauldron: The South China Sea and the End of a Stable Pacific*. Random House.

Karaosman, H., Marshall, D., & Ward, I. (2024). *For the many not the few: introducing just transition for supply chain management.*

Karcıoğlu, R., & Öztürk, S. (2022). Sustainable cost management in the supply chain: A case analysis. *HOLISTIC ECONOMICS*, *1*(1), 49–64. DOI: 10.55094/hoec.1.1.05

Kaur, J., Kumar, S., & Joshi, R. (2023). Is supply chain finance an antidote to SMEs in the economic crisis? - A qualitative inquiry. *International Journal of Logistics Management*, *34*(6), 1890–1910. DOI: 10.1108/IJLM-10-2021-0496

Keohane, R. O. (1984). *After Hegemony: Cooperation and Discord in the World Political Economy*. Princeton University Press.

Khan, T., & Hasan Emon, M. M. (2024). Determinants of AI Image Generator Adoption Among Marketing Agencies: The Mediating Effects of Perceived Usefulness. *2024 IEEE 3rd International Conference on Robotics, Automation, Artificial-Intelligence and Internet-of-Things (RAAICON)*, 177–182. DOI: 10.1109/RAAICON64172.2024.10928548

Khan, T., Emon, M. M. H., & Rahman, S. (2024b). Marketing Strategy Innovation via AI Adoption: A Study on Bangladeshi SMEs in the Context of Industry 5.0. *2024 6th International Conference on Sustainable Technologies for Industry 5.0 (STI)*, 1–6. DOI: 10.1109/STI64222.2024.10951050

Khan, T., Emon, M. M. H., & Rahman, M. A. (2024a). A systematic review on exploring the influence of Industry 4.0 technologies to enhance supply chain visibility and operational efficiency. *Review of Business and Economics Studies*, *12*(3), 6–27. DOI: 10.26794/2308-944X-2024-12-3-6-27

Khan, T., Rahman, S. M., & Hasan, M. M. (2020). Barriers to Growth of Renewable Energy Technology in Bangladesh. *Proceedings of the International Conference on Computing Advancements*, 1–6. DOI: 10.1145/3377049.3377086

Kim, E., & Lee, Y. (2021). The role of blockchain in sustainable supply chains: Enhancing transparency and accountability. *Technological Forecasting and Social Change*, *170*, 120892.

Kinsey Report, Mc. The State of AI: How organizations are requiring to capture value https://www.mckinsey.com/capabilities/quantumblack/our-insights/the-state-of-ai

Kirchherr, J., Yang, N.-H. N., Schulze-Spüntrup, F., Heerink, M. J., & Hartley, K. (2023). Conceptualizing the Circular Economy (Revisited): An Analysis of 221 Definitions. *Resources, Conservation and Recycling*, *194*, 107001. DOI: 10.1016/j.resconrec.2023.107001

Kraus, S., Jones, P., Kailer, N., Weinmann, A., Chaparro-Banegas, N., & Roig-Tierno, N. (2021) Digital transformation: An overview of the current stateof the art of research. Sage Open, 11(3), 21582440211047576. *(PDF) The Importance of Digital Transformation (5.0) in Supply Chain Optimization: An Empirical Study*-https://www.researchgate.net/publication/378427870_The_Importance_of_Digital_Transformation_50_in_Supply_Chain_Optimization_An_Empirical_Study [accessed Apr 20 2025].

Kretzschmar, M. E., et al. (2020). *Impact of COVID-19 Control Measures on the Spread of the Virus*. Science.

Kreutzer, R. T. (2024). Sustainability in Corporate Governance and on the Customer Side. In *The Path to Sustainable Corporate Management* (p. 1–59). Springer Fachmedien Wiesbaden., DOI: 10.1007/978-3-658-43974-3_1

Krugman, P. (2021). *Arguing with zombies: Economics, politics, and the fight for a better future*. W. W. Norton & Company.

Kumar, J. (2024). Psychological mechanisms behind access-based luxury brand consumption: Empirical investigation from the lens of new ownership paradigm. *Journal of Business Research, 175*, 114539. DOI: 10.1016/j.jbusres.2024.114539

Lakshmanamoorthy, S., & Athinarayanan, S. (2024). Balancing Act: Exploring the Relationship between Inflation and Consumer Behaviour. *Shanlax International Journal of Economics, 12*(2), 8–12. DOI: 10.34293/economics.v12i2.7194

Lalitha.B.S & Ramanarayan.C.S (2016) "Effectiveness of Innovative Retail Banking Services in Karnataka "https://shodhganga.inflibnet.ac.in/handle/10603/219112#

Lambourdiere, E., & Corbin, E. (2020). Blockchain and maritime supply-chain performance: Dynamic capabilities perspective. *Worldwide Hospitality and Tourism Themes, 12*(1), 24–34. DOI: 10.1108/WHATT-10-2019-0069

Lee, J., Siahpour, S., Singh, J., & Azamfar, M. (2020). Integration of digital twin and deep learning in cyber-physical systems: Towards smart manufacturing. *IET Collaborative Intelligent Manufacturing, 2*(1), 34–36. DOI: 10.1049/iet-cim.2020.0009

Ling, G. H. T., Md Suhud, N. A., Leng, P. C., Yeo, L. B., Cheng, C. T., Ahmad, M. H. H., & Ak Matusin, A. M. R. (1704). binti Md Suhud, N. A., Leng, P. C., Yeo, L. B., Cheng, C. T., Ahmad, M. H. H., & Ak Matusin, A. M. R. (2021). Factors Influencing Asia-Pacific Countries' Success Level in Curbing COVID-19: A Review Using a Social–Ecological System (SES) Framework. *International Journal of Environmental Research and Public Health, 18*(4), 1704 DOI: 10.3390/ijerph18041704 PMID: 33578829

Lin, W., Zhao, S., Lu, B., Jiang, F., Lu, Z., & Xu, Z. (2024). Structures, performances and applications of green biomass derived carbon in lithium-ion batteries. *Energy Materials, 4*(5). DOI: 10.20517/energymater.2024.09

Liu, H., Shi, Y., Yang, X., & Zhang, W. (2023). The Role of Business Environment and Digital Government in Mitigating Supply Chain Vulnerability—Evidence from the COVID-19 Shock. *Sustainability (Basel), 15*(3), 2323. DOI: 10.3390/su15032323

Liu, M., Liu, H., & Lee, C. (2023). An empirical study on the response of the energy market to the shock from the artificial intelligence industry. *Energy, 288*, 129655. DOI: 10.1016/j.energy.2023.129655

Lorenzoni, G. (2009). A theory of demand shocks. *The American Economic Review, 99*(5), 2050–2084. DOI: 10.1257/aer.99.5.2050

Loxton, M., Truskett, R., Scarf, B., Sindone, L., Baldry, G., & Zhao, Y. (2020). Consumer Behaviour during Crises: Preliminary Research on How Coronavirus Has Manifested Consumer Panic Buying, Herd Mentality, Changing Discretionary Spending and the Role of the Media in Influencing Behaviour. *Journal of Risk and Financial Management, 13*(8), 166. DOI: 10.3390/jrfm13080166

Lučić, A., & Uzelac, M. (2024). Addressing global overconsumption: Positioning the anti-consumption through communication appeals. *Corporate Communications, 29*(2), 187–205. DOI: 10.1108/CCIJ-08-2023-0114

Luthra, S., Sharma, M., Kumar, A., Joshi, S., Collins, E., & Mangla, S. (2022). Overcoming barriers to cross-sector collaboration in circular supply chain management: A multi-method approach. *Transportation Research Part E, Logistics and Transportation Review, 157*, 102582. DOI: 10.1016/j.tre.2021.102582

Lyu, J., He, Y., & Zhou, F. (2023). Digital Technique-Enabled Container Logistics Supply Chain Sustainability Achievement. *Sustainability (Basel), 15*(22), 16014. DOI: 10.3390/su152216014

Madanchian, M. (2024). Generative AI for Consumer Behavior Prediction: Techniques and applications. *Sustainability (Basel), 16*(22), 9963. DOI: 10.3390/su16229963

Mageto, J. (2021). Big Data Analytics in Sustainable Supply Chain Management: A Focus on Manufacturing Supply Chains. *Sustainability (Basel), 13*(13), 7101. DOI: 10.3390/su13137101

Maguire, S., & Robson, I. (2023). Business Innovation and Change for Circular Economy. In *Sustainable Development Through Global Circular Economy Practices* (p. 113–132). Emerald Publishing Limited., DOI: 10.1108/978-1-83753-590-320231005

Mahdavian, A., Shojaei, A., Mccormick, S., Papandreou, T., Eluru, N., & Oloufa, A. A. (2021). Drivers and barriers to implementation of connected, automated, shared, and electric vehicles: An agenda for future research. *IEEE Access : Practical Innovations, Open Solutions*, *9*, 22195–22213. DOI: 10.1109/ACCESS.2021.3056025

Maria Teresa Espinosa Jaramilo, Manuel Enrique Chenet Zuta, Chaitanya Koneti, Jayasundar, S, Soledad Del Rosario Olivares, Z, Flor Marina Carvajal Ordonez (2024)" DTin Supply Chain Operations Bridging the Physical and Digital Worlds using AI", Journal of Electrical Systems 20-10s1764-1764-1774. .DOI: 10.52783/jes.5434

Mariotti, S. (2024). "Open strategic autonomy" as an industrial policy compass for the EU competitiveness and growth: The good, the bad, or the ugly? *Economia e Politica Industriale*, 1–26.

Mariotti, S. (2024). "Win-lose" globalization and the weaponization of economic policies by nation-states. *Critical Perspectives on International Business*, *20*(5), 638–659. DOI: 10.1108/cpoib-09-2023-0089

Marmot, M. (2020). The COVID-19 pandemic and the social determinants of health. *Lancet*, *395*(10238), 1181–1183.

McKinsey & Company. (2021). The economic challenges of decarbonization. https://www.mckinsey.com

Mearsheimer, J. J. (2019). *The great delusion: Liberal dreams and international realities*. Yale University Press.

Meghrajani, I., & Shah, S. (2022). Product extension or channel extension – a case of Cronos Industries Pvt Ltd. *Emerald Emerging Markets Case Studies*, *12*(4), 1–28. DOI: 10.1108/EEMCS-10-2021-0350

Meng, X., & Yu, Y. (2023). Does the Russia-Ukraine conflict affect gasoline prices? *Energy Economics*, *128*, 107113. DOI: 10.1016/j.eneco.2023.107113

Miceli, A., Hagen, B., Riccardi, M. P., Sotti, F., & Settembre-Blundo, D. (2021). Thriving, Not Just Surviving in Changing Times: How Sustainability, Agility and Digitalization Intertwine with Organizational Resilience. *Sustainability (Basel)*, *13*(4), 2052. DOI: 10.3390/su13042052

Mishra, P., & Sharma, R. (2022). Green bonds and investor behavior: Trends and challenges. *Journal of Environmental Management*, *316*, 115315.

Mollenkopf, D., Stolze, H., & Tate, W. (2020). Managing Supply Chain Risks During the COVID-19 Pandemic. *Journal of Business Logistics*, *41*(2), 103–121.

Monge, M., Lazcano, A., & Infante, J. (2024). Monetary policy and inflation rate in the behavior of consumer sentiment in the us. A fractional integration and cointegration analysis. *Research in Economics*, *78*(3), 100981. DOI: 10.1016/j.rie.2024.100981

Nam, K. (2024). Digital Transformation and Inter-Regional Dynamics: Accelerating Chinese Multinationals' Internationalization in the De-globalization Era. *Global Business & Finance Review*, *29*(8), 31–45. DOI: 10.17549/gbfr.2024.29.8.31

Nasirian, K., & Taheri, H. (2019). *EPRA International Journal of Research & Development (IJRD). EPRA International Journal of Research & Development.* IJRD., DOI: 10.36713/epra2016

Ncube, L. K., Ude, A. U., Ogunmuyiwa, E. N., Zulkifli, R., & Beas, I. N. (2020). Environmental Impact of Food Packaging Materials: A Review of Contemporary Development from Conventional Plastics to Polylactic Acid Based Materials. *Materials (Basel)*, *13*(21), 4994. DOI: 10.3390/ma13214994 PMID: 33171895

Ndalu, T. C., & Umennaihe, V. (2024). Port Infrastructure Quality and Economic Growth in Nigeria. *IIARD International Journal of Economics and Business Management*, *10*(9), 141–158.

Negm, E. M. (2023). Consumers' purchase behavior reactions: A focus on the steady devaluation of currency, compounding increase in inflation rates in Egypt. *Journal of Humanities and Applied Social Sciences*, *5*(5), 383–401. DOI: 10.1108/JHASS-05-2023-0054

Nicolaou, C. (2022). Generations and Branded Content from and through the Internet and Social Media: Modern Communication Strategic Techniques and Practices for Brand Sustainability—The Greek Case Study of LACTA Chocolate. *Sustainability (Basel)*, *15*(1), 584. DOI: 10.3390/su15010584

Niu, Y., Ying, L., Yang, J., Bao, M., & Sivaparthipan, C. B. (2021). Organizational business intelligence and decision making using big data analytics. *Information Processing & Management*, *58*(6), 102725. DOI: 10.1016/j.ipm.2021.102725

Noussan, M., Raimondi, P., Scita, R., & Hafner, M. (2020). The Role of Green and Blue Hydrogen in the Energy Transition—A Technological and Geopolitical Perspective. *Sustainability (Basel)*, *13*(1), 298. DOI: 10.3390/su13010298

Nsude, C. C., Loraamm, R., Wimhurst, J. J., Chukwuonye, G. N., & Debnath, R. (2024). Renewables but unjust? Critical restoration geography as a framework for addressing global renewable energy injustice. *Energy Research & Social Science*, *114*, 103609. DOI: 10.1016/j.erss.2024.103609

Nwokedi, T. C., Nwachukwu, J. O., Eru, J. U., & Ogwo, N. E. (2022). Elongated Cargo Dwell Time in Nigeria Ports, the Root-Source and Economic Implications. *European Journal of Maritime Research*, *1*(1), 11–18. DOI: 10.24018/maritime.2022.1.1.2

Nygaard, A. (2022). The Geopolitical Risk and Strategic Uncertainty of Green Growth after the Ukraine Invasion: How the Circular Economy Can Decrease the Market Power of and Resource Dependency on Critical Minerals. *Circular Economy and Sustainability*, *3*(2), 1099–1126. DOI: 10.1007/s43615-022-00181-x

OECD. (2020). *The Economic Impact of COVID-19 on Global Economies and Strategies for Recovery*. OECD.

OECD. (2021). Economic implications of decarbonization. https://www.oecd.org

Ojadi, F. I., & Walters, J. (2015). Critical factors that impact on the efficiency of the Lagos seaports. *Journal of Transport and Supply Chain Management*, *9*(1), 1–13. DOI: 10.4102/jtscm.v9i1.180

Okogwu, C., Agho, M. O., Adeyinka, M. A., Odulaja, B. A., Ufoaro, O. A., Ayodeji, S. A., & Daraojimba, C. (2023). Adapting to oil price volatility: A Strategic review of supply chain responses over two decades. *International Journal of Innovation and Scientific Research*, *X*(X), 68–87. DOI: 10.51244/IJRSI.2023.101007

Onma Enyejo, J., Peter Fajana, O., Sele Jok, I., Judith Ihejirika, C., Olusola Awotiwon, B., & Motilola Olola, T. (2024). Digital Twin Technology, Predictive Analytics, and Sustainable Project Management in Global Supply Chains for Risk Mitigation, Optimization, and Carbon Footprint Reduction through Green Initiatives. International Journal of Innovative Science and Research Technology (IJISRT), 609–630. DOI: 10.38124/ijisrt/IJISRT24NOV1344

Oritse, G. & Bivbere, G. (2018, April). Persistent Apapa gridlock: Stakeholders blame NPA. *Vanguard Newspapers*.

Ossio, F., Salinas, C., & Hernández, H. (2023). Circular economy in the built environment: A systematic literature review and definition of the circular construction concept. *Journal of Cleaner Production*, *414*, 137738. DOI: 10.1016/j.jclepro.2023.137738

Oyewole, F. O. (2019). Technology adoption and performance of Nigerian ports. *RSU Journal of Strategic and Internet Business*, *4*(2), 714–746.

P, A. (2023). *Artificial Intelligence in Energy Market Size, Share, Growth & Industry Analysis, By Component (Solutions and Services), By Deployment (On-Premises and Cloud-based), By Application (Robotics, Renewable Management, Demand Forecasting, Infrastructure, and Others), By End User, and Regional Analysis,* https://www.kingsresearch.com/artificial-intelligence-in-energy-market-849

Páez, L. (2024). The Political Economy of Preferential Trade in the Global Economy: Why Africa Needs to Refrain from Mega-regionals and Other FTAs with Third Parties. In *The African Continental Free Trade Area* (p. 241–284). Springer Nature Switzerland. DOI: 10.1007/978-3-031-66605-6_8

Paltiel, A. D., Zheng, A., & Walensky, R. P. (2009). Assessing Cost-Effectiveness in HIV Prevention. *Journal of the American Medical Association, 302*(10), 1095–1101.

Papamichael, I., Voukkali, I., Economou, F., Liscio, M. C., Sospiro, P., Naddeo, V., & Zorpas, A. A. (2024). Investigation of customer behavior regarding circular fashion. *Sustainable Chemistry and Pharmacy, 41*, 101675. DOI: 10.1016/j.scp.2024.101675

Pape, R. A. (2021). Why economic sanctions do not work. *International Security, 22*(2), 90–136. DOI: 10.1162/isec.22.2.90

Park, Y. W., Blackhurst, J., Paul, C., & Scheibe, K. P. (2022). An analysis of the ripple effect for disruptions occurring in circular flows of a supply chain network*. *International Journal of Production Research, 60*(15), 4693–4711. DOI: 10.1080/00207543.2021.1934745

Patti, A., Cicala, G., & Acierno, D. (2020). Eco-Sustainability of the Textile Production: Waste Recovery and Current Recycling in the Composites World. *Polymers, 13*(1), 134. DOI: 10.3390/polym13010134 PMID: 33396936

Pérez, M., Lieder, M., Jeong, Y., & Asif, F. M. A. (2025). A simulation-based decision support tool for circular manufacturing systems in the automotive industry using electric machines as a remanufacturing case study. *International Journal of Production Research*, 1–20. DOI: 10.1080/00207543.2025.2464912

Pinyol Alberich, J., Pansera, M., & Hartley, S. (2023). Understanding the EU's circular economy policies through futures of circularity. *Journal of Cleaner Production, 385*, 135723. DOI: 10.1016/j.jclepro.2022.135723

Polack, F. P., Thomas, S. J., Kitchin, N., Absalon, J., Gurtman, A., Lockhart, S., Perez, J. L., Pérez Marc, G., Moreira, E. D., Zerbini, C., Bailey, R., Swanson, K. A., Roychoudhury, S., Koury, K., Li, P., Kalina, W. V., Cooper, D., Frenck, R. W.Jr, Hammitt, L. L., & Gruber, W. C. (2020). Safety and Efficacy of the BNT162b2 mRNA Covid-19 Vaccine. *The New England Journal of Medicine*, *383*(27), 2603–2615. DOI: 10.1056/NEJMoa2034577 PMID: 33301246

Popov, V. (2025). Is Globalization Coming to an End Due to the Rise in Income Inequality? *Journal of Risk and Financial Management*, *18*(3), 138. DOI: 10.3390/jrfm18030138

Pretner, G., Darnall, N., Testa, F., & Iraldo, F. (2021). Are consumers willing to pay for circular products? The role of recycled and second-hand attributes, messaging, and third-party certification. *Resources, Conservation and Recycling*, *175*, 105888. DOI: 10.1016/j.resconrec.2021.105888

Quarton, C., & Samsatli, S. (2020). The value of hydrogen and carbon capture, storage and utilisation in decarbonising energy: Insights from integrated value chain optimisation. *Applied Energy*, *257*, 113936. DOI: 10.1016/j.apenergy.2019.113936

Radtke, M. L., de Almeida, S. O., & Espartel, L. B. (2022). What Brought Me Here? Different Consumer Journeys for Practices of Sustainable Disposal through Take-back Programmes. *Sustainability (Basel)*, *14*(9), 5003. DOI: 10.3390/su14095003

Rahimjonovich, M. S. (2025). THE RISE OF DEGLOBALIZATION: IS THE WORLD MOVING AWAY FROM FREE TRADE? *Web of Humanities: Journal of Social Science and Humanitarian Research*, *3*(4), 80–89.

Ramya, K., & Karthikeyan, K. (2024). A study on the usage of Artificial Intelligence technology in influencing consumer Buying Behavior with special with special reference to online shopping. *Proceedings on Engineering Sciences*, *5*(4), 13–20. DOI: 10.24874/PES06.01.002

Ranney, M. L., Griffeth, V., & Jha, A. K. (2020). Critical Supply Shortages—The Need for Ventilators and Personal Protective Equipment during the Covid-19 Pandemic. *The New England Journal of Medicine*, *382*(18), e41. DOI: 10.1056/NEJMp2006141 PMID: 32212516

Ran, Y., Nilsson Lewis, A., Dawkins, E., Grah, R., Vanhuyse, F., Engström, E., & Lambe, F. (2022). Information as an enabler of sustainable food choices: A behavioural approach to understanding consumer decision-making. *Sustainable Production and Consumption*, *31*, 642–656. DOI: 10.1016/j.spc.2022.03.026

Rathore, M. M., Shah, S. A., Shukla, D., Bentafat, E., & Bakiras, S. (2021). The role of AI Machine Learning and Big Data in Digital Twinning:A systematic Literature Review, Challenge and Opportunities. *IEEE Access : Practical Innovations, Open Solutions, 9*, 32030–32052. https://www.researchgate.net/publication/349508978_The_Role_of_AI_Machine_Learning_and_Big_Data_in_Digital_Twinning_A_Systematic_Literature_Review_Challenges_and_Opportunities. DOI: 10.1109/ACCESS.2021.3060863

Rene, E. R., Sethurajan, M., Kumar Ponnusamy, V., Kumar, G., Bao Dung, T. N., Brindhadevi, K., & Pugazhendhi, A. (2021). Electronic waste generation, recycling and resource recovery: Technological perspectives and trends. *Journal of Hazardous Materials, 416*, 125664. DOI: 10.1016/j.jhazmat.2021.125664 PMID: 33838506

Report, N. (2024) Role of AI in SMEs- https://community.nasscom.in/communities/ai/role-ai-smes-

Research Network Sustainable Global Supply Chains. (2023). *Sustainable global supply chains in times of geopolitical crises: Annual report 2023*. Stiftung Wissenschaft und Politik (SWP).

Rid, T. (2020). *Active measures: The secret history of disinformation and political warfare*. Farrar, Straus and Giroux.

Rinku, N., & Singh, N. G. (2023). Artificial intelligence in sustainable in energy industry: Status quo, challenges and opportunities. [IJMR]. *EPRA International Journal of Multidisciplinary Research, 234–237*, 234–237. DOI: 10.36713/epra13323

Ritchie, H., & Roser, M. (2021). The impact of consumer preferences on supply chain sustainability. *Environmental Research Letters, 16*(4), 045012.

Rosen, R., Von Wichert, G., Lo, G., & Bettenhausen, K. D. (2015). About the importance of autonomy and DTfor the future of manufacturing. *IFAC-PapersOnLine, 28*(3), 567–572. DOI: 10.1016/j.ifacol.2015.06.141

Rothe, C., Schunk, M., Sothmann, P., Bretzel, G., Froeschl, G., Wallrauch, C., Zimmer, T., Thiel, V., Janke, C., Guggemos, W., Seilmaier, M., Drosten, C., Vollmar, P., Zwirglmaier, K., Zange, S., Wölfel, R., & Hoelscher, M. (2020). Transmission of 2019-nCoV Infection from an Asymptomatic Contact in Germany. *The New England Journal of Medicine, 382*(10), 970–971. DOI: 10.1056/NEJMc2001468 PMID: 32003551

Saberi, S., Kouhizadeh, M., & Sarkis, J. (2019). Blockchain technology and the sustainable supply chain: A review. *International Journal of Production Research, 57*(7), 2092–2110. DOI: 10.1080/00207543.2018.1533261

Sakwa, R. (2022). *Frontline Ukraine: Crisis in the borderlands*. I.B. Tauris.

Salvador, R., Barros, M. V., Donner, M., Brito, P., Halog, A., & De Francisco, A. C. (2022). How to advance regional circular bioeconomy systems? Identifying barriers, challenges, drivers, and opportunities. *Sustainable Production and Consumption, 32*, 248–269. DOI: 10.1016/j.spc.2022.04.025

Santiago, F., Haraguchi, N., & Lavopa, A. (2024). Global Trends and World Order: Implications for New Industrial Policies in Developing Countries. *Journal of Industry, Competition and Trade*, *24*(1), 5. DOI: 10.1007/s10842-024-00419-4

SAP Insights Research Center-https. www.sap.com/india/blogs/digital-twins-at-work-

Sarfraz, M. S., Hong, H., & Kim, S. S. (2021). Recent developments in the manufacturing technologies of composite components and their cost-effectiveness in the automotive industry: A review study. *Composite Structures*, *266*, 113864. DOI: 10.1016/j.compstruct.2021.113864

Sarkis, J., & Zhu, Q. (2020). Environmental sustainability and supply chain resilience. *Journal of Cleaner Production*, *258*, 120774.

Segal, A. (2021). *The hacking of the American mind: Cybersecurity and global conflicts*. PublicAffairs.

Seyyedi, S. R., Kowsari, E., Gheibi, M., Chinnappan, A., & Ramakrishna, S. (2024). A comprehensive review integration of digitalization and circular economy in waste management by adopting artificial intelligence approaches: Towards a simulation model. *Journal of Cleaner Production*, *460*, 142584. DOI: 10.1016/j.jclepro.2024.142584

Shahadat, M., Nathan, R., Chowdhury, A., & Fekete-Farkas, M. (2023). Digital Technologies for Firms' Competitive Advantage and Improved Supply Chain Performance. *Journal of Risk and Financial Management*, *16*(2), 94. DOI: 10.3390/jrfm16020094

Sharma, K. D., & Jain, S. (2020). Municipal solid waste generation, composition, and management: The global scenario. *Social Responsibility Journal*, *16*(6), 917–948. DOI: 10.1108/SRJ-06-2019-0210

Sharma, S. K., & Singh, V. (2022). Digitization of the food industry enabled by Internet of Things, blockchain, and artificial intelligence. In *Current Developments in Biotechnology and Bioengineering* (p. 421–445). Elsevier., DOI: 10.1016/B978-0-323-91158-0.00013-2

Shishodia, A., Sharma, R., Rajesh, R., & Munim, Z. H. (2023). Supply chain resilience: A review, conceptual framework and future research. *International Journal of Logistics Management*, *34*(4), 879–908. DOI: 10.1108/IJLM-03-2021-0169

Shultz, J. M.. (2016). The Impact of Pandemics on Mental Health: A Global Perspective. *Current Psychiatry Reports*, *18*(12), 121.

Singh, M., Srivastava, R., Fuenmayor, E., Kuts, V., Qiao, Y., Murray, N., & Devine, D. (2022). Applications of Digital Twin across Industries: A Review. *Applied Sciences (Basel, Switzerland)*, *12*(11), 5727. DOI: 10.3390/app12115727

Singh, P., Arora, L., & Choudhry, A. (2022). Consumer Behavior in the Service Industry: An Integrative literature review and research agenda. *Sustainability (Basel)*, *15*(1), 250. DOI: 10.3390/su15010250

Sinha, P., Sharma, M., & Agrawal, R. (2024). AI enabled business decisions that enhance sustainability impact of an apparel and fashion supply chain. *Technology Analysis and Strategic Management*, 1–18. DOI: 10.1080/09537325.2024.2424428

Sodhi, M. S., Seyedghorban, Z., Tahernejad, H., & Samson, D. (2022). Why emerging supply chain technologies initially disappoint: Blockchain, IoT, and AI. *Production and Operations Management*, *31*(6), 2517–2537. DOI: 10.1111/poms.13694

Sohag, K., Islam, M. M., Tomas Žiković, I., & Mansour, H. (2023). Food inflation and geopolitical risks: Analyzing European regions amid the Russia-Ukraine war. *British Food Journal*, *125*(7), 2368–2391. DOI: 10.1108/BFJ-09-2022-0793

Song, Y., Yu, W., Jacobs, M. A., & Chavez, R. (2025). Pandemic-related inventory management practices and financial performance: Exploring the roles of pandemic-related production uncertainty and big data analytics capability. *International Journal of Production Research*, 1–20. DOI: 10.1080/00207543.2025.2470990

Sönnichsen, S. D., & Clement, J. (2020). Review of green and sustainable public procurement: Towards circular public procurement. *Journal of Cleaner Production*, *245*, 118901. DOI: 10.1016/j.jclepro.2019.118901

Stone, M. (2022, July 13). Decarbonized supply chains are resilient supply chains. *McKinsey & Company*. https://www.mckinsey.com/~/media/mckinsey/email/rethink/2022/07/2022-07-13d.html

Strand, R. (2024). Global Sustainability Frontrunners: Lessons from the Nordics. *California Management Review*, *66*(3), 5–26. DOI: 10.1177/00081256241234709

Sullivan, Y., & Wamba, S. F. (2024). Artificial Intelligence and adaptive response to market changes: A strategy to enhance firm performance and innovation. *Journal of Business Research, 174*, 114500. DOI: 10.1016/j.jbusres.2024.114500

Sun, M., Cao, X., Liu, X., Cao, T., & Zhu, Q. (2024). The Russia-Ukraine conflict, soaring international energy prices, and implications for global economic policies. *Heliyon, 10*(16), e34712. DOI: 10.1016/j.heliyon.2024.e34712 PMID: 39247264

Syed, A. H. Z., Khan, S. A., & Chaabane, A. (2024)" Unlocking the potential of DTin supply chains: A systematic review,"Supply Chain Analytics, Volume 7, 100075, ISSN 2949-8635, . (https://www.sciencedirect.com/science/article/pii/S2949863524000189)DOI: 10.1016/j.sca.2024.100075

Tao, F., Cheng, J., Qi, Q., Zhang, M., Zhang, H., & Sui, F. (2018). Digital Twin-Driven Product Design, Manufacturing and Service with Big Data. *International Journal of Advanced Manufacturing Technology, 94*(9-12), 3563–3576. DOI: 10.1007/s00170-017-0233-1

Tao, F., Zhang, H., Liu, A., & Nee, A. Y. (2019). Digital twin in industry: State-of-the-art. *IEEE Transactions on Industrial Informatics, 15*(4), 2405–2415. DOI: 10.1109/TII.2018.2873186

Tao, H., Sun, X., Liu, X., Tian, J., & Zhang, D. (2022). The impact of consumer purchase behavior changes on the business model design of consumer services companies over the course of COVID-19. *Frontiers in Psychology, 13*, 818845. DOI: 10.3389/fpsyg.2022.818845 PMID: 35310236

Taubenberger, J. K., & Morens, D. M. (2006). 1918 Influenza: The Mother of All Pandemics. *Emerging Infectious Diseases, 12*(1), 15–22. DOI: 10.3201/eid1209.05-0979 PMID: 16494711

Tavana, M., Raeesi Vanani, I., Kumar Gangadhari, R., & Shaabani, A. (2022). A Review of Digital Transformation on Supply Chain Process Management Using Text Mining. *Processes (Basel, Switzerland), 10*(5), 842. DOI: 10.3390/pr10050842

Teeraphantuvat, T., Jatuwong, K., Jinanukul, P., Thamjaree, W., Lumyong, S., & Aiduang, W. (2024). Improving the Physical and Mechanical Properties of Mycelium-Based Green Composites Using Paper Waste. *Polymers, 16*(2), 262. DOI: 10.3390/polym16020262 PMID: 38257061

Tesla. (2021). Tesla's sustainability report. https://www.tesla.com

Tewary, A., & Upadhyay, P. (2025). Proposing a 6R framework promoting circular strategies for platform organizations. *Digital Policy. Regulation & Governance, 27*(2), 145–174. DOI: 10.1108/DPRG-11-2023-0169

Thomas, A., Thomas, M. A. H., Turk, M. R. A., & Turk, R. (2023). *Food insecurity in Nigeria: Food supply matters*. International Monetary Fund.

Tiwari, S., Sharma, P., Choi, T.-M., & Lim, A. (2023). Blockchain and third-party logistics for global supply chain operations: Stakeholders' perspectives and decision roadmap. *Transportation Research Part E, Logistics and Transportation Review*, *170*, 103012. DOI: 10.1016/j.tre.2022.103012

Tsang, Y. P., Tang, V., Wu, C. H., & Li, F. (2024). Unlocking the Potential of Robotic Process Automation for Digital Transformation in Logistics and Supply Chain Management. *Journal of Global Information Management*, *32*(1), 1–24. DOI: 10.4018/JGIM.361710

Unegbu, P. I., & Ugwunna, O. T. (2024). Importation and manufacturing sector performance in Nigeria: An empirical analysis. *ANSU Journal of Arts and Social Sciences*, *11*(2), 43–60.

UNICEF. (2020). *COVID-19 and Children: Impact and Recommendations for Action*. UNICEF.

Unilever. (2023). Sustainability Report. https://unilever.com

Vadakkepatt, G. G., Winterich, K. P., Mittal, V., Zinn, W., Beitelspacher, L., Aloysius, J., Ginger, J., & Reilman, J. (2021). Sustainable Retailing. *Journal of Retailing*, *97*(1), 62–80. DOI: 10.1016/j.jretai.2020.10.008

van Hoek, R., & Dobrzykowski, D. (2021). Towards more balanced sourcing strategies – are supply chain risks caused by the COVID-19 pandemic driving reshoring considerations? *Supply Chain Management*, *26*(6), 689–701. DOI: 10.1108/SCM-09-2020-0498

Vaughan, R., & Tisdall, M. (2020). *Taiwan's COVID-19 Response: A Model for the World*. Financial Times.

Venkatesh, V., Gordon, B. D., & Fred, D. D. (2003). User Acceptance of information technology, towards a unified view. *Management Information Systems Quarterly*, *27*(3), 425–478. DOI: 10.2307/30036540

Vidrova, Z. (2020). Supply chain management in the aspect of globalization. In *SHS Web of Conferences* (Vol. 74, p. 04031). EDP Sciences. DOI: 10.1051/shsconf/20207404031

Vitasek, K. L., Manrodt, K. B., & Abbott, J. (2005). What makes a Lean Supply chain. *Supply Chain Management Review*, *9*(7), 39–45.

Vredenburg, J., Kapitan, S., Spry, A., & Kemper, J. A. (2020). Brands Taking a Stand: Authentic Brand Activism or Woke Washing? *Journal of Public Policy & Marketing*, *39*(4), 444–460. DOI: 10.1177/0743915620947359

Walker, H., & Jones, N. (2023). Circular economy practices in sustainable supply chains. *Resources, Conservation and Recycling*, *192*, 106828.

Wang, Q., Wang, X., & Li, R. (2024). Geopolitical risks and energy transition: The impact of environmental regulation and green innovation. *Humanities & Social Sciences Communications*, *11*(1), 1272. DOI: 10.1057/s41599-024-03770-3

Waris, I., Suki, N. M., Ahmed, A., & Barkat, W. (2024). Environmental corporate social responsibility initiatives and green customer citizenship behavior in tourism industry: The mediating roles of green trust, customer-company identification and green corporate image. *Social Responsibility Journal*, *20*(6), 1138–1156. DOI: 10.1108/SRJ-07-2023-0378

Weber, M., Franke, P., & Aumueller, U. (2023). POSSIBILITIES AND LIMITS OF DIGITALIZATION TO INCREASE SUPPLY CHAIN RESILIENCE. *Beykent Üniversitesi Fen ve Mühendislik Bilimleri Dergisi*.

WEF. (2023). Clean Skies for Tomorrow Initiative. https://weforum.org

WHO. (2021). *Mental Health and COVID-19: Impacts, Concerns, and Solutions*. World Health Organization.

Williams, M. D., Rana, N. P., & Dwivedi, Y. K. (2015). The Unified Theory of Acceptance and usage of technology (UTAUT): A literature review. *Journal of Enterprise Information Management*, *28*(3), 443–488. DOI: 10.1108/JEIM-09-2014-0088

Wilson, M., & Goffnett, S. (2022). Reverse logistics: Understanding end-of-life product management. *Business Horizons*, *65*(5), 643–655. DOI: 10.1016/j.bushor.2021.10.005

Wong, C. Y., Yeung, H. W. C., Huang, S., Song, J., & Lee, K. (2024). Geopolitics and the changing landscape of global value chains and competition in the global semiconductor industry: Rivalry and catch-up in chip manufacturing in East Asia. *Technological Forecasting and Social Change*, *209*, 123749. DOI: 10.1016/j.techfore.2024.123749

World Bank. (2013). GLOBAL ECONOMIC PROSPECTS | July 2013 Commodity markets Outlook. *GLOBAL ECONOMIC PROSPECTS*. https://thedocs.worldbank.org/en/doc/1146415876740236l9-0050022020/original/CMO2013Julyanalysis1.pdf

World Bank. (2021). *Global Economic Prospects: January 2021*. World Bank Group.

World Bank. (2022). *Improving Transport Connectivity for Food Security in Africa: Strengthening Supply Chains*. World Bank. https://documents1.worldbank.org/curated/en/099013125143525383/pdf/P1799337471740478 35/P17993919896090b31b8c71d9df51feffc3.pdf

World Bank. (2023). Global Economic Prospects. https://worldbank.org

World Economic Forum. (2020). The future of supply chain decarbonization. https://www.weforum.org

World Economic Forum. (2021). *The Impact of COVID-19 on Global Supply Chains*. World Economic Forum.

World Health Organization. (2021). *Coronavirus Disease (COVID-19) Dashboard*. World Health Organization.

XiaohongChen, Liu Liu, Dayuan Li, Yangfan Han XialiangLiu (2025) " The impact of Artificial Intelligence on the new quality productive forces of enterprise", Volume 1, Article 3, Journal of Digital Management https://link.springer.com/article/10.1007/s44362-024-00002-1

Yang, M., Chen, L., Wang, J., Msigwa, G., Osman, A. I., Fawzy, S., Rooney, D. W., & Yap, P.-S. (2023). Circular economy strategies for combating climate change and other environmental issues. *Environmental Chemistry Letters*, *21*(1), 55–80. DOI: 10.1007/s10311-022-01499-6

Yang, M., Fu, M., & Zhang, Z. (2021). The adoption of digital technologies in supply chains: Drivers, process and impact. *Technological Forecasting and Social Change*, *169*, 120795. DOI: 10.1016/j.techfore.2021.120795

Ye, M., Si Mohammed, K., Tiwari, S., Ali Raza, S., & Chen, L. (2023). The effect of the global supply chain and oil prices on the inflation rates in advanced economies and emerging markets. *Geological Journal*, *58*(7), 2805–2817. DOI: 10.1002/gj.4742

Ying-Jun, L. I. N. (2025). Changing Orders in International Economic Law Volume 1: A Japanese Perspective *Asian Journal of International Law*, 1-2, p. 223

Zali.N, Soltani.A, Najafi.P., Ebadi Qajari & Mehrju.M(2024) DTfor Smarter Iranian Cities: A future studies perspective, Computational Urban Science, 4(1), Article 43, https://pure.tue.nl/ws/portalfiles/portal/347098619/s43762-024-00155-9.pdfDOI: 10.1007/s43762-024-00155-9

Zarbakhshnia, N., & Karimi, A. (2024). Enhancing third-party logistics providers partnerships: An approach through the D.L.A.R.C.S supply chain paradigm. *Resources, Conservation and Recycling*, *202*, 107406. DOI: 10.1016/j.resconrec.2023.107406

Zhang, C., Xu, Y., & Zheng, Y. (2024). Blockchain Traceability Adoption in Low-Carbon Supply Chains: An Evolutionary Game Analysis. *Sustainability (Basel)*, *16*(5), 1817. DOI: 10.3390/su16051817

Zhou, P., Yang, X. L., Wang, X. G., Hu, B., Zhang, L., Zhang, W., Si, H.-R., Zhu, Y., Li, B., Huang, C.-L., Chen, H.-D., Chen, J., Luo, Y., Guo, H., Jiang, R.-D., Liu, M.-Q., Chen, Y., Shen, X.-R., Wang, X., & Shi, Z.-L. (2020). A pneumonia outbreak associated with a new coronavirus of probable bat origin. *Nature*, *579*(7798), 270–273. DOI: 10.1038/s41586-020-2012-7 PMID: 32015507

About the Contributors

Muralidhar L B is a professionally qualified dental surgeon. He holds a Ph.D. from Canara Bank School of Management Studies, Bangalore University, after his MBA from Christ University. He is qualified in management at UGC - NET and KSET. He has 18 years of total teaching experience spanning across dental education, healthcare management and general management and 4 years of corporate experience. He has worked as a research associate in the Institute for Social and Economic Change, Bangalore in a project entitled as "Management By and For Common Man: An Exploration of the Concept and Direction for Future"post Ph.D. He had secured 28th rank in the S.S.L.C. examination for Karnataka State in 1993. His 25 patents have been published, and 2 design patents have been granted. He has 36 research publications to his credit, of which 7 are Scopus-indexed and 5 are ABDC indexed. He has co-authored 11 books and 6 book chapters.. He is supervising Ph.D. research of 3 research scholars at JAIN (Deemed to be University). He works as an assistant professor in the Department of Business Management Studies, School of Commerce, Jain Deemed to be a University student in Bangalore.

Mehedi Hasan Emon is a research practitioner specializing in business and management, supply chain management, and digital transformation. His work has significantly contributed to the fields of marketing, artificial intelligence, and supply chain analytics, with a strong focus on sustainable business practices. Through his research, he explores the intersection of technology and business, aiming to enhance operational efficiency, digital marketing strategies, and sustainable supply chain practices. As an active researcher, he has authored numerous publications in Scopus and Web of Science-indexed journals. His research covers areas such as artificial intelligence adoption, digital marketing strategies, sustainable supply chain management, and the economic implications of technological advancements. His work has gained wide recognition, reflecting his growing influence within the academic community. He has been involved in multiple research projects, including those funded by the University Grants Commission of Bangladesh and European Union-funded initiatives. His research aligns with his vision of leveraging technology to drive sustainability, efficiency, and innovation in business ecosystems. Additionally, he has contributed to academia as a peer reviewer for high-impact journals, ensuring rigorous academic standards and fostering knowledge dissemination in his field.

Tahsina Khan is serving as Deputy Director (Research) at the Centre for Higher Studies and Research in Bangladesh University of Professionals (BUP). In addition, she is also serving as the Assistant Editor of the BUP Journal. She is an Academician in Business Studies with more than 14 years of teaching, research & consulting experience in Higher Education Institutions. Over the years, she has successfully supervised multilateral academic programs in collaboration with the Government, NGOs, and Corporations from the Business sector. As a Visiting Lecturer, she has taught in the MBA program of the University of Gavle, Sweden. She has worked as Director of the research projects funded by the University Grants Commission (UGC) under the Ministry of Education. Her research papers were presented in National and International Conferences in Canada, France, Malaysia and Indonesia. As Session Chair, she presided over the conference organized by Higher Education and Innovation Group (HEAIG). She has also been invited as a resource speaker at the United Nations affiliated conference at the Yonsei University in Wonju, South Korea. She has published a number of peer-reviewed articles in reputed international journals and her policy brief paper on Rural Development has been included in the knowledge hub of the UN Task Force on SDG implementation. She is a member of International Sociological Association (ISA) which is associated with UNESCO, Economic & Social Council of the United Nations.

V Lava Kumar is an accomplished academician with a diverse educational background and over 13 years of enriching experience in the field of education. Holding an impressive array of qualifications including an MBA, M. Com, PhD in Management, PGDTTM, along with certifications from APSET in Management and APSET in Commerce. His area of specialization is Finance and Accounting. Currently serving as an Assistant Professor at GITAM School of Business, GITAM Deemed to be University, Bengaluru, Dr. Lava Kumar is dedicated to nurturing the minds of future business leaders. His teaching methodology is grounded in both theoretical knowledge and practical insights, ensuring that students receive a holistic understanding of their subjects. Dr. Lava Kumar's contributions extend beyond the classroom, evident through his prolific research endeavours. He has authored numerous research papers, with 3 publications in prestigious Scopus-indexed and ABDC journals, and an impressive tally of 10 research articles in international and peer-reviewed journals. He co-authored a Book which is published in Surana publications. His research interests primarily revolve around contemporary issues in management and finance, where he strives to contribute to the academic discourse with valuable insights and innovative perspectives.

Sheneni Maiyaki is a Research and Teaching Assistant at Lagos Business School. With a background in Entrepreneurship, his primary research focuses on Institutional Entrepreneurship and Process Innovation.

Frank Ojadi obtained a bachelor's degree in Engineering Physics from the University of Ife in 1981 (now Obafemi Awolowo University), an MBA from the Maastricht School of Management, Netherlands and PhD in Transport Economics from the Department of Transport and Supply Chain Management of the University of Johannesburg, South Africa. He has been a faculty member at Lagos Business School, Nigeria, for 24 years. He has also provided leadership in the school's DBA programme. Prior to entering academia, he worked at various times as an Operations Planning, Logistics and Supply Chain Manager in the steel, aluminium, paper, pharmaceutical, tobacco and hospitality sub-sectors of the Nigerian economy. Professor Ojadi's teaching and research interests are in operations management, design and implementation of logistics and supply chain management improvement methodologies. His research works have been published in Supply Chain Management: An International Journal; International Journal of Production Research; Journal of Transport and Supply Chain Management; International Journal of Logistics: Research and Applications.

ArunR is an Assistant Professor in the Department of Commerce at Jain (Deemed to be University), Bengaluru. Holding a Master of Commerce (Finance) from Mangalore University, Arun has demonstrated academic excellence through prestigious qualifications, including successful clearances of the UGC NET (Commerce) thrice and KSET once. Dedicated to fostering academic excellence, Arun is passionate about teaching and research, striving to inspire students and contribute valuable insights to the field of commerce and finance.

Varanasi Rahul is an Assistant Professor at JAIN University (Bangalore), a semi-qualified Cost Accountant, holding three postgraduate degrees: M.Com (Accounting & Taxation), M.Com (Management), and an MA (History). He has cleared the UGC NET in Commerce twice and has also cleared the AP SET in Commerce, History, and Management, as well as the TS SET in Commerce. With 3 years of experience as an Assistant Professor and 6 months as a Corporate Tax Associate for Australian Taxation at PwC (Big 4), he brings both academic and professional expertise to his field. Additionally, he is a freelance archaeologist, practicing epigraphist in Brahmi script, and a numismatist. His scholarly and creative contributions include over 30 newspaper articles published in Deccan Chronicle, Times of India, and other local newspapers. He has presented and participated in 25 national and international seminars and has published 1 research article in ABDC Journal, 1 in SCOPUS-indexed journals and 4 in peer-reviewed journals. As a story writer, 5 of his stories have been published in top magazines of Andhra Pradesh. Furthermore, he has authored 3 books. He has also contributed 9 book chapters to various academic publications. In addition to his extensive achievements, he has applied for 13 patents and designs, of which 2 has been granted one Indian design and one UK Design and 11 patents have been published.

N Sathyanarayana has over 15 years of teaching experience at the UG and PG levels. He holds a Master's in Business Administration and Commerce and is pursuing a Ph.D. He currently holds the position of Assistant Professor in the School of Commerce at Jain (Deemed-to-be University), Bangalore. He has published 22 research papers in international journals, 7 research papers in national journals, and presented 14 research papers at international conferences and 11 research papers at national conferences. He has co-authored 2 books at national level and 8 book chapters.

Lalitha Srinivasarao is an academician and researcher, currently serving as an Assistant Professor at SSMRV, Jayanagar in Bangalore. She has also Authored and Published a textbook on "Strategic Cost Management" from Himalaya Publishing House for M.Com students under Bangalore City University. She has also authored another e-book titled "Challenges of Filing GST Returns" from Lambert Academic Publishing, USA

Index

A

C

D

E

G

I

L

M

N

O

P

R

S

T

V

www.ingramcontent.com/pod-product-compliance
Lightning Source LLC
LaVergne TN
LVHW081337300926
849161LV00008B/1996
* 9 7 9 8 3 3 7 3 1 9 8 2 7 *